Cambodian Buddhism

Cambodian Buddhism

History and Practice

Ian Harris

University of Hawai'i Press
Honolulu

Printed in the United States of America
10 09 08 07 06 05 6 5 4 3 2 1

Library of Congress Cataloging-in-Publication Data

Harris, Ian Charles.
Cambodian Buddhism : history and practice /
Ian Harris.
p. cm.
Includes bibliographical references and index.
ISBN 0-8248-2765-1 (hardcover : alk. paper)
1. Buddhism—Cambodia—History. 2. Buddhism and politics—Cambodia. 3. Political atrocities—Cambodia. I. Title.
BQ466.H37 2005
294.3'09596—dc22 2004018492

University of Hawai'i Press books are printed on acid-free paper and meet the guidelines for permanence and durability of the Council on Library Resources.

Designed by University of Hawai'i Press
Production Staff

Printed by The Maple-Vail Book Manufacturing Group

Contents

Preface

Surprisingly little material specifically related to Cambodian Buddhism has been written in English. A brief glance at the bibliography accompanying this book demonstrates the truth of this assertion. Rather more is available in French, as one would expect from the ex-colonial power, but much is out of print and can be consulted only in specialist libraries. In addition the bulk of French-language materials tends toward the recondite, and no introductory overview exists. The present book represents a modest attempt to fill the gap.

In 1853 the Catholic priest Jean Claude Miche had been responsible for drafting King Ang Duang's letter to Napoleon III, asking for French protection and aid in retrieving the provinces of Cambodia that had been lost to the neighboring powers of Thailand and Vietnam. Thus he was instrumental in establishing a European presence in the region. But he was also an early observer of the religious scene. Yet to his prejudiced eyes Cambodian Buddhism appeared a "vast and absurd Pantheism, which covers with its veil a hopeless atheism." He wrote that it "defies the whole of nature," for its sacred writings ranked "man in the same class with the brutes." Its conception of heaven was likewise problematic, in that the blessed were supposed to experience various joys that "for the most part consist in carnal pleasures of which decency forbids the mention" (Miche 1852, 605, 607–610). Such attitudes must be seen in their historical context, but they were quite long-lived and influential. Indeed, some of them have persisted down to the present. But they were soon to be challenged by a more careful and less ideologically charged approach to the study of Buddhism in the region.

Adhémard Leclère had begun service as a *fonctionnaire* in Cambodia in 1866, but he is principally known today for his seminal work of 1899, *Le buddhisme au Cambodge*. This remarkable book is one of the very few works of Western scholarship to treat the subject in the round. It covers matters as diverse as cosmology and metaphysics, the annual cycle of the Buddhist year with its various festivals, and monastic ordination and contains materials that illuminate both ecclesiastical organization and discipline. It is therefore a fundamental starting point for anyone seriously wishing to understand the nature and practice of Buddhism in Cambodia. Yet it does, to my mind, suffer from a number of problems. From a practical perspective it is available only in French and, despite a relatively recent reprint, continues to be rather difficult to obtain. It is also quite weak from the historical standpoint, and it reveals a tendency, particularly in the more doctrinally oriented sections, to indulge in somewhat tangential discussion of issues of more interest to the Christian theologian than to the student wishing to know more about the nature of traditional beliefs and practices. Admittedly, Leclère has abandoned the coarser forms of Christian missionary rhetoric found in Miche, yet an unexamined European triumphalism remains. Leclère admits the "elevated" character of Buddhist philosophy and ethics yet regards the mass of ordinary Cambodian Buddhists as lacking intellectual strength: "[they] are excessively contemplative, slack, without initiative, very imaginative; they seem always to have had for their sacred domain absolute respect for their ancestors, even the most barbaric" (1899, xiii). Thus, his work acted as a lens through which Cambodian culture and history were refracted in support of those anxious to extend French influence in the region.

Much of Leclère's oeuvre is concerned with the traditions of the Cambodian court, but he also shows a strong concern for ethnology. Although many of the rustic practices he describes are no longer attested, his ethnological instincts appear to have been sound. In this respect he may also be identified as the progenitor of a line of fine scholars interested in Khmer folk traditions. The work of Éveline Porée-Maspero, culminating in her three-volume study entitled *Étude sur les rites agraires des Cambodgiens* (1962–1969), is the most obvious example, although more recently the baton has been taken up by Ang Chouléan, particularly in his *Les êtres surnaturels dans la religion populaire khmère* (1986). Both scholars shed new light on the nature of Cambodian religiosity, and, when relevant to Buddhist history and praxis, their insights have been incorporated into the fabric of my own work.

Having acknowledged these debts, by far and away the most significant scholar in the field of Cambodian Buddhist studies is François Bizot. In a continuous stream of work beginning in the mid-1970s, precisely the time when the country had entered its descent into collective madness, Bizot produced studies of outstanding competence, range, and originality. Bizot's output must be considered a major landmark in Buddhist and Cambodian studies, since it clearly demonstrates that, at core, the religious traditions of the country are at some variance with Theravada orthodoxy of the sort now found in neighboring countries like Sri Lanka and Thailand. However, and notwithstanding its importance to Buddhist scholarship, his writing is rather technical, especially for those not already accustomed to this very specific scholarly terrain. I have tried to make some of these findings more accessible, particularly in the fourth chapter of this book, where I attempt a synopsis of relevant aspects of nonorthodox praxis, a tradition that appears to have been almost entirely neglected by earlier investigators such as Leclère. The present book would have been severely impoverished had I not been able to depend on Bizot's work. It will be up to others to decide how well I have represented his views.

Far be it from me to undermine the brilliance of Bizot's investigations of the religious folkways of traditional Cambodia, but it must be admitted that he adopts a rather dismissive attitude toward those strands of Buddhist doctrine and practice that have emerged over the last century or so. I am thinking here of Buddhist modernism, a phenomenon that has, in one way or another, exercised a significant presence in all the countries of Buddhist Asia since the end of the nineteenth century. Put simply, Buddhist modernism has a preference for those modes of thought and behavior specifically authorized by the "scriptural tradition" of Theravada Buddhism as expressed in the Pali canon (Tripitaka) and its commentaries. It also shows a marked tendency toward laicization and the employment of modern proselytizing techniques, such as pamphlet production, distribution, and the like. Buddhist modernism, then, presents itself as a movement of purification, reform, and return to the "original truth" of the Buddha's vision. It has tended to flourish in Buddhist cultures under colonial rule and has been influential in the development of various national liberation struggles, which may be read as alternative forms of the liberation recommended by the Buddha. Bizot and his coworkers have tended to accept the traditionalist position somewhat uncritically. Thus they are inclined to dismiss the modernist position as nothing more than politics and not really much to do with Buddhism. I disagree with that assessment on the grounds that it is difficult to identify any historical manifestation of the Buddhist tradition that does not, on detailed examination, possess some element of the political. The story of the tension between modernism and traditionalism is, consequently, assigned a prominent place in my discussions.

No one can write about the early phases of Cambodian history without an enormous debt to the labors of George Cœdès. This remains as true today as it was in the past, despite Vickery's recent and persuasive criticism of Cœdès' Sanskrit-oriented approach to the study of the inscriptional record. My debt is particularly manifest in the early portions of this book, even where the great savant's conclusions have been reconsidered in the light of Vickery's more recent investigations; for it will be obvious to the careful reader that I have tried to take onboard some of the findings of the latter's *Society, Economics, and Politics in Pre-Angkor Cambodia: The Seventh–Eighth Centuries* (1998).

The post-Angkorian period is undoubtedly the least well-understood phase of the region's historical record. Mak Phœun's and Khin Sok's works on the royal chronicles are the most obvious guides to the period and have been very useful. Regrettably, the chronicles shed a rather anemic and unreliable light on the development of Theravada Buddhism before the arrival of the French, and it was with some trepidation that, in due course, I turned to this most intractable part of the whole book. During my flounderings in the middle period of Cambodian history, I had the good fortune to stumble upon the work of Ashley Thompson, particularly her 1999 doctoral thesis, "Mémoires du Cambodge." In it she examines the manner in which ancient temples, originally constructed during the Angkor period, were reappropriated by an expanding Theravada tradition with strong probable links to a reinvigorated cult of kingship. By connecting her work with previous studies on post-Angkorian epigraphy ("Inscriptions modernes d'Angkor" [IMA]), especially those conducted by Saveros Pou [Lewitz], I have been able to give an admittedly sketchy account of this shadowy period of Buddhist history.

The second half of the book explores the issue of politicized Buddhism in Cambodia since the middle of the nineteenth century in some detail and from a chronological perspective. If the work has any claim to originality, it is to be found here. As one moves closer to the present, so the resources grow in number and quality. In terms of primary sources, Ven. Huot Tath's *Kalyānamitt roboh kñom* (My intimate friend, 1970)—a partial account of the career of the influential monk Ven. Chuon Nath, the leader of the emerging Buddhist modernist cause—is crucial to the understanding of the tensions that developed in the Buddhist order, and to a lesser extent in wider Phnom Penh society, in the first half of the twentieth century. But I must also acknowledge my dependence on materials contained in a recent doctoral thesis by Penny Edwards, "Cambodge: The Cultivation of a Nation, 1860–1945" (1999); though not concerned specifically with Buddhism, it nevertheless fills in many of the gaps that were previously missing from the overall historical picture of the time. For reasons of completeness, Jean-Samuel Try's 1991 École Pratique des Hautes Études doctoral thesis, "Le bouddhisme dans la société khmère moderne," is also worthy of mention in this context. It covers a fair amount of relatively contemporary material, not all of which may be easily found elsewhere, but it is not really available for public scrutiny. It is also slightly compromised by the fact that, as a Khmer Christian, Try seeks to engage in the kind of interreligious dialogue that characterizes some of Leclère's writing.

Most secondary sources related to the modern period are tangential to the main thrust of my account. But no one can embark on a serious examination of recent Cambodian history without significant reliance on the writings of David Chandler, Steve Heder, Ben Kiernan, and Michael Vickery. Although none of these four shows any great interest in Buddhism, voluminous references to their scholarly output at crucial points in my discussion demonstrate that this book is no exception.

• • •

In terms of its coverage, the book is organized as follows. The first chapter considers evidence for the existence of Buddhism in the earliest phase of Cambodia's history, a period stretching from the first significant polity in the region, Funan, to the fall of Angkor. It surveys available epigraphic, art historical, and other documentary evidence, particularly that located in Chinese literary sources, in an attempt to evaluate the oscillating fortunes of Buddhism when set beside the various forms of Hinduism that also flourished around the time. The chapter examines what we can know about the sectarian affiliations of early Cambodian Buddhism and considers the forms of Hindu-Buddhist syncretism that appear to have developed at crucial points in the history of Angkor. It concludes by looking at the manner in which Buddhism participated in the life of the state, with special emphasis on the dominant role of tantric Mahayana concepts and rituals under Jayavarman VII (r. 1181–c. 1220). The second chapter continues the historical thrust with consideration of the factors that led to the emergence of a distinctively Theravada form of Buddhism in Cambodia following the collapse of Angkorian power. Resolution of the question as to whether the Theravada should be regarded as a popular tradition operating at the grass roots or as yet another elite system with its locus in courtly circles is given some prominence. Drawing on a more limited inscriptional base, though complemented by relevant materials from later Cambodian royal chronicles, the chapter looks at the ways in which significant Angkorian-period temples dedicated to other cults, Angkor Wat most notably, were remodeled and reappropriated so that they could serve as significant beacons of the new Buddhist faith. It also considers the symbolism of Angkor's various successor capitals and the link between the Theravada and the cult of kingship up to the reign of King Ang Duang in the mid-nineteenth century.

In the following two chapters the discussion is loosened from a purely historical framework in an attempt to isolate and describe the distinctive features of Cambodian Theravada Buddhism. Chapter 3 examines the way that the premodern Khmer interpreted their environment from both the physical and the mythological perspectives. It becomes clear that, despite the shift in religious priorities at the end of the Angkorian period, certain key preoccupations and dichotomies were preserved. The chapter demonstrates that, in its popular manifestations, Theravada cult activity owes a significant debt to probably quite archaic ways of understanding reality. The discussion also covers the nature of the monastic economy in the premodern period and concludes with a short examination of the basic structural and sociological features of the tradition that have persisted down to the present. Chapter 4 surveys some of the literary resources and practices characteristic of the Cambodian Buddhist tradition. The discussion steers away from detailed examination of the kinds of mainstream Theravada beliefs and practices rooted in canonical sources and performed in all the regions of South and Southeast Asia, for such accounts may be readily found elsewhere; instead it focuses on several distinctive Cambodian literary genres before detailed attention is turned to the baroquely esoteric traditions mentioned previously in connection with the work of François Bizot.

In chapter 5, with its focus on the ways in which Cambodian Buddhists reacted to the challenge of colonial rule, we return to historical narrative. The chapter explores the impact of various foreign influences on the nineteenth-century monastic order *(sangha)*, including the establishment of a new Thai-based and reformed monastic fraternity, the Thommayut. The mechanisms through which the *sangha* became polarized and fractured into two camps—the modernizers *(thor thmei)* and the traditionalists *(thor cah)*—are traced, and the issues dividing the two parties considered. At the heart of the chapter is a characterization of the career of Ven. Chuon Nath, probably the most influential monk of the twentieth century and a major champion of modernization and reform. It shows how the modernizers, in some but by no means all cases, cooperated with the colonial power to bring about significant reforms in monastic education and administration. But not all members of the order were enthusiasts for change, and some appear to have bitterly opposed it.

The Buddhist contribution to an emerging sense of nationhood is covered in chapter 6, which begins with discussion of a number of insurrections in the late nineteenth and early twentieth centuries that appear to have had a Buddhist element. Some, but not all, of these insurrections may also have been motivated by anticolonialist sentiment. The establishment and impact of Cao Dai, a new Vietnamese religion founded just across the Cambodian border at Tay Ninh and conceived as a "renovated" Buddhism, are also considered. Cao Dai was viewed with concern by the colonial authorities, but it also appears to have focused the minds of some senior Cambodian Buddhists, who both condemned it and saw in it a model for a new and more challenging relation with the French.

The first real manifestation of organized anticolonialism in Cambodia materialized in 1942, when a monk-led demonstration challenged various reforms being imposed on the Khmer people. In a sense this event opened the floodgates, and it may not be too bold to assert that the country moved toward independence on a breaking wave of Buddhist activism that had its seeds in the late nineteenth century. The chapter concludes with an examination of the Buddhist socialist movement instigated by Prince Sihanouk in the early decades of the newly independent state.

Following the overthrow of Sihanouk in 1970, Cambodia slid quite rapidly into disorder and violence, a process that culminated in the fall of Phnom Penh to extreme nationalistic communists in April 1975. The resulting state of Democratic Kampuchea lasted only until the end of 1978, when it was toppled by a fraternal invasion of Vietnamese communists. The devastation and horror of the Democratic Kampuchea period have achieved notoriety and are widely known, at least in general outline. Chapter 7 may be the most surprising part of the book to the reader with little prior knowledge of modern Cambodian history, for it suggests that the Buddhist-inspired nationalist movement discussed in the previous chapter provided fertile ground for the germination of Khmer communism. As the communist movement grew and developed, some of its leading members sought to break their links with the past by shedding all prior connections. As is quite well known, the regime developed a vehemently antireligious policy, yet even at the height of the Democratic Kampuchea period subliminal Buddhist influences remained. These are treated in some depth, as are the phases in the elimination of institutional Buddhism under the Khmer Rouge. The chapter also explores the manner in which Buddhism was manipulated by various political groupings in the civil war period, which consumed the first half of the 1970s.

In the concluding chapter, attention is focused on the gradual reemergence of Buddhism after the darkness of the Pol Pot years. The slow recovery of organized Buddhism, its ideological manipulation, and its attempts to gain a toehold within the political system prevailing in the early years of the 1980s are all described and analyzed. The great easing of restrictions following the withdrawal of Vietnam from the country at the end of that decade, and the impact that preparations for the 1993 elections had on the restoration of the *sangha*'s prerevolutionary institutional forms, are given similarly detailed treatment. The chapter ends by cataloguing and evaluating the forms of Buddhism that have emerged in recent years, with particular reference to their political contexts. An earlier version of this final section first appeared in 2001 as an essay entitled "Buddhist *Saṅgha* Groupings in Cambodia" in the *Buddhist Studies Review* (vol. 18, no. 1, pp. 73–106), and I would like to thank the editor, Russell Webb, for his permission to include it here.

• • •

Over the course of the last few years I have engaged in discussion and correspondence with many individuals well placed to offer good advice. Many are mentioned in the endnotes. It is wise to maintain the anonymity of others. However, I would like to thank the following for their criticism and wise counsel at various points in the composition of this work: Olivier de Bernon, David Chandler, Youk Chhang, Chin Channa, William Collins, Penny Edwards, Alain Forest, Peter Gyallay-Pap, Hean Sokhom, Steve Heder, Judy Ledgerwood, John Marston, Caroline Nixon, Thonevath Pou, and Peter Skilling. I am also grateful to Alex Watson for her help in tracking down obscure research materials. The views and errors contained herein are purely my own responsibility.

My appreciation also goes to the individuals and grant-awarding bodies who have variously supported my efforts over the last five years; in particular the British Academy Committee for Southeast Asian Studies and its chairman, Professor Ian Brown; my departmental and faculty research committees at the University College of St. Martin, Lancaster; the Trustees of the Spalding Trust; and, last but by no means least, the Becket Institute at St. Hugh's College, Oxford, and its executive director, Dr. Jonathan Rowland, who for the last two years has provided me with a Senior Scholarship that guaranteed the time, space, companionship, and intellectual refreshment to bring this project to its completion. Finally, many thanks to my long-suffering wife, Gwen, and our three children, Joe, Saoirse, and Catherine, for tolerating extended absences and lengthy pontificating on all things Cambodian and Buddhist over a protracted period.

Note on Transliteration

My approach to the representation of Asian terms was determined by three separate considerations: scholarly norms, the most widespread form of proper names, and reader recognition. With a few very common exceptions, the transliteration of Pali and Sanskrit terms accords with accepted academic conventions. The rendering of Khmer terms is more problematic, because no universally recognized system of transliteration exists. Some systems aim to give an accurate representation of Khmer orthography, while others provide a clearer account of pronunciation. Publications of the École Française d'Extrême-Orient have tended in the former direction, and in order to avoid confusing readers who may wish to consult these important sources, I have retained this rendering in relevant sections of the book. Elsewhere I have employed a simplified rendering with stronger emphasis on oral articulation. It is impossible to square the circle, but khmerologues may refer to the word list at the end of this work, in which the majority of terms occurring in the text are also given in Khmer script.

1

Buddhism in Cambodia

From Its Origins to the Fall of Angkor

The great pioneering works of French scholarship on ancient Cambodia were primarily concerned with the construction of royal chronologies and with the problem of how Hinduism had been transplanted in an alien setting.[1] The towering figure in the field, George Cœdès, had been trained as a Sanskritist and regarded Southeast Asia as a tabula rasa for the reception of Indic religious and cultural ideas and practices, which, rather astonishingly, appeared to bear exactly the same meanings as they had in their land of origin. This is odd, for old Khmer inscriptions are actually slightly more frequent in Cambodia than those in Sanskrit, even from the earliest period. One of the earliest, found at Angkor Borei [K. 600] and dated 611 CE, is written entirely in Khmer, for example.[2] For the joint Sanskrit/Khmer inscriptions, it is a rule of thumb that "the Sanskrit text is concerned only with the spiritual benefits acquired by some pious act or other, while the Khmer text is to some extent a notary's deed placed under divine protection" (Jacques 1970, 24). The Khmer portion, then, is addressed to living men and women; the Sanskrit, to the gods. Given this fact, Vickery (1998, 139) has argued that the ancient Khmer were materialists "overwhelmingly concerned with practical, not religious, affairs." Jacques (1982, 40; 1990, 15), on the other hand, regards the inscriptions as "exclusively religious documents." Here, then, are some of the quandaries facing the investigator exposed to divergent and incompatible readings of the most basic kind. What can we know about religion in ancient Cambodia? Were the old Khmer effectively "Indianized," or did autochthonous deities survive their exposure to foreign influences by putting on a suit of Indic clothing? There are no clear answers here, although Mabbett (1997, 350) has persuasively suggested that the storehouse of imported mythologies would have provided a rich resource for the

Map of Cambodia.

forging of a unified identity in the expanding polity that emerged in the lower Mekong region in the early centuries of the Christian era.

Little is known about the domestic life of ancient Cambodia. The inscriptions and other material remains are the work of elites and were often associated with the king himself. The efforts of several generations of archaeologists have quite naturally been directed at the clearance, reconstruction, and interpretation of grand temples. The spaces between these impressive structures and much of the larger Khmer region—spaces in which ordinary people can be assumed to have lived, worked, and worshipped—have been largely ignored.[3] Any reconstruction of this enormous period will have many lacunae, and, in consequence, it would be unwise to claim that one could offer a coherent account. As Mus (1975, 7) once sagely observed, "One sometimes risks confusing a library with a country."

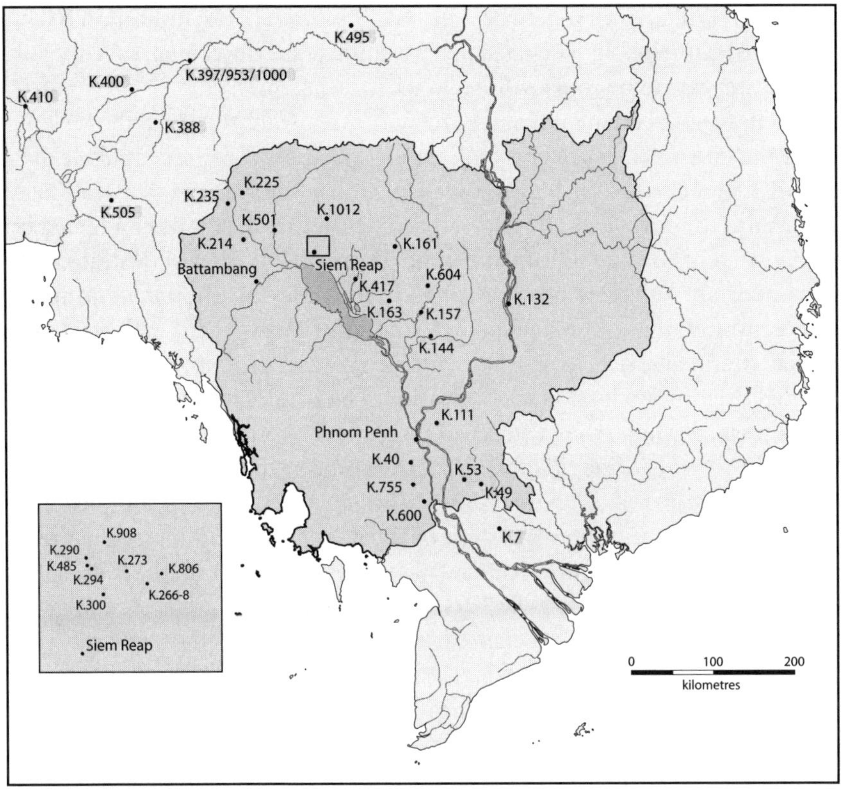

Locations of old Buddhist inscriptions.

Funan

The earliest known settlement in Cambodia, dating from c. 4200 BCE, is Laang Spean, near Battambang. The site appears to have been occupied down to the ninth century CE (Mourer 1977), yet the first significant polity in the region is generally known as Funan. The word is thought to be the Chinese equivalent of the Khmer "*bnaṃ*," meaning "mountain." Evidence relating to Funan is restricted to a small body of Chinese writings from differing periods of history, some roughly contemporary epigraphic materials in Khmer and Sanskrit,[4] and the growing data assembled through recent archaeological investigation. The paucity of sources has meant that considerable imagination has been used in the reconstruction of Funan's history. Even Cœdès fell into the trap when, with little evidence at his disposal, he argued that the kings of the region who employed the Khmer title "*kuruṅ bnaṃ*" (= Sanskrit *śailarāja*, or "king of the mountain") ruled from somewhere near Ba Phnom. This identification is now known to be untenable. The most likely candidate for the capital, called Vyādhapura, appears to be Angkor Borei (Vickery 1998, 19).

At its height, Funan's influence probably extended throughout the Mekong Delta and into much of present southern Vietnam, as well as the central Mekong region. It may also have included some of the Chao Phraya valley and the Malay Peninsula (Cœdès 1968a, 36–37). Archaeological investigations conducted by Malleret at Oc Eo and related coastal sites during the 1940s demonstrated that this important Funanese port was a link in the Indo-Roman trade during the early centuries of the Christian period. Certainly, Funan seems to have been a socially stratified society in which rice production and hydraulic works had both reached a significant level of sophistication. The ethnic character of the people is unknown, although the existence of inscriptions from the early seventh century points to the Khmer identity of at least some of the inhabitants, probably for many centuries prior to this period. Vickery (1998, 19–20) has argued that, possibly for reasons of prestige, some of the village chiefs of the region, previously known under the Mon-Khmer title of *poñ,* began to take the Indic suffix "*-varman,*"[5] from perhaps as far back as the fifth century CE. These individuals were probably ritual and clan chieftains who claimed descent from predominantly female, pre-Sanskritic deities *(kpoñ).* These, in turn, slowly transmogrified into higher-status divinities designated by the honorific term "our lord" *(vraḥ kamratāṅ añ)* (Vickery 1998, 153).

Present levels of knowledge make it impossible to be certain about when Buddhism first arrived in Cambodia. The evidence is "at best sketchy" (Skilling 1997, 93), but around forty carved buddha images from the Mekong Delta region and from areas of Thailand associated with Funan[6] have been found in a variety of materials, including stone, wood, glass, clay, bone, and metal. Their iconography is varied.[7] Given the concentration of finds around Wat Romlok, near Phnom Da, this area has been regarded as a focus of Buddhist cult activity, although both Angkor Borei and Tra Vinh Province in Vietnam must also have been important (Bhattacharya 1961, 18). Dating must remain tentative,[8] but other significant discoveries include a fine standing buddha in *varamudrā,* probably dating from the seventh century, discovered at Tuol Tahoy, Kompong Speu Province; two images of buddhas in *parinirvāṇa,* dating from the fifth–sixth centuries, one from Oc Eo and the other from Angkor Borei; and a roughly contemporary image of the Buddha seated under a multiheaded *nāga,* also from Angkor Borei.

According to Boisselier (1967), the Tuol Tahoy buddha shows many similarities to Dvāravatī statues, a fact that could be used to support the generally accepted thesis that Cambodian Theravada Buddhism was originally influenced by Mon culture. However, the most characteristic element of Dvāravatī art, the wheel of the law *(dharmacakra),* is not attested in ancient Cambodia. This need not imply that there were no links between Funan and Dvāravatī, but the evidence is slender. Nevertheless, a few pieces imported from India and China have been found, indicating Funan's position as the hub of complex trading connections. Of particular note is a Gandhara-style buddha head of probable Indian origin, dated to the fifth–sixth centuries and discovered at Wat Kompong Luong, Angkor Borei (Tranet 1998, 439).

Scholars of an earlier generation tended to regard these finds as evidence of Indianization in the sense that Brahmanical and Buddhist artifacts were exported from their place of origin by powerful individuals intent on establishing familiar religious and cultural ideas in alien lands. Cœdès (1968a, 55–56), for instance, postulates waves of emigration of southern Indians to Funan in the first half of the fifth century, perhaps as a result of the campaigns of Samudragupta (r. c. 335–375) and the resulting submission of the Pallava dynasty. But we know that the people of coastal Indochina were skilled seafarers from early times, and it is perfectly possible to envisage mariners bringing back familiar images as souvenirs from their trading activities around maritime Asia. This theory has a number of attractions. It obviates the need to establish why Indians might have been motivated to engage in Hindu-Buddhist missionary activity, and it fits with what we know about the seafaring traditions of early Southeast Asia.[9] But, most significantly, there is little evidence that imported Buddhist objects had any great influence on the evolution of Cambodian sculptural styles (Boisselier 1966, 266). Certainly much of the Buddhist imagery from Funan reflects, though not slavishly, the schools of Buddhist art that were flourishing within greater India at the time, but native aesthetics were not compromised. Had such images been introduced with specific missionary intent, one would surely have expected them to have exercised a more substantial influence on the indigenous artistic tradition.

Scattered Chinese sources illuminate the scene a little further.[10] A fifth-century account given by an individual named Che suggests that "two *hundred* Fo-du (probably Buddhists) . . . from India" were living in Tuen-siun, a vassal state of Funan (Pelliot 1903, 279n5; italics mine). *History of the Southern Qi Dynasty (Nan Qi shu),* written between 479 and 502 CE, preserves a poetical account of the religion of Funan by a Buddhist monk Nāgasena (Na-kia-sien). It seems that in 484 he had been sent as an envoy to the Chinese emperor by a king of Funan, perhaps called Kauṇḍīnya-Jayavarman, in an unsuccessful attempt to induce the Chinese to provide military aid. Nāgasena is reported to have told his hosts that Brahmanism and Buddhism both flourished in Funan. Although he emphasizes that "the custom of this country was to worship the god

Maheśvara (Śiva)," he uses a number of technical terms when speaking of Buddhism, such as "*pāramitā*" and "*bhūmi,*" which strongly suggest a Mahayana presence (Cœdès 1968a, 58–59). A further point worthy of note is that, in both this embassy and its successor in 503, the Funanese king is said to have sent Buddhist presents to the emperor, including two ivory *stūpas* and a coral buddha image (Majumdar 1953, 32), a sound indication that Buddhist ideas and practice had, in some form, infiltrated royal circles.

Another two Buddhist monks from Funan, named Saṅghapāla (460–524) and Mandra,[11] arrived at the court of Liang in Nanjing in 506 and 503, respectively. The Sanskritic forms of their names give no indication of their ethnic identity, and there is little justification in assuming, as some scholars have done, that they were Indians. Having said that, both had competences in Sanskrit, for translations into Chinese of Indic canonical texts are ascribed to them, and they appear to have stayed at the Bureau of Funan (Funan-guan) while at Nanjing. As was the case with Nāgasena, it is difficult to derive a feel for the doctrinal affiliations of these important early intermediaries. Of the two, Saṅghapāla appears to have been the more able scholar, yet both tended to work on Mahayana sources. This is, however, insufficient evidence to conclude that they were Mahayanist monks. Saṅghapāla's biography tells us that the majority of his translations concerned Mahayana doctrine, although he was also interested in the Abhidhamma.[12] One of the texts he brought from Funan and subsequently translated, although from what original language it is difficult to be certain, was the *Vimuttimagga,* a work probably composed by a certain Upatissa in the second century CE in northern India. This work will be of interest to us when we start to examine the much later features of traditional Theravada Buddhism in Cambodia. The *Vimuttimagga* has widely, though not universally, been thought of as a text associated with the heterodox Abhayagirivihāra of medieval Sri Lanka, which may have played some role in shaping the forms of Buddhist practice in Cambodia following the fall of Angkor in the fifteenth century.[13] The presence of the *Vimuttimagga* might suggest the existence of both Mahayana and Śrāvakayāna styles of Buddhism in Funan.

One other Funanese monk is known to the Chinese sources. His name was Subhuti, but his activities are not recorded (Yang Baoyun 1998, 141). We also hear of the Chinese monk Yunbao, who made a reverse journey from the court of Liang to Funan in response to a series of six embassies sent by King Rudravarman (r. c. 514–c. 550) to China between 517 and 539 (Mabbett 1986, 295).[14] He returned to China bearing the gift of a Buddhist relic, a twelve-foot-long hair of the Buddha. However, the most famous name to be associated with Buddhist contacts between Funan and China is undoubtedly the celebrated Buddhist translator Paramārtha (c. 499–569). According to the second volume of

Biography of Eminent Monks (Xu gaoseng zhuan), composed in the late seventh century, Paramārtha was a native of Ujjain in western India but spent a period of time in Funan before arriving in China in 546 CE. It appears that the Chinese emperor had requested—some sources suggest a higher level of coercion—that the king of Funan, probably the same Rudravarman, might wish to supply his country with Buddhist texts and eminent teachers of the Buddhist *dharma*.[15] Paramārtha was subsequently chosen, arriving in China with 240 bundles of texts. It is unclear whether he had brought them all the way from his native India or had collected them in Funan itself.

Paramārtha never returned to Funan; indeed we have no idea how long he had been there when he received the call from China. But this evidence, particularly when taken together with the translation interests of Saṅghapāla and Mandra, points to the strong likelihood that the rulers of Funan were somehow involved in the patronage of Mahayana Buddhism. It is difficult to be more precise, although it is certainly tempting, given Paramārtha's own doctrinal propensities and the much later practice-oriented and quasi-tantric trajectory of Cambodian Buddhism, to wonder whether the Yogācāra school of thought, as represented in India by the Valabhī monastic center, might have found a toehold in Funan.

A Sanskrit inscription at Ta Prohm of Bati [K. 40], probably from just before the middle of the sixth century, mentions both Jayavarman and Rudravarman and begins with an invocation addressed to the Buddha. This is followed by mention of holy relics, the Buddhist triple jewel *(triratna)*, and details of how a Brahmin court official became a Buddhist lay-disciple *(upāsaka)* (Cœdès 1931, 8; Majumdar 1953, 41). A roughly contemporary inscription from Prasat Pram Loveng, Thap Muoi, in the Plaine des Joncs [K. 7],[16] on the other hand, commemorates the installation by Prince Guṇavarman[17] of Vaiṣṇava cult objects at the temple of Cakratīrthasvāmin in a ceremony presided over by Brahmins well versed in Indic sacred writings and traditions. The text also mentions the existence of Hindu priests of the Bhāgavata sect (Majumdar 1953, 40).[18] From this evidence it seems likely that both Buddhism and Brahmanism were supported by influential figures. However, the presence of Buddhist artifacts and inscriptions from Funan is greatly outweighed by those influenced by Brahmanism. Indeed, the finest works of art associated with the region are statues of Kṛṣṇa Govardhana, Viṣṇu Balarāma, Viṣṇu Paraśurāma, and Lakṣmī, probably dating from the early to mid-sixth century (B.-P. Groslier 1962, 61).[19] For most of its history, then, Funan had some of the characteristics of a Hindu state in which an atmosphere of religious tolerance seems to have operated. Bhattacharya's view (1961, 16) that the kings of Funan sponsored Buddhist activity for "purely political imperatives" seems a little harsh and difficult to justify on the basis of available evidence. Both Vaiṣṇava and Śaiva cults certainly operated at the level of the court, but Mahayana and Śrāvakayāna styles of Buddhism also oscillated in importance. It goes without saying that the majority of the population continued to practice ancestral cults.

Zhenla

According to Chinese sources, Funan was eventually subdued by a neighboring vassal state called Zhenla. Like Funan before it, there is no mention of such a place in Cambodian epigraphy, yet it must certainly have existed, given that an enormous growth in the inscriptional record in the seventh century confirms the existence of a polity very like that described by the Chinese. In Funan the *poñ* had not claimed ownership of the land, which remained communal property, but this type of local authority figure was eventually supplanted by a different form of ruler, the *mratāñ-varman,* who became a distinctive element in the early Zhenla political landscape. These changes appear to be associated with transformations in the religious cult. In the words of Russian scholars, "[Earlier temples developed] from the sacred place of lineage god ancestors of the commune into a focus of wealth separated from the commune, and held by a privileged commune upper class. This was conducive to the replacement of pre-Indic local beliefs by Hinduism and the formation of a priesthood."[20]

A fair quantity of statuary has survived from the early Zhenla period. It retains earlier features but is characterized by a certain stiffness and "frontality." This mild degeneration into the so-called Phnom Da style B is nicely illustrated by an early eighth-century image of Avalokiteśvara from Rach-Gia, near the Mekong Delta.[21] A number of buddha images, mostly from the south, also date from this transitional period. The most important of these is a Buddha image from Tra-vinh, the hair of which is rendered by large, flat spiral curls with an almost absent *uṣṇīṣa* (B.-P. Groslier 1962, 64, 71). The architecture, on the other hand, usually consists of lone or grouped brick towers with stone-framed doors. The earliest of these exclusively Brahmanical sites are the brick tower of Preah Theat Touch in Kompong Thom Province and the sandstone structure of Asram Maha Rosei on the slope of Phnom Da, near Angkor Borei.[22]

These structures have been regarded as the first examples of a truly Khmer art, the initial phase of which is sometimes termed the Sambor style after Īśānapura (modern Sambor Prei Kuk, to the north of Kompong Thom), an early capital of Zhenla that was founded by Īśānavarman I (r. c. 616–635). The southern group of temple buildings at Īśānapura certainly seems to date from this reign. Although in a ruinous state today, the brick core of its central shrine is supposed to have housed a gold *liṅga*, while the eastern enclosure tower acted as a stable for Śiva's mount, Nandin. Both were oriented to catch the rays of the rising sun.[23]

According to *History of the Sui Dynasty (Sui shu)*, the original capital of Zhenla was on the middle Mekong at Bassac. Cœdès (1968a, 66) has identified the site with Wat Ph'u. At a sacred mountain nearby, human sacrifices were made to the spirit P'o-to-li (probably Bhadreśvara, a form of Śiva); the king visited the temple once a year to perform the rite at night. *History of the Sui Dynasty* also confirms the existence of Buddhist monks and nuns in Zhenla. They appear to have participated in funerary rites during the reign of Īśānavarman I (Cœdès 1968a, 74–75), but by the time that Bhavavarman II came to power around 639, the veneration of Śiva had begun to eclipse both Buddhism and all other Brahmanical cults. This seems to fit the observations of the Chinese pilgrim Yijing in the late seventh century regarding the region. Although he never actually visited Cambodia, Yijing's Southeast Asian informants had told him that in Funan "the people . . . venerated many gods." Then "the law of Buddha prospered and spread about" until an unidentified "wicked" king "expelled and exterminated them all, and there are no members of the Buddhist Brotherhood at all" (*I Tsing* 1896/1982, 12). Cœdès (1968a, 67) has offered the opinion that this king may have been Bhavavarman II. Actually, there is some evidence that devotion to Viṣṇu and Harihara did continue, although the inscriptions of the next king, Jayavarman I (r. c. 655–681), point to an increased emphasis on the *liṅga*.

Vickery's survey (1998, 140–141) of extant Khmer inscriptions dating from Zhenla lists ninety differently named Indic gods *(vraḥ)*. More than half, given their *-īśvara* suffix, are probably references to Śiva. Of those remaining, fourteen concern Viṣṇu, eight mention Śiva-Viṣṇu combinations (i.e., Harihara), and there is one reference to the sun god, Sūrya. But there are also seven specifically Buddhist inscriptions: K. 828, K. 49, K. 505, K. 755, K. 163, K. 244, and K. 132. To these we should add a few scraps of epigraphical material written in Sanskrit.

K. 828 need not detain us, for it is only a small piece of graffiti, but in K. 49—a dual Sanskrit/Khmer inscription from Wat Prei Val, Kompong Trabek, Prey Veng Province, dated 664 CE—two monks *(bhikṣu)*, Ratnabhānu and Ratnasiṃha, are named and described as brothers. In the Sanskrit portion we discover that they have donated slaves, animals, and land toward the foundation of a religious property.[24] In addition, King Jayavarman will guarantee that a certain Śubhakīrti is to have hereditary rights over the establishment. The Khmer portion of the text ascribes the title "*pu caḥ añ*" (= *sthavira*), or "elder," to both monks. Bhattacharya (1961, 16) has suggested that this means they must have belonged to the Theravada. This is possible, but the term, although monastic, really implies monastic seniority and is not convincing evidence of sectarian affiliation. Of rather more significance as evidence of possible Theravada presence in Cambodia is a portion of Pali text [K. 820] engraved on the back of a seventh-century buddha figure from Tuol Preah Theat, Prey Veng Province.[25] Pali is, of course, the canonical language of the Theravada. Furthermore, Dupont (1955, 190–221) believes that the figure shows some Dvāravatī influences.

Another Khmer inscription from Prachinburi Province, Thailand, dated 761 CE, is not listed by Vickery, because it was discovered fairly recently (Rohanadeera 1988). It contains three Pali stanzas in homage to the triple jewel that appear to come from the *Telakaṭāha-gāthā,* a poetical text believed to have its origin in Sri Lanka. As such, it represents the strongest evidence of a Theravada presence at this period of time. To this one might add a final, though not conclusive, piece of support from a dual Sanskrit/Khmer inscription [K. 388] from Hin K'on, Nakhon Ratchasima, in the Korat region of Thailand.[26] The Sanskrit portion mentions the donation of ten *vihāras,* four stone boundary *(sīmā)* markers, and some *caityas* by a royal monk *(rājabhikṣu)* to "provide for the body of Sugata [= Buddha]." Also mentioned is the donation of two sets of monastic robes *(cīvara)* in a *kaṭhina* ceremony. Filliozat (1981, 84) has, dubiously in my opinion, interpreted this as a reference to Theravada practice.

Two more inscriptions refer to the long-standing practice of monastic slavery.[27] One—in joint Khmer and Sanskrit from Khlau Rang, Prachinburi Province [K. 505], dated 639 CE—enumerates the gift of pagoda slaves *(kñuṃ vihāra),* plantations, and treasure to a *vihāra* by a certain Sinãhv.[28] The roughly contemporary K. 163 from Prasat Ampil Rolum, Kompong Thom, is more specific. Poñ Prajñācandra is recorded as having donated slaves to a trinity of Buddhist deities: *vraḥ kamratāñ añ śāstā* (= Buddha), *vraḥ kamratāñ añ Maitreya,* and *vraḥ kamratāñ añ śrī Avalokiteśvara.* The presence of Avalokiteśvara as one of the triad has led some scholars to regard this inscription as the earliest explicit evidence for the existence of the Mahayana in the region. Bernard-Philippe Groslier (1962, 77) has gone somewhat further, suggesting that the gradual increase in production of Mahayanist images throughout the Zhenla period could represent a gradual broadening of Buddhist practice beyond the confines of the court into the mass of the people. Cœdès (1968a, 94), on the other hand, has chosen to characterize K. 244 from Prasat Ta Keam, Siem Reap Province, as the first explicit piece of evidence for the existence of Mahayana Buddhism in Cambodia; it is specifically dated 791 CE and mentions the erection of an image of Lokeśvara, consecrated with the title *jagadīśvara.* Both theories are problematic, most notably because the veneration of Avalokiteśvara is attested in Theravada settings and cannot be taken as a decisive indication of Mahayanist activity.[29]

Although these specific inferences may not be correct, there does appear to have been a considerable expansion of the Mahayana throughout the Southeast Asian region from the mid-eighth century, perhaps as a result of the sponsorship of the Pāla kings of northeast India and the growing influence of Nālandā university. In some ways it would be surprising for there not to have been a resurgence in Buddhist contacts with Southeast Asia during the Pāla period, for these royal patrons of Buddhism controlled and made accessible the major Buddhist pilgrimage sites. In consequence, Nālandā became a mecca for Buddhist scholars, so much so that Bālaputra, king of Śrīvijaya, built a monastery for monks from his realm in the precincts of the great monastic center around 860 CE (Kulke and Rothermund 1990, 119).[30] It seems that a combination of tantric ideas and symbols contained within a Hindu-Buddhist syncretism, common to Bengal and surrounding regions, began to make its presence felt in Cambodia from around this time.[31] The erection of an image of Śrī Vidyādhāraṇī (= Prajñāpāramitā) by a physician—mentioned in K. 132, from Sambor Prei Kuk and dated 708 CE—may conceivably fit this context, while a Sanskrit inscription from the same location [K. 604], dated 627 CE, tells us that a Brahmanical teacher of the Śaiva Pāśupata sect, Vidyāviśeśa by name, had studied Buddhism, although it is impossible to say whether this study took place in Cambodia or in India.

Angkor before Jayavarman VII

The founding figure of the Angkorian period, Jayavarman II (r. c. 802–850), was connected by blood to earlier rulers. He arrived in the region from a place named Javā[32] around 800 CE, setting up a power base at Indrapura, a not completely identified location but probably Banteay Prei Nokor, to the east of Kompong Cham. He then gradually extended his influence across much of Zhenla, subsequently moving his capital to Hariharālaya, fifteen kilometers southeast of modern-day Siem Reap, and finally to Mahendraparvata (Phnom Kulen), where a Brahmin named Hiraṇyadāma "learned in the magical science *(siddhi vidyā)*" ordained Śivakaivalya as royal chaplain *(purohita)*[33] so that he might perform rites associated with the cult of *devarāja*.[34] Earlier scholars, such as Cœdès and Dupont, understood the *devarāja* to be either the deified king himself or a singular image of Śiva standing in the king's stead. The matter has not been adequately resolved, but it now seems more likely that the *devarāja* was a special mobile image *(calantī pratimā)* of a protective deity (Kulke 1993, 355) or, perhaps, some sort of sacred fire (Woodward 2001, 257–258).

It was on Kulen that Hiraṇyadāma also performed a ritual that sacralized Jayavarman's claim to be a universal king *(cakravartin)*[35] and symbolically broke his dependency on Javā. According to an important and very long Sanskrit and Khmer inscription from Sdok Kak Thom [K. 235], dated 1052, this ritual derived from four Indic texts: *Vināśikha, Nayottara, Saṃmoha,* and the *Śiraścheda.*[36] These were probably tantric, with a sixth- to seventh-century northern Indian provenance. We do know that many Angkorian inscriptions, from as early as the beginning of the ninth century, mention texts of the Śaiva Āgama corpus (Bagchi 1930). These describe the proper construction of the various classes of *śivaliṅga,* and this expansion of Śaivism fits in well with what we know about religious developments toward the end of the Zhenla period. The Āgamas make it clear that the priests conducting such rites must be drawn from Brahmanical families of northern Indian origin, and it looks likely that there would have been significant intercourse with India itself at this stage of Cambodia's history. Indeed, the Phum Ta Tru inscription [K. 538], dated 978 CE, underlines this, for another royal chaplain, Bhaṭṭa Divākara, is said to have come from the banks of the Yamuna River in northern India. Such an arrangement operated, however sporadically, for a considerable time; even as late as the last Sanskrit inscription in Cambodia [K. 300], dating from the fourteenth century, the priest Sarvajñāmuni is said to have come from Āryadeśa, that is, India. Having said all this, we should avoid assuming that either Śivakaivalya or Hiraṇyadāma was definitively Indian.

Only the ruins of Jayavarman's Krus Preach Aram Rong Chen—the temple-mountain on Phnom Kulen, which housed the *devarāja*—remain today. However, the king did not reside there. It was too sacred and, on a more pragmatic level, rather inhospitable. He died at Hariharālaya and was deified with the posthumous name "Parameśvara." His funerary temple,[37] Preah Ko, was erected at his death, though not completed until 879. Preah Ko comprised six towers in two rows on a low platform. The three towers at the front contained images of Śiva, while the back three housed representations of the god's female consort Gaurī. In addition, the central tower of the front row was dedicated to Jayavarman, and the one behind to his wife, who had also been given a posthumous name, "Dharaṇīndradevī." In this way the royal couple were incorporated into a *maṇḍala* of divinities, a characteristic feature of Angkorian religion, both Brahmanical and Buddhist, that was to become increasingly complex as the period unfolded.

The next important king, Indravarman (r. c. 877–889), had a chaplain *(purohita),* Śivasoma, who was not only a member of the royal lineage but also appears to have been a disciple of Śankara (c. 788–820), the great Indian Śaiva founder of the Advaita Vedānta school of orthodox Hindu philosophy.[38] Like Jayavarman II before him, Indravarman clearly favored Śaiva cults, dedicating a temple to Śiva at the already sacred site of Phnom Bayang in the south of the country. But his most important monument is the Bakong, dedicated at Hariharālaya in 881.[39] Although also a Śaiva shrine, the Bakong resembles the Buddhist temple-mountain of Borobudur on the island of Java, which had been constructed by the Śailendra kings around the middle of the ninth century (B.-P. Groslier 1962, 99). Inscriptional evidence from the reign certainly demonstrates that Buddhism had not entirely disappeared as an element in the religious life of the region. A Sanskrit inscription from Ban Bung Ke—near Ubon in the Mun valley [K. 495], dated 886 CE, and erected by one Somāditya—mentions Indravarman as the reigning king and describes the donation of fields, gardens, slaves, and buffalo to make merit for Somāditya's deceased father. The text also notes the installation of a stone image of "the master of all the *munis,* Trailokyanātha." As Majumdar (1953, 74) notes, Trailokyanātha is "evidently a Buddhist god."

Indravarman was also the originator of the great hydraulic schemes that so graphically typify the material and symbolic aspects of Angkorian civilization. The technical and managerial resources that he must have commanded in order to construct the Lolei Baray[40] (Indrataṭāka)—a rectangular tank of three hundred hectares containing ten million cubic meters of water, aligned on an east-west axis to the north of Hariharālaya—remain quite remarkable even from the contemporary perspective. This artificial body of water was not simply a reservoir. It had a clear symbolic significance, given that some of its water was diverted along canals to nearby sanctuaries,[41] the whole design evoking the oceans surrounding Mount Meru in traditional Hindu and Buddhist cosmology.

Indravarman's successor, Yaśovarman (r. 889–900), was associated with another enormous hydraulic project: the Eastern Baray (Yaśodharataṭāka), to the northeast of his new capital, Yaśodharapura. One of Śankara's great practical achievements had been to establish monasteries *(maṭha)* in the four corners of India, and it was perhaps in imitation of this that, in the year that he acceded to the throne, Yaśovarman commissioned one hundred hermitages *(āśrama),* some of which have been discovered by recent archaeological investigation.[42] It seems that these *āśrama* catered to a variety of religious sects. The inscriptional record makes it clear that the southern shore of the Yaśodharataṭāka was the site for a number of *āśrama,* including one for each of the assorted Śaiva and Vaiṣṇava groupings that flourished in the kingdom. However, a Sanskrit stele found at Tep Pranam, Angkor Thom [K. 290], dated from the end of the ninth century, suggests that one of the structures in this area was a Buddhist monastery (Saugatāśrama).[43] Its remains have not yet been identified—they were probably replaced when Tep Pranam was constructed—but the existence of organized Buddhism so close to the symbolic heart of the state points to official toleration of the religion. It is difficult to be certain of the factors that contributed to this situation, but a close study of the text of K. 290, alongside the very similar and roughly contemporary inscription of nearby Prasat Komnap [K. 701], the site of a Vaiṣṇavāśrama, suggests that the religious landscape of the period had syncretic features. It seems that the establishment of both Vaiṣṇava and Buddhist structures is preceded by an invocation to Śiva, but it would be incorrect to push the notion of interreligious tolerance too far. Residents at the Vaiṣṇavāśrama seem to have held some Buddhists in low regard, for K. 701 warns that ignorant Buddhists with bad morals, possibly with regard to celibacy, are not welcome in the hermitage. Bhattacharya (1955a, 112–113) notes that the same stipulation is not made for Śaivas.

The construction of the Śaiva Śikharīśvara temple at Preah Vihear and the sanctuary of Lolei dedicated to his parents apotheosized as Śiva and Umā was begun during the reign of Yaśovarman, but his finest achievement was the construction of the Bakheng in 893 CE. With some 108 towers arranged around the central shrine, this seven-level temple-mountain, surmounted by five sanctuaries arranged in quincunx, appears to be overflowing with complex Indian cosmological significances. This is certainly the view of Filliozat (1954),[44] although Vickery (1998, 59, 172) has suggested that Indic cosmological norms may have been imperfectly known in Cambodia at the time of the construction but have been anachronistically transposed onto the structure without consideration of other possible and more culturally compatible factors. The squared arrangement of the Bakheng does seem problematic from an Indic perspective, although it makes perfect sense in the context of what we know about traditional Southeast Asian spatial concepts.[45] Like many of the important architecture structures at Angkor, the Bakheng had a dynamic history, in that it has been significantly remodeled on more than one occasion. Indeed, we know that by the mid-sixteenth century it had become a Buddhist temple.[46]

During the reign of Rājendravarman (r. c. 944–968) a high-ranking Brahmin named Kavīndrārimathana, the only named architect in the epigraphical record, was charged with the construction of the Eastern Mebon temple on an island in the middle of the Yaśodharataṭāka. Kavīndrārimathana is described as an emissary *(chāra)*, but it is also clear that he was a devotee of the Buddha.[47] In this capacity he was involved in the establishment of the previously mentioned Saugatāśrama, to which he donated slaves. He also founded the temple of Bat Chum in 953 CE. According to Sanskrit and Khmer inscriptions on its three towers [K. 266–268], Bat Chum enshrined a triad of deities: the Buddha, Avalokiteśvara-Vajrapāṇi, and Prajñāpāramitā.[48] A mystical diagram (yantra) of forty-eight Sanskrit syllables arranged on a lotus blossom was engraved on one of the foundation stones of the temple, appearing to emphasize further that the cult practiced at the site was Mahayanist and tantric (Cœdès 1952). However, some caution is required in this context, for we know that later forms of Theravada Buddhism practiced in the region[49] employed similar imagery. Whether Bat Chum represents an early manifestation of this latter tradition or was fully Mahayanist must, given our present state of knowledge, remain an open question. Whatever the answer, there can be little doubt that Buddhism was patronized at the highest level, for one of Kavīndrārimathana's relations, Vīrendravikhyāta, was also associated with the Buddhist cult. Furthermore, the foundational inscription of Kdei Car, Kompong Thom Province [K. 157], dated 973, tells us that the *vihāra* was constructed to house pure bronze images of Lokeśvara and Devī (= Prajñāpāramitā) donated by Rājendravarman himself.[50]

A number of very significant Brahmanical structures were also completed in Rājendravarman's reign. The best-preserved of these today, Banteay Srei (Citadel of Women), is a Śaiva temple in miniature that was dedicated in 968 by two Brahmins, Yajñavarāha and his younger brother Viṣṇukumāra. An undoubted architectural gem, it is richly decorated with numerous scenes, including many derived from the *Mahābhārata* and *Rāmāyaṇa*. Rājendravarman, on the other hand, constructed Baksei Chamkrong and Pre Rup. The latter's inscription [K. 806], dated 961, is of particular interest. Bhattacharya (1971, 99) has described its author as probably the most erudite figure of the Sanskrit epigraphy of ancient Cambodia. An adherent of the Brahmanical philosophical tradition, he demonstrates a broad understanding of the great range of Indian literary and philosophical thought, even referring to two important concepts of Mahayana Buddhist philosophy, representation-only *(vijñaptimātra)* and emptiness *(śūnyatā)*.[51] It is clear that quite sophisticated understandings of Buddhist intellectual categories flourished among the religious elites of the period, even though the evidence indicates that Buddhism occupied a subordinate position in the religious imagination of the early Angkorian period.

The situation begins to change from the second half of the tenth century, when we witness a steady increase in the production of Buddhist statuary and, for the first time, we discover Buddhist episodes inscribed on temple lintels. Little of this material has been discovered with supporting epigraphy, and it has consequently been rather neglected. Nevertheless, much of the material exhibits stylistic parallels with Brahmanical statuary, most of which has been more fully studied and stratified, so it is possible to arrive at some fairly accurate datings (Boisselier 1966, 271).[52] On this basis we can say that sculpted images of buddhas and bodhisattvas were quite common in the late tenth century. Good examples are the seated Buddha from Peam Cheang, encircled and protected by the *nāga*-king Mucalinda, now in the Phnom Penh National Museum, and a bronze Maitreya from Wat Ampil Tuk (Girard-Geslan 1997, 182). Both show Indic influences, particularly in the way that the conical *uṣṇīṣa* is composed of many fine braids of hair in the style of a tiara *(mukuṭa).*

During the reign of Rājendravarman's son, Jayavarman V (r. 968–1001), Śaivism was still in the ascendant. However, a detailed Sanskrit inscription from Wat Sithor [K. 111], dated 968, indicates the extent to which Buddhism was percolating the region. The first section (vv. 1–9) starts with an invocation to the Buddha, dharma, and bodhisattvas, followed by verses expressing adoration for the Buddha's triple body *(trikāya)*. The statement that "this world is nothing but mind *(cittamātra)*" (v. 8) indicates that we are in Mahayanist territory. The author of the text, Kīrtipaṇḍita, is a servant of the king. Thanks to the latter's efforts, "the law of Buddha reappeared from the darkness, as autumn brings out the moon that up to a short time before had been veiled by the clouds of the rainy season." The servant continues, "In his [the king's] person the doctrines of emptiness *(nairātmya)* and subjectivity *(cittamātra)* . . . reappear like the sun that brings back the day. He reignited the torch of the true law, the *śāstra Madhyantavibhāga,* and the other, that the destructive gusts of sin had extinguished. He brought in from foreign lands, in order to spread their study, many philosophical books and treatises, such as the *Tattvasaṃgraha* commentary" (vv. 26–29). There is a strong suggestion here of an attempt to reestablish the intellectual credentials of Buddhism in Cambodia after a period of persecution. It is difficult to be precise about the context, although the occurrence of Mahayanist concepts in K. 806 only six years before could suggest that any harassment of Buddhism may have occurred before 961 CE. The missionary strategy outlined by Kīrtipaṇḍita appears to be based around the importation, possibly from India, of relatively sophisticated philosophical concepts and supporting texts. Specific mention of the commentary to the *Tattvasaṃgraha* and the *Madhyantavibhāga,* a key work of the Mahayanist Yogācāra school, is particularly intriguing, given that Paramārtha, a great champion of the same school, had a connection with the region some four centuries before. Could it be that Kīrtipaṇḍita was trying to revivify this earlier tradition? K. 111 concludes with a series of royal ordinances relating to various aspects of the Buddhist cult, such as the correct performance of monthly rituals to the constellations [vv. 52–55], procedures for the dedication of a monastery [vv. 58–65], daily rites [v. 67], ceremonial ablutions of buddha images at the full moon and other occasions [vv. 70, 71, 74], copying sacred writings [v. 82], and much else besides.

The inscription of Phnom Banteay Nan [K. 214], dated 982, is also connected with Jayavarman V's reign.[53] The text's author, Tribhuvanavajra, is "celebrated for his discipline *(vinaya).*" In Sanskrit he praises the Buddha's triple body *(trikāya)* before invoking Lokeśvara and Prajñāpāramitā, the "mother of the buddhas." The Khmer portion also mentions his many donations to Trailokyavijayāgīśvarī (= Prajñāpāramitā). Another purely Buddhist inscription from Thmar Puok [K. 225], dated seven years later, invokes an even more complex set of six Buddhist deities—the Buddha, Prajñāpāramitā, Lokeśvara, Maitreya, Vajrin (= Vajrapāṇi), and Indra—said to have been enshrined by the sage Padmavairocana.[54] A preoccupation with Mahayanist pantheons, then, is a distinct feature of the period.

Sūryavarman I (r. 1002–1050) was accorded the posthumous title "Nirvāṇapada," clearly Buddhist in inspiration. Both epigraphy and the northeastern Thai Pali chronicles of the fifteenth and sixteenth centuries, such as the *Cāmadevīvaṃsa,* suggest that Khmer power began to extend to the Chao Phraya basin during his reign. Despite the evidence of K. 701, relations between various religious sects fell into a more settled pattern. Sūryavarman I's Lopburi inscription [K. 410] tells us that Mahayana and Sthavira Buddhist monks lived in proximity to Brahmanical ascetics. They are all ordered to offer the merit of their austerities to the king, and anyone hindering their holy retreat is to be expelled and punished heavily.[55] A more markedly syncretic outlook is revealed around this period. An early piece of evidence from Preah Khan of Kompong Svay [K. 161], dated 1002, starts with an invocation to Śiva Naṭarāja and is followed by one to the Buddha. It contains a mélange of Buddhist and Śaiva ideas (Bhattacharya 1961, 35–36). Similarly, the inscription from 1041 CE at Phimai [K. 953] has a Sanskrit invocation to Śiva on one side of the stele, while a Khmer verse honors the Buddha on the reverse. That this state of affairs persisted is evidenced by the Trapan Don On inscription [K. 254] of 1129, which lists offerings to Śiva, Viṣṇu, and the Jina (victor) of Vaṅśārāma—an epithet of the Buddha (v. 30). A probable explanation is that it is related to the growth of tantrism in the region. Indeed, a recently discovered bilingual inscription from Sab Bāk near Nakhon Ratchasima, present-day Thailand, dated 1066,[56] provides clear evidence of the presence of tantric Buddhist concepts. The Sanskrit part of the text refers to the five buddhas *(pañcasugata),* together with Vajrasattva in his capacity as their chaplain *(purohita)*. We also read of a powerful individual, possibly Sūryavarman I, who has eliminated a threat to Buddhism and consolidated the religion in the country. The Khmer portion informs us that nine images of Buddha-Lokeśvara, formerly erected on a mountaintop to forestall a threat from Java, have been renovated. This all appears quite consistent with what we know about the protective and exorcistic character of many tantric rites. A final interesting feature of the inscription is a reference to a secret tree *(guhyavṛkśa)* from which the fruit of truth may be eaten (Chirapat Prapandvidya 1990, 12). There is, perhaps, some connection between this and other magical trees mentioned in the esoteric Buddhist texts of a much later period.[57]

We know virtually nothing about the reign of Jayavarman VI (r. 1080–1107), but later inscriptions link him both to Śaiva constructions, particularly at Preah Vihear and Wat Ph'u, and to Buddhist structures at Phimai and Preah Pithu.[58] Phimai (Vimāya) is the most important and imposing Khmer monument to survive in present-day Thailand.

Started around 1000 CE and architecturally representing an early transition between the Baphuon and the Angkor Wat styles, the site was probably associated with Buddhism before this date, as attested by the incorporation of a stone inscribed in Sanskrit [K. 1000], dating from the eighth century and mentioning a statue of the Buddha *(munirāj)* in the masonry of the first gallery (Dagens 1988, 18). Phimai once contained a large amount of Buddhist tantric imagery,[59] most significantly a figure of Vajrasattva surrounded by a profusion of Brahmanical iconography and an image of Trailokyavijaya ("conqueror of the three worlds"), who, in a Khmer inscription [K. 397] of 1110 CE, is described as the general *(senāpati)* of the *kamrateṅ jagat* of Vimāya.[60] This use of military terminology fits the tantric and exorcistic context quite nicely. The temple still boasts fine Buddhist scenes on the lintels of the sanctuary, including the first known Khmer Buddha in *bhūmisparśamudrā* (Boisselier 1966, 274).

Banteay Samre and Beng Mealea, both Buddhist foundations dating from the early to mid-twelfth century, are similar to Phimai in structure and iconographical arrangement. Erected during the reign of Sūryavarman II, at about the same time that the great Vaiṣṇava temple of Angkor Wat was being constructed, both have a central tower adorned with Buddhist imagery surrounded by Vaiṣṇava structures and devices. These caused problems for earlier investigators who tended to misidentify the small number of Buddha figures on the lintels of Beng Mealea, concluding that the temple must have been exclusively Brahmanical.[61] As Boisselier (1952–1954, 218) sagely notes, the iconography of Beng Mealea and Banteay Samre is sufficiently problematic to make it difficult to form any clear hypothesis about the type of cult practiced there, but, given the obvious parallels with Phimai, the most likely explanation is that they were all conceived as three-dimensional *maṇḍalas,* instantiating elaborate Mahayana Buddhist-dominated pantheons arranged to provide a religio-military protective function in accord with the prevailing tantric mood. When we turn to the reign of the greatest Angkorian king, Jayavarman VII (r. 1181–c. 1220), we shall have more evidence at our disposal to indicate how Mahayana Buddhism performed this apotropaic role.

Jayavarman VII: Symbolism of Temple and State

The various capitals of the Angkorian kings may be read symbolically as miniature images of the universe. The rivers and *barays* represented the cosmic ocean; the enclosing walls, the iron-mountain chain *(cakravāla)* at the limit of the world's golden disk; and the temples, the central world mountain, Mount Meru. The various hydraulic projects at Angkor may all be reduced to a simple form of a *baray* surrounding a temple-mountain. In essence the mountain collects heavenly water and is fructified by the encounter. The water then runs down into a *baray*, from where it fertilizes the surrounding soils. We find this arrangement first at Kulen, but it may also be observed at Angkor Wat and the great Buddhist temple complexes of Jayavarman VII. From his cosmic center the king ruled; he both "consumed" his domains and, by the proper performance of the royal cult, radiated back quasi-divine power. In this way, order and prosperity were sustained. At death he was absorbed back into the immaterial realms above the central world mountain and replaced by a new king. The great cosmic cycles of origination and dissolution so typical of the Khmero-Indic worldview were recapitulated as one reign followed another. This basic pattern worked whether the cult performed at the center was Brahmanical or Buddhist, the system reaching its apogee during the reign of Jayavarman VII.

The temple of Ta Prohm,[62] one of Jayavarman's first great Buddhist temple projects, was constructed in 1186 to house an image of his mother, Jayarājacūḍāmaṇi, in the form of Prajñāpāramitā, the mother of the buddhas. Its foundational inscription [K. 273] includes invocations to the triple jewel, Lokeśvara, and Prajñāpāramitā. It also tells us that Ta Prohm was supported by enormous royal donations, including 3,140 villages and their 80,000 residents, plus more than 600 female dancers. The king and various landed proprietors *(grāmavant)* also supplied more than 5,000 kilos of gold plate, 4,500 jewels, and much else besides. However, the cosmology of temple design is best illustrated at Preah Khan of Angkor, founded several years later on the basis of the astonishing donation of 13,500 villages and 306,372 male and female slaves from various foreign regions.[63] In its foundational inscription [K. 908], dated 1191 CE, we read that the great temple housed an image of Lokeśvara, rendered in the form of Jayavarman's father, as its central divinity. Its cosmological significance is that it lies in the neighborhood of three *barays*, or sacred tanks *(tīrtha)*, representing Buddha, Śiva, and Viṣṇu [K. 908, v. 33]. In one of these, the Preah

Khan *baray*, or Jayataṭaka, Jayavarman built another temple, Neak Pean.[64] The structure is a reference to the mythological Lake Anavatāpta, whose waters were deemed so pure and inaccessible that anything coming into contact with them must be thoroughly cleansed. Only those with advanced magical powers, like the Buddha, who supernaturally transported himself to Anavatāpta for his daily ablutions, can journey there, and it is said that gods brought sixteen pots of its holy water for the daily use of Aśoka, the archetypal Buddhist king (*Sp.* i.42). Kingship, then, is strongly linked to the mythology of the lake.[65]

According to Boisselier (1970, 94–95), the construction of an artificial version of Anavatāpta was de rigueur for any self-respecting Buddhist monarch. The Chinese pilgrim Xuanzang, for instance, is supposed to have seen such a structure fed by both hot and cold springs on the outskirts of Rājagṛha when he visited India in the seventh century, and the Sinhalese tradition also describes something similar built by Parakkamabāhu I (r. c. 1153–1186), who was an almost exact contemporary of Jayavarman VII (*Cv.* lxxxix.49). According to Buddhist traditions, the four great river systems of the world issue from Anavatāpta, so canals oriented in the four cardinal directions also naturally flowed from Neak Pean. Its sanctuary incorporated an image—Balāha, the horse avatar of Avalokiteśvara, with human figures clinging to him for dear life—to the east of a central lotus-throned Buddha. These figures appear to be the shipwrecked merchants mentioned by the *Kāraṇḍavyūha sūtra*, one of the principal Indic sources of the cult of Avalokiteśvara. To the west is a reclining male figure identified as Viṣṇu; to the north is a block holding sculptures comparable to the thousand *liṅgas* found at Phnom Kulen and clearly related to Śiva.[66] Unfortunately, the southern image is too eroded to be identified, but Boisselier (1970, 99–100) has concluded that this architectural *maṇḍala* is a political statement of the universal power of the kingdom committed to the ideology of Mahayana Buddhism founded on, and not antagonistic to, the veneration of both Śiva and Viṣṇu. The arrangements at Phimai, Banteay Samre, and Beng Mealea, although not so explicit, were probably inspired by similar considerations.

We have already had cause to note that the cult of Avalokiteśvara had been around in Cambodia for some considerable time. Indeed, the two Sanskrit inscriptions K. 214 (dated 982, from Banteay Nan, Battambang Province) and K. 417 (dated 970, from Prasat Chikreng, Siem Reap) mention the bodhisattva specifically.[67] K. 908 also mentions that Jayavarman VII erected twenty-three images, named Jayabuddhamahānātha, around the principal towns of his domains. Woodward (1994–1995, 106–107) has suggested that these were the "radiating" Avalokiteśvara figures covered with small buddhas and a Prajñāpāramitā on the chest, many of which are still extant. The iconography, with buddhas emerging from every pore of the bodhisattva, is also based on the

Kāraṇḍavyūha sūtra.[68] The likelihood, then, is that this or similar texts were well known in Cambodia, a likelihood reinforced by the iconographic evidence of Banteay Chmar, a late temple of Jayavarman's reign in the far northwest of the kingdom. Banteay Chmar once possessed eight unique two-meter-high figures of Avalokiteśvara, carved in low relief on the southern side of the western gallery.[69] Iconographically, they are in surprising conformity with the *Kāraṇḍavyūha.*

Jayavarman's great temple-mountain, the Bayon,[70] was constructed quite late in the reign. It housed a colossal stone image of the Buddha protected by the *nāga* Mucalinda. But its most distinctive external features are its towers, each with four faces.[71] Unfortunately, there is little consensus over their identity. It has customarily been believed that they are the faces of Lokeśvara. However, to Bernard-Philippe Groslier (1962, 183), and to Mus before him, the 54 towers with their total of 192 faces are an architectural expression of the Buddha's famous miracle at Śrāvastī, where he manifested multicolored beams of light from every pore. To these scholars the faces are those of the historical Buddha, whereas Thompson (2000, 261), if I understand her correctly, suggests a link with Maitreya. Woodward (1981, 62) has argued that the faces were originally conceived as representations of Vajrasattva, though, when sometime later the Bayon was redesigned under the influence of resurgent Brahmanism, they were reinterpreted as images of Brahmā. It is difficult to decide among the various identities advanced in scholarly circles, yet Filliozat (1969, 47) has noted one striking parallel. The appearance of face-towers in both Cambodia and the Himalayan region, where eyes facing the four directions are painted on temple towers, occurs at around the same time. It may be that during the Muslim conquest of Bengal at the end of the twelfth century Buddhist monks fled not just to Nepal and Tibet, as is widely known, but also to Indochina.[72] Dominant Buddhist philosophical and aesthetic notions, many of them connected to the tantric current that had run strong in northern India for many centuries, would inevitably have spread and adapted to local conditions in the process. There is certainly clear evidence that the tantric divinity Hevajra and his elaborate pantheon were venerated during the Bayon period (Boeles 1966). Contemporary Khmer bronze *vajras* and other ritual implements of the type associated with tantric cult activity are also well attested. It is possible that these were additions to the current of Buddhist tantrism that had already been active in Cambodia since at least the reign of Rājendravarman.

The Lokeśvara-Buddha-Prajñāpāramitā triad is found in earlier strata of the inscriptional record, but, as we have already noted, Jayavarman VII specifically associated Lokeśvara and Prajñāpāramitā with his father and mother. What we seem to have here is a Buddha family in which the central figure in the triad, the Buddha, equates to the king himself. To put it another way, father/Lokeśvara and mother/Prajñāpāramitā act as the bodhisattva lieutenants of the king/Buddha. If Woodward is correct about the identification of the Jayabuddhamahānātha images, and if the *Kāraṇḍavyūha* or related texts really do support the iconography of extant Avalokiteśvaras of the period, we may well be looking at a symbolic representation of kingship extending from its Angkorian center to the farthest extremities of the realm. This notion is picked up and extended by Hawixbrock (1998, 76–77), who argues that the total religious symbolism of the monuments constructed by Jayavarman VII expresses the king's status as a righteous ruler *(cakravartin)* in the classical Buddhist mold. The *cakravartin* ideal is given added resonance by the fact that Jayavarman VII also constructed 121 "houses of fire" (probably rest houses) along the principal roads of his kingdom and 102 hospitals, perhaps in imitation of Aśoka.[73] Hawixbrock believes that there is good reason to regard some of Jayavarman's temples—Ta Prohm and Preah Khan at Angkor, Banteay Chmar, and Wat Nokor are good examples—as sites of important victories over the Cham. They each act as three-dimensional cosmograms symbolizing the restoration of order through the power of a righteous king, but the ensemble of religious foundations can also be read as an overarching *maṇḍala* by which the realm was restored and purified following its violation during the Cham invasions. Through their construction and accompanying rites, the kingdom was transformed into an ideal realm. At the center of the great city Angkor Thom stands Jayavarman's pantheon, the Bayon, representing Mount Meru; the nearby Royal Palace is homologized to the residence of Indra; and Neak Pean, to the sacred lake Anavatāpta. We do know that the Siem Reap River, which flows through the city, had been identified with the Ganges sometime previously.[74] To complete the vision, the great provincial temples of the reign, like Ta Prohm of Kompong Svay and Banteay Chmar, represent the various islands surrounding the world mountain of traditional Buddhist cosmology. Symbolically, then, the Angkorian state has become coextensive with the entire world. Jayavarman VII's cult of state Buddhism was undoubtedly the high-water mark for the Mahayana in Cambodia.[75]

The Late Angkorian Period and the Rise of Theravada Buddhism

It seems that Jayavarman VII had inherited a strong attachment to Buddhism from his father, Dharaṇīndravarman II (r. c. 1160), who "found his satisfaction in this nectar that is the religion of Śākyamuni."[76] The construction of Preah

Palilay may have occurred during the father's reign. Unlike previous examples, this temple appears to have been conceived as a uniquely Sravakayanist structure, since it contains no tantric imagery, such as crowned buddhas, and its narrative scenes depicting incidents in the life of the Buddha are quite reminiscent of those found in much more recent Theravada contexts. Indeed, the scene on the eastern pediment of the north entrance to the *gopura*—depicting the Buddha being served by an elephant, Pārileyya, and a monkey—gives the structure its modern name.[77] Preah Palilay may have been an inspiration for some of Jayavarman's later Buddhist structures like Banteay Kdei, probably the Pūrvatathāgata (Buddha of the East) mentioned in K. 485, the western *gopura* of which includes a carved depiction of a robed monk that some scholars have held to be characteristic of the Theravada. Although quite what inspired the incorporation of such elements remains a subject of speculation, Dupont's thesis (1935) that the influence is from Dvāravatī is unproven, but we know that the Theravada had been present in the Pyu and Mon regions of Southeast Asia since the fifth century and that in the mid-eleventh century it had challenged and defeated the tantric Āri sect that had established itself at Pagan several centuries earlier. Contact between Mon and Khmer regions may have catalyzed similar processes during the high to late Angkorian period, yet, as we have seen, Mahayanist forms of the tradition were not abandoned overnight.

Other members of Jayavarman VII's immediate household also had a strong attraction to the teachings of the Buddha. One of his wives, Indradevī, was an important Buddhist patroness, described as having "surpassed in her knowledge the knowledge of philosophers." Her almost faultless Sanskrit inscription at Phimeanakas [K. 485][78] tells how she taught Buddhism to nuns at three named convents: Nagendratuṅga, Tilakottara, and Narendrāśrama. She also converted the king's first wife, Jayarājadevī, who is said to have organized dramatic enactments of stories of the Buddha's previous lives *(Jātakas),* performed by young nuns recruited from outcaste families. How large the nuns' order was at this time is impossible to say, but the involvement of two principal wives of such a powerful king must have had a beneficial impact. According to the Burmese *Glass Palace Chronicle* (1960, 143–144), in 1180 CE one of Jayavarman's sons, Tāmalinda, traveled in a party of Mon monks to Ceylon, where he received monastic ordination into the lineage of the Theravada Mahāvihāra, which had been recently purified by Parakkamabāhu I. Tāmalinda seems to have died in Burma, never returning to his homeland, so it is difficult to know whether the consequences of the journey were felt in Cambodia itself. However, the event may indicate that Angkor now felt the need to reach out, both diplomatically and spiritually, to other influential regions of the Theravada world.[79] There is some reinforcing evidence in this connection. The *Cūlavaṃsa,* a Sinhalese chronicle, informs us of significant tensions between Parakkamabāhu and the Burmese ruler, Narapatijayasūra, in the early to mid-1170s (*Cv.* lxxvi). One consequence of the deteriorating relations was that a Ceylonese princess was seized by the Burmese while on her way to Cambodia, perhaps to marry a member of the Cambodian royal family. From what we know of the religious situation in Cambodia at the time, there would have been good reasons to establish alliances with other powerful Theravada polities. The benefits from the Ceylonese perspective would, no doubt, have been equally desirable. Some Ceylonese inscriptions, particularly those from the reign of the next king, Nissanka Malla (1189–1197), also suggest a Cambodian connection. One mentions a group of fowlers, called Cambodi, who were bribed by the king in an effort to discourage them from their scandalous way of life. Some scholars have suggested that they may have been Cambodian mercenaries. In itself this does not constitute very strong evidence of a link between the two regions, but other tantalizing clues reinforce the suspicion. Of particular interest is the appearance of Khmer motifs in contemporary Ceylonese architecture. The Satmahalprāsāda and the Potgul Vihara, for example, seem to exhibit a Khmer character,[80] and one of the gates of Polonnaruva was apparently called Kambojavasala (Panditha 1973, 143).

From the evidence of widespread damage to Buddhist images and their replacement by *liṅgas* or figures of praying ascetics, it looks probable that a muscular Śaivism had an Indian summer during the mid-thirteenth century.[81] The anti-Buddhist iconoclasm was rather more selective than has sometimes been thought, however. Geographically isolated structures, such as Banteay Chmar, escaped harm completely, while even at Angkor itself some sites, such as Preah Palilay, were left intact. The probable explanation is that the reaction was directed at images of a syncretic or tantric nature representing concepts quite recently imported into the country from an India convulsed by Muslim invasions (Boisselier 1965, 82–83). The opposition, then, was to alien ideas and practices rather than to long-standing Buddhist traditions. This may account for the rapid disintegration of Jayavarman VII's style of state Mahayana fairly soon after his death. The Śrāvakayāna, on the other hand, had been a presence prior to these developments and seems not to have been adversely affected. Whatever the true state of affairs, its rise to prominence in Cambodia dates from the post-Jayavarman period.

The inscriptional record for the early thirteenth century is rather bare, but when Zhou Daguan, a member of a Chinese ambassador's entourage, arrived in Cambodia in 1296 CE, he reported the presence of three separate religious groupings active in the country: Brahmins, who wore the sacred thread; ascetic worshippers of the *liṅga* (i.e., followers of Śiva); and individuals he called *zhugu*, who "shave their heads, wear yellow lower garments, uncover the right shoulder, fasten a skirt of material around the lower part of the body, go barefoot."[82] This is a pretty clear reference to Buddhist monks, and, given the color of the robes, they could possibly have been Theravadins. Zhou Daguan observed that there were no Buddhist nuns in the country, which is odd, for they are mentioned in the Jayavarman VII epigraphy, as noted above. But the king went on a journey where he first had to visit "a small golden tower in front of which is a gold Buddha."[83] The king was probably Śrīndravarman, a pious Buddhist who seems to have abdicated the throne and withdrew to the forests in 1307 CE.[84]

A Pali inscription [K. 754] at Kok Svay Chek, near Siem Reap, dated 1308 CE, indicates a possible Theravada presence. It states that King Śrīndrajayavarman (r. c. 1307–1327) donated a village to a senior monk *(mahāthera)*, Siri Sirindamoli, and an additional four villages and slaves of both sexes for the funding of a monastery.[85] One must beware of an oversimplistic equation of language and religious affiliation, for it might be falsely assumed that Buddhist Sanskrit inscriptions are always Mahayanist whereas materials in Pali are Theravadin. Yet even in a comparatively well-studied area like medieval Sri Lanka such assumptions cannot be easily supported, as Bechert (1998) has convincingly shown. Nevertheless, by the time Jayavarmādiparameśvara took the Angkorian throne around 1327 CE, Theravada Buddhism was well established. The Laotian chronicles tell of an exiled prince from Lan Chang, called Fa Ngum, who spent time in the Cambodian court being taught by a Buddhist monk called Maha Pasaman. Fa Ngum subsequently married one of Jayavarmādiparameśvara's daughters before returning to his homeland with a collection of Pali scriptures donated by her father. In due course Fa Ngum, now king of Lan Chang, sent a return embassy to Cambodia, led by his old monk teacher. Eventually he returned to Lan Chang with the famous Phra Bang Buddha image and another collection of sacred writings (Sirisena 1978, 107).

In the century following the construction of the Bayon, Buddhist statuary also begins its move in a more definitively Theravadin direction. In particular, wooden buddha images with both hands outstretched in *abhayamudrā* are produced in large numbers. Dupont (1959) has pointed to several examples from Preah Pean, Angkor Wat, which were constructed using the same technique of attaching the hands by a tenon joint as at Dvāravatī. Wheels of the law *(dharmacakra)*, another characteristic of the Dvāravatī art, also start to appear in Cambodia around this time, notably at Phnom Kulen. The last inscription in Sanskrit at Angkor dates from 1327, and Mahayana Buddhism itself largely disappeared after the fall of Angkor in 1431.

2

The Middle Period and the Emergence of the Theravada

The Problem of Sources

Śrāvakayāna Buddhism had been present in Cambodia well before the fall of Angkor, but the precise nature of its occurrence remains elusive and it is difficult to divine any social influence the movement might have exercised. Whether the Śrāvakayāna was represented by one school or by many is impossible to say. It is also hard to get a clear perspective on the movement's oscillating fortunes over the lengthy period stretching from Funan to the opening of the fifteenth century. The occurrence of scattered fragments of Pali inscriptional evidence, with isolated examples from as far back as the seventh century CE, has inclined some to believe that the Theravada was active in the region at a relatively early point, but this can hardly pass muster as convincing evidence. As noted in the previous chapter, we are on firmer ground from the opening of the fourteenth century.

In an influential essay Benda (1962) has argued that Theravada Buddhism gained the power to replace a Mahayano-Brahmanical ancien régime that had become "either deficient or declining, if not both" toward the end of the Angkorian period. The strength of the Theravada in these changed circumstances was considerable. Benda asserts that it made possible the creation of "a quasi-egalitarian religious community of which even the monarchs themselves became, albeit for short times and mainly symbolically, members." This new community in turn acted as an effective mechanism for the restraint of excessive kingly authority, particularly since those committed to this new form of religious life "practiced the principles of other-worldly simplicity and frugality, in sharp contrast to the Mahāyāna monks of the classical age" (Benda 1962, 120–121).[1] Other scholars have taken a similar line, with Kulke, for instance, attributing the decline to Jayavarman VII's "frenzy of [Mahāyāna] missionary zeal" combined with a heady Buddhist-inspired apotheosis of kingship. The people, exhausted by the economic consequences of the experiment, then wearily "turned to the Ceylonese Theravada Buddhism which from the twelfth century began to spread across Burma to the rest of mainland Southeast Asia" (Kulke 1993, 375–376). The *Jinakalamali*, a Southeast Asian Pali chronicle, certainly mentions eight Khmer in a larger party of Thai monks who received higher ordination in Sri Lanka in 1426,[2] but we should be a little careful about reading this as evidence of a fundamental shift in emphasis for Cambodian Buddhism as a whole.

Benda characterizes the Cambodian Theravada of the late and immediately post-Angkorian periods as a grassroots movement, its populist and antiaristocratic message supporting its spread through a previously neglected rural environment. Under its benign influence the peasantry gained a new sense of solidarity and were able to break free from the confines of "the world of local spirits and traditions" to a wider understanding of their place in the historical process. In this, Benda perhaps unconsciously endorses the presuppositions of earlier French scholarship. Leclère (1899, 497), for example, believed that Buddhism had been responsible for the destruction of the Angkorian caste system, although it must be said that contemporary inscriptions do provide some evidence of interethnic and interclass marriages with good levels of interaction between social groupings.[3]

Benda's analysis of this major change in direction for Cambodian society has wide currency but suffers from a thin evidential base and too romantic a reading of Theravada history and metaphysics. Theravada karma theory, for instance, links social rank with merit accrued in previous lives. This means that it offers limited opportunities for advancement to those from the lower strata of society. Indeed, its innate conservatism is a key feature of attack by its opponents, most notably the communists of the modern period. If we look elsewhere, it is not at all clear that Buddhism in Sri Lanka around the same period successfully operated beyond aristocratic control, and the same holds good for Thailand, although admittedly somewhat later. It is probable that Cambodian Buddhism operated in much the same pattern.

Another problem relates to the unanswered question, if the Śrāvakayāna had been present in the region for many centuries, what caused it to break through at this specific point? Furthermore, the velvet revolution through which the Theravada is supposed to have risen to prominence does not fit the established pattern of social and political change in the region. Up to this point, radical adjustments in the religious domain had been driven by a strong centralized authority, not by popular demand. Indeed, an inscription [K. 177] in Khmer and Pali from Preah Theat Khvao, Kompong Thom Province, probably dating from the mid-fifteenth century, records a monk's ecclesiastical advancement by the king in time-honored fashion. Nevertheless, "Cambodia was becoming post-Angkorian well before the abandonment of Angkor" (Chandler 1996, 78), and Theravada Buddhism undoubtedly played an influential and sustained role in this transformation. Since that time its roots have been strong enough not to be dislodged by competing religious traditions.

Hard historical evidence from Cambodia's middle period is, if anything, thinner than that for the preceding periods. Epigraphy does exist, but it has received significantly less attention than earlier materials. Conclusions to be drawn from architectural and art historical studies are also compromised by a number of factors. Many religious structures were built from perishable materials, such as wood and thatch, and have not survived down to the modern period. Other material remains have suffered badly from vandalism, both intended and unintended, as evidenced by an enduring Khmer mania for reconstruction. Historical writing has not been a major genre in Cambodian literature, but chronicles *(bangsavatar)*, particularly royal chronicles *(rajabangsavatar)*, exist in a number of versions. However, they contain large quantities of legendary material, are somewhat contradictory, are not especially old, and tend to retroject the customs and practices current at the time of composition into the period described. They were not designed for general consumption or even for recital, but they seem to have been part of the ritual items in the king's postmortem regalia. The genre flourished from the late eighteenth until at least the mid-twentieth century, after which, in Chandler's words, "foreigners took more interest in Cambodia's history than the Cambodians did themselves" (1979, 208). Nevertheless, the chronicles can be important sources of historical knowledge, especially when read judiciously alongside the reports from foreign travelers.

Benedict Anderson's observation (1990) that Southeast Asian chronicles focus on continual bloodletting and generalized violence and thus provide a "reassurance of fratricide" is confirmed in the Cambodian context. Redactors of the chronicles were either mandarins who focused on the doings of the court, or monks who were more concerned with Buddhist traditions, the king's involvement in agricultural and Buddhist rituals, and provincial matters.[4] The interpretation of such texts, however fraught with methodological difficulties, must be regarded as an important key to the understanding of Buddhism in Cambodia before the arrival of the French.

Legendary Materials: Preah Thong and the Emerald Buddha

The chronicles generally start in mythic time before moving on to a discussion of more solidly historical figures. The region's first ruler, Preah Thong,[5] is anachronistically held to have built a *stūpa* at Angkor to house Buddha relics sent from India by Aśoka.[6] Another mythic figure, Dāv Vaṅs Ascāry,[7] gained the boon of a male child after observing the Buddhist precepts. The child, Kaetumāla, really the son of Indra, had been sent to earth to protect the country and Buddhism.[8] Sometime later the divine artificer Viśvakarman[9] was reborn under the name "Cau Citt Kumār." Offering his services to the king, he built the Bayon, Baphuon, Phimeanakas, and "all the temple towers decorated with the faces of Brahma." Dāv Vaṅs Ascāry practiced the ten royal virtues and lived until he was 108, after which Kaetumāla became king and built Nagar Vatt (i.e., Angkor Wat).[10] But he came under the spell of women, and his passions led him to ignore the norms of Buddhist kingship. Indra, in distress, ordered Viśvakarman to invite Ānanda, a disciple of Mahinda Thera,[11] and seven other monks to travel from Lanka to Angkor, where they performed a royal consecration rite *(indrābhiṣeka)*, reciting Buddhist verses while Indra and Brahmā acted as Brahmanical priests. By this act Kaetumāla was released from the women's power, the eight monks constituted an ecclesiastical bureaucracy *(rājāgaṇa)*, and the kingdom prospered once more (Mak Phœun 1984, 59–64).

During the reign of Padum Suriyavaṅs,[12] a junk loaded with copies of the Tripitaka and an Emerald Buddha given to the Laotian king by the king of Ceylon ran aground in a storm near the great city *(maha nagar)*. Becoming aware of Padum Suriyavaṅs' kingly virtues, monks offered him the junk's contents, and he installed the Emerald Buddha and the sacred writings in Angkor Wat. Copies of the Tripitaka were then made and distributed to all the monasteries of the land. In due course the Lao king recovered the original copy of the Tripitaka, but the Emerald Buddha stayed in Cambodia until it was forcibly recovered following a serious flood at Angkor (Mak Phœun 1984, 79–80, 83–84, 114–115).[13]

In another version of the story, Nāgasena, a monk from Pataliputra in northern India, wishes to make an emerald image of the Buddha from the *maṇijoti*, the precious jewel of all the *cakravartins* located at the summit of Mount Vepulla. On Indra's orders Viśvavarman carves the image in seven days, and Nāgasena predicts its future peregrinations around South and Southeast Asia.[14] An interesting feature of this version is that the great Theravadin exegete Buddhaghosa and five colleagues who had previously supervised the copying of the Tripitaka in Lanka have become members of the shipwreck party. Now washed ashore near Phnom Penh, the junk contains the sacred *uṇṇaloma* Buddha relic—the jewel of sacred fire *(kaev preah phloeung)*—and the Vinaya and Abhidhamma,[15] alongside the Emerald Buddha. The sacred cargo is distributed to monasteries in Phnom Penh. The sacred writings go to Wat Langka, Wat Unnalom gets the Buddha relic, and the Emerald Buddha is installed in Wat Preah Budd Mān Puṇy.[16] Buddhaghosa himself resides at Wat Buddhaghosa, where the king honors him with the title of *sanghareach,* before he moves to Angkor Wat with the Emerald Buddha and a collection of sacred writings copied onto gold and silver (Mak Phœun 1984, 358–359). Similar tales with the same massively retrojected themes designed to antiquate and authenticate recent traditions are told across the Theravada world and must be taken with a pinch of salt. However, since both versions seek to represent Angkor Wat as a Buddhist structure from its inception, it seems likely that their composition may be traced to a time when that important temple was actually undergoing a major personality change.[17]

Thai Influences and Middle-Period Kings

At its height the Angkorian empire had extended over much of what is now Thailand. But the population of outlying areas had been largely non-Khmer. During the eleventh and twelfth centuries Thai groups moved down into the central Mekong valley, in due course throwing off weak Khmer overlordship and establishing a first independent state at Sukhothai around 1238 CE. There seems to have been little cultural discontinuity, however. The earliest Theravada monastery at Sukhothai, Wat Aranyik, employed Khmer-style stonework (Gosling 1991, 22–23), while Wat Phra Phai Luang consists of three Khmer-style towers aligned north-south, to the east of which was once a terrace and a wooden *vihāra* dating to the reign of Jayavarman VII.[18] However, as Thai power increased, Angkor suffered a number of attacks. It seems to have been temporarily abandoned in the 1430s, when the Cambodian king Bañā Yāt (c. 1417–1463) moved south to the more easily defended region around Phnom Penh, but it would be incorrect to assume that Angkor was entirely forgotten and overwhelmed by jungle, even though the traumatic reverberations of the event are still felt to the present.

The Cambodian royal chronicles, in their quasi-legendary description of the Thai capture of Angkor, state that monks, buddha images, and other statues, including the sacred cow *(preah go),* were taken as booty (Mak Phœun 1984, 144).[19] A long-standing tradition among the Khmer is that *preah go* was part of the king's regalia and that it contained a hidden library of writings that gave him his powers and granted access to all areas of learning for the Khmer people

Shrine of Preah Go and Preah Kaev—Chhlong District, Kratie Province.

(Mak Phœun 1995, 61n70). From a symbolic perspective the story underlines the reality that both power and learning had now been lost to the Khmer and passed to the Thai. But it also raises some interesting questions about the direction of Theravada influence in the fifteenth century. The inclusion of human and cultural assets of a specifically religious character in the booty may suggest that the Thai desired to strengthen their own fledgling affiliation to the Theravada.

Evidence that the Thai came to regard Cambodia as a repository of important cultural and religious knowledge is plentiful. This curious schizophrenia is nicely illustrated in the career of King Prasat Thong (1629–1656), who on the one hand built Wat Chaiwatthanaram at Ayutthaya to commemorate a victorious campaign in Cambodia, yet on the other hand sent architects to Angkor to study temple construction so that they could build Prasat Nakhon Luang to the east of the capital when they returned (Fouser 1996, 31).[20]

The Thai also quickly came to embrace Angkorian principles of statecraft, Khmer was adopted as the language of the aristocracy, and the court operated with a terminology derived from both Khmer and Sanskrit. Indeed, Khmer inscriptions are found in the central Thai region well after the fall of Angkor, until as late as the late seventeenth century (Vickery 1973, 52–53). The legacy is also revealed in the importation of the *Rāmāyaṇa* into royal circles and in the fact that, until well into the nineteenth century, most Pali texts that were used in the Theravada monasteries of central Thailand were written in the Khmer *(khom)* script.[21] The Thai fascination with all things Angkorian endured into the modern period, when Mongkut (r. 1851–1868) had a model of Angkor Wat constructed[22] and installed alongside the shrine of the Emerald Buddha. He also sponsored a bungled attempt (the leader of the team was murdered by locals) to dismantle two towers from Ta Prohm and reerect them in Bangkok (Chandler 1976a, 55n4).

According to the Phnom Penh foundation myth, a certain Lady Penh established Wat Phnom around 1372 CE after she found a bronze buddha image and a stone carving of Viṣṇu embedded in a tree floating downriver. The carving of Viṣṇu was installed in a shrine at the foot of the *phnom,* and the Buddha image in a *vihāra* at the top (Khin Sok 1988, 70–71). After her death the sanctuary fell into ruin but was restored by Bañā Yāt when he fled from Angkor. It is said that he built a large *stūpa* to house the bronze Buddha, and other powerful images were brought from the old capital for the purpose. He also sponsored *sīmā*-laying ceremonies at nearby monasteries.[23]

The chronicles describe the reign of Dhammarāja (1486–1504) as a Buddhist golden age. He committed many pious acts, including a three-year suspension of taxes, and the country was at peace. He knew the Tripitaka by heart, and around 1496 CE he arranged the transfer of Buddha relics from Preah Thong's *stūpa* at Angkor to a new home in the village of Khvav Brah Dhatu near Phnom Santuk, Kompong Thom. He subsequently spent three months there as a monk and made a number of large donations to the *sangha,* including a gift of twenty-one male and twenty-one female slaves to look after the *stūpa* and its associated structures (Khin Sok 1988, 95–97).

Following an unsettled period during which Thai incursions into Cambodia became the pattern, King Ang Chan[24] established a new capital at Longvek[25] in the first half of the sixteenth century. According to a royal chronicle, the king had been wandering in a forest one day when he saw an unusual large stone in the branches of a *koki* tree. He ordered craftsmen to carve it with four Buddhas facing out from its four sides. The resulting piece was enshrined in the cruciform Wat Tralaeng Kaeng, Longvek, in 1530 CE (Khin Sok 1988,

149–150, 294n530).[26] There is some reason to suppose that the stone had been part of an earlier Angkorian temple left abandoned in the forest. If this is indeed the case, Ang Chan appears to have rededicated an earlier cult object for Theravadin usage. Signs of Buddhist regeneration are also shown by the significant numbers of Cambodian monks who traveled to Luang Prabang to study Theravada Buddhism, particularly during the reigns of kings Pothisārāt and his son Setthāthirāt (Condominas 1975, 253). Several years later, perhaps around 1533 CE, Ang Chan undertook more substantial construction works on and around the nearby hills *(phnom preah reach trop)* at Udong. *Barays,* originally left incomplete at the death of the king's father, were finished, and a number of monasteries, such as Wat Brah Dhammaker, were built. It seems that at least one of these was dedicated to the Buddha's disciple Kassapa in 1536 (Marquis 1932, 477–478). The construction of a colossal north-facing Buddha, Preah Put Attaroes,[27] on the south summit and a temple housing an enormous figure of the Buddha in *parinirvāṇa*[28] to the east completed the ensemble. A senior monk named Uk, or Brah Nagga Thera, was appointed to take care of the complex (Khin Sok 1988, 150). Although the site has never been studied in depth, it is perhaps not too imaginative to read it as a second Angkor, with some of the same cosmological significances previously noted in connection with the reign of Jayavarman VII.

The chronicles are clear that Ang Chan was a pious Theravadin. However, he is also known to have executed a series of Brahmanical bas-reliefs at Angkor Wat, including depictions of Kṛṣṇa's victory over Bāna and Viṣṇu's victory over the Asuras. It is worth bearing in mind that the Buddha was regarded as an incarnation of Viṣṇu in Brahmanical circles and that there had been a tendency to associate him with Rāma, another incarnation of Viṣṇu, since the time of Sūryavarman II (Thompson 1999, 249). Ang Chan was merely continuing the tradition. On the other hand, some previously Brahmanical structures such as the Bakheng and Baphuon were rededicated to Buddhism. The former was invested with a giant seated Buddha at its summit, the latter with a similarly enormous *parinirvāṇa* figure. The majority, however, were simply neglected and left to deteriorate, though previously Buddhist structures such as Banteay Kdei and Wat Nokor were remodeled and brought back into use. A vogue for Buddhist rock-carved images, particularly large images of the Buddha lying in *parinirvāṇa,* is an emerging feature of the public art of the period. Good examples are found at Phnom Santuk (Dalet 1934, 796)[29] and the famous Preah Ang Thom of Phnom Kulen, dating from 1568 CE (Boisselier 1966, 280).[30]

Khleang Moeung is supposed to have been a general in Ang Chan's army.

Preah Ang Thom—Phnom Kulen, Svay Leu District, Siem Reap Province.

Facing defeat against the Thai, he threw himself into a ditch of stakes with his wife and three sons at Bakan in Pursat Province. Transformed into an army of ghosts, they sowed the seeds of cholera in the enemy, who were subsequently defeated. His death by unnatural means transformed him into a powerful protective spirit *(neak tā)*.[31] During the reign of Saṭṭhā (Paramarāja IV, 1576–1594), Longvek itself came under Thai attack. The king protected his capital by venerating the potent Buddha Kaya Siddhi image at Wat Brah Inda Deba and worshipping at the shrine of Khleang Moeung. To counter these supernatural defenses, two wizards disguised as Buddhist monks were sent to Cambodia by the Thai king, probably Naresuan (r. 1590–1605). Gaining the king's confidence, they drove Saṭṭhā insane, convincing him that his problems emanated from the malign influences of the Buddha Kaya Siddhi and the previously mentioned Buddha of Wat Tralaeng Kaeng. Saṭṭhā ordered both images to be broken and thrown into the river. The chronicles tell us that this caused the sacred sword of Khmer kingship, *preah khan,* to rust;[32] the waters of a sacred spring at Banon, Battambang Province, dried up; a Buddha image at Vihear Suor, Srei Santhor, cracked and bled; and the leaves of a *bodhi* tree at Longvek fell out of season. Cholera spread across the land, and the Thai gained control. Only when the pieces of the sacred images were recovered, reassembled, and restored to their rightful place was the enemy repulsed (Khin Sok 1988, 188–193).[33]

The Buddhist Appropriation of Angkor

A number of Khmer inscriptions from Saṭṭhā's reign provide brief insights into the nature of Buddhism at the time.[34] IMA2, dated 1577 CE, contains a number of Pali phrases. Its author, a pious queen mother named Mahākalyānavattī Srī Sujātā, refers to herself as of "righteous faith, threefold." She has participated in much merit making and meditated on impermanence *(aniccā)*. Her son, the king, has piously restored Preah Pisnulok, that is, Angkor Wat (Lewitz 1970).[35] IMA3, written two years later, confirms this. Here a royal figure, probably Saṭṭhā,[36] has rebuilt the temple's central tower and covered it with gold. Four inscriptions [IMA4] dated 1586 CE also relate how a high dignitary and his wife restored statues at the Bakan, built a *stūpa*, planted a *bodhi* tree, and had copies of the Abhidhamma and the Great Jātaka made as part of their merit-making efforts (Lewitz 1971). Independent evidence supports the idea that the central sanctuary of Angkor Wat—the Bakan, an arrangement of five towers in quincunx—was significantly remodeled and invested with great images of Buddha in high relief and giant Thai-influenced *buddhapāda* around this period (Boisselier 1966, 281).

The tenth-century Brahmanical Preah Indr-Kosiy to the south of Angkor Wat gradually metamorphosed into Wat Preah Indr-Kosiy (Pou 1987–1988, 341) at this time, and Buddhist structures began to multiply within the precincts of the temple itself. Indeed, its current name, meaning "city with monasteries," indicates that middle-period monastic foundations flourished within its compound (Pou 1990, 19). Epigraphy from 1566 to 1744 CE mentions a variety of high-ranking Buddhist dignitaries active in the area, a good indication that it was the locus of very significant religious activity.[37] A general resurgence of Buddhist activity is confirmed by the accounts of European adventurers, some of whom had established themselves at Longvek at the end of the sixteenth century. One of them asserted that a third of the male population were Buddhist monks. This must be a massive overestimate, but the report of sizable monastic estates (B.-P. Groslier 1958, 160) suggests that institutional Buddhism was prospering.

Angkor Wat was becoming a pilgrim magnet,[38] as is well illustrated by fourteen inscriptions in Chinese ink left by Japanese visitors in its central cruciform gallery, Preah Pean,[39] during the first half of the seventeenth century. In the most legible of the records, Morimoto Ukondayu Kazufusa writes that he arrived in January 1632 CE after a lengthy sea journey to make offerings to four buddha images, to perform rituals for the repose of the soul of his father, and to pray for the long and peaceful life of his mother. It appears that some of these pilgrims believed that Angkor Wat was the true site of the Jetavana Vihāra, which had actually been located at Śrāvastī in northeastern India.[40] Unfortunately, the *vihāra* had already been destroyed by fire by the time the Chinese traveler Faxian visited India in the fourth century, so it is perhaps unsurprising that its location was shifted to a more convenient spot, particularly when we realize that this had not been the first time that a mystical Indic geography had been transposed upon the physical contours of Southeast Asia. It is difficult to be precise about when the flow of international pilgrims ceased, but the instabilities of the next two centuries undoubtedly had a deleterious effect. Ironically, the flow resumed once more in the colonial period, although by then the efforts of French conservators had led to a removal of all Buddhist imagery and a relocation of monks to a safe distance beyond the central sanctuary in a sterile gesture to return the structure to its original Brahmanical purpose (Edwards 1999, 203).[41]

The process of buddhification was not confined to Angkor Wat. Many early Theravada monastic sites emerged through the conversion of preexisting structures. These "Buddhist terraces" (Marchal 1918) generally consist of a rectangular stone platform and a temple, previously dedicated to Brahmanical or Mahayanist use, laid out on an east-west axis. A wooden *vihāra* to the east and a colossal seated Buddha image with its back turned to the ancient sanctuary and occupying the extreme western edge of the platform, the ensemble encircled by stone boundary markers *(sīmā),* are the Buddhist additions. One of the most interesting features of the transformation is the opening up of a previous ritually and physically closed space, for the temple had formerly been available only to a priestly elite. The new Theravada boundary, on the other hand, demarcates but does not block access.[42] The change may, perhaps, reflect the more democratic tendencies of the new tradition.

Some of the oldest Theravadin statues of the middle period are preserved in the Vihear Banon, the northern sanctuary of Wat Sithor, Srei Santhor District, Kompong Cham Province. A tenth-century Mahayanist inscription [K. 111], mentioning the restoration of Buddha images under Rājendravarman and Jayavarman V, suggests that Wat Sithor also occupied an earlier Angkor-period temple.[43] A particularly interesting fact about this region is that it appears to have been the center of a *stūpa* cult. The great *stūpa* behind the central *vihāra* at Wat Sithor, for example, is supposed to house the relics of the Buddha's disciple Ānanda.[44] Another structure, Wat Nokor, also in Kompong Cham Province, had originally been built as a Mahayanist temple during the reign of Jayavarman VII, but the four pediments of the central sanctuary date from the latter part of the sixteenth century. That to the east has a particularly early image of the earth goddess, Nang Thorani, in a niche underneath an enthroned buddha.[45] The Wat Nokor inscription [K. 82], dated 1566 CE, records the conversion of Jayavarman's original sanctuary into a *stūpa*. Examples of similar conversions include Vihear

Great *stūpa*—Wat Sithor, Srei Santhor District, Kompong Cham Province.

Prampil Lvaeng and Tang Tok, both at Angkor Thom, and Preah Theat within the precincts of Wat Unnalom in Phnom Penh.

Intriguingly, *stūpas* appear very late in Cambodia. The oldest—at Sasar Sdam, thirty miles southeast of Siem Reap—probably dates from the late twelfth century.[46] They are not attested in the Funan, Zhenla, or early to high Angkorian periods. But the construction of *stūpa*-like structures in perishable materials, such as sand, is a definite feature of popular Buddhism in the modern period, so it is perfectly possible that ancient *stūpas* did exist but have not survived.

K. 82 at Wat Nokor contains the first explicitly Theravada reference to the future Buddha, Maitreya *(preah si ar maitrey)*. It also seems likely that he is depicted on the western pediment of the central sanctuary (Thompson 2000, 249). We have other evidence for the development of a Maitreya cult around that time. Gaspar da Cruz, a Portuguese Dominican who visited Longvek between 1555 and 1557 before being driven out by hostile Buddhist monks, confirms that the deity

The future Buddha, cutting off his topknot—southern pediment of central *prasat;* Wat Nokor, Kompong Siem District, Kompong Cham Province.

was the focus of significant attention (Thompson 1999, 164n63). With these facts in mind, Ashley Thompson has suggested that some post-Angkorian *stūpas* of the sort mentioned above were connected with the Maitreya cult. At Wat Nokor, four Buddha figures were arranged so that they faced out from the four antechambers of the cruciform structure. Similar configurations may be found in adjacent chapels (Thompson 2000, 246–247). The pattern also occurs at Angkor Wat, where the four doorways of the central tower were closed with sandstone blocks carved with images of standing buddhas at around the same time. Contemporary residents regard these images as representations of the

(left) Arrangement of four standing Buddhas—Wat Tralaeng Kaeng, Longvek, Kompong Tralach District, Kompong Chhnang Province.

(below) Arrangement of four Buddhas—Vihear Yiey Peou, Wat Nokor, Kompong Siem District, Kompong Cham Province.

buddhas of previous epochs, and Thompson (2000, 253) concludes that the central figure hidden between the other four must be Maitreya, the buddha to come. It seems that Ang Chan's earlier iconographic experiments with the fourfold buddha at Wat Tralaeng Kaeng may be read in a similar light. The significance of the iconographical development is not entirely clear, but it is possible that Maitreya's princely and messianic character may have been borrowed by rulers of the period anxious to enhance their own status, to point to their quasi-mythological status, and to reinforce a sense of continuity with a glorious Angkorian past.[47] This is a recurring leitmotif in Cambodian history all the way down to the present.

The Late Middle Period

The progress of Theravada Buddhism in Cambodia certainly encountered setbacks. The chronicles tell us that when Cau Bañā Ñom (Kaev Hvā I, r. 1600–1602) came to the throne at the age of sixteen, he neither observed the ten royal virtues nor supported Buddhism. He drank alcohol, hunted, and engaged in debauchery, and in consequence the kingdom suffered drought, famine, disease, and brigandage. Tigers entered the villages, and meteors fell on the Royal Palace. His grandmother called on the Thai king in Ayutthaya for help. As a result, Bañā Ñom was tied in a sack and drowned at Phnom Penh. There is some evidence linking a famous senior monk, Kaev Brah Bhloen, with the act (Mak Phœun 1995, 95n59), perhaps demonstrating that at this period the assassination of an unrighteous king could be justified from the Buddhist perspective.

The next king, Srī Suriyobarm (Paramarāja VII, r. 1602–1619), had been living in Ayutthaya, probably as a monk. The chronicles tell us that he was very respectful toward his royal Thai protector and did his utmost to revive Buddhism on his return to Cambodia. Around 1607 CE, after he and his court observed the Buddhist precepts for three days in order to purify the kingdom, Suriyobarm received a royal consecration *(prāptābhiṣeka)*. He also reconstituted an ecclesiastical hierarchy *(rājāgaṇa)* (Mak Phœun 1981, 118, 255). Around 1606 CE, Suriyobarm ordered the establishment of Wat Sambok in present-day Kratie Province, to which he made donations of a Buddha image, *chedis,* and forty families of slaves.[48] According to the *wat*'s foundational document, Suriyobarm conferred the title of "Samdech Preah Naganvan"[49] on the monastery's chief monk, Ariyagāthā. It is clear from the text, however, that this dignitary's duties were not entirely religious, for he also had responsibility for surveillance of the eastern "door to the kingdom" (Tranet 1983, 90). This seems to imply that he collected border and customs duties from river traffic coming down the

Mekong from Laos. Certainly, Christian missionaries writing around 1775 CE described the chief monks of Sambok as "seigneurs de toutes ces provinces-ci," and even in the nineteenth century their feudal powers remained considerable.[50] It is difficult to know whether the dual role played by senior monks started in the early sixteenth century, but it seems to have been fairly widespread at that time, for another monk, Preah Buddhavaṁsā of Wat Chrei Bak, Kompong Chhnang Province, is also recorded as having brought about the submission of a rebellious local governor around 1608 CE (Mak Phœun 1995, 126–127, 246).

At the age of seventy-one, Suriyobarm relinquished the throne "in conformity with ancient tradition," entering the monastic order and handing the kingdom over to his son, Jayajeṭṭhā II (1619–1627). Before coming to the throne, Jayajeṭṭhā had lived under Thai "protection" in Ayutthaya, possibly as a monk at Wat Phra Chao Phanam Choeng, where between the ages of sixteen and twenty-one he engaged in both scholarship *(ganthadura)* and meditation *(vipassanādhura)*. On being defrocked, he was obliged to become the Thai king's head of elephants. Indeed, he is widely supposed to have been the author of an important work on the classification of elephants. While out on a chase one day, he stumbled upon an ancient Buddha image at the top of a mountain. There is a possibility that it may have dated from the Angkorian period, for Jayajeṭṭhā is said to have taken a vow before it that he would return to his homeland to reestablish the cults of the *prateyekabuddhas,* the *arhats,* and the great buddhas of the past. The Cambodian chronicles comment that his companions saw a smile appear on the face of the Buddha in confirmation of the vow (Mak Phœun 1981, 102–118). Around 1620 this new king transferred his capital from Longvek to Udong,[51] a site that had first received attention during the time of Ang Chan. Suriyobarm died soon after, and he was cremated with great ceremony. Jayajeṭṭhā invited a thousand monks to recite the *Sattapakaraṇa*[52] for his dead father. A few years later a funerary monument *(chedi traitrins),* decorated around the base with elephants' heads and coated with three layers of lead, silver, and gold, was built on the holy mountain to house the relics of Suriyobarm. In due course it would contain those of Jayajeṭṭhā. Jayajeṭṭhā also consecrated a number of monasteries on and around the mountain, inaugurating their ritual boundaries *(sīmā)* in an elaborate seven-day ceremony during which both settled monks and tree-dwelling ascetics *(anak dhutun rukkhamul)* were offered lavish gifts (Mak Phœun 1981, 148–149). It seems possible that the mountain had attracted solitary religious practitioners before it became a royal center. Indeed, this may have been one of the reasons behind its selection as a capital, for ascetic and royal powers have often been related in the Cambodian context.[53]

Eventually another Thai king, possibly Prasat Thong, attempted to invade

Cambodia but was driven back. The chronicles describe how Thai captives, having sought sanctuary at Wat Preah Put Leay Leak, Babaur, were spared and made slaves of the triple jewel. To celebrate his victory, Jayajeṭṭhā commissioned a Buddha image, made to his own measurements, for the same monastery (Mak Phœun 1981, 139). It seems that another tranche of slaves, sent to Wat Preah Put Leay Leak around 1639 following the rebellion of a wizard named Pālaṅk Ratn, gained it the reputation of having more slaves than any other monastery in the kingdom (Mak Phœun 1995, 227).

A son, Cau Bañā Tū (Srī Dhammarāja I, r. 1627–1632), followed Jayajeṭṭhā to the throne. He had also been a learned monk, and the chronicles describe his righteous reign in archetypically Buddhist terms. He is also the first Khmer king to be described as a poet and a Pali scholar. A didactic work, *Cpāp' Trīnetr,* and various *Jātaka*-based stories are attributed to him.[54] According to one chronicle version, Bañā Tū had been ordained at Angkor Wat. Other traditions link him to Wat Neak Ta Soeng[55] at Udong. This seems to have been the monastery of a learned *sanghareach,* Preah Sugandh Mean Bonn, who was the author of another didactic text, *Cpāp' Kram.* He and the king are said to have been in the regular habit of debating Buddhist doctrine and Pali (Mak Phœun 1981, 149–159).[56] Further evidence of close links between the court and organized Buddhism at this time comes from a short inscription [K. 75] at Wat Preah Nippean, Kompong Speu Province, dated 1628 CE. It records the gift of rice fields to Samdech Preah Bodhiñān, its chief monk, by Bañā Tū's mother (Mak Phœun 1995, 203).

In 1642 CE some Malays[57] are recorded as supporting the rebellion of a Khmer prince who subsequently seized the throne as Rāmādhipatī I (Cau Bañā Cand, r. 1642–1658). As king of Cambodia, he embraced Islam and changed his name to Sultan Ibrahim,[58] even though he had been initiated into meditational practice *(kammaṭṭhan)* at Wat Preah Put Leay Leak, Babaur, as a young man (Mak Phœun 1995, 253). The chronicles refer to him as Rama the Apostate (Rāmā cūl sāṣ). However, an inscription [K. 166] at Wat Srei Toul, Kompong Thom Province, seems to indicate that he continued to support Buddhism after his conversion, for he made donations of a hundred pagoda slaves, a hundred rice fields, and musical instruments to Wat Prasat Pi (Mak Phœun 1981, 351; Mak Phœun 1995, 263; Mak Phœun and Po Dharma 1984, 291). His Buddhist identity was also reconfirmed after death, and his ashes were interred in royal funerary monuments, either in Prei Nokor (Saigon) or in Udong (Mak Phœun 1995, 305).

Subsequent tradition has it that Rāmādhipatī's apostasy happened after Tuan Chai, a famous Cham-Javanese priest, used a love philter to cause the king to fall in love with a Cham princess (Hickey 1982b, 129).[59] In essence, then, Islamic magic made the king forget his ancestral responsibilities to Buddhism.[60] During his short reign Rāmādhipatī declared jihad against the Dutch East India Company (Buch 1937, 219–221), many prominent Muslims entered the court, and there was a surge in mosque building. Having said that, there is no evidence of significant Muslim proselytism in the period, and when Rāmādhipatī was eventually overthrown, with Vietnamese assistance,[61] Buddhism regained its previous status with little obvious fuss. Cambodia's Muslims do not appear to have suffered any systematic persecution around that time (Mak Phœun 1990, 65–66).[62]

After this short and faintly traumatic Islamic interlude, Ang Sūr (Paramarāja VIII, r. 1659–1672) reestablished the royal patronage of Buddhism, a fact demonstrated by an upsurge in Khmer inscriptions at Angkor shortly after his inauguration. For instance, IMA25, dated 1663 CE, deals with the manumission of two slaves on the recommendation of the recently deceased Mahāsaṅgharāj Sīlācāry (Lewitz 1973a). Père Louis Chevreul, a Catholic missionary who was in Cambodia from 1665 to 1670, also noted the high regard paid by Ang Sūr to the *sangha* (Mak Phœun 1995, 310). However, the wider political picture in Indochina was beginning to change as the Vietnamese continued their "march to the south" *(nam tien)* and, in the process, began to vie with the Thai for influence over Cambodia. As has already been noted, a number of late sixteenth- and seventeenth-century Khmer kings had been obliged to spend a period under the "protection" of the increasingly powerful Thai during their minority. It is also clear that the Thai significantly manipulated their "guests" once they had reached the throne. The arrival of the Vietnamese complicated matters. High-level Buddhist patronage of the sort witnessed over the previous century largely ceased, and pro-Thai and pro-Viet factions began to develop within the Khmer court. As Chandler (1972, 168) sagely observes, "All Cambodian history, at least since the eighteenth century, is colored by the fact that Udong and Phnom Penh are more accessible to Saigon than to Bangkok." The difficulties are indicated by an event witnessed by Nicolas Gervaise in 1677 CE when a large number of monks who had gathered to conduct the funeral rites of King Ang Jī (Kaev Hvā II, r. 1673–1677) were massacred by the pro-Vietnamese faction of the court. Monks were also killed, and monastery buildings containing a great deal of Buddhist literature were destroyed during a particularly bloody Vietnamese-led attack on Udong in November 1682 (Mak Phœun 1995, 364, 372).

Illness is supposed to have been the cause of the first abdication of Jayajeṭṭhā III (1677–1695, 1696–1700, 1701–1702) in favor of his mother. That this occurred on further occasions gives a possible insight into the instability of the time. Jayajeṭṭhā III, assisted by the supreme patriarch, revised the country's laws on the grounds that they were too severe and not in accord with the Buddha's teachings (Leclère 1899, 506).[63] He also spent much of his time in robes at Wat Preah Sugandh Mean Bon, Udong, away from state affairs (Mak Phœun 1995, 381). The attitude of withdrawal appears to have been shared by other high-ranking individuals at this difficult time. For instance, IMA38 (dated 1701 CE), the so-called Grande Inscription d'Angkor, records that a minister, Jaiya Nan, was ordained a total of five times.[64]

We can pass over the next few reigns with little comment. Ang Eng (r. 1779–1794) is noteworthy in that he gave French Catholic missionaries permission to proselytize the country. Indeed, they asserted that the king had received a conditional Catholic baptism in the 1770s (Chandler 1973, 80), although this seems unlikely. As a young man, Eng had been well initiated into the Thai Buddhist thought universe, having Preah Thamma Vipassana Kong, a Bangkok-educated chief monk from Phnom Santuk, as preceptor (Yang Sam 1990, 59, 73). His successor, Ang Chan (r. 1794–1835), came to the throne as a child invested with the title by the Thai king Rama I. Chan's Thai teacher, a senior monk from Bangkok, made a visit to the court around 1811 CE, and Chan's three brothers, one of whom subsequently became King Ang Duang, entered the Buddhist order as monks. Vickery (1982, 83–84) suggests that Chan may have set up a commission to revise the Buddhist canon around this time. It was intended as an offering to Preah Thamma Vipassana Kong, although the chronicle of Sitbaur monastery, which mentions the event, is unclear about whether there was a successful outcome or even which texts were selected. We do know that Chan appointed two Buddhist patriarchs, Pech and Nong. The latter was chief monk *(chau adhikar)* of Wat Chatuli.[65]

When Chan died with no male offspring, the Vietnamese appointed his daughter, Ang Mey (r. 1835–1841), to rule Cambodia. Truong Minh Giang, the general of the occupying force, had already embarked on a policy of Vietnamization by replacing traditional religious rites with those imported from Vietnam. It is said that he forced monks from their monasteries, destroyed Buddha images, cut down *bodhi* trees, and ordered *chedis* to be demolished (Barrault 1927, 74).[66] The Vietnamese emperor also suggested that walls be raised around monasteries, ostensibly to beautify them, though more likely so that they could not be easily fortified in the event of an insurrection (Chandler 1973, 139). Certainly a monastery to the east of Wat Phnom, Phnom Penh, was dismantled, and a Vietnamese temple called Ong Choeurng was built on the site (Yang Sam 1990, 61). An attempt was also made to build a Vietnamese citadel higher than Wat Phnom, so that the latter would be eclipsed in the eyes of the populace (Tully 1996, 73).

The Vietnamese suspicion of Khmer Buddhism needs to be read against a background of political instability. A rebellion in 1820, led by Kai, a monk originally from Wat Sambaur who claimed supernatural powers, was probably related to the oppressive conditions endured by 5,000–odd Khmer laborers on the reconstruction of the Vinh Te Canal. Kai was subsequently declared king at the holy site of Ba Phnom. His followers seem mainly to have been recruited in the area around Tay Ninh, an area with a long history of millennial uprisings. He intended to take Phnom Penh but was killed with a number of other monks by a Vietnamese military force near Kompong Cham.[67] A Khmer poem of 1869 glorifies the exploits of Kai and his assistant, the novice monk Kuy, who eventually escaped to live among the Lao. The two seem to have recruited followers through a combination of sermonizing, the practice of magico-medical rites, and prophecy. The poet tells us that Kai's store of religious merit was high at the beginning of the campaign but was soon used up. His "amulets and charms had lost their power" (Chandler 1975a, 22). In true millennial fashion, when Kai's force was defeated, "the sky grew dark and serious floods broke out elsewhere in the kingdom" (Chandler 1973, 105). Another short-lived anti-Vietnamese insurrection broke out in 1840, with fighting particularly heavy around Prey Veng and Ba Phnom. It also seems to have had a Buddhist inspiration, for a high official *(oknya)* at the time is reported to have said, "We are happy killing Vietnamese. We no longer fear them; in all our battles, we are mindful of the three jewels—the Buddha, the *dhamma* and the *sangha*" (Chandler 1973, 154).

Around 1838 the Thai had begun to fortify the Battambang area against a possible Vietnamese invasion. Hedging their bets, they purchased cannons from England and placed stone blocks *(sīmā)* carved with mantras in the surrounding rivers as protection against waterborne attack (Tauch Chhuong 1994, 9, 28). A contemporary letter by Rama III, in which Chan is accused of betraying Buddhism by taking sides with the Vietnamese, underlines Thai irritation at the situation (Chandler 1973, 158). It is unsurprising, then, that the issue became the pretext for Rama III's attempt to place Duang, at that time a captive in Bangkok, on the throne around November 1840. From the Thai perspective, Vietnamese political control of Cambodia meant that Buddhism was without a royal sponsor. But the crowning of the new king was problematic because the royal regalia had been taken off to Saigon in 1812 and was not returned until the end of 1847 (Chandler 1972, 165–166). Ang Duang's coronation ceremony finally took place in Udong on April 8, 1848.

When Duang returned to Udong from Bangkok, he found a culture on the brink of extinction. As a contemporary chronicler, Tā Mās, noted, "[The] novices and priests also suffered because the *vihāras* had been plundered. The gold and silver buddhas had been taken from them and the soldiers had set fire to many *vihāras*. In many places the *wats* that remained often did not have roofs. The roofs had sunken down and broken apart and the rain came down on the monks." Those who remained in robes were largely ignorant of the Buddha's teachings, and very few sacred writings remained intact.[68] Tā Mās could easily have been describing the situation immediately after the Pol Pot period. Duang refurbished the royal funerary monuments and reinvigorated surrounding monasteries (Chandler 1983, 108) by recasting buddha images, encouraging the people to pay respect to monks once again, and ordering a census of monks and *wats*. The results of the census disappointed Rama III, who observed, "Where there are only hundreds of monks there should be thousands" (Chandler 1973, 190n28). The withdrawal of Vietnam from Cambodia in 1846 was marked materially by the construction of seven monasteries with rubble from demolished Vietnamese fortifications near the capital of Udong,[69] and psychologically by an enduring Khmer hostility to all things Vietnamese. Like Chan before him, Duang created two patriarchs in 1847 CE. Nou, *chau adhikar* of Wat Rajapabbajit,[70] was appointed *saṅghanayaka* in charge of spiritual training *(vipassanādhura)* in four appanages *(samrap)*, while Ouk of Wat Tep Pranam[71] became *mahāsaṅgharāja* in charge of scholarly studies *(ganthadura)*.[72]

Theravada Buddhism was placed on a sound footing again, and a minor renaissance in Cambodian art, literature, and culture was stimulated. The duties of high-ranking officials *(oknya)* were not especially demanding, for Cambodia, unlike Vietnam, was not a bureaucratic culture. This meant that some *oknya* were happy to direct their financial resources to the sponsorship of Buddhism and the arts (Chandler 1973, 47). Duang himself had a scholarly bent. He knew Pali and the canonical texts well (Huot Tath 1962, 12) and wrote poetry, including the narrative *Nieng Kakei* (Lady Kakei), a work of some literary merit that is based on two traditional *Jātaka* stories[73] and a Thai court poem, *Ryang Kaki* (The story of Kaki), by Phra Khlang.[74] But the most significant literary figure of the period was the previously mentioned Nong.[75] His high ecclesiastical office under Chan has already been noted. He was also Ang Duang's preceptor. After leaving the *sangha*, he occupied important administrative and political roles, including being the official in charge of the royal treasure. However, he is principally known today as a writer whose works comprise *Cpāp' Subhāsit* (1790), a didactic poem in the traditional genre of a moral treatise; *Lokanayapakar* (1794), a cosmological work; *Puññasār Sirsā* (1797); *Bhogakulakumār* (1804); *Varnetr Varnuj* (1806); *Preah Samudr* (c. 1850); and an early version of the royal chronicles. Nong's writings reflect the conventional ordering of Cambodian society with a sharp eye for details of the natural world. He also drew heavily on both Buddhist ideas and Buddhist writing genres. Dhanañjay kumār, the hero of the *Lokanayapakar*,[76] for example, seems to be directly modeled on Mahosadha, the central figure of the *Mahāummagga Jātaka*,[77] who strives to protect his kingdom from the depredations of enemies both internal and external. *Bhogakulakumār* is considered to be the most original of the versified romances that circulated in the early nineteenth century, with themes ranging from kingship, daily life, and traditional customs and sentiments to the depiction of nature. It gives a first-person account of the Buddha's former existence as the eponymous hero and is sprinkled with many words in Sanskrit, Pali, and Thai, reflecting the custom of the court at Udong. It also covers certain points of Buddhist doctrine, including karma theory, merit accumulation through donation to the *sangha,* the three marks of existence, and the moral precepts, as well as descriptions of inhabitants of heaven and hell.

The chronicles tell us that Duang indefatigably encouraged the Buddhist virtues. He forbade his ministers to consume alcohol; toured the country, discouraging drinking and opium smoking;[78] condemned hunting and the ill treatment of animals; and laid down guidelines on the proper size for fishing nets. He personally prepared food for monks (Yang Sam 1990, 64–67), taught them liturgical chanting (Brunet 1967, 201), and urged them to provide accommodation for the homeless. Acting on a model already established by Aśoka and Jayavarman VII, Duang had rest houses built along the principal roads of the kingdom. He also designed costumes for the Royal Ballet (Jeldres and Chaijitvanit 1999, 97). It is said that he meditated in the middle of the night and spent a significant portion of his fortune freeing 350 slaves and providing support to learned monks and literati.[79] Taking his lead from Bangkok, Ang Duang instituted a twelve-month-long cycle of agricultural rites in 1855.[80] In the same year he appears to have participated in an ordination ceremony on a raft at Kompong Luong, near Udong. This led to the introduction of a new Thai monastic fraternity, the Dhammayutika Nikāya, to Cambodia—an event that would have serious repercussions, as we shall discover in chapter 5.

A Muslim presence in Cambodia, fluctuating in its influence, since at least the early seventeenth century has already been noted. One prominent Muslim, Tuan Sait Ahmit (Shaykh Aḥmad), had risen to the position of viceroy *(yomareach)* under Ang Chan but was executed by decapitation in 1820 CE. His three sons subsequently rose in revolt, intending to gain independence for the Thbaung Khmum region to the north and the east of Phnom Penh. This conflict festered on throughout Duang's reign and was brought to an end only with the accession of Norodom (Cabaton 1906, 39–40). This did not stop Duang from taking an interest in Islamic affairs. He intervened in a conflict between traditionalists and modernizers, recommending the translation of Islamic texts into Khmer so that local Muslims would no longer have to submit disputes to Malay or Arab legal authorities ("Election," 13). He also had positive dealings with the Jahed, the most heterodox of the three principal Muslim groups of Cambodia.[81] The Jahed are followers of Imam San, and their central place of worship is the Ta San mosque, set among the royal tombs at Udong. It seems that the forest-dwelling mystic Imam San was originally invited to the capital by Duang to answer charges that he and his followers were endangering the stability of the state. But the king was so impressed by a demonstration of mystic powers that he allowed Imam San to settle on Phnom Preah Reach Trop, where the mosque bearing his name was subsequently built. The sacrality of the site is demonstrated by the fact that both male and female Jahed ascetics lived rather like Buddhist monks on the hillside until the Pol Pot period (Baccot 1968).[82]

When Ang Duang fell mortally ill in 1860, he ordered slaves to be released as a merit-making act. He also expressed the wish that flesh be cut from his body at the moment of death and fed to voracious animals. This was done, the knives having been purified by lustral water sacralized by chanting monks. The meat was subsequently served on golden plates to birds of prey (Moura 1883, 1:345).[83] Leclère (1906, 72–73) was a witness to such rites at the turn of the century and believed them to be quite common in the past. With Duang's death the modern epoch began. From this point on, Cambodia and Cambodian Buddhism were forced to grapple with new and entirely unexpected influences.

3

Theravada Buddhism in Cambodia
Territorial and Social Lineaments

Land, Authority, and Sacred Space

In common with most cultures of the region, the Cambodians contrast the world of settled, rice-growing existence with the wilderness beyond. From the end of the Angkorian period until the 1840s the country had no roads of significance, and a royal chronicle relates: "In former times there was little dry land here, and people would go everywhere in boats, but never farther than the sounds of dogs barking in their village could be heard. There were no canals then, and no paths: there were only forests with tigers, and elephants, and wild buffaloes: no people dared leave their village."[1] The social world may have been safe, but the savagery of the world beyond was not conducive to organizational principles. For this reason the wilderness was avoided and feared (Chandler 1982b, 54). The Khmer were not as antagonistic toward hill tribes as the Vietnamese and Chinese have been.[2] The Angkorians, for example, appear to have had good relations with the Kui, who supplied them with iron (B.-P. Groslier 1985, 72). But modern Khmer reject any common ancestry with the montagnards—whom they designate by the word "*phnong,*" a term that conveys a sense of savagery and wildness[3]—and prefer to regard themselves as descendants of Hindu princes.

Insofar as the land belonged to anyone, it belonged to the spirits of the ancestors *(neak tā)*. This meant that kings and other important personages did not claim ownership of the territory of Cambodia. Instead they consumed it.[4]

We should not assume that the arrangement lacked equity. As Thion (1993, 98) has remarked, authority in premodern Cambodia was paradoxical in that "great anarchic individual freedom prevailed in a society in which there was no formal freedom at all." Neither did the arrangement inevitably damage the national economy, for the wealth extracted from the common people as a consequence of the arrangement tended to remain in the country. Such resources were used for the construction of opulent residences but most importantly for lavish donations to temples that acted as the primary engines of social security and education, as well as to patronize traditional literati, craftsmen, and artists. Wealth then was expended either in immediate consumption or in religiously meritorious donation. The notion of long-term wealth accumulation was alien to this way of being.

Since the emergence of Theravada Buddhism as the dominant religious tradition, the Cambodian king has been regarded as "one who has merits" *(neak mean bon),* a notion connected to the doctrine of karma, which sees present worldly merit as the result of the accumulation of beneficial deeds in previous existences.[5] Kingship was largely hereditary, yet the practice of primogeniture was not always applied. It seems that "election" of a new king by a committee of royal family members, senior officials, and monks probably predates the modern period (Osborne 1973, 169). In the Theravada ideology of kingship the right to rule is a consequence of spiritual maturity. From this perspective, the prerogatives of the king, once appointed, may not easily be challenged by this-worldly considerations, such as political expediency. The king also possesses the power to "master the earth spirits" (Forest 1980, 57). Therefore he may bend the forces of nature to his will. In this way rain will fall at the correct time, good harvests are guaranteed, and calamity is avoided.

The king's possession of a set of powerful fetish weapons, most likely fashioned toward the end of the Angkorian period (Boisselier 1966, 357), reinforced this supernatural authority. The power conferred by the regalia was of considerable interest to neighboring states. We have already seen how, in 1783, the Thai took the collection to Bangkok as a way of emasculating Cambodian royalty. It was returned only in 1847.[6] Tradition holds that the hilt of the sacred sword *(preah khan)* had once been in the possession of the so-called king of fire *(sdach phloeung),* while its sheath belonged to the king of water *(sdach toeuk)*—two Jarai tribal chiefs from the northeastern region of the country. It seems that the post-Angkorian kings paid tribute to the tribe every three years, and the Jarai reciprocated with gifts of forest products, including rhinoceros horn and wax. The latter was used to make special candles deemed efficacious in protecting the country from epidemic, flood, and war.[7] The Cambodian monarch's exercise of power, then, depended on maintaining good relations with a mysterious power manipulated by tribal peoples at the periphery of the state.

The cosmological centralization of Southeast Asian kingdoms around a capital city tended to mean that the king and his court rarely penetrated the surrounding countryside (Solomon 1970, 3), and there were certainly occasions when the Cambodian monarch's writ extended no farther than the boundary of the city itself. He did not deal with his people on any conventionally political level but was largely absorbed in the performance of rites.[8] Neither were the corps of royal scribes expected to transcribe the actual or reported words of the monarch. That their function was more ritual than administrative is demonstrated by the fact that one of their duties was to "supervise the manufacture of sugarcane sticks used to expel evil spirits, and the cotton cords beaded with bits of paper inscribed with sacred texts on the 13th, 14th, and 15th days of the waxing moon in the month of *phalkun* (February–March)."[9] Yet the king was not entirely isolated from his subjects. The sixteenth-century Portuguese writer Gaspar da Cruz noted that Ang Chan held regular audiences to adjudicate on his people's grievances, a practice that continued down to the modern period. Traditional writings, such as the *cpāp'*, also list many occasions on which it may be appropriate for the king to be drawn into legal proceedings (Ebihara 1984, 284).

Traditional law codes saw the kingdom as a body in which dignitaries represented its mouth, eyes, and bones; the rich, the flesh; and the common people, the skin (Leclère 1898, 1:99).[10] In Nong's *Royal Chronicle (Rapāl ksatr),* written between 1813 and 1818, a fairly rigid hierarchical social structure is described. Members of the immediate royal family are at the top, immediately followed by the Buddhist patriarchs *(sanghareachs)*[11] and court Brahmins *(baku).*[12] Next come the literati, sages, high-ranking officials (including the four principal ministers), and functionaries. Ordinary people constitute the final level of the structure (Mak Phœun 1980, 144). This harmonizes well with Buddhist categories. The king, then, is classified alongside the Buddha; the *sanghareach* is the Buddha's chief disciple; the royal family, the pantheon of highest gods; ministers, deities of the second rank; provincial chiefs, godlings of regional significance; local functionaries, diverse local spirits; and the peasants, the laity.[13]

Unlike its neighbors Vietnam and Thailand, Cambodia did not possess pictorial maps before the colonial period, but nineteenth-century texts that are connected with the performance of royal ceremonies contained place-names—organized in a clockwise spiral centered on Udong—that may have served the same purpose. These lists indicated locations where tutelary spirits *(neak tā)* were honored by sacrifice, while they also articulated notions of sacred space, ethnicity, and jurisdiction. They survived in one form or another until 1969, when government officials called on the spirits to witness their oath of allegiance to Sihanouk. Nineteenth-century Cambodia was arranged into five regions *(dey):* Thboung Khmum, Ba Phnom, Treang, Pursat, and Kompong Svay (i.e., Kompong Thom) (Leclère 1894a, 183–185).[14] Ba Phnom was probably central

(Chandler 1976b, 175), a patterning of space in accord with Theravada cosmology, where four regions are grouped around a central hub in a *maṇḍala* arrangement. It also mirrors the topology of Angkor. As we have already seen, the Angkorian capital was the center of a complex and interlinked *maṇḍala* through which wilderness space was appropriated to human civilization. Communication between the center and its satellites was achieved by a variety of ritual acts. In particular, the king was expected to make regular pilgrimage to satellite temples dedicated to chthonian deities so that he might draw their power back to the capital (B.-P. Groslier 1985–1986a, 66). Similar ritual mechanisms appear to have operated until quite recently.[15]

There is remarkable historical continuity in the way the land has been patterned by the Khmer people. Angkorian capitals were positioned to the south of a sacred mountain and open to the east. They were also at the confluence of two rivers, where the male and female serpent deities *(nāga)* were supposed to meet. Such an auspicious site would ensure fertility, in every sense of the term, throughout the kingdom. If the correct natural features did not exist, they could be built; this partially explains the temple mountains and reservoirs *(barays)* so typical of the Siem Reap region. Precisely the same arrangement of space can be discerned in the more recent centers of Longvek, Udong, and Siem Reap (B.-P. Groslier 1985–1986a, 66–67).

Neak Tā and Other Spirits

As is the case in other countries of Buddhist Southeast Asia, village Cambodia is protected by a network of tutelary spirits *(neak tā)* who, though they lack any explicit association with Buddhism from a purely doctrinal perspective, nevertheless have important and complementary functions at the level of popular ritual (Forest 1992). They are mundane deities—that is, gods of the realm of men *(devatāmanussāloka)*—and cannot intervene in the process of final salvation, but they may be induced to bring about significant change in the human and physical realms. Some *neak tā* are related to specific locations, such as a tree, a pond, or a ruined village, while others have vaguer associations. Powerful *neak tā* may protect a large geographical area, governing their territory from a central location. Some are solitary, while others are hierarchically organized into families.

Individual *neak tā* may be called *cah srok*, "the old one of the country," indicating the archaic nature of their cult. A powerful *neak tā* called Toeuk Lic, for example, dwells in an Angkorian-period Buddha statue now placed at the foot of the cascade on Phnom Kulen (Bizot 1994a, 121). Some have a personal name, while others are merely called *loak cah,* "old gentleman." For convenience they can be divided into three categories. The first contains spirits associated with natural phenomena, such as mountains *(neak tā phnom),* rivers *(neak tā tuk),* trees *(neak tā dam),* paddies *(neak tā sre),* swamps *(neak tā beng),* and forests *(neak tā prey).* Ancestral spirits, both male and female, come next, while *neak tā,* derived from Brahmanical gods and various mythical heroes, make up the final category (Souyris-Rolland 1951a, 162).

The world of spirits is a particularly dynamic place. New *neak tā* may be created, and established spirits are known to shift their place of residence. The shrine of *neak tā ā'c chke* (literally, "dog shit," a name indicating the spirit's ability to protect from pollution), close to Wat Prey Kral, Banteay Meas, illustrates the former tendency. According to a popular account, not long ago a man who saw some dog excrement underneath a tree covered it with branches. Travelers subsequently took this to be an abode of a *neak tā,* and a shrine or altar *(ktom)* was constructed. The movement of a *neak tā* may be an economic necessity. Trees are the dwelling places of *neak tā,* and it is particularly dangerous to cut them down. However, if the wood is required, a *ktom* is erected and all nearby spirits called on to enter it. Only after they have abandoned the trees, received appropriate offerings, and been placed elsewhere is it safe to begin the job.[16]

The most famous *neak tā* in the country is Khleang Moeung, the tutelary spirit of Pursat. Believed to have been a general in Ang Chan's army, he defeated Thai invaders after he, his wife, and their three sons immolated themselves by falling into a ditch of stakes. Returning as the head of an army of ghosts, Khleang Moeung spread cholera among the enemy, who were subsequently defeated. His shrine is five kilometers northwest of Pursat town, and the annual ceremonies of homage can be particularly impressive. *Neak tā* Khleang Moeung's exploits once formed part of the repertoire of the National Theater and were often performed during times of tension with Thailand. In this sense, he may be regarded as the protector of the realm (Ang Chouléan 1986, 207, 209–210). Indeed, when Cambodia gained independence, Sihanouk had an enclosure built around Khleang Moeung's statue. It was broken up and thrown into a nearby pond during the Pol Pot era but has now been recovered and reconstituted.[17]

Of the *neak tā* derived from Brahmanical deities, the most significant today is *neak tā* Ganeś, better known as Siddhi-Suost,[18] also sometimes considered as a national protector. Another example of the transformation of Indic gods and goddesses is Me Sa, the white mother of Ba Phnom. Her name is probably a contraction of the Sanskrit Mahiṣāsura, thus revealing her true identity as Durgā or Umā Mahiṣāsuramardinī, the destroyer of the buffalo demon.[19] It

Shrine of Preah Nang Cek and Preah Nang Cam, Siem Reap city.

is known that ritual suicide and probable human sacrifice were linked to goddess cults practiced in the Indian Pallava kingdom of the seventh through ninth centuries. It is possible that such rites were exported to Cambodia, for the last human sacrifice in the country took place at Ba Phnom in April or May 1877[20] when two prisoners of war were beheaded during a royally sponsored ceremony of "raising up the ancestors" *(loeng neak tā)*, a festival still held in a highly modified form at the beginning of each growing season. It is significant that the rite occurred in *pisakh,* the month sacred to Kālī, the Brahmanical deity most particularly associated with *neak tā* Me Sa. Indeed, the human sacrifice of a criminal seems to have occurred annually at a sacred spot on the northeastern slope of the mountain site. Evidence also suggests that Buddhist monks based at nearby Wat Vihear Thom were involved in a number of unspecified prayer rituals, including prayers for the dead, during the first few days of the rite.[21] However, they withdrew sometime before the coup de grâce on the final day, a Saturday. The direction that blood spurted from the severed neck was used to predict the nature of the coming rains. Ritual decapitation is also attested in two other nineteenth-century Cambodian locations,[22] but as the century progressed, human sacrifice fell into abeyance and a rutting buffalo was replaced as victim.[23] Nevertheless, the basic association with rainfall and fertility remained (Chandler 1974, 216–202).

Neak tā may be represented aniconically. In this case, stones *(thmar)* are placed on the altar *(ktom)* to represent them. When there is more than one *thmar,* the largest represents the main spirit, and smaller stones represent his or her retinue *(beisach)* (Souyris-Rolland 1951a, 164, 166). But *neak tā* are frequently depicted in anthropomorphic style. There are three basic types of rite associated with their cult. The first is a vow or promise *(ban sran)* performed to gain a blessing for a minor undertaking or to find a missing object. The second *(bon banchan neak tā)* is a more formal ceremony designed to counteract more serious difficulties, such as major illnesses, famine, or drought.[24] It involves a priest *(rup)* and an orchestra. The final category *(bon banchan neak tā oy sok sabai)* is reserved for *neak tā* with a regional or national significance. Also known as "raising up the ancestors" *(loeng neak tā),* it generally takes place in January–February and is oriented toward general protection, health, and peace throughout the coming year.[25] Such rituals may entail the recitation of protective verses *(parittas)* by Buddhist monks, but it is usual for the Buddhist section of the ceremony to end after a few hours, particularly when alcohol, a substance much appreciated by many *neak tā,* is then offered.

Bray are another class of exclusively female and highly dangerous spirits of virgins or of women who have died in childbirth. Although malevolent by nature, individual *bray* may be domesticated. This happens when a Buddhist monk ritually encourages her to take up residence in the pedestal of the main Buddha image *(bray pallangk bray)* of the *vihāra.* In this transformed role she acts as the guardian of the temple *(bray preah pāramī, boramei,* or *boramei vat).*[26] The *boramei* is explicitly connected to the Buddha, his teachings, or his religious community, and Bizot (1994a, 119) has observed that her rites require the presence of a Thai orchestra *(phleng siem),* whereas non-Buddhist godlings may be entertained by a Khmer ensemble *(phleng khmaer).* In the modern Cambodian context, Thailand signifies orthodox Theravada values. On the popular level the distinction between pedestal and image may be somewhat blurred, so

The earth goddess, Nang Thorani—Wat Buddhaghosa, Phnom Penh.

that the *boramei* is often held to indwell the central Buddha image of a monastery. Thus it is she who receives the food offerings made each day to the image. A *boramei* may be installed in a Buddhist setting by other means. In an interesting example of changing sexual identity, Ven. Chan Cheung, a famous monk who spent most of the early 1970s meditating at Wat Unnalom, Phnom Penh, became a *boramei* after his death and is now venerated accordingly (Sok Sahom and Bertrand 1998, 1133).

Some Cambodians see a close connection between the *boramei vat* and Nang Thorani *(nāṅ kanhīṅ preah dharanī),* the earth goddess. Nang Thorani is frequently seen in Cambodian monasteries, in mural paintings both within and without the *vihāra,* and on carved Buddhist boundary markers. She is depicted standing, wringing water out of a thick braid of hair soaked with water libations made in testimony of the Buddha's liberality in previous lives and

The earth goddess, Nang Thorani, destroying Vietnamese troops, who are represented as the horde of Māra—Phnom Penh wall poster, February 1972. Courtesy of François Bizot.

pulled over her left shoulder. This distinctive iconography cannot be traced to Indian or Sri Lankan sources but seems to be based on the Pali *Paṭhamasambodhi,* an anthology of biographical accounts of the Buddha's life known only in Southeast Asia. The image is old, as carvings at Beng Mealea, Ta Prohm of Angkor, and Ta Prohm of Bati, all dating to the twelfth century, testify.[27] The traditional account of the Buddha's enlightenment also tells how Nang Thorani emerged from the soil after Māra's daughters failed to excite the Buddha's sexual passions so that he could remain tied to the world. She turned them into old women before drowning the rest of Māra's minions with water wrung from her hair. It is clear, then, that she is the principal guardian of the Buddha and his teachings. She also retains an earlier function connected with the sphere of fertility (Harris 2000b, 140).[28]

According to legend, Wat Vihear Thom, Srok Sambaur, Kratie Province (also known as the pagoda of one hundred columns), is guarded by one hundred *bray* so committed to their task that when the chief monk of the monastery makes a journey, they always accompany him. This is why he cannot travel by car but must ride in a truck. The *bray* are popularly supposed to have been one hundred virgins in the service of Princess Krapum Chhuk. They were sacrificed, and their bodies placed under the hundred pillars of the monastery after their mistress was swallowed by a crocodile.[29] A *stūpa* containing her remains became an important royal pilgrimage site, and in time the princess transmogrified into the main protective spirit of the monastery, under the name "*boramei krabuṃ jhūk.*" She performs a number of important functions. When a new *chau adhikar* is selected, *boramei krabuṃ jhūk* appears to the local community in dreams and tells them the identity of the replacement (Ang Chouléan 1986, 132–133). She has also acted as an oracle *(snang),*[30] particularly during the 1960s, when her messages sometimes informed the policy of Sihanouk and his government. However, when, in 1969, her priestess *(rup)* received the unwelcome message that Sihanouk's regime would come to an end before the year was out, she mysteriously disappeared (Meyer 1971, 44, 88, 92).

Wat Vihear Suor was another locus for various royal rites until the late 1960s, when some *snang* claimed that their powers had become severely limited by Sihanouk's absence from the country.[31] The association of *boramei* and kingship is illustrated at the Royal Palace in Phnom Penh, where relics of all the kings of the present dynasty from Ang Duang to Suramarit have been placed in their respective busts.[32] The nearby equestrian statue of King Norodom also contains relics. All of these statues are believed to have their *boramei* who issue oracles that may sometimes affect state policy. The same principle also applies to leading members of the monastic order. Paradoxically, given *sanghareach* Chuon Nath's known opposition to unorthodox practices (discussed further in chapter 5), a small Buddha image was made after the cremation of the *sanghareach* in 1970 to incorporate some of his remains. The image is now venerated as an abode of a *boramei* (Bizot 1994a, 120).

A great range of additional spirits are known in the village setting. Godlings known as *neak saccam* seem to have lived as ascetic and peripatetic monks *(loak dhutang)* in a previous life (Ang Chouléan 1986, 190–191),[33] while *arak* are a class of benign and malevolent spirits that speak through a female medium *(rup arak)* during possession ceremonies *(cuen arak)* that usually take place during January and February. A *rup arak* has no training but is regarded as a woman with particularly good character and a natural tendency to fall into trance. A variety of different kinds of ghost *(khmoc)* are especially feared. These include the *kmauit long,* a ghost of someone who was murdered or committed suicide; the *baysayt,* a ghost that lives on dirt and excrement and is capable of taking human or animal form; the *priey,* a ghost living in a large tree with the ability to turn into a ball of fire; and the *pret,* a ghost of an individual who infringed Buddhist ethical norms, such as killing animals, while alive (Ebihara 1968, 428–429).[34] For completeness, one might also mention the ancestral spirits *(meba)* that, though not related to individual ancestors, protect specific families; elflike guardians of various animal species *(mrenh kongveal);* and the purely benign house guardians *(mneang phteah).*

The human body is thought to mirror the external world and is also a locus for spirits or souls *(braling).* It is traditionally held that the body is animated by nineteen *braling,* a number difficult to harmonize with any of the customary categories of orthodox Theravada metaphysics. Despite the superimposition of the Hindu and Buddhist psychological notions since the region's first historical contacts with India, then, an older indigenous conception of selfhood has been retained. As Thompson (1996) has observed, the Indianization of the Khmer self was never entirely completed. The *braling* have a tendency to wander from their proper seat within the body, and it may be necessary to invite them back or to reintegrate them from time to time through a "calling of the souls" *(hau braling)* ritual. This is especially so during periods of personal transition, such as rites of passage, sojourn in a foreign land, or illness.[35]

Spirit Priests, Amulets, and Protection

We have already mentioned the role of female spirit priests. Another class of practitioners, the *gru,* are almost always male. They work in a variety of differing religious idioms, some from a vaguely Śaiva perspective and others from a Vaiṣṇava orientation. Eisenbruch (1992, 285n11) mentions a *gru* who was "an expert in invoking the previous incarnations of the Buddha"—hardly surprising, given that many *gru* are former monks and that others claim to have learned their healing techniques from Buddhist ascetics. Those working in a Buddhist idiom tend to draw principally on the notions of Abhidhamma,[36] an area of doctrine and practice that holds a strong fascination for traditionalist monks, as we shall see in chapter 4. *Gru* generally follow written texts containing details for the preparation of botanical medicaments, symbolic diagrams (yantras),[37] and mantras. Such texts cannot be regarded as mere recipe books, for a great deal of supplementary knowledge is also required. It is quite common, for instance, to invite an elaborate ritual pantheon of deities and spirits to the preparation of a medicine so that it will become effective.

The ritual space has a cosmological significance. It the case of a healing ritual, the patient kneels on a wooden board balanced on a central bell representing Mount Meru, the central world mountain. Other ritual objects representing the continents are arranged at the four cardinal points. As Eisenbruch (1992, 312) notes, "There seems to be a parallel between the spaces of the *yantra,* the patient, the *gru*'s ritual arena, the village space, and the universe: all these spaces are addressed in healing ritual." Some *gru* draw on other features of Buddhism in their practice. They may, for instance, invoke Nang Thorani while lustrating the patient in repetition of the goddess' defeat of Māra. But by no means do all *gru* have an affinity toward Buddhism. The *dhmap'*, for instance, specializes in malevolent or black magic. He can cause a knife or other sharp object to enter a victim's body, resulting in intense pain or even death. To preserve his powers, he may never penetrate the ritual boundary of a monastery or pass in front of or make obeisance to a Buddha image. Neither may he wash for his entire life.[38]

The *gru*'s magical skills may extend to the making of love potions and amulets *(katha),*[39] the finding of lost objects, and exorcism. A monk who feels that he lacks eloquence may also obtain a love philter *(sneh)* from a *gru* to improve his ability to deliver a sermon.[40] The use of magical protection has a long history in Cambodia. A yantra of forty-eight syllables arranged on a lotus blossom engraved on one of the foundation stones of the temple of Bat Chum dates from the middle of the tenth century (Cœdès 1952), and the late thirteenth-century Chinese writer Zhou Daguan also noted that the Khmer king was protected from arrow and sword wounds by an amulet implanted under his flesh (Pelliot 1951, 34). The implantation of amulets persists, and many vernacular texts[41] describe how to inscribe *katha* of lead, silver, or gold with Pali syllables in the round Khmer script deemed particularly efficacious. The five syllables of the *namo buddhāya* formula are frequently used. To charge the *katha* with power, mantras are chanted during its construction, and its maker, usually a *gru,* must observe three strict rules: incense sticks and candles must be kept burning throughout the ritual, he must not be troubled by human intercourse or noise, and the stylus must remain in contact with the plates continuously until the job is complete (Khin Sok 1982, 117). Protective amulets come in a variety of forms. They may consist of small buddha images carved from a variety of materials such as ivory, pyrites, or wild boar tusk. The tooth of a parent may also be worn as a *katha.* The amulets may be worn around the neck, around the waist, or over the genitals.[42] It is important for its possessor that the *katha* be kept pure. This means that it must not be taken into a latrine. Similarly, the wearer should avoid the consumption of inauspicious foodstuff such as zucchinis, lavender, and gourds. He should also aim to observe the five lay Buddhist precepts. Observing the first two of these precepts, which prohibit killing and stealing, may not be possible for soldiers, pirates, and brigands in the course of their professional duties.[43] To compensate and ensure the continuing power of their protective devices, they must make frequent offerings of alms to the *sangha*. Protective devices may also be inscribed on a piece of cloth called a *kansaeng yantra*. These are often prepared by charismatic monks, despite a royal ordinance of December 24, 1920, forbidding monks from engaging in medicine, astrology, sorcery, tattooing, and the making of amulets (Bizot 1976, 11).[44]

Some masters of tattooing *(bidhi sak)* are monks, while others are laymen. Tradition holds that only men may have the skin of their upper body inscribed in this way.[45] Typically the ritual begins with Buddhist refuge-taking, the lighting of incense, and the chanting of mantras. One of these—*i, ka, vi, ti*—comprises the first, last, and two middle syllables of the first portion of the *itipiso* formula from the protective *paritta*, the *Dhajaggasutta*. In the past the stylus was the same as that used for inscribing sacred texts onto palm leaves. The ink is a thick Chinese ink sometimes mixed with other substances. Human bile collected from a courageous enemy is sometimes mentioned; so too is the skin of a monk.[46] On completion, the tattoo must be consecrated. The most effective method is to receive ritual aspersions *(sroc toeuk)* from seven senior monks at seven separate monasteries (de Bernon 1998c, 88).

Certain magical potions may also confer invulnerability when they are drunk. *Toeuk thnam kong*—a mixture of oily liana, dried python, the feces of a red vulture, and water—was once especially prized for its ability to resist spear or bullet penetration of the skin (Souyris-Rolland 1951b, 182–185). But the most effective protection device is an amulet made from a desiccated human fetus *(goan krak)*. It is believed to whisper words of advice to its wearer during times of danger. Ang Chouléan (1986, 160) has noted that the use of *goan krak* tends to be greater during periods of national instability; the Issaraks, for instance, are known to have used them during the independence struggle. A husband is supposed to cut a fetus from his wife's uterus after several months of pregnancy. In theory she has previously agreed to offer herself up to him and dies in the process.[47] The *goan krak* is then dried out over a fire and generally worn in a small wooden ball of two halves *(danlap)* around the neck. Its power is multiplied by leaving it for a while in front of the principal Buddha image of a monastery (Ang Chouléan 1986, 157–158). Again the power is even greater when the ritual takes place in seven different monasteries.[48]

Mountains

Although the ancient Khmer often built temples on the summits of hills and mountains, they generally avoided habitation in these places. Many of these Angkorian hilltop sites were eventually converted to Theravada usage.[49] Ba Phnom is a good example. It had been a sacred site from an early point, as a number of inscriptions make clear. The earliest, dating from 629 CE, associates it with Śiva, and another from the tenth century calls the place a "holy mountain" (Chandler 1974, 211). In more recent times Ba Phnom's relatively remote location has been attractive to ascetic monks *(loak dhutang)* who had a tenuous connection with national *sangha* administration. It has also been an occasional center from which ultimately unsuccessful Theravada-oriented millennial movements have radiated.

Phnom Kulen was the holiest mountain of the Angkorian period, but it has also been appropriated by the Buddhist cult. According to local legend, the Buddha visited the mountain and left his footprints *(preah pād)* when crossing a natural arch at nearby Kbal Spean. These are still revered today (Boulbet 1970, 15). Both Phnom Kulen and Kbal Spean are famous for their Brahmanical rock carvings, but the vogue for rock-carved images at the site did not cease with the victory of the Theravada. A large image of the Buddha in *parinirvāṇa*, Preah Ang Thom, carved into the top of a boulder, dates from 1568 CE, according to an inscription at its base (Boisselier 1966, 280).[50] A similar *parinirvāṇa* figure dating from the same period may also be found on Phnom Santuk, Kompong Thom Province.[51] When Bareau (1969, 23) visited Kulen in the 1960s, he met a long-haired hermit who, after ten years in various Thommayut monasteries in and around Phnom Penh, had joined the Khmer Issarak independence movement around 1945. Eventually he escaped the fighting and lived in a cave, where he practiced meditation. He claimed descent from the bearded Brahmanical ascetics depicted at the base of numerous pillars at Angkor and, although no longer in monastic robes, taught meditation to monks and laypersons alike. Bareau describes a variety of other ascetics on Kulen at that time. Some were married and spent at least part of the day engaged in agricultural activity in nearby clearings.[52] My own investigations on Phnom Bayang, Takeo Province, suggest that a similar pattern of practice was established at the end of the Pol Pot period.

About thirteen kilometers west of Battambang on the Pailin road is Phnom Sampau, "hill of the junk." According to legend, Sovann Meccha, a beautiful woman with a tame crocodile, was jealous of the king's love for Princess Nang Sok Koop, who had the power to turn water into land by simply passing her hand through her hair. One day, when the king had sent a junk full of gifts to his lover, Sovann Meccha unleashed her crocodile, which frightened the sailors and sank the boat. To avert this danger, Nang Sok Koop magically transformed the junk into Phnom Sampau, the crocodile becoming nearby Phnom Krapau. The region appears to have had a special significance for many centuries. In modern times its monastery served as a base for a few rustic monks led by the charismatic Ven. Kev Chuon. However, when Kev Choun died in 1947, some of his monastic followers were forced to leave the holy mountain and remove themselves to Wat Unnalom in Phnom Penh. It is not clear why, but the resonant association of wilderness, ascetic monks, and potential insurrection is a likely factor. Another monastery, Wat Phnom Sampau (originally called Wat Savann Kiri Phetra), was constructed at the base of the mountain sometime early in the twentieth century, and after Kev Chuon's death a new superior, Ven. Duong Set, developed the precincts to accommodate a growing number of pilgrims and tourists attracted by the impressive scenery in the neighborhood. Bizot (1980, 232) has argued that the development proved fatal to the site, particularly because a number of archaic practices observed on the mountain were gradually replaced by activities more in tune with the outlook of the "reformed" *sangha* authorities in Phnom Penh. It seems that traditional rites centered on a number of natural grottoes in the limestone hillside, such as Laang Teng Kloun, Laang Lkoun, and Laang Pka Sla.[53] These "caves of [re]birth" *(raang prasut)*, were particularly frequented over the New Year period. When Bareau visited, he met a monk who meditated in a cave every day for four hours in the morning and three hours in the afternoon, hoping to see the "light of the Buddha." This is a probable reference to the "noble radiance of *arahat*ship," a notion specifically mentioned in one of the Cambodian Buddhist visualization texts connected with traditional initiatory practices (Bizot 1980, 249).[54] Phnom Sampau was also the site of a hermitage for women, although they tended to meditate in cabins rather than caves (Bareau 1969, 14–15).

Another cave-oriented complex once flourished on the slopes of Phnom Sia, Kampot Province, quite close to the Vietnamese border. It is perhaps for this reason that when Bareau visited it, the majority of hermits in residence were Mahayanists from Vietnam. However, Theravada laypersons and a couple of Mahanikay monks, most refugees from Kampuchea Krom, were also in residence, and chapels representing both forms of Buddhism were scattered about. One old monk had previously lived in a hermitage on Phnom Kulen but, finding it too cold, had moved farther south.[55]

Phnom Preah Reach Trop, the sacred hill at Udong, had also been a cult center long before any Cambodian kings used it as their residence. Eleventh-century lintels and a column have been discovered at the site, and an image of

Śiva's mount, the bull Nandin, had been venerated there for many centuries (Giteau 1975, 148). Today all trace of the Royal Palace has disappeared, and it is a pity that no proper scholarly study of the site has been made. Nevertheless, Preah Reach Trop is unique in that ascetic practices of the sort associated with most other hilltop sites appear to have existed side by side with elements of the potentially hostile royal cult. It is popularly believed that a secret tunnel leads from Udong to a grotto on nearby Phnom Baset that had supposedly been consecrated to Buddhism by the legendary king Baksei Chamkrong (Mak Phœun 1984, 105–106).[56] By the middle of the twentieth century the hillside sheltered more than ten monasteries, including at least two royal foundations—Wat Vihear Luong and Wat Chaudotes.[57]

Monasteries

A lot of modern monasteries, particularly in Kompong Cham, Svay Rieng, Takeo, and Kandal provinces, have been constructed on the site of Angkorian and pre-Angkorian temples, many reusing the original building materials. However, apart from a few *stūpas* and ancillary structures, few monastic buildings today are older than the mid-nineteenth century. The unthinking destruction of monastic buildings and, in many cases, the paintings and sculptures that they housed was not simply a feature of the Pol Pot period. Giteau (1975, 6) notes that between 1964 and the early 1970s at least four monasteries in Battambang town alone were pulled down and replaced by new structures. A similar situation applied in the old capital of Udong. Whether artworks were preserved was often merely a matter of chance. It is a fair bet that the custom, perhaps supported by the Buddhist emphasis on impermanence, stretches back several centuries.

Typically, a monastery consists of a group of buildings within a stockade or masonry enclosure *(mahāsīmā)* provided with several entrances. Monks have tended to dwell in communal houses,[58] although in some monasteries simple individual huts *(kdei)*, which are clearly more conducive to the contemplative life, may also be found. The chief monk *(chau adhikar)* usually has a separate residence. Some of these residences can be quite elaborate, and they may also act as the monastic library *(hotrai)* (Étudiants 1969, 37), a meeting place, or a depository for ancient images.[59] Most monasteries possess a tank *(srah)* in which monks may bathe; a cooking shed; shrines to tutelary spirits *(neak tā)*, often situated in the northeast of the compound (Ang Chouléan 1986, 218); family funerary monuments *(chedi)*;[60] and one or more, often open-sided pavilions *(sala)* used for a variety of purposes such as a refectory, a classroom, or lodging for travelers. The principal structure, however, is the ceremony hall, or *vihāra*. This tends to be oriented on an east-west axis and is more richly decorated than the other structures. It houses Buddha images and is the place where important monastic rites must be conducted. Paradoxically, given its purpose as a residence for male celibates, Bizot (1992, 34n1) has noted considerable sexual and embryological symbolism in the spatial layout of the monastery.[61]

Monasteries often possess racing canoes that are stored in a special shed, awaiting the annual races in the month of *kattik* (November–December) at the end of the three-month Buddhist retreat *(vassa)*. This is the time that the flow of the Mekong River becomes so great that it forces the Tonle Sap to back up, significantly increasing the perimeter of Cambodia's Great Lake. Winning the race has an enormous effect on the prestige of the monastery and its surrounding community, so great efforts are made in securing success. Wat Svay Chum on the eastern bank of the Mekong upstream from Phnom Penh is particularly renowned in this regard.[62] According to popular belief, its canoe is the residence of a *bray* who is "nourished" by offerings supplied by the monks and the *chau adhikar* of the monastery throughout the rest of the year. Racing canoes are also said to represent *nāgas* who ensure that the earth will accept the floodwaters without the rice's being drowned. Their power may be increased by the application of a set of eyes on either side of the prow for the duration of the race.

The ritual boundary *(sīmā)* of a *vihāra* must be properly laid out and consecrated before it can be used for monastic purposes. Verse chronicles outlining the circumstances of the foundation, such as that from Wat Srolauv, Kompong Thom Province, are sometimes attested in the historical record (Chandler 1982b, 59). According to Buddhist tradition, the site of the first monastery was donated by King Bimbisāra. The Buddha then permitted his two principal disciples, Sāriputta and Mahā Mogallāna, to trace out the *khaṇḍasīmā,* the area within special marker stones *(nimitta)* in which recitation of the monastic rules and confession of infractions could take place. The area within the *khaṇḍasīmā* is a sanctuary that is still, at least theoretically, felt to be beyond the reach of the secular power. In Thailand, for example, it is the custom for the king to cede this space to the *sangha* (No Na Paknam 1981, 57). That this has also been an important matter in Cambodia is attested by Ven. Huot Tath's short work on the topic, *Sīmāvinicchayasaṅkhepa* (Summary of opinions on the *sīmā*), first published in 1932.

The ritual for establishing a *khaṇḍasīmā (thvoeu bon banchho sema)* is thought to be highly meritorious and is one of the most popular of Cambodian festivities. It traditionally takes place during the month of *pisakh, ches,* or *assath* (May–July) (Leclère 1899, 370). The central act of the elaborate rite is the positioning of eight stone boundary markers *(nimitta),* in the four cardinal and four intercardinal directions, around the *vihāra*'s perimeter. Another stone, the so-called *indrakhīla* (or *sīmā kil*), is then placed at the center.[63] Although monks are involved and recite relevant passages of scripture, the ceremony is actually led by a lay ritual specialist *(achar)*.[64] Altars are erected to various directional deities at the eight positions around the *vihāra,* with the eastern position having as many as three.[65] The *achar* encircles the altars and their offerings with a protective thread of cotton before pits are dug. Offerings, such as shards of mirror, perfumed water, hair, nail clippings, musical instruments, or money, are thrown into the pit to make merit. Those present may also cut their finger to allow a few drops of blood to drip in before a circular block of stone, consecrated the previous night, is dropped down after being cut free from a supporting bamboo cross-member.[66] Both activities seem to point to an archaic and sacrificial origin for the rite. The ceremony is concluded by covering the round stones with soil, after which distinctive carved boundary stones *(sloek sema)* are positioned over the burial as a visible marker. The central position is left unmarked (Giteau 1969b, 44).[67]

Most monasteries of the early post-Angkorian period were built of wood and thatch and have not survived. Even those constructed from more durable materials have, as previously mentioned, been periodically dismantled and reconstructed. A detailed understanding of the historical development of monastic architecture is not helped by the total absence of any ancient textual sources relating to iconography and related matters. Nevertheless, in 1954 the Buddhist Institute in Cambodia commissioned a text on monastery construction by a craftsman employed at the Royal Palace, Ieng Sioeng.[68] Giteau (1975) was subsequently able to supplement this work with detailed stylistic analysis and comparison of monastic architecture in neighboring countries. In this way she began the task of constructing a precise chronology for Cambodian Theravada architecture.[69]

Some of the oldest Theravada monasteries appear to have been founded by powerful individuals. Vihear Banon—the northern sanctuary of Wat Sithor, Srei Santhor, one of the medieval capitals—and nearby Wat Vihear Suor both share an early post-Angkorian date and a royal foundation (Giteau 1975, 63–64). Indeed, both have been associated with the royal cult down to the present. According to local traditions, a commoner named Kan usurped the power of the ruling family in the early sixteenth century. Kan used a powerful racing canoe named "floating algae" *(saray andaet)* as his royal vehicle.[70] When Kan consecrated Wat Preah Put Leay Leak around 1529 CE as a way of legitimating his power, the canoe was cut into three pieces and its middle portion used to construct the central Buddha image of the monastery. The front and back were carved into flanking figures (Khin Sok 1988, 130, 144).[71]

Prince Sihanouk, cutting *indrakhīla*—Wat Ang Chum, Kompong Speu Province, February 10, 1968.

Similar royal foundations have continued into the modern period. Thus Wat Koh, Kien Svay District, Kandal Province, was founded by Sisowath's favorite wife, the king himself participating in the boundary *(sīmā)* demarcation ritual (Meas-Yang 1978, 44).

Some monasteries rose to prominence by virtue of their possession of important relics. Wat Unnalom in Phnom Penh, now the headquarters of the Mahanikay order, is the old site of a *stūpa* popularly believed to have been constructed by a certain Ven. Assajit to house one of the hairs *(loma)* of the Buddha's *uṣṇiṣā*, a hairy whorl between his eyebrows believed to be one of the marks of a great man (Cœdès 1913a, 11).[72] Over time the fabric of the monastery has been overlain with elements of the royal and protonational cult. Medieval kings are supposed to have donated buddha images to the monastery, and a *sala* under a *bodhi* tree near the riverbank was dedicated to *neak tā* Khleang Moeung fairly early on (Khin Sok 1988, 71–72). Until recently a statue of the Leper King also stood in front of Unnalom as a sort of protective deity (Giteau 1975, 25).

All *vihāras* possess at least one buddha image, and most house many more. The modern inscriptions of Angkor [IMA] make it clear that the donation of such artifacts was a highly meritorious act, and wealthy donors were often prepared to offer quite large numbers of buddha images made of precious materials if the monastery was sufficiently prestigious (Giteau 1975, 151–152). The royal chronicles bulge with accounts of high-profile donations by kings and members of the ruling elite. Regrettably, many high-quality buddha images of the past are now in museums and private collections or have simply been broken up. The standard of craftsmanship of those that remain in situ is often mediocre, although they may still act as reservoirs of supernatural power.

Two famous wooden statues of the Buddha in the fear-dispelling posture *(abhayamudrā)*[73] once housed in a monastery in Siem Reap, have had a checkered recent history. They were removed to Phnom Kulen in the 1950s by Dap Chhuon, a local warlord, politician, and mystic. In the early 1990s they were recovered and ceremonially reinstalled in a shrine on the edge of a public park, though now detached from their original monastic context (Bizot 1994a, 121). But once again they act as the dwelling place of a female protective spirit *(boramei)* who has the power to possess a number of oracle-priests *(snang)* (Sok Sakhom and Bertrand 1998, 1131).

Images of the Buddha's early monastic followers, particularly Sāriputta and Mahā Mogallāna, are frequently found flanking the central image of a *vihāra.* Their deposition at important monasteries seems to be quite an old practice, as an inscription at Angkor Wat dating from 1586 CE makes clear (Giteau 1975, 197). Perhaps the most interesting of these subsidiary images is the small figure of Preah Kam Chay, or Mahā Kaccāyana. Although not as widespread as Sāriputta and Mahā Mogallāna, Preah Kam Chay is a distinctive figure, generally positioned behind the main Buddha image. According to Pali canonical sources (*DhA.* i.324–326), Mahā Kaccāyana was once seen adjusting his robe by the wealthy merchant Soreyya, who conceived a desire to make the monk his wife, upon which the monk turned into a woman. After many years Soreyya confessed his fault, and the monk became a man once more. In Cambodia it is believed that Preah Kam Chay took an unattractive form to prevent the same thing from happening again. This is why he is depicted as short, fat, and ugly.[74] But Preah Kam Chay possesses great protective power. Naive images of him are printed on pieces of cloth or shirts for protective purposes. He also has the ability to help a supplicant seduce girls (Étudiants 1969, 48). By way of comparison, the range of female figures found on Buddhist altars is more limited. Statuettes of the earth goddess, Nang Thorani, are fairly common, and one might also mention a nineteenth-century stuccoed image of a nun *(bhikkhuṇī)* once occupying a space behind the main altar at Wat Samrong Thong, Battambang (Giteau 1975, 241).

Prasat Neang Khmau near Phnom Chisor, dating from the second quarter of the tenth century, is the only surviving Angkor-period monument to retain painted murals, but these are ubiquitous in the Theravada period. It seems

Shrine of Neak Tā Khleang Moeung, Bakan District, Pursat Province.

that many of the customary motifs of monastery art were already present in Cambodia in the seventeenth and eighteenth centuries. Carved wooden panels from Babour now in the National Museum in Phnom Penh, for example, depict the Buddha's conception and various sylvan deities *(yakkha)*, as well as scenes from the *Rāmāyaṇa* and the *Jātakas* (Giteau 1975, 209–214).[75] Today the interiors of most *vihāras* are painted with narrative depictions. They may also have murals on their outer walls.[76] The interior walls generally illustrate key incidents from the life of the Buddha. It is particularly common to find the defeat of Māra *(māravijaya)* immediately behind the altar. Depictions of the Buddha's previous lives, as recorded in the 547 stories of the canonical *Jātaka* collection, are also frequent. Particularly common are the final ten *(dasajātaka)*, with pride of place given to the Buddha's penultimate existence as the embodiment of generosity, Prince Vessantara. Apocryphal *Jātakas,* like the stories of Vorvong and Saurivong (*Vorvong and Saurivong* 1971) and of Preah Chinavong,[77] have circulated in Cambodia for many centuries and appear to be unique to the region. They are also occasionally depicted in monastic murals. Indeed, the *sala* at Wat Kieng Svay Krom, in Kandal Province, was decorated with tableaux covering the entire story of Preah Chinavong until they disappeared some twenty years ago (Jacq-Hergoualc'h 1982, 1988).

Buddhist sites associated with less mainstream practices seem to have displayed this identity iconographically. Until the late 1960s, Phnom Sampau near Battambang had been a locus for the esoteric practices discussed in chapter 4. Many of the painted scenes in its various shrines abounded with skeletons, dead bodies, executions, murders, and decomposition. Photographs of dead Buddhist monks and Christian saints whose bodies had been miraculously preserved were also displayed. The arrangement was clearly designed to underpin the central Buddhist insight of impermanence. One of the painted scenes representing the Buddha's alms-gift of a shroud *(paṅsukūl)* from Suvaṇṇadāsī underlines this. Phnom Sampau also had a hermitage for women. Its decorations depicted the lives of various early Buddhist nuns and prominent laywomen such as Subhaddā, Dhammadinnā, Khemā, Pesakāradhītā, and Saṅghamittā (Bareau 1969, 14–15).

Thailand has been the principal influence on Cambodian Buddhist art since at least the nineteenth century, but both Lao and Vietnamese elements are also present along the relevant border areas. Some of the oldest murals dating from this period appear to have been at Wat Chaudotes at Udong, Wat Sisowath Ratanaram on the Bassac River, and Wat Phnom Del on the Mekong.[78] However, the earliest dated religious paintings were fourteen temple hangings depicting the *Vessantara Jātaka* on fabric suspended between pillars at Wat Kraing Chek, Moha Saing, Phnom Sruoch, Kompong Speu, created in 1877 (Dupaigne and Khing 1981, 27). Unfortunately, none of these artworks appears to have survived the upheavals of recent decades. Apart from the famous *Rāmāyaṇa* sequences at the Royal Palace and Wat Bo, Siem Reap, it seems that the only old and relatively intact Buddhist murals still extant are at Wat Kompong Tralach Leu.[79]

Little is known of the identity of most mural painters, although frescoes at Wat Tep Pranam, Udong, were once signed by two Phnom Penh–based artists—Um, who seems to have been a monk, and Ket.[80] On the basis of internal evidence such as clothing styles and the like, they appear to have completed their work around 1910. The most famous figure in this connection was Oknya Tep Nimit Māk (b. 1856). He started his career with six years as a Thommayut monk at Wat Botum, Phnom Penh, before traveling to Bangkok to study architecture (Nafilyan and Nafilyan 1997, 76).[81] In 1897 he became architect of the Royal Palace, and in 1918 the director of the School of Arts in Phnom Penh. Today he is known for directing the team of forty artists who created the *Rāmāyaṇa* murals at the Royal Palace in 1903–1904. The murals of Wat Sisowath Ratanaram and the rich and elegant work at Wat Chaudotes are also generally attributed to his school (Jeldres and Chaijitvanit 1999, 47).

The Monastic Economy

The work involved in constructing the Angkorian *barays* and their associated temples had been enormous and required the services of a massive pool of manpower. This manpower seems to have been largely supplied by the institution of slavery, a practice that survived in Cambodia in one form or another down to the beginning of the twentieth century. The Khmer word "*kñuṃ*" possesses the semantic resonances to justify its translation by the term "slave," but one must be aware of potential anachronism. Western notions of freedom and slavery may not always be appropriate in judging the institutions of medieval Southeast Asia (Ebihara 1984, 290–291), and as Vickery (1998, 226) has observed, the old inscriptions never make reference to "explicitly free commoners." Given this background, is it reasonable to suppose that because the *kñuṃ* were not free, they must have been slaves? Jacques (1975) has suggested that they were not, for slaves would never have had their names engraved on temple records, nor would they have been allowed to defile the temple precincts.[82] We need to know far more about the nature of old Khmer society and its notions of property in particular before the matter can be more precisely resolved, but for the purposes of this discussion I shall accept the translation of "*kñuṃ*" as "slave," subject to these qualifications and for want of a better alternative.

A probable mid-seventh-century Khmer inscription [K. 163] from Kompong Thom mentions the gift of *kñuṃ* to a Buddhist foundation (Vickery 1998, 147, 221–222). *Kñuṃ* came in a variety of categories. Some were slaves of the god *(kñuṃ vraḥ),* others slaves of the temple *(kñuṃ vihāra).* The latter seem to have been donated by a powerful owner, probably as a merit-generating act. Temple slaves could be employed as singers, dancers, or musicians in the cult of the deity. Alternatively they might be assigned roles as cooks, administrators, or secretaries. They could also be mobilized in time of conflict (Jacob 1993a, 281). How they fell into slavery is not entirely clear, but some were captured in war, often against various tribal groupings (Jacob 1993b, 304).[83]

It might have been expected that, with the fall of Angkor and the adoption of the new tradition of Theravada Buddhism, the practice of monastic slavery would have come to an end. However, this was far from the case. We know that, in Sri Lanka, medieval Theravada kings such as Aggabodhi IV (r. 658–674) had donated slaves and endowed land for the upkeep of the *sangha*. The same principle applied in Cambodia. According to a manuscript once housed at Wat Sambok ([Keo-Han 1951], King Paramarāja VIII [r. 1659–1672]) decreed that 40 families of condemned persons forced into corvée for the king *(neak na)* and "slaves of the Buddha" *(pol preah)* be responsible for the upkeep of the monastery and a large *stūpa* in perpetuity. Indeed, descendants of these slaves were still around in 1951. Similarly, in Thailand, Rama I (r. 1782–1809) bestowed 224 families, 66 corvée laborers *(phrai luang)* who were required to donate three months' labor each year, and 7,672 baht for the upkeep of Wat Phrachetuphonn; the custom of monastery slaves *(lek wat)* came to an end only with the first emancipation act of August 21, 1874, in the reign of Chulalongkorn. In Cambodia itself a virtual disappearance of *kñuṃ vihāra* was envisaged in a royal ordinance of July 11, 1897. Despite this legislation, they were still being used in the Thai-administered provinces of northwest Cambodia, particularly in the monasteries around Angkor, until the end of the nineteenth century. Indeed, a letter from Angkor-based monks to the Bangkok authorities, dated November 28, 1900, complained that with the emancipation of the *lek wat* there was no one left to care for the temples (Reynolds 1979, 197–198).

In the middle period of the Khmer inscriptional record, between the sixteenth and nineteenth centuries, *kñuṃ* donated by powerful individuals for the care of sacred images are regularly given Pali-derived names of the form "Mrs. Suddh" (pure) or "Mr. Jet" (best) (Jacob 1986a, 118). Works of moral and political instruction like the *cpāp'* are also surprisingly rich in varied but quite specific terms relating to slavery. In his pioneering work on Buddhism in Cambodia, Leclère (1899, 399–400) distinguishes four categories of monastery slave: those condemned for an act of sacrilege *(pol preah)*,[84] prisoners of war *(komlas preah)*, those donated by their masters *(bamros preah)*, and individuals who had taken the role voluntarily *(nhom preah)*, perhaps as a penance. Children born to monastery slaves would generally become slaves in their turn (Leclère 1890, 279). Monks could also become pagoda slaves if found guilty of committing a variety of offenses, including killing and stealing sacred objects. For fornication, adultery, incest, bestiality, administering a drug to bring about an abortion, falsely claiming to have achieved various spiritual powers, plus a number of other heinous offenses, the monk was obliged to become a slave in a royal monastery (Leclère 1890, 241–242).

Criminals might fall into permanent and hereditary slavery, whereas debt slavery was temporary (Tauch Chhuong 1994, 32). Slavery might also be a punishment for an individual engaged in unpatriotic behavior, so if a woman persisted in sexual relations with a non-Buddhist foreigner after a tribunal had ruled that she should desist, she could be punished by becoming a royal slave (Vollman 1973, 181). By the 1870s there were still thousands of *kñuṃ* in Cambodia classified under three headings: royal slaves, child slaves, and temple slaves. Although hereditary slaves were theoretically unable to buy their freedom, in practice this did sometimes happen. Manumission of debt slaves was quite common, and we hear of such persons joining the *sangha* or being attached to temple work parties.[85] Evidence also exists that wealthy persons bought an individual slave's freedom as a merit-making act (Lewitz 1973a, 184–185). It seems that this was a relatively common procedure for ensuring the future felicity of a recently deceased member of the family and would be recommended by monks dealing with the funeral rites. A slave who had looked after his master during the master's final illness might also be granted his or her freedom (Leclère 1899, 502).

A monastery's real estate was termed *sambat preah*. Such sacred lands *(dey preah)* were not taxed when worked by slaves but might be subject to taxation when tended by freemen. The arrangement clearly perpetuated the institution of monastic slavery. However, because monastic slaves were part of the property of a monastery, they were ultimately the property of the Buddha and this partially explains their reasonably tolerable treatment.[86] Although traditional Cambodian Buddhism never dreamed of the complete abolition of slavery, a study of the history of legislation and religious practice in the country reveals a continuous effort both to ameliorate the lot of the slave and to limit the freedom of cruel masters. Monastic lands were generally donated by wealthy and influential figures to maintain the foundation in perpetuity, although other forms of land and property bestowal are also attested in the historical record.[87] Ebihara (1984, 292) believes that such donations were motivated by two basic considerations: merit making and tax avoidance. When the latter was uppermost, the most appropriate locus for liberality would be a monastery whose chief monk *(chau adhikar)* was a brother or other close family member, because the control of donated land could then be effectively maintained. Some of these monasteries could become magnets for further land donation over the generations. As such, they became quite powerful, even though, as Leclère (1899, 400) implies, monastic lands were not managed effectively, for the majority of monks had no clear idea of the responsibilities of ownership.

Monks, Ritual Specialists, and Laity

In the mid-1960s Kalab (1968, 521) studied a village, Prek Por, of around 4,500 inhabitants. It consisted of a number of hamlets variously supporting three separate local monasteries. One of these, Wat Prakal, possessed three high-ranking monks—the chief monk and his two deputies. She tells us that the former spent most of his time in meditative and intellectual pursuits, one deputy taught in the government school and spent his spare time collecting and preserving fragments of old palm-leaf manuscripts, and the other deputy was involved in the construction of a village medical center at which novice monks provided much of the unskilled labor. The description nicely encapsulates the spiritual, educational, and social welfare–oriented functions of a typical rural monastery several years before the country erupted into civil war.

The chief monk *(chau adhikar)* is also known as the head of the monastery *(mevat)*. In modern times he has been part of the provincial *sangha* hierarchy. His responsibilities include the overall maintenance of monastery buildings, the supervision of personnel and properties, and the upholding of good levels of monastic discipline. As was the case at Wat Prakal, the work of the *chau adhikar* is often supported by two monastic assistants *(gru sot)*, one in charge of the instruction of monks and the other with responsibility for the teaching of children (Meas-Yang 1978, 45). Monks *(loak song)* constitute the heart of the community, but other categories of person also reside in a typical monastery. Temple boys *(kmeng vat)* between seven and twelve years of age carry out various domestic tasks and gain a basic education, while at the same time accruing merit for themselves and their families. The monastery is also a refuge for the old and pious of both sexes. Thus women who have renounced the household life may live in the compound. These *don chi* (or *yiey chi*) are not nuns *(bhikkhuṇī)* in the strict sense, for a valid ordination rite for female religious died out many centuries ago. Therefore they are not bound by the 311 rules laid down in the nuns' code of discipline by the Buddha.[88] They are, accordingly, not always granted an especially high status, even though they observe most of the precepts of a novice monk. They perform various menial functions and may be excluded from certain aspects of the monastery's spiritual routines. In the past, *don chi* were allowed to study liturgical texts but not to practice meditation (Étudiants 1969, 52).

As if to underline this inequality between the sexes, village traditions hold that a boy around the age of twelve should become a novice monk *(samne)* and observe the ten precepts for a short period in honor of his mother. Full ordination as a *bhikkhu* around the age of twenty, on the other hand, is undertaken in honor of one's father (Ebihara 1968, 385n2). One of the distinctive features of Theravada Buddhism in Cambodia and Thailand, as opposed to that in Sri Lanka, is the ease with which one can enter and leave the monastic life. A range of differing novice ordination rituals has been practiced in twentieth-century Cambodia, including ordination entered to fulfill a vow *(puos ṭinguṇ)*;[89] the "fire ordination" *(puos phloeung)*, in which a boy takes robes temporarily on the death of a close relative; and the shortest of all, a rite that involves the taking of robes in the morning and a return to lay life the same afternoon *(puos muoy saṃkāṃṅ taṃrī)*.[90] It would be a mistake to assume that everyone taking ordination has a strong vocation for the contemplative life. A variety of other motives, including the desire to secure a basic education or to try to escape from alcoholism, are common. A popular saying holds that an individual may become a monk "just to get rid of lice," a consequence of having his head shaved (Smith-Hefner 1999, 49).

The customary time for temporary ordination is the rainy season *(vassa)*. The rest of the agricultural year is punctuated with Buddhist festivities, but once the rains arrive, a more somber mood pervades the village, the agricultural work rate increases, and the *sangha* enters a three-month period of increased ascetical character. As I have suggested elsewhere (Harris 2000b, 149–154), this highly focused period of male renunciation is believed to aid the growth of rice. At the end of his temporary period in the monastic order the novice is also able to return to the world well primed for life as a householder. Temporary ordination, then, can be read as a mechanism for focusing male reproductive energies.[91] The ordination ritual for novices is often explicitly termed the ordination of the *nāga (puos nag)*. A *nāga* is the preeminent symbol of the earthly power of fecundity, and in some traditional forms of the rite a serpent's vital spirits *(braling)* are explicitly called upon to enter the candidate's body (Porée-Maspero 1951, 147–148).[92] Perhaps unsurprisingly, modern reformers have been hostile to this interpretation of the rite. One of the great monuments to the reforming spirit, Chuon Nath's *Dictionary* (1938), describes the calling of souls *(hau braling)* as "performed according to a Brahmanical treatise"[93] and not in accord with the true intentions of the Buddha. Cambodian modernists have taken their lead from King Mongkut (Rama IV, r. 1851–1868), who tried to eliminate fertility elements from Buddhist agrarian traditions in nineteenth-century Thailand. Mongkut was also concerned about counteracting rural women's tendency to regard monks as "fatted pigs ready for the slaughter."[94] The issue nicely illustrates a tension that has come to characterize monasticism over the last century. In the traditional rural setting, the monk is not regarded as a figure especially withdrawn from the world. He participates in a wide variety of agrarian and other annual rituals, and even at the point of maximum detachment he is felt to be focusing his energies for some potential future reengagement. The reformers have systematically sought to break the connection between the practice of Buddhism and its agrarian environment. In the process the modernist monk has achieved a greater authenticity and dignity but, paradoxically, is also more detached from his social milieu. Naturally, such an individual can thrive best in the relatively impersonal setting of a modern city like Phnom Penh, where he will be less dependent on the support of a village community.

In the past, *sangha* members were accorded considerable deference, no matter how high the social or economic standing of the layperson might be.[95] The penal code of King Sisowath prescribed the death penalty for anyone who killed a monk while he was exercising his religious functions (article 209), and the injury of a monk in similar circumstances drew the penalty of forced labor for life (article 210).[96] Conversely, monks guilty of serious monastic offenses would, in the first instance, be dealt with according to ecclesiastical law *(vinaya)*. Should they be expelled from the *sangha,* they could then be tried in a civil court.[97] Before the 1970s it was quite common to see ordinary people walk in a crouch when passing a monastic seated on the ground, so that their head was lower than that of the monk. These attitudes of deference were so widespread that Chinese or Vietnamese drivers would regularly offer the best seat on a bus to a monk, even though they were not practicing Buddhists (Ebihara 1968, 376). The events of the last three decades, combined with the creeping influence of global forces, have caused a great attenuation in this outlook. Having said that, respect has always been tempered by the knowledge that monks may occasionally go astray. Traditional stories, for instance, often ridicule individual monks, particularly those with untamed sexual desires, but Buddhism as an institution has rarely become the focus of satire (Jacob 1982). This distinction is clarified in the case of the chief monk of Wat Angkor Chrey, Kompong Cham Province, who in August 1900 had been condemned by both the laity and his fellow monks for having a relationship with a local woman. The governor of Srei Santhor, after taking advice from interested parties, imposed a fine and confiscated the monk's property, transferring ownership to the monastery itself (Forest 1980, 56). There is no conception here that the misdeeds of an individual might adversely affect the condition or standing of the monastic order as a whole.

It is sometimes said that, for a monastery to prosper, "either the villagers around must be rich or modestly well-off, or the abbot must be very skilled in religious magic" (W. Collins 1998a, 21). In the latter case, the *chau adhikar* may be able attract visitors and pilgrims from far and near, thus supplementing the meager income generated locally. Of course this will be possible only if he possesses a range of traditional skills, and it is difficult to see how a modernist monk could be successful in such an undertaking. We have seen that some monasteries have royal foundations and, until relatively modern times, were not so dependent on local economic vicissitudes. But these are rather special cases, and all monasteries must generate and administer significant funds to guarantee their future survival. This is a task that neither the *chau adhikar,* his monastic assistants *(gru sot),* nor the community of ordinary monks can easily perform, for their monastic discipline prevents all engagement in commercial and financial activity. This is a job for a lay functionary, the *achar.*

The *achar vat* is generally selected in a consultation process between the *chau adhikar* and the village community. Ideally, he must be a pious older man who keeps the first eight precepts of the novice monk. In addition he must be known for his financial probity. His prime responsibility is the general management and maintenance of the temple and its properties. He also negotiates the interactions between monks and the outside world, particularly in matters connected with money, and he acts as the villagers' spokesman in their dealings with the *sangha.* Some larger monasteries, given their varied activities, may have more than one *achar,* so a chairman *(achar thom)* is elected from their midst. However, whether a monastery is big or small, the *achar* is expected to cooperate with the senior monks and to work hand in hand with a management committee consisting of a number of village elders *(cah thom)* who keep the five lay precepts. *Achars* must always be male, but members of the *cah thom* may be of either sex. Indeed, in recent times it is increasingly common for women to serve on the management committee.

Another important role of the *achar* is as organizer of the seven major annual festivals. These celebrations are important opportunities for fund-raising, although ad hoc flower festivals *(bon pgah)* in which flowers made of banknotes are offered may also be arranged if a major item of expenditure, like a new building, is planned. It is quite usual to speculatively invite wealthy outsiders to these events. The *achar*'s final responsibility is to lead the laity in acts of worship. In this role he must be proficient in the requisite Pali formulae and must be something of a ritual specialist. For this reason, *achars* are often ex-monks.[98] Indeed, an officiating monk will not rise to deliver a sermon until invited to do so by an *achar,* who recites a series of verses describing how the deity Brahmā Sahaṃpati requested the Buddha to preach the *dhamma* for the very first time.[99]

Lay specialists, like monks, come in a variety of styles.[100] It is not uncommon for a traditional *achar* to act as astrologer *(hora),* and many monasteries once contained a good range of works on the subject in their libraries. However, those with modernist tendencies scrupulously avoid all reference to magic and related arts (Étudiants 1969, 50–51). Try (1991, 170) asserts that *achars* fall into one of five basic categories: those responsible for the ordination of novices, reciters of *dhamma* during the ceremony of entry into the monastery, Pali teachers, those responsible for pupils at the monastery school, and teachers of Buddhist *dhamma.* Ebihara (1968, 439), on the other hand, distinguishes between an *achar kar* (also called *moha*), who specializes in marriages, and an *achar yogi,* whose expertise is in funerals. Clearly, most of these roles may be appropriated by one individual in the course of various of his duties. The *achar yogi*, however, is different, for he is connected with an esoteric or initiatory *(yogāvacara)* tradition that will be discussed in more detail in chapter 4. He is the most knowledgeable of the various village ritual specialists and should not be confused with the *achar vat* (Porée-Maspero 1954, 620).

The term "leader of the wind" *(mekhyal)*[101] is sometimes deployed in connection with the roles played by *achars* and *cah thom*. It implies that a position of authority is transient and related to specific situations. Thus, an *achar* may become *mekhyal* to accomplish a particular task. Conversely, not all *mekhyal* are *achars*. A *mekhyal* is expected to become involved in a definite undertaking and should not act solely in a supervisory capacity. However, like the wind, he may act with daring to overcome obstacles, even if this implies some defiance of customary norms (W. Collins 1998a, 26–27). This may explain why in the past, though very much less so today, *achars* were frequently associated with "mouvements de contestation" (Forest 1992, 88).

Because the monastic order is deemed to be the most fertile ground in which to sow the seeds of good actions, much Buddhist lay practice revolves around ceremonies that involve the gift of food, clothing, lodging, medicine, and other necessities to monks. Agriculture-related rites, such as those connected with rain making and the harvest, also incorporate acts of generosity.[102] All donations are meritorious and are held to lead to favorable consequences. As has already been noted, kings and other influential individuals are thought to have earned their current status through the accumulated merit of many such actions performed in previous existences. Lay rituals may also be performed for purely this-worldly ends, for, as an eighteen-year-old girl told Ebihara (1968, 383), "I will go to three or four Kathun[103] festivals this year so that I will be reborn as a rich American." No matter the motivation, expenditure of large sums of money and energy in support of elaborate rituals, even by those who are not especially prosperous, was and continues to be an important element in the life of all Buddhist communities. Whereas *achars* officiate at all major rites of passage, the *sangha* is far less involved in ceremonies relating to birth, marriage, and adult initiation. However, the ritualization of death is very much a monastic preserve. Since both crematoria and lay funerary monuments are sited within the monastery compound, this is the obvious location for obsequies that tend to be detailed, lengthy, and lavish. If the deceased individual happens to be a senior monk, proceedings can be very lavish indeed.[104] Funerary rites, then, provide an ideal context for monastic entrepreneurialism. At the same time, the merit generated by the sponsors is transferred to the deceased to ensure an auspicious transition to his or her next existence.

The layperson tries to support the Buddhist triple jewel *(triratna)*—the

Buddha, his teachings, and the monastic order—by the observation of certain set rituals[105] and donations of one sort or another. He or she is also expected, at least theoretically, to observe five moral precepts. These are to abstain from taking life, to avoid taking what has not been given, to abstain from sexual misconduct, to refrain from lying, and to refrain from liquor and other intoxicating substances. On certain occasions a particularly pious layman or laywoman may extend the number of precepts they observe in order to live a life approximating that of a monk. However, for many Cambodian Buddhists, indeed for Buddhists as a whole, the demands of the precepts may sometimes seem excessively onerous. Under these circumstances all kinds of casuistry come into play. Most villagers do at least try to observe the first precept when it comes to eating the meat of domesticated animals. Engaging in butchery would clearly be unacceptable, yet chickens and other poultry are often reared. Their killing is a job done by children, usually boys of twelve or thirteen years of age who, by virtue of their nonadult status, are regarded as incompletely subject to Buddhist ethical injunctions (Ebihara 1968, 312). Higher animals such as pigs are normally slaughtered by non-Buddhist members of the Chinese or Cham Muslim community, but restrictions are lighter when it comes to wild animals, with fish, some birds, snakes, frogs, and toads forming important ingredients in the rural diet (Martel 1975, 231). Nevertheless, it does seem as though the first precept is the most strongly observed of the five.[106] As is the case in many other Asian Buddhist societies, the practice of one precept is deemed significantly better than nothing. Certainly, the fourth precept is difficult to hold to in a culture where bribery and mendacity in the face of officialdom are endemic. Similarly, the widely acknowledged failure to heed the third and fifth lay precepts, especially among men, has a strong cultural component.

Recent Cambodian religious traditions retain much that is archaic. The cult of the *neak tā* may be regarded as a foundational layer upon which later traditions have been overlaid. Some of these tutelary spirits probably predate the arrival of Indic influences, though it is also clear that Brahmanical deities have themselves sometimes been assimilated into the folk level. Although much of the cultic activity associated with the *neak tā* is not specifically Buddhist, it is nevertheless incorporated into a generalized Buddhist world picture both spatially, in the sense that the shrines of *neak tā* are often located within the perimeter of Buddhist structures, and conceptually, in that the *neak tā* are assigned worldly powers that complement the salvific influences of the Buddha and Buddhist saints. In the case of the *boramei,* the latter relationship is the most closely integrated, in that originally malevolent spirits have been transformed into Buddhist protector deities.

The most visible expression of the concept of magical protection is, however, embodied in the person of the king. Indeed, the role of the monarch as the guarantor of justice and order, interpreted in the widest possible sense, is characteristic of all vigorous phases of Cambodian history. Therefore the king had always been regarded as a repository of merit symbiotically linking, through his person, the state and the cosmos. In the Angkorian period it appears that he was thought of as divine. But as Theravada Buddhism extended its hold, the Brahmanical mythology that had underpinned the concept of the *devarāja* diminished, though it was never entirely abandoned. The sacred character of kingship has persisted, although Buddhist influences led the righteous king to be thought of as a *dhammarāja* imbued with the charisma of the universal monarch or *cakravartin*. His benevolent power over both his people and the natural order was no longer considered so much an expression of his divinity; rather, it was considered a register of how closely he adhered to the eternal laws of existence *(dhamma)*, as discovered and enunciated in the teachings of the Buddha.

We can identify a general trend toward assimilation and accretion in the way that the Cambodian landscape has been sacralized over the centuries. Worship at high places is a feature of most religious traditions, and Cambodia is no exception, for mountain cults are attested in the region from the earliest period. After the collapse of Angkor, many of these ancient sites were transformed and converted for the performance of Buddhist cultic activity. The same general principle applies in the rest of the country, where significant Theravada structures eventually appeared on sites originally dedicated to other gods. In the process, old deities were absorbed into a new Buddhist cosmological and conceptual framework. We have seen that the rituals employed for the foundation of new Buddhist monasteries still preserve many archaic and sacrificial features. But the retention of the institution of sacred slavery until well into the modern period also demonstrates that social and political arrangements of the Angkorian period were retained by the post-Angkorian Theravada dispensation. Such examples point to the essential conservatism of Cambodian religious traditions.

4

Literary and Cult Traditions

Cambodian Literary Tradition

Cambodian literature is customarily divided into two major categories. The first encompasses all explicit works of religious instruction *(gambhir),* including canonical, cosmological, and ritual Buddhist texts; commentaries on these; annals and chronicles; works of moral and political instruction *(cpāp'),* and juridical literature *(kram).*[1] The second *(lpaeng)* is equally large and diverse. It includes legends, fables, epic stories, poems, and novels. *Lpaeng* were used widely in the monastery-based education of the laity, and even today traditionalist monks continue to chant versified romances based around the Buddha's past lives and the like, in a spare and stylized manner *(smut)* that takes several years to learn (Khing Hoc Dy 1990, 1:25, 1:94). Not all of Cambodia's Buddhist literature falls into the former grouping, and it would be incorrect to assume that *lpaeng* is purely secular. This distinction can be meaningfully applied only to works that have emerged over the last fifty years, for the Buddhist background pervaded all elements of Cambodian culture until very recently. Therefore the majority of classical Khmer novels *(rioeng lpaeng)* are based around popular Buddhist tales, particularly those contained in the apocryphal *Jātaka* collection, the *Paññāsajātaka.*[2] A good example is the well-known story of Vorvong and Saurivong (*Vorvong and Saurivong* 1971).

Traditional manuscripts exist in a number of forms. The largest and most imposing of these are the *satra,* which comprise large bundles of prepared and dried palm leaves *(sloek)*[3] that have been inscribed by a stylus and washed with ink before being bound between wooden boards. Particularly lengthy *satra* may be made up of a number of fascicles *(kse).* Shorter texts, on the other hand, are bundled in an identical manner but are called *vien.* The other common traditional form is the *krang,* a book written with ink on paper made from the bark of young branches of *Streblus asper*—a plant commonly found growing among rice fields—which is then folded in a concertina arrangement.[4] A variety of Khmer script styles are used, but the general rule is that Pali texts are rendered in a round style *(mul),* whereas Khmer itself is given in the slanted style *(crieng)* (Khin Sok 1982, 114).

By and large, no extant Cambodian manuscripts are especially old. Occasionally, one may find something dating back to the end of the eighteenth century, but most are somewhat later. There are a number of reasons for this. In the first place, the climate is not conducive to the longevity of traditional writing materials. If damp and mold do not get them, insects and rats probably will. Another reason relates to the custom of burning old manuscripts on the funeral pyres of ecclesiastical dignitaries as a merit-making activity (Ang Chouléan 1997, 57).[5] They may also be housed in funerary monuments *(chedi)* alongside fragments of statues and other sacred items, once their useful life is over. A good example of the practice may be found in the *chedi* of Ven. Chuon Nath at Wat Unnalom, Phnom Penh. Vandalism during the Khmer Rouge period as a cause for the disappearance of ancient texts may not, therefore, be quite as significant as once thought.[6] Certainly, many important collections of relatively modern Buddhist manuscripts were destroyed or otherwise lost during the period, but French scholars had already noted the absence of ancient texts in Cambodia at the end of the nineteenth century (Filliozat 2000).

The arrival of the French and the gradual imposition of the conditions of modernity on the Buddhist *sangha* had a profound impact on all aspects of Cambodian culture, particularly in the field of writing. Traditional literary activity was one of the immediate casualties, as monks turned away from the laborious and ritually circumscribed techniques associated with traditional manuscript production to adopt writing in European-style notebooks. In time many turned to printing, and the old copyists' craft with its merit-making underpinnings began a dramatic decline. In addition, an archaic and essentially magical vision of the universe, in which inscribed Khmer characters are assigned occult powers, was largely undermined.[7] As de Bernon (1998a, 879) has noted, it is rare today to find monks who have any confidence in reading traditional cosmological works, such as the *Traibhūm,* which once formed the core of the Khmer literary canon.

Pali Literature

Finot's detailed investigation (1917) into the condition of the libraries of Laotian Buddhist monasteries revealed that none contained a full set of writings from the Pali canon or the Tripitaka, although many held a complete Abhidhamma. The reason appears to be that the latter contained the texts necessary for the proper conduct of death rites and related ceremonies.[8] On the surface this appears rather puzzling, for the scholarly consensus has been that the Tripitaka is the sine qua non of Theravada Buddhism. One explanation could be that Buddhism in Laos was in such a degenerate condition that its monks could not be bothered to preserve its sacred patrimony. Yet when we turn to Cambodia, the situation was much the same. Finot had begun collecting Cambodian manuscripts in the late nineteenth century. Indeed, he seems to have given a small boost to tradition by conscripting monks into making copies of extant works for him. However, in an inventory of 1902 he lists a total of 256 palm-leaf writings, of which only around 40 (about 15 percent) were in Pali (Filliozat 2000, 447). The majority of the rest were written in Khmer. It seems that this proportion remained pretty constant down to the middle of the century.

Despite Cambodia's history of upheaval and social disruption since the fall of Angkor, the country did possess some significant Buddhist libraries. In a survey conducted in 1912, Cœdès identified a number of important collections. In the capital, Wat Unnalom possessed several separate libraries, some 150 manuscripts were housed at the Silver Pagoda, and 350 works, admittedly mainly Thai, were held at Wat Botum. In Battambang, the former Thai viceroy Phya Katathon had donated around 120 manuscripts to Wat Damrei Sar, Wat Po Veal[9] maintained an impressive collection, and the library of Wat Văt was clearly well established with old, yet hardly read texts, probably constituting the best collection in the country. Cœdès concluded that learned monks had once lived at Wat Văt, although the library was now rather neglected. Other libraries also existed at Udong and elsewhere, while copyists based at the Royal Library and the École Supérieure de Pali supplemented these collections by making new versions of old texts between 1927 and 1936 (Filliozat 2000, 448–449).

Cœdès believed that most of the scattered Pali manuscripts in these collections had their origin in Thailand. This idea reinforces the notion that the Tripitaka was hardly known in its entirety in Cambodia until modern times. Indeed, unless a monk had come under direct influence of Theravada reformers, either in Sri Lanka or Thailand, it is very likely that he would have had a poor grasp of Pali. Insofar as Pali literature was read at all, it was generally restricted to the rote learning of certain manuals that contained extracts from the Tripitaka. Cœdès' observation (1915, 2) that the *Dhammapada* commentary *(Dhammapadaṭṭhakathā)* and two works containing apotropaic writings *(parittas)*—the *Sarātthasaṅgaha* and the *Maṅgalatthadīpanī*—were the basis of Pali culture in premodern Thailand also holds good for Cambodia.[10] The vast majority of canonical and noncanonical concepts, as well as the rules and regulations of the monastic order, were clearly transmitted in the vernacular.

A Mon monk, Phra Sumet (aka Buddhavaṅsa), had convinced King Mongkut (Rama IV, r. 1851–1868) that the Thai monastic order was in need of reform in line with King Dhammacetī's fifteenth-century campaign of purification in Burma. Mongkut attributed the moral decline of the Thai *sangha* to the aftereffects of the Burmese sack of Ayutthaya in 1767. From that point until the establishment of the Chakri dynasty in 1782, civil wars had raged in which clans of monks with swords and guns, some led by high-ranking ecclesiastical dignitaries, attempted to carve up the country.[11] Although the problem of marauding monks had been solved long before Mongkut came to the throne, in his eyes the intellectual and spiritual life of the *sangha* had not improved. If monks could be persuaded to study the words of the Buddha in their original form rather than in late vernacular reworkings, the perceived decline in Buddhist fortunes would be reversed. The establishment of a Pali canon embodying those authentic words of the Buddha is the key act of reform. Thai Buddhist literature had always been written in the Khmer *(khom)* script, but as the reforms began to bite, Prince Patriarch Vajirañana arranged for the Tripitaka to be published in the Thai script. It finally appeared during the reign of Rama V (r. 1868–1910), but the more conservative segments of the Thai *sangha* were opposed to the initiative because the sacred *khom* script was thought to possess a magical efficacy hallowed by traditions stretching back many centuries.[12] In another reform, a pronunciation of Pali along the lines preserved by Mon-Burmese monks was introduced, even though no one really knew how Pali had originally been uttered. The reformers came to refer to themselves as members of the Dhammayutika Nikāya (Thommayut)—that is, "the group who hold to the teachings [of the Buddha]"—while in course of time the unreformed majority, or "order of long-standing habit," became known as the Mahānikāya (Reynolds 1973, 81–82).[13] The close involvement of the Thai court in Cambodian affairs meant it was inevitable that similar changes and tensions would manifest themselves in Cambodia.

We have already had cause to observe that the royal chronicles talk of editions of the Tripitaka in Cambodia at quite an early date. A number of sources, both Khmer and Thai, mention the legendary king Padum Suriyavaṅs, who had the Tripitaka copied onto leaves of gold and silver and distributed around the kingdom after a Laotian junk loaded with sacred Buddhist literature and the Emerald Buddha ran aground in a storm near the great city of Angkor.[14] Clearly, we do not know what the term "Tripitaka" implies in these contexts. In addition, the reports are late, contain many anachronisms, and must be treated with great caution. But we do know that Pali inscriptions are found in the country from the thirteenth century on. Given all this, it would be unwise to rule out the possibility that quantities of Pali literature circulated in Cambodia before the modern period. However, it is unlikely that these materials were ever formed into a canonical collection or that they possessed the grand significance assigned to them by modern reformers.

Insofar as Pali texts were known, it was their apotropaic and symbolic significance, rather than any explicitly didactic content, that seemed most relevant. Indeed, many of these works appear quite heterodox from the modernist standpoint. Jaini (1965), for instance, describes the *Mahādibbamanta,* an undated palm-leaf *paritta* text in the National Museum of Bangkok that is written in Cambodian characters and probably of Cambodian origin.[15] It consists of 108 verses, an auspicious number also specifically mentioned in the work itself (v. 10). One of the unusual features of the text is that it describes a *maṇḍala* of the eight chief disciples of the Buddha (vv. 18–20).[16] It also includes a mantra, *hulu hulu hulu svāhā* (vv. 38–39), and some verses of benediction *(siddhi-gāthā),*[17] which glorify a range of deities, including the earth goddess (v. 4), the Buddha, Hara, Harihara, and Rāma and the *nāgas* (vv. 78–89).[18] The *Mahādibbamanta* equates the Buddha with various major and minor divinities and concludes with an assurance of the magical efficacy of the text's recitation, particularly in counteracting enemies (vv. 90–98). When Jaini was working on the text, his Cambodian informant, the chief abbot of Wat Unnalom, informed him that the work was "Mahayanist."[19] This seems reasonable, since its obvious concern with *maṇḍalas, mantras,* and a highly syncretic pantheon of divinities certainly does look rather tantric. Yet the work is not uncharacteristic of the Pali Theravada literature that had circulated in Cambodia for several centuries.

What we do know is that in 1854 Ang Duang petitioned Bangkok to send a complete version of the Tripitaka in the pure form of Pali recently championed by the monastic reformers of that country, on the grounds that nothing of the sort existed in Cambodia at the time. A party of Thai monks subsequently brought some eighty bundles of sacred writings to Udong, and the Thommayut was established there under royal patronage. Interest in this new source of literary authority did ultimately percolate out beyond the boundaries of the Thommayut, with senior figures in the unreformed order taking a key role in advancing the modernist agenda as the new century unfolded (a topic to be discussed in chapter 5). Having said that, the Cambodian interest in sacred texts has not taken the critical path characteristic of the Theravada in other parts of South and Southeast Asia, where the Tripitaka has occupied central ground since the onset of the modern period.

Khmer Literature—The *Cpāp'*

Buddhist works of moral instruction are well attested throughout the Asian region. In Cambodia the genre began to emerge possibly as early as the fourteenth century and continued as a vigorous mode of writing well into the modern period.[20] These works seem to have been mostly composed by Buddhist monks in a variety of verse forms. This is hardly surprising, given that monks who taught in monastic schools had to prepare their own materials, and it is to be expected that any *gru* with literary talent would have been widely copied or imitated. These texts, known as *cpāp'*, are typically quite short, between twenty-nine and a hundred stanzas, and were primarily designed for the moral education of children of both sexes. They were learned predominantly in sung oral form. The earliest extant representatives of the genre, such as *Cpāp' Kerti Kāl,* date from around the sixteenth century, are reasonably short, and are anonymous, but as time went on, texts in the genre became longer and often gave the names of their author or redactor. *Cpāp' Ariyasatthā,* for instance, purports to be the work of the eponymous author Ariyasatthā (Pou and Jenner 1975, 371). The longest extant *cpāp'* is Nong's previously mentioned *Lokanayapakar* (1794), comprising some two thousand stanzas in which the author skillfully interweaves themes from a variety of earlier works on political ethics, such as the Pali *Lokanīti,* which he had presumably studied in Thailand, and the Sanskrit *Nītiśāstra* corpus,[21] with an assortment of *Jātaka* materials (Pou 1981, 466).[22] Nong was also responsible for *Cpāp' Subhāsit,* a didactic poem dating from around 1790 CE.

Cpāp' may be grouped into two categories: those designed for general consumption, and those specifically oriented toward a political or aristocratic elite. The latter are sometimes referred to as *cpāp'-neti* (Pou 1981, 458), whereas the former provided the basis for traditional monastery-based Buddhist moral education until very recent times. Indeed, a proposal to reinstate the study of *cpāp'* in schools was floated in the early 1990s (Martin 1994, 10, 259). We can get some idea of the nature of this curriculum from the testimony of two individuals, given shortly before the disintegration of the country in the 1970s. The chief monk of Wat Tep Pranam, Udong, remembered learning *Cpāp' Kram* and *Cpāp' Kerti Kāl* alongside the *Jinavaṃsā Supina,*[23] *Bhāṇavāra,*[24] and the ten great *Jātakas* when he first entered the monastery at the age of eight (Choan and Sarin 1970, 127), and Bhikkhu Meas-Yang (1978, 46) reports that in his own monastery children were taught three *cpāp'* in the following order: *Cpāp' Kram, Cpāp' Srī,* and *Cpāp' Prus.* These texts were meant to apply across the whole of society, and, as such, they are quite useful from the historian's perspective. Their detailed study might well plug some of the many holes left by the more elitist royal chronicles. Extant *cpāp'* reflect a Buddhist milieu heavily influenced by Khmer cultural norms. As Chandler (1984, 279) notes, they teach a view of society "where deference and fatalism take up more space than rebelliousness or hope," but other influences may also be discerned.[25]

Cpāp' Kram appears to be the most widely known and well circulated text in the genre. It is ascribed to a *sanghareach* of the early seventeenth century, Preah Sugandh Mean Bonn of Wat Neak Tā Soeng, Udong. It also possesses a modern commentary, *Cpāp' Kram Pariyāy,* written by Nhik Nou (1900–1974), a teacher and noted traditionalist who worked hard to illuminate the Buddhist traditional literature of the country and to prevent its being swamped by Occidental influences. The text takes the form of a monk-teacher's address to an audience of young novice monks. He is aware that many will be ordained for a temporary period only, so he recommends a three-stage approach to the acquisition of virtue. As a first step, one must understand the "social code," before moving on to gain worldly wisdom: "Even if you are not of high rank . . . by force of application and deference you will gain certain glory" (v. 14). The final stage concerns the teachings of the Buddha, which alone lead to supreme perfection *(boramei)* (Pou and Jenner 1979, 133, 150n5). The work is particularly eloquent on the value of the teacher-pupil relationship:

> To know by oneself
> Is like being lost
> In the middle of the forest, or like a blind man
> Left to himself, who sets out on his way
> With no one to take his hand.
> And when he looks for the path
> He never finds it,
> But wanders into the forest instead
> Because he has learned things by himself
> With no one to take his hand. (vv. 24–25)[26]

Cpāp' Kerti Kāl has a rather more specific focus. It recommends that well-born persons should utilize slaves *(kñuṃ)* and clients *(kaṃtar)* of both sexes for various agricultural tasks (vv. 4, 5, 10, 19). There is no hint of disapproval of the custom of slavery in the text, and there are no general recommendations regarding the humane treatment of *kñuṃ*. Indeed, verse 19 suggests that one should observe slaves carefully to determine those who are to be trusted and those who are not. Individuals from the former category should be treated sympathetically (v. 23). Elsewhere the text urges a middle way with regard to material possessions: "Too many goods will be difficult to look after, too few will give you worries" (v. 22).

Cpāp' Prus is a text directed toward young boys, and, unusually, its author, Mai, is mentioned in the colophon. It starts by stating that human birth poses difficult problems for men and for women (v. 3), but the Buddha has also taught that there are three great follies to be avoided: women, alcohol, and certain games of chance.[27] Various card and other betting games are mentioned, and some anti-Chinese feeling is expressed (vv. 52–53). Hunting and other blood sports are also condemned (v. 53), and the dangers of alcohol are rendered in detail and with great accuracy (vv. 78–79). Mai also wrote a better-known and more widely taught companion work for girls, *Cpāp' Srī*.[28] The text purports to be the advice given by the *nāga* Queen Vimalā to her daughter Irandatī as she prepares to leave her home to dwell in the world of men with her husband, the sylvan deity *(yaks)* Paṇṇak. In most respects the advice is quite predictable, following the line taken by remote ancestors, such as the Indic *Laws of Manu*. A young woman should respectfully tend three fires, representing her parents, her mother, and the "master of the chamber" *(gamtaeng kralā)*, that is, her husband (vv. 34–37). In her dealings with the latter she should eschew shrewishness, sarcasm, and impudence (vv. 71–73) and should strive to occupy four beneficial roles in her marital relationship: mother, friend, fellow, and servant (vv. 126–148). Success in this project will ensure rebirth in Tusita, the heaven of the future Buddha, Maitreya (v. 150). If, on the other hand, she is a tyrant or an enemy of her husband or if she steals his property, she will be reborn as a hermaphrodite in hell (v. 186). When appearing in public, she should comport herself properly and avoid ten inauspicious forms of behavior, such as laughing loudly (v. 107). This is clearly a tall order, and readers are reminded that the *cpāp'* for women is very difficult to follow (v. 8). But the gains are great; success could lead to rebirth as the mother of the future Buddha (v. 215).

Let us conclude this brief survey with two *cpāp'-neti* texts. *Cpāp' Rājaneti*, or *Cpāp' Braḥ Rājasambhār*, may possibly be the work of a royal author. Alternatively, given that the term "*rājasambhār*" is used to designate chief monks of important monasteries in both Laos and Thailand, it may have originated with a high ecclesiastical dignitary.[29] The second possibility seems a little more likely, for the work explicitly claims to be based on Pali texts (v. 1)[30] and advises its royal readers not to place confidence in Brahmanical ascetics (v. 3). Statecraft is clearly a serious matter. The text seems to hint at the possibility that the assassination of a king who neglects his duty to defend Buddhism might, under some circumstances, be justified:

> The *dhamma* is the way
> Which protects and defends beings
> And assures them success.

It is better to lose a fortune
Than to die: but it is better to die
Than to lose the essence of the law. (v. 28)[31]

We have already seen that the royal chronicles, particularly in their treatment of the fate of Cau Bañā Ñom (r. 1600–1602), seem to endorse a similar outlook.[32]

In *Cpāp' Trīneti* a royal tutor *(rājagrū)* teaches a great prince *(mahāksatr)* how to train himself to take on the task of ruling the kingdom:

If there is an evil minister,
According to the sacred Pali texts
The king will perish.
If the grand dignitaries
Do not practice reflection
The prince will be reduced to nothing
And will not be remembered. . . .
The subjects of the king are like fish.
The officers of the king, both civil and military,
May be compared to the water.
Now, if the latter becomes hot
They get overheated to excess
And the people will feel in danger
[because the king] failed to give them support.
(vv. 5 and 7)[33]

The text is supposed to have been written by Cau Bañā Tū (Srī Dhammarāja I, r. 1627–1632), who had been a learned monk before ascending the throne. Like other *cpāp'-neti,* it was evidently not designed for general consumption.

Reamker

The Indian epic poem *Rāmāyaṇa* has exercised an influence in Cambodia for more than a millennium. A seventh-century Sanskrit inscription [K. 359] from Veal Kantal, Stung Treng, mentions daily recitations of a clutch of Indic writings donated to the sanctuary, including the *Rāmāyaṇa.* It appears to be the first specific reference to the text (Bizot 1989, 26). Epigraphical and artistic evidence also shows that the story was well known in Angkorian times. Carved narrative reliefs illustrating elements of the epic are widespread, occurring at the Bakong, Banteay Srei, Baphuon, Phimai, Thommanon, and Banteay Samre, to name but a few prominent temples. The scenes depicted in bas-reliefs of the northwest corner pavilion and the adjoining north wing of the western gallery at Angkor Wat are justly renowned, the latter section being given over entirely to a vivid depiction of the climax of the *Rāmāyaṇa,* the battle at Lanka between Rāma and his monkey allies and the army of the demon-king Rāvaṇa. However, it is clear that even at this early period, the Khmer version of the story was somewhat different from those that circulated in India and in other regions of Asia (Boeles 1969, 169).[34]

The Cambodian *Rāmāyaṇa* has persisted into modern times and exists in a number of forms. A literary text known the *Reamker (Rāmakerti),* written during the middle period of Khmer literature, consists of two separate, incomplete, and anonymous compositions in verse. The first, composed in a variety of meters, probably dates from the sixteenth to the seventeenth century. The second, written in one meter throughout, is more verbose and somewhat later (Jacob 1986b, ix–x). There are some grounds for believing that the *Reamker* was originally composed as the libretto to a masked dance drama (*lkhon khol;* literally, "covered-face theater") performed solely by men (Pou 1980, 20). The text is also an important subject for Buddhist monastery frescoes, and the large leather puppets *(spaek thom)* associated with traditional shadow theater are used exclusively to tell the story.

A number of painted representations of the *Reamker* still exist today, although the figure was significantly greater before the Khmer Rouge period. The most famous is the 604 meters of fresco stretching around the cloisters of the Silver Pagoda in Phnom Penh.[35] Painted in 1903–1904 by a team of forty artists directed by Oknya Tep Nimit Māk (Giteau 1975, 231), it is directly modeled on the Thai *Ramakien* murals at the royal palace in Bangkok.[36] Given that these had, in turn, been influenced by the bas-reliefs at Angkor Wat, the project demonstrates the complex recycling of ideas common to the region. Another monastic structure, Wat Kdol in Battambang, is also still surrounded by forty-eight separate cement reliefs of scenes from the *Reamker* that were produced sometime toward the end of the nineteenth century, when the region was under Thai control. Both seem to follow an oral *Rāmāyaṇa* tradition that deviates somewhat from that preserved in literary sources (Giteau 1975, 230, 266; 1997).

It seems that paintings from the *Reamker* were usually located in the cloisters surrounding a Buddhist sanctuary, but there are exceptions to this rule. A complete set of *Reamker* scenes based on those at the Silver Pagoda could once be viewed in the sanctuary of the originally eleventh-century temple at Phnom Chisor, Takeo Province, before it was destroyed during military operations in 1970. The extraordinary murals at Wat Bo, Siem Reap City, are also inside the *vihāra*. They are quite unusual in that the various incidents, which certainly do not follow the Indian version of the story, are arranged in a unique patchwork of squares and rectangles. Giteau (1975, 291) believes that they were probably inspired by shadow theater.

As was the case at Angkor, it is clear that the Cambodian *Reamker* is not a simple copy of the more famous Indian *Rāmāyaṇa*. In the Indian text Sītā emerges from the earth during a royal plowing festival, whereas in the Cambodian version she is discovered by King Janaka as she sails down the River Yamuna on a raft. Another striking difference concerns the ending. Unlike Vālmīki's Sanskrit *Rāmāyaṇa*, the *Reamker* concludes on a happy note, for the two lovers, Rām and Setā, are reunited. It also contains many indigenous elements. The god Agni's mount *(vāhana)* is a rhinoceros, not a ram, for the ram plays no part in Cambodia's traditional agricultural environment (Pou 1992, 91). In addition, the Indic etymology of the name "Rāma" seems largely to have been a mystery to the Khmers. Its pronunciation as "*riem*" was connected with the homophone "*rīem,*" meaning "elder brother," which had the consequence of transforming the relationship between Rām and Laks into "one of the most revered themes in the Khmer people's mind" (Pou 1980, 25). The Khmer spelling of the name "Setā" is also significant here. The Indic form "Sītā," meaning "furrow," relates back to the myth of Setā's birth, whereas the Khmer form derives from the Pali "*seta,*" a term connected with the concept of "purity."

More significantly, the form and content of the original text have been reshaped by a mentality strongly imbued with the teachings of the Buddha.[37] As Pou (1992, 93) notes, "It was made of a Valmikian warp into which Khmer authors wove a gamut of weft-yarns drawn from their Buddhist culture." More specifically, Rām is no longer simply an incarnation of Viṣṇu but has been assimilated to the Buddha. He has been reborn in this world at the request of ascetics and gods who fear that Buddhism *(preah sasana)* is about to be destroyed by demons (vv. 211–213). He carries the marks of a great man, such as the imprint of wheels on the palms of his hands (v. 2141) and is said to come from the "lineage of Nārāy [= Viṣṇu] and the Buddhas" (v. 2342). He is regularly referred to as a bodhisattva. Elsewhere he is described as the bud of the Buddha *(Buddhaṇkūr)* (v. 368), "of the lineage of the *tathāgatas*" (v. 1796), and "of the lineage of those who have accumulated the elements necessary for awakening." He tells Setā that he intends to lead her to the knowledge of "supreme *nirvāṇa*" (v. 538). The various hermits *(ṛṣī)* in the tale appear to be modeled on forest-dwelling Buddhist monks, and all of the allies of Rāb (= Rāvaṇa) are referred to as *māras*. When faced with an enemy, Rām manages to channel his fiery energy *(tejaḥ)* in nonviolent directions by the performance of miracles and the use of skillful words. If this is not feasible, it is his brother Laks and various monkeys who fight in his stead, for Rām, as the embodiment of the ideal Buddhist bodhisattva-king, must stand above physical struggle. The cosmographic setting is also fully in line with Theravada teachings, where sentient beings, heavens, hells, world mountains, forests, and so on must all be ultimately dissolved by the inexorable logic of impermanence, for all conditioned things are marked by birth, old age, suffering, and death (vv. 832–842). One further example is instructive. The battle between Rāb's demon-brother, Kumbhakār, and Rām's army is commonly depicted. Older versions, such as those carved at the Baphuon and the Thommanon, stay close to the Indic original, while those at the Silver Pagoda and Wat Bo inject a novel element into the story. This concerns Kumbhakār's struggle with Indrajit, and the death of Kumbhakār in meditation, a sequence clearly designed to introduce a more strongly Buddhist flavor into the narrative (Giteau 1995).

The *Reamker* is also important at the level of popular religiosity. It is the custom to perform auspicious excerpts during funerals of eminent monks. Scenes concerning the deaths of heroic characters are naturally avoided. Another popular episode, the "release of waters"—in which Hanumān and Aṅgad use their magical powers to defeat Kumbhakār, who has denied the monkey army their water supply—is performed to alleviate drought (Pou 1992, 99).[38] Major characters of the *Reamker* are also associated with the twelve-year animal cycle, the days of the week, and the directions, while various topographical features—such as Phnom Preah Bat, which is believed to have been used by Hanumān to supply the rock for the construction of the causeway to attack Rāb's island fortress—litter the Cambodian countryside (Porée-Maspero 1983, 20–21).

Allegorical and esoteric interpretations of the *Rāmāyaṇa* are known in India.[39] A comparable tradition has flourished in Cambodia for centuries (Bizot 1983, 271–272). Bizot (1989, 47–48) breaks the allegory down into a number of stages representing the path of initiation that leads to full enlightenment. The appearance of the key characters in the story represents an embryological stage in which the psychophysical constitution of the initiate *(yogāvacara)* is formed. The marriage of Rām and Setā leads to the conception of a special crystal globe *(tuong kaev)* that holds the elements for the attainment of enlightenment. The subsequent battle and defeat of the demon-king Rāb equate to the perfection of spiritual praxis *(samathavipassanākammaṭṭhan)* and the completion of the initiatory phase, while Setā's banishment from the city of Ayodhya, seat of the initiate's spirit, demonstrates the impossibility of union with the crystal globe while still embodied. The *yogāvacara* must first die to his old identity. The final stage, then, involves Rām's faking of his own funeral, his recovery of Setā, and the birth of their twin children. This is the ultimate attainment of *nirvāṇa*.

Traditional Literature and Esotericism

We have already seen that a Pali work like the *Mahādibbamanta* focuses more heavily on ritual and experiential factors than on the doctrinal and the didactic. The same general principle holds true for many of the Buddhist writings in Khmer, which represent the vast bulk of literary output until recent times. Such vernacular works present a number of challenges to the casual reader. They are difficult to date, are generally anonymous, and describe rites and notions somewhat out of line with standard accounts of orthodox Theravada. They may contain terms with a Mon origin, sometimes overlaid with traces of Thai influence, suggesting a current of religiosity common to the wider region.[40] Their terminology can be quite opaque, and the abbreviated character of much of their contents implies that they can be properly understood only when provided with the oral commentary of a teacher. Clearly this commentary has been difficult to obtain since the events of the 1970s.

All of these factors have contributed to a lack of scholarly concern for these traditions, with one exception. Over the course of several decades the outstanding research of François Bizot has revealed the existence of nonorthodox Buddhist meditational practices that have been largely secret, although not necessarily confined to members of the monastic order. The texts underpinning the tradition are often obscure, are clearly symbolic, and may be subjected to multiple interpretations. They have much to say about ritual and frequently contain mantras in Pali. The tradition is clearly old and certainly predates the reform movements of the nineteenth century.

According to Cousins (1997, 189), a "rich ceremonial and elaborate ritualism" was a feature of South and Southeast Asian Śrāvakayāna Buddhism prior to the systematizations of Buddhaghosa in the fifth century. Apotropaic elements, such as the chanting of *parittas,* were a distinctive feature of this tradition.[41] Others have suggested that at a later period additional influences—possibly Śrāvakayānist, Mahayanist, or Brahmanical—might have overlaid, intermingled with, or otherwise interacted with this early stratum.[42] The genealogy is rather complex and does not always fit the little we do know about the early history of Buddhism in Cambodia. As a way of clarifying the matter, let us consider the ingredients one at a time.

Both Brahmanical and Buddhist tantrism, consisting of highly ritualized and esoteric religious practices with a strong emphasis on activating potentialities within the practitioner's own body, had a significant purchase on the state religion of the Angkorian period. The esoteric texts and traditions currently under discussion concern similar practices, and this has led some commentators to suggest that they represent a form of tantric Theravada. This seems problematic for two reasons. In the first place, there is no independent evidence to support the idea that Theravadin and tantric ideas syncretized in Cambodia. The idea that Śaiva, Vaiṣṇava, or Mahayana influences may be present is hard to sustain, for the terminology and doctrinal background of the textual record appear to be entirely Theravada in tenor. But more importantly, the well-defined cycles of divinities characteristic of the Hindu and Buddhist tantras are largely absent from the Cambodian literary record.

Another theory is that the esoteric tradition has its origins in the nonorthodox teachings of the Ceylonese Abhayagirivihāra, a monastery that rivaled the ultimately more influential Mahāvihāra until the forced purification of the *sangha* under King Parakkamabāhu I in the third quarter of the twelfth century. The monastery's writings are said to have been burned by "pious kings in the excess of their zeal for the purity of the faith" (Malalasekera 1974, 1:133), but the fraternity had established a center at the Sīhalārāma in Java by the eighth century (Ilangasinha 1998, 187), and we also know that the *Vimuttimagga,* a text thought to be associated with the Abhayagirivihāra, had been translated into Chinese by Saṅghapāla, an early sixth-century monk associated with Funan.[43] The occasional use of the term "non-Mahāvihāravāsin" by Bizot to designate the esoteric tradition indicates that he has sometimes been tempted to establish a link to the Abhayagirivihāra. However, we should be aware that esoteric teachings are not unknown in the Mahāvihāra tradition, the putative beacon of Theravada orthodoxy. Buddhaghosa, for instance, refers to secret *(gulha)* texts on three separate occasions.[44] Crosby (2000) has also argued for a much wider existence of the tradition in Ceylon than had previously been entertained. She claims that esoteric *(yogāvacara)*[45] practices entered the country in the eighteenth century "under the auspices of the Mahāvihāra" itself and that its Thai and Cambodian sister order, the Dhammayutika Nikāya, was founded by individuals previously trained in the same traditions (Crosby 2000, 180). If this is so, the simplistic equation of esoteric practice with unreformed elements within the Buddhist Theravadin monastic order is in need of further scrutiny. Given that arguments based on the influence of one region of the Theravada world on another often suffer from the problem of circularity, the safest position to adopt, in the absence of compelling evidence to the contrary, is that we are looking at an indigenous Southeast Asian tradition that may have come under ill-defined external influences in the course of its development. Its survival in Cambodia down to the present day can perhaps be explained by the relative remoteness of centralized reforming bureaucracy from the lives of the majority of the population. This in turn sheltered them from changes that occurred in other more accessible regions.

Before turning to a discussion of specific texts, it would be as well to list some of the general characteristics of the esoteric tradition. Of prime importance is the need for initiation by a skilled master who need not be a monk. The charge of elitism customarily leveled at initiatory religion is tempered by the fact that the practices are theoretically open to all—to laywomen and laymen as well as to monks. A tendency toward the allegorical elucidation of sources is very marked, and nontraditional use of meditational practices abound. Visualization and sound are both assigned a creative function that may be used to hasten the process of spiritual transformation, often conceived as a mystic embryology involving the creation of a buddha within the practitioner's own body. A final element concerns the special significance assigned to the Abhidhamma.[46] The *Saddhavimala,* an important text studied by Bizot and Lagirarde (1996, 220), for instance, tells us that the seven books of Abhidhamma are the creative force behind the body and mind of all beings.

Esotericism and Exotericism

Two approaches to the spiritual life can, in all probability, be traced back to the earliest phases of Buddhist history. In the Mahācunda Sutta (*A.* iii.355–356), the monk Mahā Cunda manages to reunite two opposed parties representing the *dhammayogābhikkhus* on the one hand and the *jhātibhikkhus* on the other. The former are supposed to have adopted a speculative route to the resolution of existential problems, whereas the latter were ecstatics who, through the practice of meditation, "touched immortality with their bodies."[47] Other examples of this fundamental tension are easily identified. It is embodied in the Buddha's two chief disciples, Sāriputta and Mahā Moggallāna, the former oriented toward a scholastic concern for matters of doctrine, the latter known for his meditational and supernatural powers. Indeed, the current distinction between monks who engage in scholarly activities *(ganthadhura)* and those who practice meditation *(vipassanādhura)* may also be read in this light, and the need to establish an antagonistic symbiosis between these competing realms has been crucial to the long-term vitality of the tradition as a whole.

The tension may also be found in Cambodia. Among the traditional Buddhists, the teachings and practices based on a modernist interpretation of the Pali canon are held to represent an explicit or "exterior way" *(phluv krau)* to the truth. The path of the esoteric initiate *(yogāvacara),* on the other hand, is a "hidden" *(lāk')* or "interior way" *(phluv knong).* Whereas practitioners of the former way may progress to become "adepts of insight" *(neak vipassanā),* the goal of the *yogāvacara* is to become an "adept of *mūla kammaṭṭhāna*" *(neak mūla kammaṭṭhāna).* Now, in mainstream Theravada Buddhism the term "*kammaṭṭhāna*" refers to the traditional list of subjects for meditation; Buddhaghosa, for instance, lists forty of these in the *Visuddhimagga*. But in Cambodia the term has a more specialized sense in that it refers to mastery of the techniques employed on the *phluv knong*.[48] The term "*mūla*" is also said to refer to a particular use of the letters of the alphabet that denote the Buddha's teachings. To confuse things a little more, *mūla kammaṭṭhāna* practice may be pursued in two ways, the right-handed path *(phluv sdam)* and the left-handed path *(phluv chveng)*. These are determined by the motivation of the practitioner. The former path leads to otherworldly goals and ultimately to *nirvāṇa*, whereas the latter is about the attainment of worldly ends, such as gaining power over others (Bizot and von Hinüber 1994, 17).

Initiation

An important representative of the tradition, Achar Trok Din, told Bizot: "The works of the *braḥ kammaṭṭhāna* refer to the Tripitaka in ways differing from the manner employed by the modernists. The traditionalists explain nothing. They hide [what they know] and teach how to practice the spiritual life. . . . The modernists transmit their knowledge but only speak of the fruit and flowers. Of roots and stumps they say nothing."[49] The reference to silence and secrecy underlines the initiatory character of the traditional teachings. The guidance of a master, who may be either a monk or a layperson, is indispensable. He represents the ultimate teacher, Mahā Paṭṭān,[50] and is able to identify the nature of any psychic disturbances encountered by the *yogāvacara* in the course of his or her exercises and to recommend specific countermeditations.

A certain Achar Uong, an adept of the left-handed path *(phluv chveng)*, in 1938 had a total of twenty-eight disciples at his base on Phnom Damrei Roniel, Ang Ta Som District, Ta Keo Province (Bizot 1981b). This indicates the popularity of the practices at the time. One of these disciples, Gru Theng Eng, told Bizot that he quickly gained the ability to leave his body, and in this condition he undertook a mystical journey to his teacher's own secret master. His spiritual apprenticeship culminated in a seven-day retreat at the base of a dark cavern where, seated in an upright fetal position and chanting mantras all the while, he took no food and only a little water. In this way he traveled to heavenly realms, where he received visions of mystic diagrams (yantras). On his return to his home village Eng copied what he had seen, and these yantras became the basis of his subsequent magical powers. In a typically Khmer twist to the story, at some point in the 1940s Eng attended a conference organized by the French-supported Commission des Mœurs et Coutumes du Cambodge that had been convened to collect information on the use of yantras. At the same time, he was using his occult powers to aid the Issaraks, who were fighting for independence from the colonial power.

When Kalab studied the hamlet of Prathnol in Prek Por in the mid-1960s, the local Wat Prakal possessed fifty small huts for lay meditators, although these were rarely all occupied. She describes a retreat or "entry into meditation" ceremony led by a sixty-year-old *achar*. Despite the truncated nature of her account, this appears to have been connected with the same esoteric tradition. Having paid their respects to the Buddha image in the *vihāra,* the participants were led behind the altar, where incense was offered and prostrations were made to an image of the earth goddess, Nang Thorani. They then withdrew to their huts, where, having learned certain texts by heart, they meditated until they received some sort of vision. In some cases this appears to have come quite quickly. The *achar* subsequently interpreted the visions in individual interviews (Kalab 1990, 12–13).

Bizot's own participation in a pilgrimage from Phnom Penh to Phnom Sampau, near Battambang, at the beginning of the rainy season *(vassa)* in June 1971 is more vividly described (1980, 235–236). Having received blessings from Ven. Yeak, the chief monk of the monastery, in the form of ritual sprinklings of water, the party was led to a gorge in which a subterranean ritual complex was located directly beneath the modern pagoda. An *achar* who had accompanied the party from Phnom Penh was already established within. Pregnant women were not allowed to enter, but other pilgrims passed into the vestibule, where they faced a "golden door" *(dvar meas),* a term in common usage as a euphemism for the female sexual organs.[51] To pass through, it was necessary to crawl along a very narrow passage while continuously reciting the formula "*a ra ham.*" After some twelve meters the pilgrims entered a large cavern containing a prominent stalagmite next to a pool of water. The party grouped themselves around the stalagmite, or "umbilical cord," and washed their faces in the pool of "amniotic fluid." After the *achar* had led them in meditation for about an hour, they exited with due ceremony. It was made clear that they had entered the womb of the noble mother *(garbha preah mata)* and were now reborn. As a final act, the *achar* petitioned the earth mother to pardon them for having contaminated her. The archaic, perhaps even pre-Buddhist, aspects of the rite are quite obvious.

If the candidate is a monk, initiation may begin three months after higher ordination *(upasampadā).*[52] Having retired to the parental home, he makes a ceremonial farewell. The parents then accompany him to the monastery, where they build a hut on stilts large enough for him to sleep, eat, and arrange an altar. The altar is laid with an elaborate range of offerings arranged as a *maṇḍala,* each symbolizing aspects of his reborn body, for the hut represents a womb. All aspects of the rite must be kept secret, because the ceremony of rebirth is a symbolic reenactment of the copulation of mother and father (Bizot 1992, 32–34). The monk should also consider that the traditional seven-part monastic robe represents the seven elements of the fetus in the maternal womb. While meditating, the monk visualizes himself as a fetus, for, as has already been said, there is an isomorphism between embryological development and Buddhist spiritual progress in this tradition (Bizot 1980, 244).

Embryological elements may also be detected in the observance of the distinctive great probation ritual *(mahāparivāsakamma)*. According to the normal rules of monastic discipline *(vinaya)*, individuals entering the Buddhist order from another religious sect are expected to observe a period of probation *(parivāsa)* for four months. A term of probation is also required if a monk is guilty of one of the thirteen infringements of monastic discipline, a designation that can be decided only by a formal meeting of the *sangha (saṅghādisesa)*. It seems that in Southeast Asia an esoteric variation on the rite evolved, although it died out under the impact of modernity. Somewhat surprisingly, it has recently been revived by a group of traditionalist Cambodian monks. This *mahāparivāsakamma* involves a substantial group of monks, who congregate during the third lunar month *(meakh)* for collective ascetic practice. The benefits accrued through performance of the rite are dedicated to the monks' parents—in particular, their mothers, for the asceticism is thought to mirror the various sufferings connected with childbirth. The monks sleep in a sitting position *(nesajjikaṅga)* that evokes the discomfort of pregnancy and the preliminary contractions. Living without a shelter *(abbhokāsikaṅga)* in the full glare of the sun at the height of the dry season recalls the postpartum *aeng phloeung*, a common apotropaic ritual in Southeast Asia, in which hot embers are placed under the bed of a newly delivered woman. Participants also abstain from bathing for six days, another ritual observed after a child is born (de Bernon 2000, 475).

Asceticism and Death

The Chinese pilgrim Yijing noted the existence of Buddhist ascetic practices in the Southeast Asian peninsula at the end of the seventh century, and an early eleventh-century Khmer inscription [K. 410] at Lopburi mentions Theravada and Mahayana religious living alongside non-Buddhist ascetics *(tāpasa)*. One of the traditional thirteen ascetic practices for Theravada monks is to live clothed with rags from a rubbish heap *(paṅsukūl)*.[53] A shroud from a dead body may also be used as a *paṅsukūl*. Now, the standardized formulae chanted during Buddhist death rites, the *Sattapakaraṇa,* are an abbreviation of the contents of the seven books of the Abhidhamma Pitaka. They are also known as *mātikā paṅsukūl.* Monks customarily chant them while maintaining contact with the deceased by means of a cotton thread or a strip of cloth. Monastic robes placed on the pyre by relatives are subsequently donated to *sangha,* and the merit accrued is transferred to the deceased. Variations on these rites may also be used for the healing of the sick.[54]

While the reformed cremation rite is all about creating merit for the deceased, the rich combination of death, asceticism, and the Abhidhamma at a funeral is a perfect setting for spiritual praxis by those belonging to the esoteric tradition. Traditional cremation ceremonies are now quite rare. So is the ritual of offering strips of the dead person's flesh to animals.[55] The former is known as "turning the body" *(pre rup).* The ritual is conducted by an *achar yogi* who carries a staff, a banner *(tung braling),* and a cooking pot. He cooks a little rice in the dying embers of the funeral pyre, after which it is extinguished and the *tung braling* is placed on a banana leaf over the ashes. The *achar yogi* then uses his staff to draw the outline of the deceased three times, oriented in different directions. Bank notes are used to indicate elements of the face. The ritual area has been previously cordoned off by sticks tied with thread to form a sacred boundary *(sīmā).* The thread leads outside to a group of monks who chant the *paṅsukūl* formulae in the normal way. Bizot (1981a, 64–65) interprets this rite in an esoteric sense. For him the *achar yogi* represents Mahā Paṭṭān; the outlined bodies, the three collections of the Tripitaka; the cooking pot, the maternal womb; and so on.

A related unreformed rite *(chāk mahāpaṅsukūl)* entails the regeneration or rebirth of a living person. It was once performed in a variety of elaborate forms in Thailand, Laos, and Cambodia. Bizot (1981a, 26–27) witnessed it in December 1973. In a remote spot near Phnom Penh, an *achar yogi* constructed a rectangular structure, or shrine, from four sticks wrapped around with white cloth. This was encircled by a clockwise, spiral pathway, or labyrinth, of more sticks held together with thread. The postulant, a woman, was introduced into the shrine by the *achar yogi,* who explained that the rite was an inner offering *(ajjhattikadān).* Crouching with her head to the east, the postulant was entirely covered with a monastic robe (representing a caul), with offerings inserted in its folds. The *sīmā* of the shrine was closed with thread, and having recited the formulae that the postulant must chant for the duration of the ceremony, the *achar yogi* moved to a position to the northeast. Meanwhile, to the southeast a *dhutaṅga* monk visualized the postulant in various stages of decomposition. Eventually, the monk walked slowly along the spiral pathway, stopping to recite verses *(gāthās).* Coming to the shrine, he removed the caul from the embryo-like postulant with the tip of his staff while reciting the *mātikā paṅsukūl*.[56] She had been reborn.

The Fig Tree and the Crystal Globe

Achar Trok Din's previous reference to the roots and stumps of a tree has various resonances. What is the meaning here? The *yogāvacara* tradition draws correspondences between the embryo and a "fig tree with five branches." This allegorical symbol represents the human body as the physical locus of transformation, the cosmos, and it expresses and crystallizes the Buddha's teachings *(dhamma)* in the form of sound. As the human body, its trunk is the torso, its branches the arms and legs,[57] its leaves the two ears, its flower the umbilicus, its fruit the embryo, and its threefold root the penis and testicles, which give rise to future generations (Bizot 1980, 250). The fig tree with five branches is also the world tree, stretching as high as the divine *(deva)* realms, and with its roots in the infernal regions (Bizot 1976, 83). The system, then, homologizes the macrocosmos to the human body. The tree is the world axis, or Mount Sumeru, but "in the five aggregates of our bodily form, our head is Mount Sumeru, our chest Mount Giriparabat, our pelvis Mount Gijjhakūṭaparabat (Vulture Peak), [and] the two knees, the two ankles, and the two soles, the seven levels of Mount Sattaparibhaṇḍ, the enclosures of Mount Sumeru. The four lakes situated at the foot of Mount Sumeru are the four elements of our bodily form" (Bizot 1976, 120).

The tree also occurs in another allegory of the spiritual path. The twins Nāṅ Cittakumārā and Nāṅ Cittakumārī represent the "spirit" of the *yogāvacara*.[58] They take leave of Yama, the lord of death, to seek birth in the rose-apple land *(jambudvīpa)*, but they get lost on the way. While they lament their predicament, a god in the form of a man encourages them to search for a jewel called the birth globe *(tuong kamnot)*, or crystal globe *(tuong kaev)*, hidden in a fig tree with five branches. The two children make supplication to the deity and begin their quest (Bizot 1992, 28). The crystal globe is guarded by Indriy[59] birds, but its possession will confer great happiness, for it is in essence the three letters "*ma*," "*a*," and "*u*," which make up the sacred syllable "*om*."[60] These three letters are also the "noble triple *dhamma*" *(preah dhammatrai)* (Bizot 1992, 31); they correspond to the three sections of the Tripitaka (Bizot 1976, 102). In other words, the twins must create a new body out of elements of the Buddha's teaching. This new *dhamma*-body *(dhammakāya)* is the "key to *nirvāṇa*" (Bizot 1980, 250).[61]

In mainstream Theravada the term "*dhammakāya*" is interpreted in an entirely nonmetaphysical way. It is the corpus of the Buddha's teachings contained, preeminently, in the canonical writings of the Tripitaka. For the esoteric tradition, however, the concept has a special meaning. It is a transformed human body animated by the *dhamma* and understood as a series of sacred syllables. This transformed body possesses supramundane qualities, the most important being the thirty-two marks of the great man *(dvattiṃsamahāpurisalakkhaṇa)*. To create this special body, the adept must use sound to awaken the crystal globe, or "infant in the womb," which is visualized in the region of the navel. Breathing exercises are also necessary:

> *passāsa*—this denotes the wind that enters through the nose
> *assāsa*—this denotes the wind that exits from the nose
> *nissāsa*—this denotes the wind of the noble Abhidhamma of seven books, that is to say the wind that stops in the womb, at the level of the navel (Bizot 1980, 247)

Visualization techniques are, of course, not unknown in the Theravada,[62] and Bizot sees the origins of the practice in the canonical notion of a mind-made body *(manomayakāya)* that may be produced by a skillful meditator.[63] The most appropriate sounds to accompany these particular visualizations are those associated with the Buddha's teachings, more specifically the initial syllables of the titles of the books of the Tripitaka:

> *A pā ma cu;* this is the quintessence of the five books of the noble Vinaya.
> *Di mam sam am u;* this is the quintessence of the five books of the noble Sutta.
> *Sam vi dhā pu ka ya pa;* this is the quintessence of the seven books of the noble Abhidhamma (Bizot 1976, 101)

To visualize the transformation of the fleshy body into that of the *dhammakāya,* one ritually plants each sacred sound in its allotted place.

A final allegory of the progress of the *yogāvacara* is provided by an esoteric reading of the *Reamker*. In this interpretation, the spiritual master (= Mahā Paṭṭā) Bibhek helps Rām overcome obstacles in the way of his union with Setā. Rām and his brother Laks represent the twins Cittakumārā and Cittakumārī on a quest for the crystal globe *(tuong kaev),* which in this instance corresponds with Setā. The demons are the Indriy birds that prevent Rām and Setā from achieving unity, while the monkey helpers are the virtues *(guṇ)* that make the goal possible. The journey to the precious island of Lanka involves the construction of a causeway, or umbilical cord linking the *yogāvacara* with the mother's womb and the possibility of rebirth (Bizot 1989, 51–52). Rām's great ally in the struggle is the monkey king Hanumān, "the son of the wind." In this tradition he is the breath *(khyal)*.[64] The interior journey should be conducted in the following manner. During a fortnight of intensive asceticism in which the *yogāvacara* hardly eats or sleeps, he or she should recite the formula "*a ra ham*"[65] while visualizing a violet "*na*" at the opening of the nose. Passing along the nostril, he opens a door and passes down a ladder that ends at the epiglottis, where there is a blue *mo*. Descending by stages, the adept comes to a yellow "*bu*" in the neck, a red "*ddhā*" in the sternum, and a "*ya*," the color of crystal, in the umbilicus. Thus he makes homage to the Buddha *(namo buddhāya)*. At the umbilicus he visualizes the Buddha seated at the place of enlightenment while the breath is drawn down from the nostril to the navel and back again. Success in the technique means that the *yogāvacara* has arrived at the remote but "precious isle of Laṅkā" *(koḥ kaev tvīp laṅkā)*. Lanka is both a funeral monument and the mother's womb.[66] At the center of the island is the great mountain called Meru. The *yogāvacara* is fortified here prior to final release from the realms of suffering (Bizot 1992, 35–36).

We have already seen that the fig tree represents the *dhamma*. Its fruits are the sections of the Tripitaka, the leaves the ten perfections *(pāramitā)*, and so forth. It represents a universe built from sacred sound. The idea of the creative power of sound is quite widespread in Cambodian Buddhism. The *Braḥ Dhammaviṅsuṅ*,[67] an important Khmer cosmogonic text once well represented in monastic libraries, contains an allegory of how a primordial being, Divine Ear *(preah kaev dibbasrot)*, creates the syllables "*na mo bu ddhā ya; ma a u; ku sa lā; a ā i ī u ū o e*" while seated on a diamond throne at the center of the world *(jambudvīpa)*. Another figure, Buddhaguṇ, constructs the five elements out of these syllables, and using a certain "dry humor," he makes them into a boy. From the boy's shadow a girl emerges. The children are named Gato and Gatā. With Divine Ear having now disappeared from the scene, Buddhaguṇ teaches the *dhamma* to the descendants of Gato and Gatā so that they may find the path to salvation (Bizot and von Hinüber 1994, 39–40).[68]

Finally, the cosmogonic significance of sound may also be transposed into the ritual context. To put it briefly, the *Ratanamālā* describes the manipulation and intersubstitution of elements of the *itipiso* formula of the *Dhajaggasutta* (*S.* i.218–220), a well-known protective, or *rakṣā*, text that contains a series of recollections of the qualities of the Buddha, the *dhamma*, and the *sangha*, each beginning with the Pali phrase "*iti pi so.*"[69] The ritual involves the writing and subsequent erasure of a series of mantras made up of the 108 syllables of the formula. The dust generated each time the slate is wiped clean may be collected and used for protective purposes.[70] In particular, it may be used to construct a powerful powder image of the Buddha *(preah phang)*. Alternatively, the syllables can be arranged in various patterns to create complex magical devices (yantras).[71] The practice is supposed to be highly effective for both those on the right-handed path and those on the left-handed path. In the latter case the power generated is believed to be sufficient to bring about the death of an enemy (Bizot and von Hinüber 1994, 17).

Cambodia, then, possesses a rich vein of traditional literature, most of which has been directly inspired by the Buddhist tradition. Old inscriptions inform us that Mahayanist literature circulated during the Angkorian period, whereas Pali writings from the Theravada canon (Tripitaka), and its commentaries, must have become established soon after Thai influence began to make its presence felt following the fall of Angkor in 1431. Indeed, Theravada Buddhism may have been a feature of the religious landscape sometime before this point, an idea reinforced by the existence of a Pali inscription [K. 754] at Kok Svay Chek, near Siem Reap, dated 1308.

Skill in Pali was never regarded as the sole index of learning or status among Cambodian Buddhists. As was also the case in neighboring Theravada cultures, a countervailing tendency to interpret possession of Pali-based knowledge as a magical accomplishment, rather than a purely scholarly one, was quite widespread. The elaborate rituals associated with the preparation, reading, and dissemination of traditional manuscripts underline the special significances attributed to Buddhist literature, and as we shall discover in chapter 5, the decision to edit and translate most Pali canonical writings into Khmer came very late. The project was first conceived by King Monivong in 1929, and the enormous undertaking was completed only in 1969. As part of the wider phenomenon of modernism that had been sweeping across Theravada Buddhist Asia for about a century, it represented an attempt to excavate some pristine authenticity from a bewildering mélange of literary materials in order to recover the original teachings of the Buddha. But it also entailed the rejection, or at the very least the demotion, of previously significant elements of customary practice on the grounds that they were not sanctioned by the Pali tradition.

Yet, insofar as literacy existed and was prized, vernacular writings were widely consulted by both *sangha* and laity alike. The *cpāp'* are particularly good examples. These texts provided the source from which the majority of the population received their moral education until very recent times. Naturally, given their composition by monks, the *cpāp'* reveal strong Buddhist influences, but, a little more surprisingly, so too do the versions of a Hindu epic poem, the *Rāmāyaṇa*, that have circulated and provided impetus for artistic and cultic expression in Cambodia since the Angkorian epoch. Not only that, but we know that the *Rāmāyaṇa* was subjected to an esoteric interpretation that coheres well with both vernacular and Pali representations of the so-called *yogāvacara* tradition, which, as Bizot's research makes clear, appear to have flourished in the region for at least a couple of centuries. It is not too much of an overstatement to suggest that this initiatory and highly ritualized strand within Cambodian Theravada, with its strong emphasis on interiority, represents the defining feature of the region's religiosity, although, as we shall shortly see, the impact of the dominant modernist paradigm was to relegate, marginalize, and render "unorthodox" these traditional teachings and practices.

5

Cambodian Buddhism under Colonial Rule

Traditionalism versus Modernism: Splits in the Monastic Order

Cambodia's weakness after the fall of Angkor meant that it could offer little resistance to the oscillating influences and rivalry of its two stronger neighbors, Vietnam and Thailand, which tended to dominate its internal affairs. The Cambodian royal family periodically divided into antagonistic pro-Thai and pro-Vietnamese factions, further undermining the coherence of the state. But the Vietnamese were viewed with more trepidation than the Thai, who at least shared the same traditions of orthography, aesthetics, and religion as the Khmer. The metropolitan outlook, Sinitic worldview, managerial genius, and ruthless efficiency of the Vietnamese were a world away from the Indianized thought universe inhabited by both Thai and Khmer.

King Norodom (r. 1864–1904), like Duang before him, had spent considerable time as a hostage in Bangkok before coming to the throne. There can be little doubt that Thai traditions in religion and culture flourished, as they had under Duang, when Norodom returned. But in August 1863, shortly before his coronation, Norodom signed a secret treaty of protection with French officials, effectively inaugurating the colonial era. It is difficult to get a clear insight into his motives, but even though he was no great lover of the French, it seems that he wished to counteract undue Thai interference in Cambodia. Some vestigial sympathy for Thailand is revealed in his attitude toward religion. He is reported as having said, "It is the king of Siam [i.e., Mongkut] in Bangkok who put the monastic robe on me; he is my religious preceptor, and there is a powerful bond between our two countries" (Fillieux 1962, 307). This implies that Norodom had been ordained in the newly established Dhammayutika Nikāya (Thommayut). But he was very angry when the northwest provinces of Battambang,

Sisophon, and Siem Reap—including Angkor, the historical and symbolic heart of the kingdom—were ceded to Thailand by the Franco-Thai convention of 1867, an agreement that ended the Thai claim to suzerainty over the rest of Cambodia. This event coincided with Mongkut's death. It ensured that significant Thai influence on Cambodia waned from this point on, although it never entirely disappeared.

The three ceded northwest provinces had, in reality, been incorporated into the Thai administrative region of Monthon Burapha sometime before. Therefore they were affected by the Thai religious and administrative reforms toward the end of the nineteenth century. This meant that the northwest effectively became the first part of Cambodia to come under rationalist and reformist influence. The local ecclesiastical hierarchy was integrated into a national pattern, and monastery-based schools were absorbed into a national curriculum (Yang Sam 1998, 254–255). Regular reports concerning religious and ethical observance were made for the first time. These were not encouraging, for they revealed that the newly introduced festivals of *magha* and *visakha pūja* were not widely observed and that Khmer monks attempted to subvert the use of the Thai language. A significant proportion of monasteries did not possess a proper *sīmā*, rendering many of their rituals ineffective from the strict perspective of *vinaya* observance, and morning readings from the Buddhist canon were neglected. Indeed, study of the Tripitaka simply did not take place in around half of all of the *monthon*'s monasteries.[1] Many monks appear to have been illiterate, and a significant proportion did not possess a full complement of monastic robes. Finally, monastic decorum was found to leave a good deal to be desired. Despite the modernist emphasis, the practices of martial arts, kite flying, chariot and boat building, and firework manufacture remained traditional monastic pursuits.[2]

In 1854 Ang Duang had petitioned the Thai king to send a complete version of the Tripitaka in the pure form of Pali recently championed by the monastic reformers of that country, on the grounds that nothing of the sort existed in Cambodia. Led by Mahā Pan (1824–1894), a Khmer based at Wat Bowonnivet, Bangkok, a delegation of eight monks representing Mongkut's rationalist and reformist Thommayut subsequently arrived at the royal court of Udong, carrying bundles of some eighty sacred writings. A Cambodian branch of the Thommayut was established at Wat Neak Tā Soeng[3] under royal patronage, probably around 1855. Mahā Pan became its first chief.[4]

There is little to distinguish the Thommayut and the Mahanikay in terms of doctrine, but they do disagree over the interpretation of some elements of monastic discipline *(vinaya)*, such as the wearing of sandals, the carrying of the begging bowl *(bat)*, and the consumption of drinks after midday.[5] The most obvious differences to the casual observer relate to the wearing and composition of the monastic robe. The traditional Mahanikay upper robe *(cīvara)* is made up of fifteen individual pieces, whereas the Thommayut equivalent has only ten. In the latter order, both *bhikkhus* and *samaneras* are allowed to wear an outer robe, covering both shoulders, whereas Mahanikay *samaneras* must have their right shoulder uncovered at all times (Bizot 1976, 18).[6] There is also a marked lack of uniformity in the ways that the two groupings intone Pali. Thommayut monks employ a technique of liturgical delivery *(pad)* in which the recitation is cut at the end of each word by a very brief silence and the end of each sentence is emphasized. The Mahanikay, on the other hand, chant rhythmically on the same note and without interruption.[7] Bizot's major study (1988b, 107) of differences in the formulae and pronunciations connected to the lower ordination ritual *(pabbajjā)* also demonstrates that the Mahanikay tend to interpret such formulae in an esoteric manner in line with the doctrines discussed in chapter 4. In all of these matters, as one would expect from a group who claim to "adhere to the law" *(dhammayutika)*, the Thommayut believe that their observance comes closest to the Buddha's own practice.

As time went on, it was inevitable that elements of Thommayut practice and outlook would rub off on reform-minded members of the Mahanikay. A few examples should suffice. The triple celebration of the Buddha's birth, enlightenment, and death *(vissakh boca)* had first been instituted in Thailand around 1817 under King Rama II. The festival was introduced to Cambodia by Mahā Pan[8] in 1855 but observed only by the Thommayut. The Mahanikay eventually took on the practice during the reign of King Sisowath (Commission des Mœurs et Coutumes du Cambodge n.d., 32). A royal chronicle also relates how some young members of the Mahanikay began to adopt the manners and customs of the Thommayut, including their particular pronunciation of Pali and their style of wearing monastic robes. Bizot (1976, 17) has noted that the practice became popular around 1918 among young Mahanikay monks keen on appearing more progressive, but it is also worth noting that the ubiquitous tattoo, something that had a clear potential to embarrass possessors among upwardly mobile sections of the monastic population, is more easily hidden if a monk wears his robe according to the practice of the Thommayut.[9] This process of borrowing accelerated in the monastic schools that began to emerge in the early twentieth century, for these were places in which members of both monastic orders worked shoulder to shoulder. A curriculum largely confined to a diet of Pali canonical literature also inclined in a Thommayut direction.

Religious tolerance was not universal during the period. Any antipathy the newcomers may have had toward the Mahanikay was tempered by the paucity of its membership. But there is evidence of opposition in the other direction.

Unlike the situation in Thailand, where the introduction of the new order was unopposed, in Cambodia there were frequent skirmishes, often initiated by Phnom Penh–based Mahanikay monks (Bizot 1976, 9). The hostility is illustrated by the fate of the *Vinayavaṇṇanā,* the foundation document of the Thommayut, which tells how King Mongkut came to see the need for reform of monastic Buddhism in Thailand. It was first translated from Thai into Khmer in 1912, but this first edition is now quite rare[10] because traditionalist members of the Mahanikay were successful in ensuring its systematic destruction (Bizot 1976, 5n1).

In 1866 the French created a new capital city for Norodom at Phnom Penh. Previously the king's role had been expressed through the magico-religious performance of traditional rites, but with the move to a modern capital new forces penetrated the inner sanctum of the state. In time the process would turn the monarch into "the living incarnation, the august and supreme personification of nationality" (Aymonier 1900–1904, 1:56). Almost immediately after the move, Wat Khpop Ta Yang, an old monastery next to the freshly constructed Royal Palace, was renamed Wat Botum Vaddey and rededicated in accord with the demarcation ritual *(nadī sīmā)* of the Thommayut (Lewitz 1966–1967, 436). Now styled Samdech Preah Sugandh, Pan was installed at Wat Botum as the Thommayut *sanghareach* (Meas-Yang 1978, 38).[11]

Since that time, the Thommayut has enjoyed considerable prestige, despite its relatively small size, in part because of its close ties with the monarchy but also because of its association with the new concentration of power in Phnom Penh. But the new order has never enjoyed "unquestioned preeminence" (Keyes 1994b, 47) over the older and larger fraternity. The French were particularly aware that monks of the Thommayut persuasion were easily able to exploit their close links with Thailand and should, in consequence, be treated as potentially intransigent.[12] Nevertheless, the Mahanikay has sometimes felt disadvantaged by the aristocratic support enjoyed by the Thommayut, even though the Mahanikay actually enjoys far greater influence in most parts of the country. As we shall see, rivalry between the two orders has affected the unity of the *sangha* and has tended to reinforce the distinction between urban elites and the peasantry throughout most of the modern period.[13]

In May 1887, Norodom sent a small group of senior Khmer monks to Ceylon with gifts, including a diamond-encrusted golden royal umbrella.[14] There they met several chief monks[15] before offering the umbrella to the Buddha's tooth relic in Kandy. Sometime in 1889 the party returned, accompanied by Ven. Ratanasara,[16] a high-ranking member of the Ceylonese *sangha* who brought Buddha relics and a cutting from the *bodhi* tree. These were installed at Wat Botum as symbolic imprimaturs for the implantation of the new Buddhist order. Mahā Pan built an elaborate structure called the *chedi* of the eight directions, just to the east of the sanctuary, for the relics. It was finally completed by his successor, Iem, and is still standing today, despite the upheavals of the past three decades. The upper part of the structure houses the relics themselves, while the ground floor enshrines the ashes of Thommayut patriarchs.[17]

Norodom was not an especially devout Buddhist, even though he had previously been a monk. His principal leisure interests seem to have been the consumption of opium and brandy. When in 1880 his son, Sukunabat, was ordained at Wat Botum, the king admitted his ignorance of the Buddha's teachings to the two patriarchs presiding at the ceremony. It is difficult to establish the reasons behind this admission, yet there is evidence that a rekindled interest in Buddhism, particularly in its more magical manifestations, was beginning to make its presence felt in Norodom's life. It is known, for instance, that between 1872 and 1882 he made four visits to a cave on Phnom Chriev in search of powerful Buddha images supposedly hidden there by the legendary king Ta Trasak Pha'em (Yang Sam 1990, 112).

Palace annals inform us that in 1880 Norodom ordered erudite Buddhist monks to assemble in the Royal Palace to begin an inquiry into the knowledge of the Tripitaka within the Cambodian *sangha* and to begin the translation of canonical works from Pali into Khmer ("Le Bouddhisme Khmer," 16). A convocation of scholars was also established to draft a Buddhist catechism in Khmer, and the two patriarchs Pan and Tieng were commanded to restructure the *sangha*. The latter act mirrored similar historical reorganizations in Thailand and other regions of South and Southeast Asia. Its effect was to confirm the seniority of the Mahanikay *sanghareach* Tieng over Pan, who was assigned second place in the new ecclesiastic hierarchy. This was hardly surprising, given the short time the Thommayut had had to put down roots in Cambodia. However, the order quickly overcame the handicap by extending its sway in influential circles.

Sanghareach Tieng (1823–1913) had been the son of peasants from Kien Svay.[18] When he was a young child, his parents were captured by Thai forces and led away into slavery in Mongol-Borey. Tieng entered a monastery at the age of eight and followed his teacher to Bangkok four years later, where he enrolled at Wat Amarin. He was fully ordained at age twenty, and he stayed in Bangkok until the age of twenty-seven. As a particularly able scholar-monk he came to the attention of King Rama III in 1850 or thereabouts and was given permission to return to Cambodia, presumably on a mission. On arrival he entered Wat Prang, Udong, becoming its abbot quite quickly. In 1857 he was appointed patriarch by Ang Duang, although, because of the previously mentioned confusion over the precise date of establishment of the Thommayut in Cambodia, it is difficult to determine whether at this stage his primacy extended over the whole of the Buddhist *sangha*.

When Norodom moved his capital to Phnom Penh, Tieng also left Udong, reestablishing the Mahanikay headquarters at Wat Unnalom, where he remained until his death. He was widely praised for fluency in Pali, Sanskrit, and Thai and also seems to have been an accomplished mathematician. He took an interest in astronomy and is the author of a work on cosmology. Tieng had a reputation for being an ardent patriot and in 1883 acted as a peacemaker between Norodom and his former student, the king's rebellious brother, Sivotha. Given Tieng's facility with languages, this seems to form a piece with the information that he "completely ignored French," although this should not lead us to conclude that he was entirely hostile to the colonial power. Indeed, he received the cross of a Chevalier de la Légion d'Honneur during his lifetime (Flaugergues 1914c). When he died in 1913, the *résident supérieur* wrote that Tieng had "always exercised a beneficial influence toward our Protectorate" and that the French had lost a "sincere helper" (Forest 1980, 143).

As a result of Norodom's desire to restructure Cambodian Buddhism, a royal ordinance had been issued on October 2, 1881, stating that all Mahanikay monks should follow the precepts and methods established and observed by Samdech Tieng. This suggests that not all of the monks nominally under Tieng's jurisdiction were following his directions. We certainly know of wide fractures in the Cambodian *sangha* around this time. Loosely speaking, two camps were beginning to resolve themselves around the twin poles of traditionalism and modernism. The traditionalists appear to have been monks opposed to the introduction of the Thommayut, which they regarded as a Thai import that was damaging to the unity of the country and the monastic order (Bizot 1993, 66). Bizot refers to this segment as the "ancien Mahānikāy."[19] The modernist grouping, on the other hand, consisted of members of the Thommayut but also contained influential members of the Mahanikay who were generally pro-Thai and open to the project of reform along rationalist lines. Not surprisingly, given his strong links with Bangkok, Tieng was the prime representative of this camp. The previously mentioned royal ordinance, then, was a thinly coded way of tackling anti-Thai and anti-modernist dissidents within the Mahanikay.

An inventory of 1901 submitted by the royal official Oknya Senarit to the *résident* of Phnom Penh estimated that around 2,300 monasteries, including about 400 in the Thai-controlled provinces of the northwest, operated in Cambodian territories at the turn of the century. In Kompong Cham Province at around the same time 193 pagodas were officially listed, containing a total of 2,724 monks and 648 novices (*Monographie* 1907, 21–22). This amounts to about

14.1 monks per pagoda, a figure that tallies well with Leclère's figure of 10.6 in Kampot. On this basis it has been calculated that around 1.7 percent of the population were monks at that time (Népote and Tranet 1983, 51, 53, 56).[20] Interestingly, Senarit's document covers only Mahanikay monasteries. Independently we know that 97 percent of all *wats* were Mahanikay at this time. On that basis we can calculate the existence of another 70 affiliated to the Thommayut. Having said that, the proportion of Thommayut monasteries was much greater, perhaps up to 15 percent of the total, in some of the regions within a hundred-kilometer radius of Phnom Penh. The situations of Wat Phnom and Wat Preah Keo Morokat, also known as the Silver Pagoda, however, were unique. The former had been renovated and landscaped by *résident supérieur* de Verneville in 1894 so that it might be transformed into a "national pagoda" (Edwards 1999, 90–91). Wat Preah Keo Morokat was built within the precincts of the Royal Palace,[21] and monks are not normally resident.[22] In consequence, it has no sectarian affiliation. This makes it the most appropriate setting for the performance of the many rituals of state Buddhism in which representatives of both orders are expected to participate.[23] As such, the Silver Pagoda points to the fact that the king and the state must, at least theoretically, stand above the rivalries between the two orders.

Népote and Tranet (1983, 70) have suggested that the concentration of Thommayut monasteries in the area around the Quatre-Bras implies that this was the only part of the country effectively controlled by Cambodia's ruling family in the second half of the nineteenth century. Some support for the thesis is afforded by a careful rereading of Oknya Senarit's document, which also indicates that the responsibility for geographically proximate groupings of monasteries around the country lay in the hands of individual members of the ecclesiastical hierarchy. Elsewhere, Leclère describes the situation as one in which a "multitude of *sanghas*" flourished. His account points to the existence of a set of largely independent appanages *(samrap)*, fourteen for the Mahanikay and eleven for the Thommayut. The way in which authority was parceled out reflected the general administrative arrangements of the court and the state into right and left halves, rather than a more straightforward differentiation based on monastic affiliation. According to this rather confusing arrangement, Tieng had authority over the appanage chiefs and the monasteries of the right, while Pan had equivalent powers in relation to the monks and the monasteries of the left (Leclère 1899, 391, 396). It is likely that this system had been in place since the mid-nineteenth century, when the Thommayut had been introduced from Thailand, and perhaps much longer in the case of the Mahanikay. To the anticlerical eyes of the French, who were looking to improve administrative efficiency—and probably also to a royal family anxious to extend its control over a much wider range than had recently been possible—the authority over significant numbers of able-bodied men by figures from within the monastic aristocracy beyond any obvious means of control was potentially dangerous. Some reform was clearly necessary.

The current system of ecclesiastical hierarchy has its origin in the importation of new bureaucratic notions from Thailand in the 1850s. However, the colonial power's first explicit involvement in restructuring the *sangha* may be traced to a royal ordinance of November 24, 1904, which bound the construction of new monasteries to an official registration process. In 1916 a parallel system for the authorization of both novices *(samaneras)* and fully ordained monks *(bhikkhus)* through the issuing of ordination certificates was introduced. *Achars* were made responsible for administering the process. They were expected to check inaccuracies in the documents, while local officials had to witness the good character of applicants. In this way, tabs could be kept on troublesome monks, and undesirables could be kept out of the monastic order. They could, of course, be a danger to the body politic in other ways. In the early 1920s, for instance, an official report had identified monks as having a complete ignorance of basic rules of hygiene (Tully 1996, 240n87). Wat Unnalom, it seems, was a major breeding ground for infectious diseases.

The appanages were suppressed by a royal ordinance of August 7, 1919, and a pyramidal ecclesiastical structure—in which provincial chief monks *(mekun)* were appointed by one of the two national patriarchs *(sanghareach),* in consultation with the Ministry of Religious Affairs—was imposed. In actual fact, old appanage chiefs were permitted to remain in office until their death, when they were replaced in the approved fashion. Head monks of individual monasteries *(chau adhikar)* could still be selected on a local basis, however. Nevertheless, the cumulative effect of the changes reduced the authority of largely independent abbots and put them under the control of a provincial bureaucracy. Because many of the former were strongly traditionalist, the new system contributed to the undermining of the Buddhist ancien régime in Cambodia. In September 1920 the various regulations were reviewed and extended by a series of official orders, most notably the royal ordinance of December 24, 1920 [no. 73] (Bizot 1976, 11), which forbade monks to learn or teach martial arts. It also undermined their ability to conduct apotropaic rites involving healing, astrology, sorcery, and tattooing, and it proscribed the making of amulets to confer invulnerability (Forest 1980, 55, 144–145). The threat of monks massing into an insurrectionary movement looked to be a thing of the past.

At the highest level of the state, Buddhist norms continued to exercise a traditional influence. King Norodom's will provided funds for the construction of rest houses along the principal roads of the kingdom, in imitation of the archetypal Buddhist king Aśoka and of Jayavarman VII. It also directed that a golden Buddha image in *abhayamudrā* be cast to his own bodily proportions (Osborne 1997, 254). This statue, Preah Chinreangsei Reachea, represents the king in the form of Maitreya, the Buddha of the future, underlining a popular belief that Norodom will be reborn as a savior figure in the five thousandth year of the Buddhist era (Jeldres and Chaijitvanit 1999, 43).[24] The construction of the statue seems to have caused Norodom's half-brother Sisowath (r. 1904–1927) some financial headaches when he came to the throne at the age of sixty-four, but Sisowath was more religiously observant, and certainly less antagonistic toward the French, than his predecessor. From the beginning of Sisowath's reign the colonial power began to recruit Cambodian men into newly formed local militias *(gardes indigènes),* with recruitment ceremonies in the presence of the provincial governor usually taking place at a local monastery, where offerings were made to the Buddha image (Forest 1980, 137). During the First World War, Sisowath also ordered public prayers for the French cause (Tully 1996, 170).

Sisowath was a stronger supporter of the Thommayut than his brother, apparently flying into a rage when informed that one of his grandsons planned to enter a Mahanikay monastery. He was calmed down only when he was reminded that both he and Norodom had first entered the Mahanikay Wat Prang, Udong, as young men—unsurprising, given that the Thommayut did not exist in Cambodia at the time.[25] Sisowath seems to have encouraged monastic defections from the Mahanikay to the Thommayut (Osborne 1997, 255). In September 1908 he was obliged to intervene in a dispute at Wat Kas Andet, Kompong Cham Province. The monastery had recently shifted its allegiance to the Thommayut, and not everyone in the locality believed this to be a good thing. Sisowath ruled that in the future all rites should be performed according to the traditions of the Thommayut, but the judgment does not appear to have satisfied all those involved in the dispute (Forest 1980, 50). Similar disputes could drag on for many decades.[26]

After the unsettled times associated with the previous king, Sisowath's reign has widely been regarded as a period of general stability. Admittedly, the king's power was narrowly circumscribed, but in some senses this had always been the case, for rival members of the aristocracy ensured that he could never exercise absolute power (Thion 1987, 152). Nevertheless, with a pious Buddhist on the throne the kingdom began to prosper along the lines congruent with the Theravada theory of kingship. As if to underline this fact, the northwestern provinces previously ceded to Thailand in 1867 were returned to Cambodia in 1907. The ancient temples could now be restored, and the splendors of the past co-opted to augment the resurgent national spirit. The year 1914 was a particularly auspicious one. Peace flourished, and abundant harvests were produced throughout most of the country. In correspondence with the felicity of the times, the explorer Henri Maitre entered the capital with an albino elephant captured in the northeastern forests as a gift for the king (Tully 1996, 159). Sisowath's possession of the elephant, a traditional item in the regalia of a righteous Buddhist king, further reinforced the feeling that Cambodia had, after many false dawns, regained its destiny as a powerhouse of Buddhist faith and culture.

When Sisowath left the country in 1906 to visit the Colonial Exhibition at Marseilles, his entourage included two Buddhist monks. En route their ship stopped in Ceylon so that he could pay respects to the Buddha's tooth relic at Kandy. The entire party was transported there on a train specially provided by the British governor. Sisowath's connection with this island stronghold of the Theravada continued, for in 1909 he visited again, dedicating a new temple, the Preah Thiangkaum Kew, to house Buddha relics (Tully 1996, 8–9). Many of his provincial governors also remained pious Buddhists, sponsoring seasonal rites and often entering the monkhood on retirement. Forest (1980, 106), for example, mentions Governor Nhek of Choeung Prey, who wrote to the *résident* on September 27, 1910, describing a Buddhist rain-making ceremony he had personally supervised two weeks earlier on a sacred mountain nearby. It also seems that in 1912 Sisowath unsuccessfully planned to abdicate and enter a monastery (Osborne 1973, 173).

In 1914, the year after his death, Tieng was cremated with great ceremony. Chief monks of all the monasteries in the realm were required to furnish materials for the construction of the incredibly elaborate funerary edifice *(men)*. The lavish ritual was attended by a great convocation of monks, including many from Annam, who wore sumptuous costumes of silk and were coiffed with delicately worked headdresses. Brahmanical priests *(baku)*, attached to the Royal Palace and tending subsidiary altars dedicated to deities of the Hindu pantheon, were also involved (Flaugergues 1914a, 486–487). The monk with overall responsibility for the proceedings was Ven. Mahā Vimaladhamma Thong (1862–1927). Thong was another modernist. He had traveled to Thailand around the beginning of the century, searching for Buddhist manuscripts, and seems to have spent much of his time studying and writing a number of works dealing with the tricky subject of monastic discipline *(vinaya)*, a topic at the heart of the reforms embodied in the establishment of the Thommayut (Finot 1927).

Thong was open to the use of modern European methods of critical judgment in the interpretation of Buddhist doctrine and practice. Perhaps more surprisingly, he had been a prominent champion of the Protectorate's efforts to reform the Cambodian writing system, an initiative bitterly opposed by traditionalists in the *sangha* who regarded this as an attack on the literary foundations of the religion. Thong is generally regarded as the "founder" of the first organized modernist grouping within the Mahanikay. This movement, called the Thommakay or "new Mahanikay" *(mohanikay tmae)*,[27] would in time become hugely influential in the shaping of Cambodian Buddhism and more widely in the development of an emerging sense of national identity, particularly through its association with the work of the Buddhist Institute.

Poor relations between the two camps simmered on well into the 1960s.[28] When Thong died on August 2, 1927, Ven. Preah Sirisammadivansa Lvi Em, a senior monk at Wat Langka, was appointed his successor as director of the École Supérieure de Pali. Described at the time as Phnom Penh's best-educated monk, Em, although something of a Mahanikay modernist, seems to have been a little suspicious of the political ambitions of some of his contemporaries.[29] One of his first tasks on taking up his new post was to ensure that places in the elite Buddhist schools became the preserve of serious-minded monks and that monks with a more careerist attitude were discouraged from attending. Also around the same time, legislation had been introduced to bring the *sangha* under the jurisdiction of secular courts, another development that concerned Em. The result had been a great increase in the number of monks who complained about their treatment by superiors. Many of the complaints naturally revolved around ongoing hostilities between the two parties (Edwards 1999, 310).

Ven. Chuon Nath

There had been an interregnum of more than a year at the head of the Mahanikay following the death of Tieng. Eventually Sisowath appointed Dhammalikhit Ker Ouk, although he was never awarded the title of *sanghareach*.[30] The appointment was not a popular move, for many in the modernist camp regarded Ker Ouk as ill educated (Huot Tath 1970). When Ker Ouk eventually died in 1936, it was widely assumed that Em, who was by now second in the Mahanikay hierarchy, would take his place. However, the royal family and the French opposed this, and the position remained vacant until 1948. It is difficult to know the precise reason for this, but it is likely to have been connected with the fact that the nationalist monk-martyr Ven. Hem Chieu, of whom we shall hear more in due course, was a close disciple of Em's.[31] Whatever the true state of affairs, Ven. Chuon Nath, a rising star on the modernist side of the Mahanikay and more sympathetic to the various reforms being imposed on the *sangha* by the French, was eventually appointed to the post.[32]

Prominent modernist monks of the early to mid-twentieth century: *(left)*, Ven. Chuon Nath; *(right)*, Ven. Lvi Em; *(opposite left)*, Ven. Huot Tath; *(opposte right)*, Ven. Oum Som.

In May 1898, Chuon Nath (1883–1969) became a novice at Wat Polyum, Sangkat Roleang Ke, Kandal Province. He subsequently transferred to Wat Unnalom in 1899, where he began his study of Pali, gaining full ordination in June 1904 and receiving the name "Bhikkhu Jotaññano." Possessing a keen intellect and a readiness to work to the French agenda for the development of Buddhism in Cambodia, his monastic career progressed rapidly. In 1915 Chuon Nath became a professor at the École Supérieure de Pali, and by 1930 he was acting as joint director alongside the more traditional Em. Chuon Nath taught Thai, Laotian, and Sanskrit, as well as Pali. Following Em's resignation over the arrest of Ven. Hem Chieu in 1942, Chuon Nath became the school's sole director.

Wat Unnalom–based scholar-monks like Ven. Chuon Nath[33] and his great friend and coworker Ven. Huot Tath (1891–1975)[34] were crucial figures in the establishment of the Thommakay grouping and subsequently did much to advance the intellectual credentials of the movement.[35] Both young monks had been specifically selected by Thong, in his capacity as director of the École Supérieure de Pali, to be schooled in modern critical approaches to the study of Buddhism and related fields. In this connection they visited Hanoi between 1922 and 1923, where they received detailed training from two major French

scholar-officials, Louis Finot, director of the École Française d'Extrême-Orient, and Victor Goloubew.[36] Another modernist monk, Ven. Oum Sou, should have joined them, but in the end he refused to go (San Sarin 1998, 127–128). In his important memoir of Chuon Nath, *My Intimate Friend,*[37] Huot Tath recalls that the friendship was cemented when they began learning French as young monks at Wat Unnalom around 1915. This they did behind closed doors, believing that their actions would be condemned by their fellows. During the rainy-season retreat *(vassa)* of 1916, Chuon Nath, Oum Sou, and Huot Tath were chosen by the new Mahanikay patriarch, Ker Ouk, to deliver nightly sermons to a royal princess. However, their preaching, particularly as it related to matters of monastic discipline,[38] was in some respects contrary to the prevailing interpretation. They also argued that many traditional texts had been contaminated by later embellishments that could not be considered to be the words of the Buddha. In the disturbances that followed, stones were thrown at Chuon Nath and Huot Tath by some of their opponents within Wat Unnalom.[39]

The events provoked letters of protest from monks representing both sides of the argument, from as far away as Kompong Cham and Svay Rieng. Ker Ouk came under considerable pressure from senior members of the ecclesiastical hierarchy to resolve the dispute.[40] He submitted the matter to Sisowath, but after a formal interview with the king and his court officials, Chuon Nath's grouping was vindicated. This did not staunch the opposition from more conservative forces, including Ker Ouk himself (San Sarin 1975, 13). As a result, on October 2, 1918, Royal Ordinance No. 71 was displayed in all the country's monasteries, to the effect that monks should either abide by the practices of Tieng and Pan or be expelled from their respective orders. More specifically, it distinguished between the group of the new *dhamma (buak thor thmei)* and the group of the old *dhamma (buak thor cah)* and forbade "teaching reforms or . . . spreading among the faithful modern ideas which conflict with traditional religion."[41] The Unnalom three bided their time, but one of the unintended consequences of the ordinance was that it encouraged more scholarly members of the *sangha* to ask themselves what precisely and critically the discipline of Tieng and Pan actually had been.

In due course Chuon Nath composed a number of works on monastic discipline *(vinaya)*—most notably *Samaneravinay,* which was critical of some of the noncanonical accretions that had grown up in the life of the order—but he had some difficulty in getting them published. It seems that the two patriarchs were required to give their permission for any work on Buddhism to be printed, and they had both refused. Modern printing presses had been introduced into Indochina toward the second half of the nineteenth century. The first had been in Saigon, but another was established in Phnom Penh at the end of the century. The presses were restricted to the production of official publications,[42] and the problem for the patriarchs was that anything they authorized might be compromised through explicit cooperation with the colonial power. However, of rather more importance was that Buddhist traditionalists opposed the influence of modern printing techniques on the grounds that they undermined the magico-religious character embodied in palm-leaf texts, which, in any case, had rarely been read for their literary, didactic, or intellectual content. Indeed, many monks were rarely literate in that sense—their interest had been in the occult power of the word itself. As such, printed books were the thin end of the wedge.[43] They would initiate a profound change in the concept of literacy and might in retrospect be seen to have undermined, in one fell swoop, Cambodia's literary and religious heritage.

Despite the opposition of the traditionalists, *Samaneravinay* began to circulate quite widely in samizdat form, and its author was forced to endure a number of hostile interviews with the Ministry of Cults and Religious Affairs on this account. This seems to show that the issues dividing the two parties actively engaged the imagination of significant segments of the *sangha.* Apart from their monastic supporters, the Unnalom three also had patrons among the aristocratic families, and before long a sympathetic official, Oknya Keth, gained permission from the *résident supérieur* to have five thousand copies of the book printed and circulated as a merit-making gesture for his recently deceased parents. When the book was released in 1920, to much consternation, it included the names of Oum Sou and Huot Tath alongside that of its actual author, Chuon Nath, on the title page as an act of solidarity.[44] The Mahanikay *sanghareach* once more tried to impose his authority. Claiming that the whole affair was a violation of Royal Ordinance No. 71, he sought permission from the king to expel all three young monks from Unnalom and was clearly put out when both Sisowath and his son, the future king Monivong Sisowath, sided with the modernizers. It was soon after these events that Chuon Nath and Huot Tath made their study trip to Hanoi. On their return to Cambodia, Louis Finot intervened on their behalf, and their careers prospered accordingly from then on.

In September 1915,[45] Sisowath appointed a team of eleven senior individuals to a royal commission charged with beginning work on a definitive Cambodian dictionary. Of the eleven, only six members played any significant part in proceedings, including chairman Ponn, the Mahanikay *sanghareach* Ker Ouk, Thong, and Achar Ind, a poet and patriot from Battambang who had been recruited because of his knowledge of the vocabulary and pronunciation of western Cambodia.[46] Given the wider context of division between traditionalists and modernizers, there could have been little surprise when disputes broke out between some members of the commission and the Council of Ministers. The latter, being largely conservative in outlook, were not supportive of various proposed reforms of orthography,[47] and consequently progress was very slow. After serious delays the king reconstituted the commission in July 1926. Of the original members, only the chairman, Ponn, and Thong were retained, but other dignitaries were added, bringing the number up to eleven again. With the enhanced status that Chuon Nath had gained from his sojourn in Hanoi, it was predictable that he would be one of the replacements.[48] The newly constituted commission then largely rejected the contentious reform proposals, and an officially approved version of the *Khmer Dictionary (Vacanānukram Khmaer)*,[49] revised under the supervision of Chuon Nath, finally appeared in two volumes in 1938 and 1943, respectively. This major work of scholarship became a quasi-official inventory of the language and an intellectual milestone (Cœdès 1938, 320). In light of the development of the Cambodian language, and ongoing ideological and linguistic disputes, the *Khmer Dictionary* was almost continuously revised throughout Chuon Nath's lifetime. Toward the late 1940s, largely prompted by the difficulties encountered in preparing the text of the 1946 Constitution, another commission was also founded to investigate the creation of new "cultural words" *(baky vappadharm)*. Most of these had been based on Sanskrit and Pali and were used to render French terms that were largely political in nature.[50] The project was not without its critics. Keng Vannsak, for example, argued that it would have been more patriotic to unearth Mon-Khmer words from the Angkorian period.[51] This antipathy toward Pali and Sanskrit, and to a certain extent toward Buddhism itself, flowed from the impression, strongly promoted by French scholarship, that Cambodia was a subservient Indianized state with no indigenous cultural resources to call its own.

However, the modernists were in the ascendant, and their most important project began on December 14, 1929, when the new king, Monivong, established a Tripitaka Commission to organize the editing and translation of Pali canonical texts into Khmer (Saddhatissa 1980, 245). Lvi Em was appointed as the first president of the commission, and the first volume to roll off the press was presented to Paul Reynaud, the minister of colonies, at a grand ceremony at the Royal Palace in November 1931, with two thousand monks in attendance (Edwards 1999, 314). The enormous undertaking, resulting in a total of 110 volumes, was finally completed some forty years after it had begun, with Huot Tath at the helm from 1966. The end of the project was marked by elaborate celebrations in the capital on April 1, 1969 ("Le Bouddhisme Khmer," 16).[52] Interestingly, the Thommayut held themselves aloof from the entire project. As far as they were concerned, they already possessed an authentic version of the Tripitaka in Thai. They regarded proficiency in Thai as a hallmark of high culture and saw the Khmer-Pali version as a work of crass vulgarization (Edwards 1999, 316). Mahanikay traditionalists reacted just as strongly but on different grounds.

The Tripitaka project may be seen as part of the wider phenomenon that had been sweeping across Theravada Buddhist Asia for about a century. Referred to by some scholars as "Pali-text puritanism," it represented an attempt to excavate some pristine canonical authenticity from a bewildering mélange of literary materials in order to recover the original teachings of the Buddha. It entailed the rejection—or, at the very least, the demotion—of previously significant elements of customary practice, on the grounds that they were not sanctioned by the canon and should therefore in effect be regarded as non-Buddhist.[53] Such a view was hardly likely to find favor with traditionalists who vigorously defended their interpretation of texts in the light of Khmer sociocultural realities and whose justification for practicing rituals not specifically authorized by the Pali canon was that they had been observed in the country for generations and were intimately connected to the identity of the Cambodian people. Indeed, the enactment of such rituals provided the most obvious means of maintaining continuity with the glories of the Angkorian past. To cut this important route of communication to a treasured reservoir of national self-worth was tantamount to treason.

Certainly, the Thommakay could make enemies. The *résident* of Kompong Thom, for instance, wrote of the "uncontrolled proselytizing" of the grouping in his 1932–1933 report. Around the same period the appointment of the Thommakay supporter Ven. Iv Tuot of Wat Po Veal, Battambang, as Mahanikay chief monk *(mekun)* of Battambang Province provoked anger from his Thommayut opposite number. Indeed, in 1934 the *résident supérieur* rebuked assembled senior monks and students at the École Supérieure de Pali for the disharmony the disputes had recently brought to the *sangha*. Still, the Thommakay was gradually extending its influence, through an increase in provincial appointments throughout the mid-1930s. As one colonial official rather paradoxically observed, the influence was "less a Buddhist enterprise than a specifically Khmer (one)." It had, for example, expressed itself in attempts to "khmerize" communities in Thai-speaking areas to the west, such as Koh Kong (Edwards 1999, 331–332).

In 1944 Chuon Nath became chief monk of Wat Unnalom, and in 1948 he was appointed *sanghareach* after the death of Ven. Prak Hin, an elderly monk who in turn had acted as a regent after the death of Ker Ouk. However, it is clear that Chuon Nath's views had held sway for some time before his official elevation was confirmed. Controversy had, for example, blown up over the use of the *Tirokuḍḍa Sutta*[54] as a protective chant *(paritta)* during the ceremony of merit making for dead ancestors *(pchum ben)* in September—modernizers were attempting to rewrite the text to eliminate its non-Buddhist elements. The suppression of the traditional New Year festivities by a royal decree of July 17, 1944, also appears to be related to the dispute over the presence of extraneous and superstitious features in popular ritual (San Sarin 1998, 119–121). Another concern seems to have been that many monasteries engaged in activities that were too intimately bound up with the agricultural economy. Pressure was exerted to end the monastic custom of keeping draft animals so that they could be borrowed by the people when their own were ill or otherwise out of action. An ordinance issued April 8, 1943, had previously defined and restricted the duties of monks to seven discrete areas of activity. Significantly, the last duty listed was "helping the government *wherever possible*" (italics mine).[55] A prescription of January 27, 1954, written by Chuon Nath and designed for display throughout the land, brought the reforms to a fitting conclusion. Its first article pointed out that the true principles and practice of Buddhism had been codified in three publications—for the laity, for novices, and for fully ordained monks, respectively—and that these should be followed without deviation.[56] The text also discouraged various unorthodox but traditional practices, such as the recitation of mantras, water sprinkling, and magical healing (Bizot 1976, 20n3).

With his position secure at the summit of the ecclesiastical hierarchy, Chuon Nath began to make frequent official trips to other parts of Buddhist Asia. In 1950 he led a delegation of Cambodian monks to Colombo to participate in the discussions that led to the formation of the World Fellowship of Buddhists (WFB). He was also invited by the Burmese authorities to help in preparations for the important Sixth Buddhist Council in Rangoon in May 1954. He was away from March 17 to April 7, 1953, and returned with a group of senior Burmese monks, led by Ven. Shinkalara,[57] bearing six marble Buddha images. After a procession around the streets of Phnom Penh, the statues were deposited in Wat Unnalom, and the delegation stayed for some time, looking at ways to strengthen links between Buddhists in the two countries (*France-Asie* 84 [May 1953], 479–480). Toward the end of his life Chuon Nath was honored both at home and in other parts of Buddhist Asia. Such was his sanctity in certain quarters that he was widely believed to be able to talk with birds and other animals (Smith-Hefner 1999, 28). At the time of his death at the age of eighty-six on September 25, 1969, after a short illness, false rumors circulated that this "impulsive and very powerful" personality had been assassinated (San Sarin 1975, 15). Some, traditionalists presumably, asserted that this was because he had made serious mistakes in his interpretation of the Buddha's teachings. Others maintained that he met his death as a punishment for his vigorous anticommunism (*PPP* 8/20, October 1–14, 1999). He was cremated in January 1970 in an elaborate crematory pavilion *(men)* representing Mount Meru that had been constructed for the occasion. Paradoxically, given his known opposition to nonorthodox practices, a small Buddha image made after the cremation, incorporating some of his remains, is now venerated as an abode of a protective spirit *(boramei)* (Bizot 1994a, 120). His funerary monument *(chedi)* still stands in Wat Unnalom, largely undamaged by the violent events that were soon to follow.[58]

Monastic Administration

Regulations for a wholesale reorganization of the *sangha* were formulated in two official orders *(kram)* of February 9 and September 18, 1943.[59] As we have already seen, the previous situation had been somewhat confused, for it contained some elements of the old appanage system—an arrangement that had theoretically come to an end with the royal ordinance of November 24, 1904—that existed alongside more recent ad hoc attempts at reform. Large increases in the numbers of monasteries and monks, combined with efforts to reorganize civil society on more rational lines, meant that the old informal arrangements were no longer desirable. Modern bureaucratic routines were beginning to affect the internal arrangements of institutional Buddhism.

Under the new dispensation the appointment of both fully independent *sanghareachs* could proceed only after they had been nominated by the king. The Mahanikay *sanghareach* then had the power to appoint senior ecclesiastics *(mahāthera)* to the post of chief monk *(mekun)* for each province *(khet)*, but only after gaining both royal approval and consent from the Ministry of Cults and Religious Affairs. Each *mekun* was then assigned to a rung on the national ecclesiastic hierarchy that reflected the size and importance of his particular province. All senior appointments had to be filled by monks who had spent a minimum of twenty uninterrupted rainy-season retreats in the monastic order.[60] As a bridge between the provincial chiefs and the two patriarchs, a number of high-ranking members of an inner cabinet with various state-related functions acted as inspectors general *(komnan khet)* for a cluster of provinces. A *kram* of October 11, 1946, made provision for the appointment of five geographically specific monastic inspectors for the Mahanikay and one for the Thommayut (Martini 1955b, 416, 423), the idea being that meetings between the *mekun* and his *komnan khet* should take place every mid-January to resolve administrative and disciplinary matters. This annual ceremony *(anusamvacchara-mahasannipat)* now takes place in Phnom Penh and involves both sections of the monastic order. Its initial stages were presided over by the king before division for *nikāya*-specific deliberations (Zago 1976b, 110).[61] Over time, minor changes were made, but in 1960 there were fifty-eight rank holders in toto: thirty-six in the Mahanikay and twenty-two in the Thommayut. In addition, each order's hierarchy was differentiated into four ranks, or *rājāgaṇa (reacheakhanac)*.[62]

To bring ecclesiastical administration into line with the government's reorganization of civil society into provinces *(khet)*, districts *(srok)*, and subdistricts *(khum)*, the post of *mekun* was later complemented by the addition of an official called *anukun* who acted as a head of either the district or the subdistrict, depending on administrative need. Owing to the smaller size and limited geographical spread of the Thommayut, neither *mekun* nor *anukun* are appointed there. Promotion to this rank, however, is less formal and does not require a royal edict. Indeed, *anukun* may be selected by the patriarch and the minister of cults and religious affairs alone, and in some cases it seems that such posts may be created by provincial governors *(chauvay khet)*, working purely on their own initiative.[63]

Ecclesiastical courts designed to settle monastic disputes operate at four distinct levels. A *chau adhikar* heads up an individual *wat* court, while at the district level a council *(sālānugaṇa)* is chaired by an *anukun*. At the provincial council *(sālāgaṇa)*, a *mekun* is helped by his right-hand assistant *(bālāt-kun)*, an elder skilled in monastic discipline *(vinaythor-kun)*, a registrar *(samuh-kun)*, and a secretary *(lekhādhikār-kun)*, while the supreme council *(therasabhā)* operates under the presidency of the relevant *sanghareach.* The supreme council is the final court of appeal in all matters pertaining to monastic discipline. It is also the only body with the authority to defrock a recalcitrant monk in extreme cases. Only after this procedure has been properly accomplished can a monk who is charged with a serious crime be handed over to the civil authorities for trial. As we shall discover in chapter 6, failure to fulfill this requirement caused great consternation in 1942 when the colonial authorities punished Ven. Hem Chieu, an early figure in the anticolonialist movement, for seditious activities.

Buddhist Education under the French

Because of the strong social dimension of village Buddhism in Southeast Asia, traditional pagoda schools had existed in Cambodia long before the establishment of the French Protectorate. In the premodern period they largely focused on teaching the scriptures by rote, although a number of practical skills, such as carpentry, could also be acquired. There was no set curriculum, and pupils could join at any time during the school year. Having said that, the observation that "a Cambodian boy leaving the pagoda school had his memory stocked with edifying passages, but could neither read, write nor count" (Bilodeau 1955, 16, 21) is not wholly accurate.

In 1884 King Chulalongkorn had begun the modernization of temple schools in Thailand, and by the early twentieth century approximately thirty such institutions were established in the Thai-controlled provinces of northwestern Cambodia. In these schools "primary education was dispensed . . . by monks . . . and other teachers . . . trained in Bangkok according to modern methods" (Forest 1980, 158–159). For the first couple of decades of colonial rule the French seemed content not to interfere in traditional educational arrangements, but this new development began to concern them.[64] If policies were not developed to shape and improve education within Cambodia itself, those whom the French claimed to protect could easily become contaminated by Thai influences. An additional worry was that the schools might become a conduit by which the British could interfere in France's sphere of influence.[65] The twentieth century, then, began with attempts to bring the traditional system of education under official control.

A first concrete attempt at reforming *wat*-based primary education started around 1908 as an experiment by the future *résident supérieur* François Baudoin, then *résident* of Kompong Cham Province.[66] Students at designated *écoles de pagode* would receive a basic Franco-Cambodian education based on a curriculum designed by E. Ménétrier, a Khmer speaker who knew a good deal about popular belief and practice and understood the need to ensure that Buddhism, particularly in its ethical dimension, should not be compromised by the new developments. It was agreed that Khmer should be the medium of instruction (Bezançon 1992, 14). As time went on, the breadth of the curriculum was gradually addressed, so that by 1912 it included the study of arithmetic, the metric system, and "general knowledge," alongside Khmer reading and writing. In due course some monks were prevailed upon to produce a textbook on moral education,[67] and additional works on geography, history, and biology, written in Khmer by French pedagogues associated with the Bibliothèque Franco-Khmer in Hanoi, followed soon after. Such developments were bound to cause difficulties for some monk-teachers because novel ideas were introduced that seemed to conflict with traditional Buddhist teachings. One obvious problem was that the new texts taught that the earth was round, a deeply problematic notion for traditionalists brought up to read Buddhist cosmological literature as literal truth.[68]

A carrot-and-stick approach was used to encourage the widest possible use of the new schools. A royal decree of November 10, 1911,[69] promoted the initiative by emphasizing that the reading and writing of Khmer, plus counting, would be taught in all the pagodas of the kingdom. The decree made it clear that the "pure ethics hitherto imparted in the pagodas should be supplemented by cultivating the minds of the young people there instructed." It also stipulated that parents found guilty of not sending boys over the age of eight to school would be punished by a fine of two piastres for the first offense. It is not clear that this part of the decree was pursued with any vigor. Indeed, the minister of education himself had complained of the lack of enforcement, in a letter to provincial governors on February 2, 1914. There is additional evidence that some local monastic officials did what they could to frustrate official policy on compulsory education, for, in a separate letter written to members of the ecclesiastical hierarchy in the same year, the minister complains about the continued existence of the old system of informal education in which children also act as unpaid servants. He urges discontinuation in favor of a methodical, uniform, class-based, and time-tabled approach to study (Bilodeau 1955, 15–16, 64). Intriguingly, there was no attempt at this stage to challenge the traditional attitudes that meant that girls were almost entirely excluded from formal education. The education of girls is simply not mentioned in the official documents.

The next step in the modernization of the system was the introduction of a standardized system of teacher training and school inspection as the best means of widening access to primary educational provision. By 1924 a school inspectorate had been formed, and initial experiments were conducted in Kampot Province, where a number of monks were given a rudimentary modern teacher training at an *école d'application* based at Wat Choeung Kriel. The institute was headed by a certain Mam Oun, although the brains behind the development was Louis Manipoud,[70] who, like Ménétrier before him, was a great respecter of Khmer traditions (Bezançon 1992, 19). By 1930, fifty-eight monks had passed through Wat Choeung Kriel, and plans to extend the "modernised pagoda school system" to the rest of the country were launched. By 1931 there appear to have been some 101 renovated pagoda schools, and by 1939 the number had risen to 908, catering to 38,519 pupils.[71] The numbers appear to have risen sharply following the creation in 1934 of a Council for the Perfecting of Traditional Education, which included both *sanghareachs* (Edwards 1999, 336).

By the academic year 1951–1952 the renovated pagoda schools sector had expanded to 1,447 schools with 1,810 teachers and 76,943 pupils (Bilodeau 1955, 24). Around 20 provincial monk teacher-training establishments had also been founded. By now these pagoda schools shared the same three-year elementary curriculum of the state schools, with the exception that French was not taught. They operated only in the afternoon, six days a week, and were overseen by a joint lay and monastic inspectorate. The entire modernization initiative had, in fact, been achieved at minimal cost. The premises were provided by the pagoda free of charge, monk-teachers received no pay, and equipment was more or less nonexistent. However, classes could be very large, containing up to one hundred pupils subdivided into three age cohorts. There was also an ongoing problem of trained monk-teachers disrobing to take advantage of emerging economic opportunities in the secular world, but this provided an ideal opportunity for the Ministry of Education, which seems always to have regarded the *écoles de pagode* as a stopgap, to begin their conversion into state schools.

Official reports show that some 1,700 pagoda schools with a total of 42,000 pupils existed in 1909. By 1911 the figure had risen to 3,000, catering to more than 50,000 students. The statistics show quite eloquently that the renovated sector at this time was a very small proportion of the whole and that most Cambodian children receiving an education were still primarily exposed to traditional forms of learning. Cross-country penetration appears to have been particularly patchy, with 87 percent of all renovated schools in existence in 1931 falling within the provinces of Kampot, Battambang, Pursat, and Prey Veng (Edwards 1999, 329). Monks from other parts of the country were distinctly cool about the reforms, with many regarding exposure to French education as "a peril for the Buddhist doctrine." They also perceived that the growing emphasis on utilitarian values in education—as expressed, for instance, in the growth of examinations and certification—might in time seriously undermine the traditional notion of knowledge acquired through age and experience (Edwards 1999, 94). Unsurprisingly, there is some evidence of organized agitation against the Franco-Cambodian schools in such circles (Forest 1980, 155).

In 1918 *gouverneur-général* Albert Sarraut instituted a secularized state educational system, closely based on the French model, throughout the whole of French Indochina. However, progress in establishing the infrastructure was particularly slow outside Vietnam, so that by 1921 only 14 such schools had been established in Cambodia, and even by 1922 only around 3,700 pupils had been recruited (Tully 1996, 237). It seems that most parents preferred to send their offspring to the local pagoda schools, where the family could be assured of earning some religious merit. The idea of education for the attainment of worldly goals, such as economic enrichment and social advancement, was still an alien concept to the vast majority of Khmer. It is against this background that the *résident supérieur* now recommended a radical shift in educational policy. Rejecting the gradualist approach of sympathetic figures like Manipoud and Ménétrier, he argued that French should be adopted as the only medium of teaching in the pagoda schools because "it is the only language capable of defeating the routine of Buddhist education," a force he regarded as retarding the economic modernization of the country (Martin 1994, 36). A recapitulation of the clash between traditionalists and modernizers within the monastic order was now playing itself out in the colonial administration, and in both cases the modernizing party was gaining ground. However, the modernizers did not have everything their own way. Although the uprooting of traditional Confucian-based schools in Vietnam had elicited scarcely a murmur of protest, the French were time and again obliged to compromise with Buddhist traditionalists over the introduction of secular learning in Cambodia (Gyallay-Pap and Tranet 1990, 363).

As the secular educational system developed as a mode for social advancement, monastic schools, both reformed and unreformed, entered a period of decline. A phase of diminishing fortunes for the monasteries—in which other traditional services such as the provision of basic health information, child care, architectural advice, and rudimentary banking facilities were also in decline—meant that the monastic sector could no longer exercise its traditional role as a "national" glue. Some of the manifestations of Buddhist militancy in the twentieth century (a topic to which we shall turn in chapter 6) are related to a perception that fundamental powers were, indeed, leaking away from the monastic sector. But there was another side to the coin. As secular schools began to take over the burden of providing the forms of education deemed appropriate to the development of a modern economy, *wat* schools could once more focus on matters for which they were best suited. Liberated from excessive bureaucratization, they could concentrate again on the transmission of basic Buddhist and Cambodian cultural elements to the bulk of the population (Népote 1974, 781).

Official concerns about the higher education of monks had led to the founding of two *écoles supérieures de théologie bouddhique* by *sanghareach* Tieng. One had opened on August 13, 1909, at Angkor Wat, in the territory returned to Cambodia by Thailand only two years earlier (Forest 1980, 145). However, it closed in 1911 (Hansen 1999, 94). Lack of funds, poor recruitment, geographical inaccessibility now that the center of national consciousness had begun its shift to Phnom Penh, and proximity to the Thai border are the most likely factors. A Phnom Penh center of higher Buddhist learning was more successful. It had been provisionally established at the Silver Pagoda in 1914, before moving to a specially constructed building on the corner of Rue Oknya Chhun and Rue Quai Sisowath, where by a royal ordinance of April 13, 1922, it was given a new name, École Supérieure de Pali.[72] The explicitly modernist mission of the school was to "favor and develop the study of Buddhist theology through a rational teaching of the ancient sacred languages, Pali and Sanskrit, and all knowledge indispensable to the understanding and explication of religious texts" (Gyallay-Pap and Tranet 1990, 363), so it was no surprise that the leading monastic reformer, Ven. Mahā Vimaladhamma Thong, should become its first director (Edwards 1999, 287). Fairly soon the range of courses offered to monks was extended beyond the original diet of Indic languages to include French, mathematics, and other secular subjects.

The advantages for the French authorities in the creation of this establishment were fairly obvious. The curriculum could be more easily monitored, and provision of good-quality facilities for the higher study of Buddhism within Cambodia itself would obviate the necessity for well-educated monks to travel to Thailand, where they might pick up bad habits (Delvert 1956, 314). To promote this message, an official campaign was launched to convince monks of the advantages of staying at home to complete their studies. They would be much closer to their family, and both indigenous and Western medical expertise would be available in the event that they fell ill (Forest 1980, 146). The supply of academically oriented monks into these higher levels of Buddhist education was improved in 1933 when a system of rural *wat*-based elementary Pali schools with a three-year curriculum was established by royal decree.[73] One of the consequences was that more and more monks were drawn into the ambit of the educational system than had been the case when a mere handful had availed themselves of the opportunity to visit Bangkok for extended periods of study. But the new institutions were located in predominantly urban environments, so the development led to a gradual derustification of large sections of the *sangha*.

As the result of pressure from Mlle. Suzanne Karpelès, who had been impressed by her visit to the National Library of Siam two years previously, King Monivong established a Royal Library on January 15, 1925 (Edwards 1999, 304). By 1930 the institution had transmogrified into the Buddhist Institute and its associated Commission des Mœurs et Coutumes du Cambodge.[74] The institute was soon to become an important catalyst in the emerging nationalist movement. It made good sense to draw together the varied strands in the Buddhist modernist project, and to this end both the institute and the Ministry of Cults and Religious Affairs were accommodated in the same building as the École Supérieure de Pali. The school had already been granted official permission to publish and disseminate approved works on Buddhism. When these publishing activities are considered alongside the parallel activities of the Royal Library, we can perceive the beginning of a boom in Buddhist literary activity.[75] This in turn prompted a definite growth in the reading of Buddhist modernist literature. To give an indication of the scale of the phenomenon, in 1928 alone the Royal Library catered to some five thousand readers, of whom around two-thirds were monks (Edwards 1999, 308).

Official sponsorship of the Buddhist modernist project had a number of tangible and significant results. The development of Buddhist higher education in the country went hand in hand with French suspicions over the motives of neighboring states, most particularly Thailand, and was used as a way of purifying the *sangha* of foreign manipulation. The fostering of a certain kind of Pali-based Buddhist scholarship also led to clearer definitions of what Buddhism actually was, and it would lead to the denunciation of heretical views, whether they had formed part of the traditional background to Cambodian Buddhism or had been newly imported, as was the case with the modern Vietnamese Cao Dai movement.[76] The growth in publishing and reading brought into being an entirely new kind of Khmer, the politicized secular intellectual *(neak cheh doeng)* who would in time come to play a major role in reformulating the idea of the nation and its national religion *(sasana jiet)* (Edwards 1999, 308). Finally, the rehabilitation of traditional culture under the auspices of the Commission des Mœurs et Coutumes du Cambodge contributed to a reinvention of Cambodian rural life.

It will come as little surprise to discover that many aspects of the project were not appreciated by the traditionalist pole of Cambodian society, including influential members of the aristocracy. As has already been noted, the Thommayut had tended to regard modernists in the Thommakay as "upstarts" (Edwards 1999, 314), and this superiority complex made it difficult for them to appreciate the new Mahanikay-inspired pretension to learning, not least because they regarded Buddhist scholarship as very much their own preserve. This meant that the Thommayut were largely alienated from the activities of the Buddhist Institute. It also seems that monks in regions of the country bordering Thailand were hostile to the project. In a 1932 report, for example, the *résident* of Siem Reap noted that "head monks persist in their blind opposition to the Buddhist Institute" (Edwards 1999, 315).

The Cambodian "middle ages" can loosely be said to have come to an end with the coronation of Ang Duang at Udong in 1847. His introduction of Thai courtly and religious culture, combined with an end to Vietnamese inference, may be said to have encouraged a kind of Theravada renaissance. This is best represented by the importation of the reformist Thommayut from Bangkok. The imposition of the French "protection" in the reign of the next king, Norodom, led to many reforms in political organization, together with a removal of the court to a newly constructed capital at Phnom Penh. Although the policies of Duang and the colonial power were unconnected and arose from vastly differing motivations, both forms of governance appear to have contributed to an increase in tension within the monastic order. But while Duang shared the reformist and Pali-oriented outlook of Mongkut, the French seem to have been especially suspicious of the political aspects of the monastic order founded on these insights and did much to frustrate its activities.

As the twentieth century unfolded, splits between modernizers, concerned about rediscovering a pure form of Buddhism free from the accretions of the past, and traditionalists, jealously guarding what they regarded as a unique cultural and religious heritage from attack by hostile external forces, came strongly to the surface. However, the structure of tension between the two camps became increasingly complex. The French intervention in Buddhist education is particularly relevant here, as are the obstacles they put in the way of Thommayut expansion. As a result the battleground for the fight became largely confined to the Mahanikay. The modernists within the Mahanikay clearly benefited from French support, and their triumph is most adequately illustrated by the career of Ven. Chuon Nath. But monastic traditionalism, though marginalized, survived into the 1970s. The political upheavals of this period would, in time, lead to an almost total elimination of the monastic sector. However, as we shall see, institutional Buddhism would reach a critical mass in the 1990s, a little more than a decade after its reestablishment following the defeat of the Khmer Rouge, and once again the old tensions would break out.

6

Buddhism and Cambodian Nationalism

Monks and Militancy in the Early Colonial Period

Southeast Asian Buddhist monks have often participated in movements of contestation. From the Burmese sack of Ayutthaya in 1767 to the establishment of the Chakri dynasty in 1782, civil war raged in Thailand. Among the combatants, clans of monks proficient in the use of swords and guns attempted to carve up the country. For example, Chao Phitsanulok of Fang, with a following of red-robed monastics, managed to establish a short-lived independent state in the north of Thailand (Lingat 1958). Meanwhile at Thonburi, Taksin (r. 1767–1782), an enthusiastic Buddhist layman who claimed the spiritual status of a stream-enterer *(sotāpanna)* and the power of supernatural flight, took possession of the throne even though he was bitterly opposed by influential sections of the *sangha*. When Rama I, the first ruler of the new Thai dynasty, finally gained power, Taksin was executed and many militant monks were defrocked (Bizot 1988b, 94).

Similar forms of militancy are attested in Cambodia for approximately the same period. A righteous king had been seen as the keystone of the premodern Buddhist polity, and it was virtually impossible for anyone to envisage a non-Khmer as the ultimate protector of the realm (Try 1991, 81–82). Monastics often led movements animated by the ideal of freedom from a foreign yoke. In 1820 a monk named Kai, popularly supposed to have magical powers, was proclaiming a vision of a millennial future free of Vietnamese influence. In due course he rebelled against the feeble monarchy, temporarily establishing himself as king at the sacred mountain of Ba Phnom in southeastern Cambodia. A more serious revolt of 1865–1867 against Norodom and his French "protectors" was incited by Po Kambo (aka Achar Leak),[1] a former monk with a following of some ten thousand, including monks in robes[2] and various holy men *(neak sel)* (Osborne 1978, 238).[3] Having rallied support at Wat Phnom, Phnom Penh, Po Kambo finally met his death after he and some followers were attacked at a monastery in Kompong Thom Province. Escaping, he was quickly pursued to the center of a lake and beheaded.[4]

It is clear that most modern Cambodian uprisings had an anti-Vietnamese or anti-French dimension, yet we should bear in mind that older antipathies toward the Thai also existed. The 1898 rebellion of cardamom collectors in Battambang Province against the high taxes imposed during the period of Thai control is a case in point. Led by a certain Ta Kae and his associate, a Vietnamese magician-monk called Sau, the uprising is celebrated in the popular poem "The Battle of Ta Kae in the Cardamom Mountains," by Achar Ind, a prominent Battambang-based intellectual.[5] In one of the more significant moments in the story, Sau manages to prevent large-scale violence by asking that some captive Thai officials be offered to him as alms, thus saving their lives.[6]

Itinerant monks are frequently connected with uprisings of one sort or another. The case of Ngo Prep is instructive here.[7] Ngo Prep was a Vietnamese who appears to have moved to Phnom Penh as a young man. We first hear of him around 1889–1890 when, posing as a traditional healer and a Buddhist monk, he unsuccessfully tried to raise a rebellion against the colonial power in the Mekong Delta region of Cochinchina. After this he withdrew to the province of Treang, where he organized various Buddhist ceremonies to raise funds to build a new pagoda. It was here that he fell in with Achar Kê, apparently a veteran of the earlier insurrection of Achar Sua (1864–1866), and Mom, a visionary. Believing that Preah Bat Thommit (the future Buddha, Maitreya) would be reborn and establish a millennial kingdom in 1899, Ngo Prep proclaimed a new unified state in which the Cambodian king and the French would serve as the future Buddha's lieutenants of the left and the right, while he would assume the role of lieutenant of the middle. Despite short spells in prison, Ngo Prep was supported by a number of prominent monks who collected funds to aid the campaign. At the beginning of 1898 we find Ngo Prep at Angkor, undergoing ordination as a novice monk, but he returned to the region around Phnom Rovieng, Treang Province, where he was reunited with the elderly Kê and Mom several months later. Following an unsuccessful bid to take control of Wat Kompong Svay, Banteay Meas Province, Ngo Prep settled at Wat Prabat Chean Chûm near Phnom Rovieng, where he held well-attended ceremonies on various nearby mountains. The chief monk of this monastery appears to have been an active recruiting officer for the movement and played an important role in supplying arms. In March 1898, following a visionary experience by Mom, Ngo Prep falsely claimed to be Ang Phim, Norodom's cousin, and distributed royal titles to his principal coconspirators. Growing concerned about the situation at Phnom Rovieng, the authorities moved to break things up. Forty-one individuals were arrested, including two *chau adhikar,* with monks and *achars* composing a significant proportion of the total.

At the beginning of King Sisowath's reign (1904–1927), an ex-monk and miracle worker named Ang Snguon adopted the identity of one of the king's uncles and declared himself the rightful ruler of Cambodia. However, after attacking the French *résidence* at Thala-Borivet, he and his followers appear to have evaporated into the mountainous Dangrek region to the north of the country and were not heard of again. In 1909 another wizard and ex-monk called Khieu had his rebellion successfully quelled by the French authorities, while Ouch, a messianic "Robin Hood figure" guided by supernatural forces and commanding a force of around a hundred tattooed and amulet-protected followers, caused official concern in early 1913 when he attacked the Apostolic Mission's plantation at Chhlong, shooting its director, Father David, in the chest (Tully 1996, 133–142).[8]

The connection between rebellion and traditional Mon-Khmer occult practices *(vethamon)* is an area of long-standing significance in the Khmer context. Coverage of Kai's 1820 anti-Vietnamese rebellion in the royal chronicles clearly distinguishes between the "cruel" Vietnamese and the Khmer "people of merit" *(neak sel),* who achieve invulnerability, strength, and invincibility through a life lived in accord with the Buddha's teachings, the practice of Buddhist ritual, and the use of powerful amulets (Chandler 1996, 121). Even today it is common to hear of soldiers who wear protective amulets or tattoos consisting of mystic diagrams (yantras) fashioned by monks or *gru.*[9] The 1916 Affair illustrates this issue quite nicely. A group of Cambodian monks, apparently trained in martial arts and believing that the ingestion of herbal medicines would render them invulnerable, cut short their studies in Bangkok to support the anti-French revolt of Norodom's favorite son, Prince Yukanthor (Forest 1980, 52, 147, 395). Two of the monks were subsequently arrested in Battambang after crossing the Thai-Cambodian border with documents from Yukanthor addressed to unknown sympathizers. They both received twenty-year prison sentences (Tully 1996, 195). French officials, believing that oath-taking ceremonies administered by monks had taken place in various monasteries prior to coordinated marches on Phnom Penh, certainly suspected a Buddhist background to the failed affair (Osborne 1978, 237). We do know that many monks resented the authorities' attempts to restrict educational visits to Bangkok and would have been sympathetic to aims of the revolt.

It is difficult to assess the degree to which a Buddhist element may have been an ingredient in the assassination of Felix Bardez, *résident* of Kompong Chhnang, on April 18, 1925, an event that proved a particular shock to the French community in Cambodia.[10] While collecting taxes in the village of Kraang Laev, the chief monk of the local *wat* had told Bardez that local people did not have the money to pay. Bardez would have none of it, and the abbot was reluctantly forced to persuade the villagers that they should pay. He used the rather unconvincing argument that one should honor one's parents and that, since the French were now the parents of the Cambodian people, the villagers were duty bound to cough up money. Bardez also allegedly insulted the villagers by suggesting that if they could afford their new pagoda, they should be able to pay taxes (Tully 1996, 284). Bardez was badly wounded in the ensuing fracas. While being tended by the abbot and the chief monk of the province, he was attacked once more and killed.[11] Bardez certainly appears to have insulted universal standards of good behavior, but it is quite possible that he would have walked away from the encounter unharmed had he managed to curb his arrogance. Although the stage on which the episode was played out happened to be a Buddhist monastery, no obvious issue of Buddhist principle was at stake, and all the evidence indicates that the few monks caught up in the disturbances did what they could to aid and protect the unfortunate official from an enraged local populace.

There has been a tendency to interpret almost all acts of monastic and quasi-monastic militancy of the nineteenth and early twentieth centuries as early examples of organized anticolonialism.[12] Yet this was not necessarily a widespread contemporary interpretation of events. Achar Ind, for example, looking back at the insurrections of his youth, comments that figures like the "contemptible" Po Kambo and Achar Sau were guilty of lèse-majesté. They were "awful persons [who] . . . incite poor people and forest people to raise up an army to betray the king." From this conservative perspective, their actions were heinous because "it is a crime to set oneself up as a king."[13] It is also odd that later revolutionary historians came to regard the events mentioned above as "people's rebellions" even though there is little hard evidence that they represented the actions of the "progressive elements" in Cambodian society. Indeed, many insurrections appear to have been "led by people who resented the loss of their traditional privileges and by pretenders to the throne of Cambodia" (Frings 1997, 813). To complicate matters further, factionalism within the monastic order also had a tendency to develop into outright hostility. A good example happened in June 1949, when a rebel band led by Achar Yi was active in Kandal and Prey Veng provinces. Yi—"a quack sorceror," according to colonial sources—burned Buddhist sacred writings, and in some cases the *wats* themselves, if he believed their monastic residents had been supporting modernizers within the Mahanikay. The governor of Kandal seems to have feared that such acts of desecration might lead to wider conflict between *sangha* traditionalists and modernists (Kiernan 1985, 70–71). Interestingly, a Communist Party of Kampuchea (CPK) document[14] from the early 1970s describes Achar Yi as a counterrevolutionary. The authors of the document have no difficulty in distinguishing differing forms of Buddhist militancy, and they clearly interpret Yi's activities as opposed both to the direction of the revolutionary struggle and to the party of monastic reform. Whether they also believed that organized anticolonialism and Buddhist modernism had a shared agenda must, however, remain a moot point.

Cao Dai

The Cao Dai movement was founded by Ngo Van Chieu (1872–1932), a Vietnamese official working within the administration of French Cochinchina, when he first entered into communication with the spirit world while serving on the island of Phu Quoc in the early 1920s.[15] He subsequently obtained a six-month leave of absence, on the grounds of ill health, and withdrew first to the Tien-Son-Tu pagoda at Ha-Tien, a Buddhist sanctuary within a large cave called Thach-Dong on the Cambodian border, and then to Mount Bokor in Cambodia itself (Meillon 184, 192). However, Ngo Van Chieu was of an ascetic disposition, and as the movement developed, he became increasingly uneasy about the rapid increase in membership. Retiring to Can Tho with a small group of followers (called Chieu Minh) toward the end of his life, he had little to do with the establishment of a Cao Dai "holy see" at Tay Ninh, close to the Cambodian border, on November 18, 1926 (R. Smith 1970a, 339–340).[16] The new leadership emphasized acting upon the social and existential aspects of suffering by fostering an atmosphere of mutual aid (Khy Phanra 1975, 322). They also underlined the healing role that the movement might be expected to play in the traditional animosities between Khmer and Vietnamese.

News of developments at Tay Ninh soon spread, and some thirty thousand peasants from Cambodia's eastern provinces are thought to have traveled there throughout 1927. Their principal aim was to pay respect to a recently erected statue of a figure on a white horse that had, perhaps miraculously, turned around to face in the direction of Phnom Penh. The horseman is a common iconographic element in popular Buddhism, most likely originally intended as an image of the Buddha immediately prior to his renunciation of the worldly life. But a millennial and nationalistic significance was soon attributed to the image. Some held that it represented Maitreya, the future Buddha. For others it was Prince Yukanthor or even perhaps Po Kambo (Kiernan 1985, 5). Whatever the correct interpretation, to the popular imagination the equestrian figure was going to be reborn imminently and renew the Cambodian nation.

On May 6, 1927, apparently quite unconnected with unfolding events at Tay Ninh, a certain Sino-Khmer named Chot led a band of Khmers to the communal house *(dinh)* of Ninh Thanh Loi, Rach Gia, the province of Cochinchina with the largest Khmer population.[17] There they mistakenly killed the father of a local tax collector and torched the land registry building. After a short battle the rebels were defeated, with nineteen dead, including Chot. Initial assumptions that this was an anti-French rebellion connected with Cao Dai turned out to be incorrect. In fact, it had been a fairly straightforward disagreement over land rights, complicated by ethnic hostilities (Brocheux 1972, 448). But the authorities were anxious about anything that might bring together Cambodians and Vietnamese in a common cause. Chot's rebellion merely reinforced their paranoia (Gouvernement-Général de l'Indochine 1933, 27, 35, 38).

In Cambodia the Cao Dai challenge was addressed in a variety of ways. On May 23, 1927, the minister of cults and religious affairs expressed the view that the movement was based on false premises and that it sought to exploit the credulity of the untutored. At the end of June the patriarchs of both Buddhist orders were prevailed upon to rule that Cao Dai was contrary to the teachings and discipline of Buddhism. Finally, on December 26, 1927, a royal proclamation was issued that underlined the movement's heretical nature from the Buddhist perspective. The document also characterized Cao Dai as a Vietnamese plot to destabilize the Cambodian throne (Khy Phanra 1975, 325). On February 8, 1928, another royal ordinance declared that involvement in ceremonies contrary to either Buddhism or Catholicism (the latter had received official recognition in 1863) would be punished. As a result a Mahanikay monk from Prey Veng Province was defrocked in June 1936, following his attendance at Tay Ninh, and it is said that small groups of Khmer pilgrims were still traveling to the "holy see" as late as 1933. But the danger had been nipped in the bud. Neither the announcement of the miraculous appearance of a new Khmer king at Tay Ninh in June 1928, nor the movement's call on devotees to settle on 500 hectares of adjacent land around August 1930, caused major official concern. In September 1930 a Cao Dai meeting in Phnom Penh was infiltrated by the Sûreté, and ninety-six persons were arrested, including the director of the movement in Cambodia, Le Van Bay (R. Smith 1970a, 344). Cao Dai soon lost its Khmer dimension, becoming enmeshed in internal intrigues of little interest to the authorities.[18] In the end the 1927 episode was an anticlimax. But it did have one significant long-term effect. It led to a wider recognition that the French were manipulating both court and ecclesiastical hierarchies. This in turn strengthened an emerging nationalist sentiment, not least within the Buddhist *sangha*.

The Umbrella War of 1942 and Its Aftermath

On May 12, 1930, in the same year that Ho Chi Minh founded the Indochinese Communist Party, the colonial authorities established the Buddhist Institute in Phnom Penh, with King Monivong and King Sisavang Vong of Laos attending its opening ceremony. Placed under the direction of Suzanne Karpelès, who had previously acted as head of the Royal Library, the Institut Indigène d'Étude du Bouddhisme du Petit Véhicule—its correct name—aimed to save Cambodian Buddhism from "degeneration" and to counteract Thai influence through the construction of a strong Indo-Chinese sense of identity. Its study of "minor differences" in practice between Thailand and French Indochina was felt to be a particularly appropriate way of achieving the latter goal. The institute was successful in addressing some of these foundational aims, but, less expectedly, it also provided a breeding ground for newly emerging anticolonialist sentiments. Whether consciously or not, Karpelès and her coworkers began to bring about "the crystallisation of an ethnically discrete rubric of nation" (Edwards 1999, 301).

Prior to the institute's establishment, the French seem to have been more favorably disposed to the traditional "cosmological" form of Buddhism than to the "modernized" rationalistic versions that were beginning to circulate in various parts of the Buddhist world. In the first place, the traditional form, by endorsing the long-standing social structures, made it much easier for the country to be efficiently administered. In addition, a generalized "fear of modernity" may also be linked to the romanticism that afflicted many French officials in their dealings with their colonies. Karpelès had a hard task on her hands, but she managed to overcome the traditional prejudices of monks and worked effectively in her capacity as director. She had studied with both Alfred Foucher and Sylvain Lévi in Paris and was competent in Pali. Having arrived in Hanoi at the beginning of 1923 to work with Louis Finot, she had come into contact with both Chuon Nath and Huot Tath, who were in the middle of their second study visit at the time. It was through the support of these arch-modernizers that the Buddhist Institute would eventually become closely linked with the modernist agenda of the Thommakay *sangha* faction.

The institute had taken over responsibility for the publication of *Kambuja Surya* (Cambodian sun). Produced since 1927 by the Royal Library, this was the first-ever Khmer-language journal. It contained articles on folklore, history, and

Buddhist literature, plus information on the royal family. Achar Ind's famous collection of traditional stories, *Gatilok,* was one of its first serialized elements.[19] Although the periodical had fairly low circulation figures, it became common for monks to read out sections during sermons and other public events. This "listening to newspapers" *(sdap-kaset)* clearly extended the influence of a newly emerging print media that was most effectively represented by another publication of the Buddhist Institute, *Nagara Vatta* (Edwards 1999, 338).[20]

Nagara Vatta was founded by two institute employees, Pach Chhoeun and Sim Var, in 1936. They were soon to be joined by Son Ngoc Thanh, an ethnic Khmer from Tra-vinh in southern Vietnam. Educated in France, Thanh had first worked as an archivist at the Royal Library. Later promoted to the Commission des Mœurs et Coutumes du Cambodge, he joined the Buddhist Institute in 1935, subsequently becoming its deputy director. Meyer (1971, 77–72) has characterized Son Ngoc Thanh and his colleagues as quasi-intellectuals who sought to develop Buddhist doctrine in such a way that it supported emerging nationalist aspirations. They actually had little knowledge of the Khmer and Pali sources, so their work tended to draw heavily on an amalgam of French and English writings on Buddhism.[21] As a result it was tinged with romanticism and theosophy. Not surprisingly, the methodology was strongly criticized by more traditionally learned monastics such as Chuon Nath.

With a readership aimed at monks—many of whom read relevant passages of the paper to the laity[22]—and low-ranking civil servants mainly educated through the monastic school system, *Nagara Vatta* began by championing the cause of a very mild and Buddhistic Khmer nationalism. As part of this agenda the newspaper was particularly hostile to the Cao Dai movement. In a series of articles in 1937 and 1938, such as "Cao Dai Religion Invades Buddhism," readers were warned that Buddhism was the nation's true religion and that Cambodians should be particularly vigilant in ensuring that the country was not taken over and perverted by the Vietnamese. A particular worry was the ongoing feuding within the *sangha,* which sapped its strength and might be detrimental to the long-term future of Buddhism by allowing non-Khmer religions, such as Cao Dai, to gain a significant foothold in the country. The article also recommended a reinvigoration of the Buddhist missionary endeavor in the eastern provinces to counteract the threat (Edwards 1999, 326).[23]

Both Thanh and Pach Chhoeun began visiting *wats* around the country circa 1939. The essence of their message was that monks should be active in the intellectual and moral awakening of the Khmer people so that they might release themselves from French rule (Kiernan 1985, 32). This activity nicely supplemented Thanh's other responsibility in the institute, a project to provide a Buddhist education for Cambodian soldiers, particularly those from his homeland in Kampuchea Krom. The institute had been clearly conceived as part of the structure of the state. It was administered by the Ministry of Cults and Religious Affairs, and those associated with its work were encouraged to use Buddhist teachings as the glue with which to bind together disparate social elements in a process of nation building. The institute's servants were expected to educate soldiers, particularly those in Kampuchea Krom, so that they might become "fervent adepts of Buddhism" and develop a disciplined frame of mind (Bunchan Mul 1982, 117–118). In this way the Khmer Krom and other peripheral groups might be incorporated into a new vision of Cambodia. But Thanh subverted the principal aim by recruiting monks who were both good orators and ardent nationalists for this work. He wanted them to be "strongly nationalist, good talkers and skilled in persuading the soldiers, using the Buddhist style of enlightenment, to love their country," and such monks were also expected to write reports naming suitable recruits in the "nationalist struggle to chase out the French" (Edwards 1999, 339). One of his most promising and articulate recruits had been Ven. Hem Chieu.

Evidence suggests that, since the beginning of the French Protectorate, competence in the Khmer language had gradually declined among colonial officials (Chandler 1996, 156). The French attempt to romanize, rationalize, and modernize written Khmer, using a system devised by the future *résident supérieur* Georges Gautier in the late 1930s, must be seen against this background.[24] The policy was never entirely successful, but some members of the intelligentsia recognized its value, as was demonstrated by the opening of a class in Cambodian romanization at Wat Botum, the headquarters of the Thommayut, in January 1944 (Edwards 1999, 345). However, in other segments of the *sangha* the idea provoked open hostility.[25] One of the most prominent opponents was Hem Chieu, a teacher at the École Supérieure de Pali and a monk of Wat Unnalom. For him the reform was an attack on both traditional learning and the status of traditional monastic educators, even though it seems that the romanization decree was not intended to apply to religious writings. Hem Chieu was arrested on July 17, 1942, and charged with involvement in organized opposition groups and with translating seditious material from Thai. Found guilty on both charges, he was imprisoned on the island of Poulo Condore, where he died in 1943 at the age of forty-six.[26]

Nationalist feeling had been rising significantly since the loss of Battambang and Siem Reap provinces to Thailand in 1941. An official announcement that monks over the age of twenty were to be brought within the taxation system had reinforced the feelings of irritation (Martin 1994, 49). In March 1941, *Nagara Vatta* had praised Hem Chieu's own institution, the École Supérieure de Pali, as a "school for the nation," arguing that without its influence "Khmer writing and religion would go to rack and ruin and eventually disappear" (Martin 1994, 49). Now the newspaper challenged Hem Chieu's arrest by calling for a demonstration to bring about his release. Part of the anger had been stirred up by the forcible defrocking of Hem Chieu and an associate, Ven. Nuon Duong, by the authorities, an action that underlined their disrespect for a prominent monk, who traditionally may be detained by the secular power only after first being allowed to disrobe in a ceremony organized by the *sangha*.[27]

More than a thousand people, around half of whom were monks, participated in the demonstration of July 20. Many of the monks were reported as representing the modernist Thommakay grouping within the Mahanikay (Steinberg 1959, 72), mainly from the Phnom Penh monasteries of Unnalom and Langka. Because they carried umbrellas, the event is sometimes termed the Umbrella War. It is generally regarded as the first coordinated act of the anticolonial forces within Cambodia, and there can be little doubt that concerns about the status, character, and external control of Buddhism were significant factors in the overall motivation of many of the participants. Other factors may, however, also have been at work. Some members of the intelligence community strongly suspected Monivong's son, Prince Monireth, of involvement in events in pursuit of his own quest for power (Lamant 1986, 192, 195), while Chandler (1991, 19) asserts that Japanese agents had been attempting to encourage certain *sangha* members to express anti-French sentiments in the lead-up to this event. Indeed, some members of the organization may have expected rather more support from the Japanese than eventually transpired. It is difficult to know whether such assertions were simply paranoid or were based on sound intelligence.[28]

After the events of 1942, there is little doubt that the official attitude toward the Buddhist Institute underwent a significant transformation.[29] *Nagara Vatta*—as a consequence of its role in calling for the demonstration, but also because of a perception that it was taking an increasingly pro-Japanese stance—was suppressed at the end of July 1942. Pach Chhoeun was sentenced to death (subsequently commuted to life imprisonment), and Thanh fled to Thailand, finally making his way to Tokyo.[30] However, Thanh did try to keep open channels of communication with influential members of the Cambodian *sangha*, including Chuon Nath himself, who it must be supposed harbored some sympathy toward the nationalist project.[31] By way of consolidation, the newly appointed *résident supérieur*, Georges Gautier, forced the king to issue an ordinance confirming the romanization of the Khmer script on August 13, 1943. At approximately the same time, monks associated with both the Buddhist Institute and the École Supérieure de Pali were forbidden to preach. As Edwards (1999, 344) comments, they were permitted to continue their intellectual work as long as they remained in their ivory tower. The institute itself was accused of being a "third sect" of Buddhism when only the Mahanikay and Thommayut had been effectively recognized, and in April 1943 the head of the Department of Propaganda, Press, and Information claimed that the institute and its Thommakay supporters had crossed the boundary between politics and religion, that it harbored an "anti-French minority," and that it was intent on spreading Thommakay influence throughout the country. Its publications were dismissed as "useless" and "lifeless" (Edwards 1999, 344). On July 17, 1944, a reform bitterly opposed by a majority in the monastic order, the official acceptance of the Gregorian calendar, was finally ushered in.

Many of the main players in the Umbrella War went on to gain a political significance, even if for some this was entirely posthumous and unintended. A number of umbrella-wagging monks, for example, entered into the spirit of rebellion. In this context we might mention Vens. Pres, Khieu Chum, and Pang Khat, all of whom had been part of Hem Chieu's immediate circle. Achar Pres seems to have fled to the Cardamom Mountains in southern Battambang immediately after the demonstrations, to "wake up the people" so that they might launch a coordinated and sustained resistance to the French (Kiernan 1985, 44). Somewhat later Khieu Chum sprang to prominence after he argued that the Buddhist religion should not depend on monarchical structures, on the grounds that the institution had been rejected by the Buddha himself when he left his own palace home to live the life of a recluse.

Pach Chhoeun was released from prison after Sihanouk declared the end of the French Protectorate and the creation of a Japanese-backed Kingdom of Kampuchea toward the very end of the war on March 12, 1945. He and Thanh returned to the capital as heroes,[32] and in July of the same year they joined Sihanouk in a national celebration of the monks' demonstration, the date becoming fixed as an annual holiday. Thanh was appointed foreign minister and subsequently prime minister, and *Nagara Vatta* reappeared, albeit in a more vigorously pro-Japanese and anti-French incarnation, in March 1945 (Lamant 1986, 196). However, Thanh had become a republican by this point and did nothing to hide these convictions from the king. On August 9, 1945, against the background of an imminent Allied victory, a group of seven agitators entered the Royal Palace to try to force Sihanouk to abdicate. The insurrection was clearly connected to the Son Ngoc Thanh circle and had the backing of many Phnom Penh–based monks and students (Kiernan 1981, 163). Following the reimposition of French rule in September of the same year, Pach Chhoeun fled to near the Vietnamese border where, with the support of the Viet Minh and a number of monks, he began propagandizing for the short-lived Khmer Independence Committee. Thanh was arrested by the British and imprisoned in Saigon.

On his release in 1951, he established himself as a maquisard, making clandestine radio broadcasts calling on monks and students to join the republican and anticommunist resistance (Kiernan 1975, 12).[33] In June 1953, monastic supporters issued a communiqué from Thanh's jungle headquarters near Battambang, threatening the French with a "holy war" if Cambodia was not granted immediate independence.

With the reimposition of French rule in October 1945 and the granting of permission to found political parties, other members of the *Nagara Vatta* group founded the Democratic Party.[34] Led by Prince Sisowath Yuthevong, it aimed to establish a constitutional monarchy along Thai lines upon winning elections set for September 1, 1946. Its strength "came in large part from the Mahanikay sect of the *sangha*, from younger members of the bureaucracy, from supporters of the Issarak movement, and from Cambodia's 'intellectual' class" (Chandler 1996, 175). Its emblem, an elephant's head and three lotus flowers, symbolized the monarchy, Buddhism, and the people (Martin 1994, 51). The party accused its detractors, particularly the Liberal Party led by Prince Norindeth, of agitating for the right for monks to vote (Preschez 1961, 18), and they in turn accused the Democrats of being anti-Buddhist.[35] The charge was vigorously denied. The Democrats argued that they merely wished monks to live an uncontaminated existence remote from the games played by politicians. Voting for the election appears to have been brisk. Given that the electorate was entirely male and that many of these men had been monks, it could be argued that familiarity with quasi-democratic procedures operating within monastic institutions may have predisposed such fledgling voters to turn out in large numbers. In any case, the Democrats, being far better organized in the countryside, won overwhelmingly, gaining fifty of the sixty-seven seats (Corfield 1994, 10–11).

Despite their success, some Democrats like Sim Var and Lon Nol appear to have lived a double life after taking power. Rumors circulated that they also belonged to a clandestine organization called the Black Star, dedicated to explicit anti-French agitation. Membership in this secret society involved a special initiation rite in which a Buddha image or a Black Star—the symbol of Son Ngoc Thanh's political police during the Japanese period, and hence the name of the society—was tattooed on the body (Lamant 1987, 87–88). Left-leaning members of the party, on the other hand, were believed responsible for organizing various anti-Sihanouk demonstrations among students, including a strike by students of the École Supérieure de Pali in January 1953 (Lee 1976, 234). Nevertheless, the Constitution, promulgated on May 7, 1947, represented an adaptation of the French constitutional arrangement of 1946 to a monarchical and Buddhist Cambodia (Thompson and Adloff 1955, 178).

For the first time Buddhism was established as the state religion and freedom of religion was guaranteed, provided that this freedom did not adversely affect public order (Preschez 1961, 24).[36]

As restrictions began to ease following the end of the war in the Pacific, increasing numbers of Cambodian monks were making study visits to India with funds supplied by the World Fellowship of Buddhists. Additional "regional religious centers," financed from the same source, were developed in Cambodia itself (Thompson and Adloff 1955, 256). Cambodian Buddhism was once more plugging into a Pan-Asian network that was beginning to take stock of a possible future free from the shackles of European domination. Buddhists were also looking forward to the important, potentially chiliastic, celebrations planned throughout the Buddhist world in connection with the twenty-five hundredth anniversary of the religion, the Buddha Jayanti, in 1956–1957. As part of the lead-up to this event, relics of the Buddha's two principal disciples, Sāriputta and Mahā Mogallāna, had circulated through Buddhist Asia, arriving in Phnom Penh during October 1952. On July 2, 1953, the famous scholar-monk Ven. Narada Mahathera donated a Buddha relic as a present from the Ceylonese *sangha* to the Cambodian people.[37] Various dignitaries—including Ven. Tong-Naga Thera, a Vietnamese Theravadin based at Wat Langka who was returning from a spell of study in Ceylon—accompanied the cavalcade as it traveled from the airport. The reliquary had been received by Ven. Chuon Nath and then driven to Wat Langka, where it was installed in the *vihāra* (Nouth 1953).[38]

It is possible that such developments may have prompted the Thai ambassador to Cambodia to deliver a speech in Phnom Penh in December 1953 in which he called for the formation of a Buddhist anticommunist bloc consisting of Cambodia, Laos, and Thailand (Thompson and Adloff 1955, 224). A Khmer Issarak (Free Cambodia) movement had been founded by Pock Khun, a retired Cambodian official, in Bangkok in 1940 shortly before hostilities between Thailand and Cambodia flared up over the former's desire to gain control of Siem Reap and Battambang provinces once more. The group grew significantly after the arrest of Son Ngoc Thanh in October 1945, when many of his supporters fled to Bangkok. Many of these new members came from the two disputed provinces and received support from Pridi Phanomyong and other prominent Thai politicians with family connections in the area. By 1947 Pock Khun had been replaced as leader by a certain Houl,[39] and the group were recognized as the "Free Cambodian Government" by Thailand in September of that year (Thompson and Adloff 1955, 173–174). Given the power bloc machinations of the time, it is quite likely that someone of Thanh's stature and political affiliation would have received some support from Thailand, South Vietnam, and the U.S. Central Intelligence Agency (CIA). Nevertheless, both he and his movement were to remain in the cold until the fall of the Cambodian monarchy in 1970, for Issarak groupings allied to the communists were making most of the running.

The most colorful of anticommunist rebels was Dap Chhuon (d. 1958), who had led a Thai-backed Issarak force since the late 1940s. By the end of the decade, he rallied to Sihanouk and was rewarded with the governorship of Siem Reap (Chandler 1991, 33, 101).[40] Dap Chhuon claimed to possess magical powers, rendering him invulnerable to injury from bullets and other sharp objects. This power derived from his custodianship of two famous "female" Buddha images that he had installed in a newly built shrine in the center of Siem Reap on being nominated minister of national security in 1957.[41]

Sihanouk and Buddhist Socialism

In the Constitution of May 1947, Sihanouk was styled "great righteous king" *(dhammika mahareach),* implying his role as protector of the Buddhist monastic order. However, quite apart from the fact that under the reestablished colonial system there could be no question of any Cambodian monarch's exercising the levels of authority apparent at certain points in the distant past, members of the Democratic Party were also anxious that any trace of absolutism was effectively neutralized within a constitutional framework. Thus, although Sihanouk often referred to himself as the king-monk, he tended to avoid any reference to the ancient Khmer concept of the god-king or Buddha-king *(buddharāja)* associated with paradigmatic monarchs such as Jayavarman VII.[42]

Chosen by the authorities as the least bad member of the royal family to succeed Monivong after his death in April 1941, Sihanouk had come to the throne under close French tutelage. Under the French influence he became more visible to his people than any other monarch had been in the past. He made frequent public speeches that managed to kill two birds with one stone, from the French perspective. In the first place, the imprimatur on official policy conferred by association with this highest expression of traditional ontology was very helpful in deflecting potential criticism, for, despite his many foibles, Sihanouk was regarded as a man of power by the vast mass of the population. Second, and arguably of more importance, Sihanouk's unenviable position ensured that he was discredited in the eyes of the anticolonial opposition, which clearly included influential sections of the newly radicalized Buddhist *sangha* (Chandler 1979, 213).[43]

Under the French the locus of kingly power in Cambodia had shifted decisively from the secular to the ritual and metaphysical realms.[44] The king was no longer required to worry about important matters such as taxation and national defense and could give himself up almost entirely to leisure and the conduct of elaborate ceremonial. In a sense, then, the colonial power merely reinforced the prevailing conception of the Southeast Asian palace as a place where the ruler assembled a vast collection of sacred persons and powerful objects such as heirlooms, weapons, elephants, incongruous animals, dwarves, and so on as a means of concentrating magic within the precincts of his dwelling place (Anderson 1990, 27). Sihanouk had inherited all of this, yet, as a beneficiary of a modern education conducted on rational lines, he shared many of the presuppositions of his European tutors. As far as Buddhism was concerned, his recorded table talk demonstrates that he endorsed the colonial power's languid assessment that it was "a sweet religion whose doctrines of resignation are marvelously suited to a tired people" (Armstrong 1964, 30). While such a sentiment could be said to point rather cynically to the manipulation of Buddhism as a form of social control, Sihanouk's understanding of recent history meant that he also appreciated that Buddhism could be employed to awaken a sense of nationhood. Evidence from the royal chronicles underlines that the historical record is full of kings who had spent some time as Buddhist monks prior to ascending the throne. But the ordination of a serving monarch is relatively rare. Sihanouk's temporary stay at Wat Preah Keo Morokat (Silver Pagoda) for three months following his ordination on July 31, 1947, is significant because it is reliably reported that this stay came about as the result of a vow that Sihanouk had made to his spiritual director, Ven. Keo Uch.[45] If his life were saved during the (short, as it turned out) Japanese occupation of Cambodia, he would become a monk (Try 1991, 167). The symbolism of the act nicely fuses the fate of the nation with the spirit of Buddhism. Sihanouk spent another brief period as a monk in 1963 after the International Court of Justice ruled that the ancient temple of Preah Vihear was in Cambodian territory. A colonial map of 1907 had put the boundary between Thailand and Cambodia along a watershed that passed through the middle of the temple (Lamb 1968, 169), but when news of the International Court's decision reached Phnom Penh, Sihanouk shaved his head (Keyes 1991a, 278n22).[46]

As the 1950s unfolded, Sihanouk became increasingly anxious to shrug off French tutelage. But his ability to exercise power was significantly frustrated by a hostile National Assembly and the depredations of various rebel groupings. His solution was to launch a crusade to break the link between the country and its colonialist overlord. In the process he would become the "father of Cambodian independence" and steal the fire from other nationalist organizations. The strategy was a success, not least because events in Vietnam meant that the

French grip on Indochina had begun to unravel decisively. Beyond the retention of a couple of economic assets, the French relinquished authority in October 1953, and in 1955 Sihanouk abdicated in favor of his father, Suramarit. Sihanouk could now enter the political arena as a private citizen. As *samdech preah upayuvareach*—the prince who has been king—he quickly formed a political movement, the People's Socialist Community (Sangkum Reastr Niyum), and, against a background of violence, intimidation, and straightforward fraud, the Sangkum won all of the seats in the National Assembly in the 1955 elections, with around 75 percent of the total vote.

To justify both his abdication and his continuing power, Sihanouk appealed to the well-known legend of Ta Trasak Pha'em, popularly supposed to have been a fourteenth-century ruler of Cambodia who overthrew the reigning dynasty with the consent of the people (Martin 1994, 63).[47] The king's name refers to his origin as a gardener from the Samre tribal people, who were famed for growing deliciously sweet cucumbers from seed received supernaturally. The reigning king was especially fond of the cucumbers and had ordered the gardener to kill any robber entering the garden. But overcome by a strong desire during the rainy season, when such foodstuffs are scarce, the king himself entered one night and was killed. The gardener, because of his skills and his obedience to the dead king's orders, inherited the throne. The allegory works on a number of levels, but by drawing on the legend, Sihanouk was able to replace the idea of rule by traditional quasi-divine right with a slightly more democratic and popular notion of exclusive political power. From around this time the affectionate term "*samdech euv*" (monsignor papa) came to be used as an epithet by Sihanouk's supporters, and he largely abandoned the use of Sanskrit or Pali-derived high-status terms, preferring a colloquial style of address. In this transmogrification the people became his "kinsmen" (Jacob 1986a, 124).

The political complexion of the Sangkum was expressed through its desire to create a Buddhist-oriented community *(sangkum niyum preah puthasasana)*, more commonly referred to as Buddhist socialism. Sihanouk stressed that the people's well-being depended on the good governance of a specifically Buddhist ruler. At the same time, he tried to repudiate the Marxist axiom that rulers represent vested interests that in time must be overcome by the will of the people. His "ramshackle ideology" (Chandler 1996, 199) stressed putatively traditional Khmer values—such as mutual help and the promotion of the welfare of the poor—linked to a full set of Buddhist principles. These would guide change while at the same time avoiding the pitfalls of state ownership and collectivization more usually associated with socialism. Sihanouk fully endorsed the concept of private property. For him, the redistribution of wealth would come about when the rich, pricked into action by Buddhist teachings, recognized their obligations to the poor. Redistribution of wealth, then, was premised on the traditional notion of merit making, through which the rich support the needy. A supporter nicely summarized the outlook when he observed that Sihanouk "regards all seven million Khmer as his fellow-members," adding that "we must guide ourselves to abolish bad customs such as those of looking down on and violating the people who earn their living serving us" (Bhi 1970, 87–88).

Sihanouk's instincts are in line with the scholarly consensus that although popular Buddhism does not promote the accumulation of capital (saving is seen as particularly unwise in the corrupt and unstable environments in which most modern Buddhists find themselves), its emphasis on merit making does stimulate the kind of spending that may act as a positive influence on economic activity.[48] Weber's insistence that the otherworldly character of Buddhism acts as a positive disincentive to economic effort is not entirely supported by the empirical evidence. The sponsorship of a religious ceremony by a wealthy individual does not increase social antagonism (see Taillard 1977, 78). On the contrary, the individual who assembles his wealth at the expense of his fellows effectively redistributes goods through ritualized merit-making activity that contributes to the social good. Having acknowledged this at the theoretical level, there is little evidence that such benefits accrued during the period in which Cambodia was supposed to have been operating under a system of Buddhist socialism.

One of the obvious features of the Buddhist socialism period was the proliferation of publications designed to inform the reading public, both in Cambodia and farther afield, of the nature of the Buddhist socialism project. The first issue of the journal *Sangkum* in June 1955 had used Buddhist karma theory to argue that the natural leaders of the country are the rich and powerful (Frings 1994b, 360). In another journal, *Kambuja,* which attempted to explain such doctrines to an essentially non-Khmer audience, Norodom Sihanouk (1965) developed the theme. In his lifetime, the Buddha had advised kings to concern themselves primarily with the happiness of the people, merchants to be honest and do good deeds for the poor, landlords to treat their tenants considerately, and highway bandits to reflect on the absurdity of their trade. In applying such teachings to the context of contemporary Cambodia, there are two basic areas of action. In terms of internal policy, Buddhist socialism is about fighting underdevelopment, eliminating social injustice, raising living standards, and promoting fraternity and concord. Peace, peaceful coexistence, territorial integrity, and independence, on the other hand, are the most important ingredients from the foreign policy perspective. For Sihanouk, all factors that frustrate these objectives—such as contempt, aggression, subversion, and interference—are the work of Māra, the Buddhist embodiment of evil. Among the Theravada texts mentioned in the article are the *Vasalasutta,* the *Tevijjasutta,* and the *Udāna,* but appeal is also made to Mahayana sources. However, the finest example of generosity is Vessantara, who was so imbued with this virtue that he gave away everything, including his wife and children. Sihanouk tells his readers that this princely figure was "a sort of Buddhist Karl Marx." Sihanouk also quotes with approval from the edicts of Aśoka, an ancient Indian ruler generally regarded as the prototypical Buddhist monarch. Sihanouk is particularly taken with Aśoka's insistence on the need for religious tolerance.[49] In this light, Marxism is a kind of religious system that should not be belittled. However, there are significant tensions between Marxism and Buddhism. The former teaches the overthrow of the strong, whereas the latter preaches righteous monarchical governance. This is why a "fusion of Buddhism-Marxism is so difficult" (Norodom Sihanouk 1965, 18). Marxism also preaches the expropriation of private property, a notion likewise incompatible with the Buddha's teaching. The adoption of Buddhist socialism would actually ensure that Cambodia was protected from the communist threat.[50]

There is little evidence that Sihanouk's political doctrines were influenced by detailed study. He had certainly been influenced by the spirit of Bandung, the Indonesian location of the Asian-African Conference in April 1955.[51] This explains his use of terms like "non-alignment" and "self-development," but as he admitted in 1967, he did not read widely and cared not "a rap about political economy, political science, or other subjects." In putting together his political ideology, he had merely studied "the veins of our nation" (Osborne 1994, 136). Because he regarded his political philosophy to be an authentic expression of the Cambodian character *(khmèritude),* he vigorously rejected the charge that it was in any way influenced by parallel developments in Burma, where a Burmese Way to Socialism had been adopted by the government in the early 1960s in what turned out to be a rather ineffective response to the twin challenges of ethnic conflict and communist insurgency. For Sihanouk, "We are socialists, but our socialism is inspired far more by Buddhist morality and the religious traditions of our national existence than by doctrines imported from abroad" (quoted in Zago 1976a, 112).

There had, of course, been a good deal of official communication between the two Buddhist states over the period. Son Ngoc Thanh, for example, had communicated with the Burmese prime minister U Nu in February 1956, asking him to persuade Sihanouk to take the Vietnamese threat seriously (Martin 1994, 46). More informally, many senior Cambodian monks are reported as having possessed radio sets that were tuned to broadcasts from Burma and Thailand through the 1950s (Steinberg et al. 1959, 147). Although Sihanouk's rejection of explicit borrowing may have been somewhat justified, comparison between the two movements is instructive. When Russian and Vietnamese communists visited Burma during its experiment with socialism, they found it difficult to recognize what was going on as socialism at all, given that so many indigenous factors appeared to be wrapped up in the overall package. Indeed, a vast majority of the Burmese population also failed to spot the socialist ingredient in the mix, preferring to regard it as simply another manifestation of traditional Buddhist values. Donald Smith (1965, 313) suggests that the Burmese failed mainly because they did not possess a prior sensitivity to ideology. On the contrary, they tended to see things in terms of practice, and for them the practice of Buddhist socialism was simply a form of meditation on a social theme. In many respects the same holds good for Cambodia under the Sangkum.

At the first meeting of the Cambodian chapter of the World Fellowship of Buddhists (WFB) at Wat Unnalom, Phnom Penh, on December 28, 1952, Ven. Lvi Em was made president.[52] The organization published a thrice-yearly bulletin, *La lumière bouddhique,* and by 1961 claimed 10,759 Cambodian members. In November of the same year it hosted the sixth conference of the WFB in Phnom Penh. In his inauguration address Sihanouk nailed his colors to the mast of a modernized and engaged Buddhism. For him the Buddha's teachings were compatible with the fundamental principles of rationality and scientific thought. The Buddha's missionary activities also underlined a concern for the alleviation of suffering within this world. Perhaps in reference to the centuries following the fall of Angkor, Sihanouk told his audience that this message had sustained and comforted the Cambodian people when "brute force and violence set out to annihilate them" (Norodom Sihanouk 1962, 27). Such remarks resonated with a rising tide of modernism, and he could count on a good level of support from the reformist faction within the Cambodian *sangha* itself (San Sarin 1998, 122). Although Ven. Chuon Nath, the Mahanikay *sanghareach,* had been a staunch royalist,[53] he does not appear to have stood in the way of attempts to co-opt monks in support of some aspects of the Sangkum project. As the most prominent monastic supporter of the People's Socialist Community, he encouraged monastic involvement in a variety of public works, including the building of reservoirs, canals, and so on. A photograph in *Sangkum* (August 1, 1965, 22) accompanying a story on road improvements, for instance, has the caption, "Monks within the framework of our Buddhist socialism participate in the work of nation building."[54] It is, however, unlikely that Chuon Nath was quite as enthusiastic when, in the same year, monks also participated in the opening ceremony of a state-controlled dance hall ten kilometers from Phnom Penh, an initiative admittedly designed to counteract the depravity of various privately owned floating dance clubs (Martin 1994, 79).

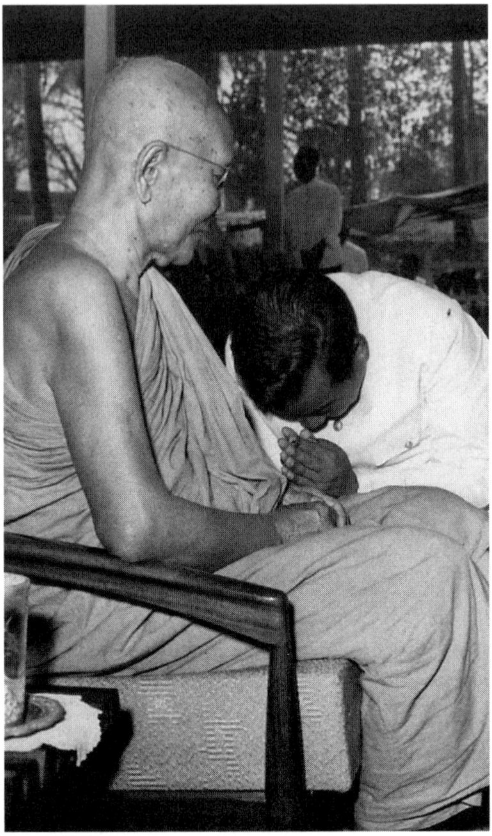

Prince Sihanouk and Ven. Chuon Nath—Wat Kompong Thmar, Kompong Thom Province, March 28, 1968.

The most obvious achievements of the Sangkum period are to be found in the expansion of both secular[55] and Buddhist education. Chau Seng is a crucial figure in this connection. On returning from studies in France in the mid-1950s, he began to take a detailed interest in the Cambodian school curriculum before being elected to the National Assembly. He eventually became secretary of state for education in Sim Var's administration of 1958.[56] By the late 1960s, three levels of Buddhist education existed. The first was represented by the Écoles Primaires de Pali.[57] There were around 570 of these, teaching both religious and secular subjects. The former comprised Pali grammar and translation from Pali into Khmer, as well as study of the *Dhammapada* commentary, the life of the Buddha, basic elements of Buddhist doctrine, and monastic discipline *(vinaya)*. Secular topics included mathematics, history, geography, sciences, civics, and basic agriculture. The duration of the first cycle was three years, the whole culminating in a national examination overseen and certified by the Ministry of Cults and Religious Affairs.[58] In 1955 the Lycée Bouddhique Preah Suramarit, or Buddhist High School, took over from the École Supérieure de Pali in Phnom Penh.[59] The number of students admitted to its second four-year cycle of study, all of whom had successfully completed the first level, was 150. The subjects taught were Pali, Sanskrit, Khmer, French, English, history, geography, mathematics, biology, hygiene, chemistry, physics, and general studies, which included civics, the history of Buddhism, Khmer civilization, and art. Similar institutions were also established in Battambang[60] in 1962 and in Siem Reap a few years later. The Université Bouddhique Preah Sihanoukreach was set up in Phnom Penh, and its first cohort was admitted in 1959. By the academic year 1961–1962 it was catering to 107 students—40 in the first year, 40 in the second, and 27 in the third (Ministre de l'Information 1962, 31). Its curriculum covered traditional and modern Western subjects divided theoretically into three cycles—lasting three, four, and three years, respectively, and roughly equivalent to bachelor's, master's, and doctoral levels of attainment. The first of these cycles had fourteen components, most of which had been studied at high school level but were complemented by in-depth study of Buddhist history, meditation, and doctrine. Other subjects included philosophy, cosmography, pedagogy, and modern Asian languages such as Hindi, Chinese, and Thai. In the second cycle, students could specialize in the study of religion, comparative philosophy, linguistics, or Khmer civilization. The final cycle appears to have been thesis based (Huot Tath 1962, 20–21).[61]

Less formal educational initiatives, often connected with Buddhist lay organizations, also flourished during the time. Prominent here were the Association of the Friends of the Buddhist Lycée, originally founded in 1949 to provide funds for students enrolled at the École Supérieure de Pali and to promote the study of Pali and Khmer.[62] In time its activities were complemented by those of the Association of Religious Students of the Republic of Cambodia (1970); the Association of the Buddhist Youth of Cambodia (1971), which organized Buddhist Sunday-school classes, radio broadcasts, and a variety of additional meetings; and the Chuon Nath Association (Zago 1976a, 111). A visitor to the northeast of the country in 1957 was surprised to find vigorous village schools that also put on well-attended evening classes for adults. When he asked a teacher why adults attended in such large numbers, he was told, "They like learning about independence, neutrality, and all that" (Pym 1959, 130). Wat Kom Pay in Battambang made courses available to monks and laypersons regardless of sex. The curriculum placed a strong emphasis on spiritual practice, and in the 1965–1967 period almost 800 students from all over Cambodia passed through the school. Its three-year program focused on the life of the Buddha and his teachings, culminating in a final year devoted to the study of meditation. Short textbooks related to these subjects were produced by the *chau adhikar* and distributed, thanks to the donations of wealthy laypersons. It seems that young girls and those suffering from ill health had not initially been allowed to enter the third year of study. However, this policy changed after the visit of a German woman who claimed to be a Theravadin nun from Burma and argued that girls had been allowed to meditate for a very long time in Burma itself.[63]

Throughout this period the monastic population had increased by 72 percent, from 37,531 in 1955 to 61,014 in 1967.[64] Yet the number of children entering monasteries over the same period declined sharply. This was partly due to the expansion of the state educational sector, combined with a lessening of the levels of prestige accruing to the monastic way of life. In the earlier part of the century, men who had experienced a period as a monk were regarded as having their "four rough edges" smoothed and, as such, were much sought after as marriage partners. The traditional scale of values was being eroded. Its place was taken by a vision of future success in a modern labor market, a situation reinforced by the state education sector's emphasis on the acquisition of vocational and technical skills. This might have been all very well had the economy taken off as had been optimistically predicted. In actual fact, economic mismanagement and corruption meant that the economy was stagnating, and many now well-educated young people were underemployed and increasingly disgruntled. The situation was not helped by the lingering influence of both Buddhist and European liberal attitudes toward education, which made these young people suspicious of what they perceived to be a pervasive Chinese-style focus on manual work (Ayres 2000, 53). The increasingly remote ideal was employment in a white-collar environment. Disaffection was also increasing in the monastic order. Many young men had entered the *sangha* during the Sangkum period to take advantage of its expanded educational provision and had prospered within the system. A significant proportion of these had also expected to take up secular careers at the end of their studies, but they were now confined to their monasteries, where they had ample leisure to discuss their grievances with like-minded individuals.

Frustration had, in fact, been a strong feature in the country's political life since the early Sangkum period. Sihanouk's capricious and foolhardy behavior was well understood in government circles. Indeed, he had become so irritated by what he regarded as factionalism within the administration that in July 1957, even though he was then serving as prime minister, he withdrew to a monastery near Angkor Wat for spiritual refreshment, handing over his duties on short notice to Sim Var (Corfield 1994, 22). Despite initial enthusiasm among the modernist segment of the *sangha,* Sihanouk was also rapidly losing the support of organized Buddhism. Chuon Nath, for example, had never been an entirely uncritical supporter, and disagreements between the two had broken out from time to time. But by the mid-1960s the patriarch had become quite agitated at a significant diminution in the numbers of functioning pagodas (Martin 1994, 72).[65]

It was not too long before the Buddhist credentials of the Sangkum were beginning to look like nothing more than window dressing. In many eyes, this is all they ever had been. Sihanouk's policies certainly seemed to involve regular violations of basic Buddhist ethics. Of significant concern was the establishment of a government casino, resulting in a generalized promotion of gambling and a number of high-profile suicides due to bankruptcy. A prophecy circulating at the time talked about the appearance of a gold-and-silver castle where people would fight for treasure until the country was consumed by war. Many interpreted this prophecy as a reference to the state casino. Most worrying was the alacrity with which the authorities turned to extrajudicial violence in dealing with their political opponents, even though Buddhist socialism was supposed to have been rooted in the principle of nonviolence. One of Sihanouk's most outrageous and bestial acts, one that particularly appalled Buddhists, was the public caging and subsequent execution on January 20, 1964, of Preap In, a Khmer Serei (Free Khmer) fighter who had been given a free pass to attend the National Congress in Phnom Penh. On Sihanouk's orders the execution was filmed and shown in cinemas for the next month (Corfield 1994, 34).[66] Rather surprisingly, Sihanouk never really tried to wriggle out of his responsibility for political assassination. Thus, in May 1968, following the summary execution of some thirty captured communist fighters in the northeast of the country, he admitted giving the orders: "I do not care if I am sent to hell. . . . And I will submit the pertinent documents to the devil himself"[67]—a statement that nicely combines both Buddhist and Christian understandings of the postmortem existence.

Following antigovernment demonstrations in the capital in August 1964, Sihanouk commented in a speech, "These demonstrations are the work of our pro-communist Khmers, who have not hesitated to press even our monks to parade in the streets, thereby infringing the fundamental discipline of their apostolate" (Norodom Sihanouk 1964, 98). Further acts of protest in which monks played a significant role are recorded in Pailin in early 1967, and Kiernan (1985, 231, 252) also reports that a monk from Prey Veng Province was arrested because of his sympathy for the communist cause the previous year. Around this period it was not unusual to find pictures of Mao Zedong decorating the cells of young monks, and Sihanouk became concerned that copies of Mao's *Little Red Book* were circulating in Phnom Penh monasteries (Chandler 1999, 79).

On April 25, 1967, around fifteen thousand students—believing that two prominent communists, Khieu Samphan and Hou Youn, had been murdered by the secret police—assembled in various schools and monasteries in Phnom Penh and Kandal Province. In late May and June, government forces drove around four thousand "rebels" from their homes in the Samlaut region of western Battambang Province. Forced to flee to the foothills of the Cardamom Mountains, the group was accompanied by monk supporters. One of the factors that may have fanned the rebellion was the high number of Khmer Krom in the area. With the escalating conflict in South Vietnam, many of them had come over the border, and by the end of 1966 a large number had relocated to Battambang. Perhaps as many as 12 percent of the group were monks. The Khmer Krom came from a quite different cultural, religious, and linguistic environment and were proud of their history of resistance to authority. The economic and security situation in and around Samlaut had been very poor before their arrival, and although it had been tolerated by locals, it infuriated the refugees. Eventually, Ven. Iv Tuot (1893–1968)—chief monk of Wat Po Veal, Battambang, and provincial *mekun*—negotiated an amnesty, and some of the "rebels" returned from their mountain hideout (Kiernan 1975, 27–35). Iv Tuot's ability to settle the matter seems to have derived from his activities during the period of Thai occupation in 1941–1946, when the monasteries under his control led resistance against attempts to draw inhabitants of the region into the Thai cultural sphere (Meyer 1969, 23).[68]

Against the background of the Chinese Cultural Revolution, some segments of the Cambodian Buddhist *sangha,* particularly those already disgruntled by a lack of prospects, were radicalized and turned to the anti-Sihanouk cause. Others, sometimes quite undeservedly, were accused as reactionary supporters of an oppressive and anti-Buddhist regime. In 1966 Prince Entaravong expressed concern about the increasing politicization of the *sangha,* particularly the Mahanikay, under Sihanouk's influence (Osborne 1979, 87). There is certainly evidence that some senior monks used sermons to extol the virtues of Sihanouk's policies. Indeed, Kalab (1976, 160) asserts that in the lead-up to the elections of that year none of the candidates running in her village held public meetings. Instead they "spent their time visiting the abbots in all the local monasteries," in the expectation that the abbots would use their influence to deliver the vote. On election day she also observed the lay meditation master leading all of his students to the polling station (Kalab 1990, 14).[69]

As early as the lead-up to the 1955 elections a certain Achar Chung, the son of a famous Cambodian poet, had been arrested for declaiming poems deemed to be insulting to Sihanouk (Chandler 1991, 81), but by the mid-1960s even something as apparently innocuous as the popular verse tale *Tum Teav* was viewed with suspicion.[70] A sort of Cambodian *Tristan and Isolde, Tum Teav* tells the story of a young and handsome sixteenth-century monk, Tum, and his fellow monk and friend Bic. One day in a village in Thbaung Khmum Province the beautiful young girl Teav overhears Tum, chanting in his lovely voice. She is smitten and sends Tum a message, revealing her feelings for him. Tum returns to his monastery, disrobes, and sets out with Bic to search for the girl.[71] Unknown to Tum, the province's powerful governor, Ârchoun, has contracted marriage between his son and Teav. When Tum finds Teav, their love is sealed even though Ârchoun is still intent on marriage. Meanwhile King Reamea has heard of Tum's wonderful voice and invites him to the palace to work as a court singer. The king is also looking for a queen, and his emissaries have identified Teav as the ideal candidate. When Teav arrives at the palace, Tum is called to perform a song. Recognizing his lover, Tum sings of his love for her. The king becomes very angry but eventually arranges for the pair to be married. However, Teav's mother devises a stratagem to lure Teav back to marry Ârchoun's son. Tum and Bic arrive in Thbaung Khmum and attempt to intervene. Ârchoun has Tum killed underneath a *bodhi* tree, and Teav, on discovering the body, cuts her throat and dies on top of her lover. The king has Ârchoun and seven generations of his relatives buried up to their necks and their heads severed by a plow. This tale of the passionate love between a girl and a monk, with subsidiary themes of official corruption, monastic persecution, and aristocratic brutality, was clearly too close to the bone for Sihanouk, and any newspaper featuring the story stood a fair chance of being closed down.

Despite his appeal to modernist values, Sihanouk had always been superstitious, and this feature of his character began to become more pronounced as the Sangkum began to unravel. Osborne (1979, 46) reports rumors that in the mid-1960s Sihanouk kept the ashes of a favorite daughter, Princess Kantha Bopha, who had died as a little girl, beside his bed as a charm. According to tradition, a sixteenth-century princess, Krapum Chhuk, had been devoured by a crocodile near Wat Vihear Thom, Srok Sambaur, Kratie Province (also known as the pagoda of the hundred columns). In time the *chedi* erected there became an important royal pilgrimage site. A female oracle able to communicate with the spirit of this princess was based there, and her services were regularly employed by both Sihanouk and his government. But when she conveyed a message she had received in 1969 to the effect that the prince's reign would come to an end before the year was out, she mysteriously disappeared (Meyer 1971, 88, 92).[72]

Sihanouk was badly shaken by a number of inauspicious events. In October 1968 an *achar* claimed to have been told by a local spirit of the location of a cache of treasure, including some magically charged objects, that would ensure that Sihanouk could live for 120 years. Excavations began at the site at Phnom Tet, Kompong Cham Province, but those involved were frightened away by the appearance from the mountain of three white phantom dogs (*Cambodge*, October 8, 1968). He was also affected by the death of twenty-four passengers killed in a train crash on the way to Sihanoukville, where he was due to inaugurate a new station. On withdrawing to a country estate, he found a flying squirrel, an inauspicious animal, asleep in his room. A group of monks were immediately convened to perform a lengthy exorcism, and the squirrel's tree was cut down. When Sihanouk left Phnom Penh for a holiday in France on January 5, 1970, he told well-wishers that he would be back in Cambodia by April in time to plow "the first furrow of the agricultural year."[73] When his mother, Kossamak, heard that he had been deposed by a coup on March 18,[74] she pulled *preah khan*, the sacred sword of Khmer kingship, from its scabbard and discovered that the blade was not gleaming but was actually tarnished a blackish color—a very bad omen. To cap it all, it was widely held that a white crocodile was seen wandering on the riverbank by the Royal Palace around March 23, and on October 9 of the same year a tree near the temporary crematorium *(men)* of the recently deceased Ven. Chuon Nath mysteriously crashed to the ground (Meyer 1971, 92, 95).

Shortly before losing power, Sihanouk admitted the failure of his Buddhist socialism. Yet he placed the blame for this failure on Buddhism itself. With its focus on nonviolence, neutrality, and compassion, Buddhist socialism had turned out to be insufficiently robust to deal with the corruption and international intrigues that Cambodia was obliged to face. His view had few supporters. As Bunchan Mul, a veteran of the Umbrella War and the new minister of cults and religious affairs, declared at a conference of Buddhist leaders in Seoul in November 1970, "[Sihanouk's] socialism was Buddhist in name only; it was diverted from its original correct path—in other words, the teachings of the Buddha were not adhered to. The ex-dictator merely sought to use Buddhism as an instrument for his personal Machiavellian, autocratic, and despotic policy."[75]

7

Liberation
The Religio-political Dimension

Origins of Khmer Communism

A Kampuchean People's Revolutionary Party (KPRP) history written in 1991 mentions a number of insurrections during the early 1930s, including the "uprising of two monks: Achar Mean and Achar Pring, etc." The Vietnamese sources on which these assertions are based acknowledge that there is no evidence that these Buddhist figures were inspired or organized by the Indochinese Communist Party (ICP). However, "the progressive thought content of these movements clearly expressed the revolutionary demands of Kampuchea in the new era" (quoted in Frings 1994a, 10–11). Having said that, after the ICP was founded in 1930, it certainly made sporadic attempts to encourage the fledgling Cambodian independence movement. Kiernan (1981, 161–162) mentions two young monks who were involved with the first known Khmer communist, Ben Krahom, in 1930. Another shadowy figure, a twenty-eight-year-old Khmer from Kampuchea Krom called Thach Chhoeun,[1] appears to have joined the ICP in 1932.[2] French intelligence sources noted that he was a monk in Takeo Province before becoming the Svay Rieng party chief at the end of the decade. These are exceptions in the colonial record. The authorities certainly took an interest in Chinese and Vietnamese communist cells in Cambodia, but their customary view of the Khmer as "nonchalant and undisciplined" (Morris 1999, 30–31) made it difficult for the authorities to believe that the Khmer could also be significant players. In the words of one intelligence officer, the Cambodians "only know how to gather together on pagoda feast-days and for funeral ceremonies, which are not very suitable for intrigues" (quoted in Kiernan 1981, 161). The struggle was certainly given a new momentum by the events of 1942, but organized communism had little substantial impact in the region until the end of the Pacific War. It had been "beaten to the punch by Son Ngoc Thanh" (Heder 1979b, 16). The earliest phase of the anticolonialist movement, then, was predominantly rightist in character. This would soon change, particularly after Son Ngoc Minh created the Unified Issarak Front (UIF)[3] in April 1950.

Also known as Achar Mean, Son Ngoc Minh had been a Pali teacher at Wat Unnalom, Phnom Penh, and had fled to Wat Yeay Tep, Kompong Chhnang Province, after the Umbrella War of 1942.[4] There he began to make contacts with an ICP cell in the nearby Thai-controlled northwestern provinces (Kiernan 1985, 44). Minh was admitted to the ICP in September 1945 and by March of the following year was commanding a Vietnamese-backed resistance group in Battambang that was designed to draw French forces away from southern Vietnam (Engelbert and Goscha 1995, 27n10, 33). At some stage he was joined by a fellow Khmer from Kampuchea Krom called Tou Samouth (aka Achar Sok). Another monk-teacher from Wat Unnalom, he had a reputation for oratory and had fled to the country soon after the monastery was hit during an attack from a U.S. B-29 warplane on February 7, 1945. Around twenty monks, plus other bystanders, appear to have been killed (Kiernan 1985, 48).

On April 17, 1950, the UIF organized the first National Congress of the Khmer Resistance at Wat Kompong Som Loeu in the southwest of the country. The conference was attended by some two hundred individuals, around half of whom appear to have been Buddhist monks.[5] In June of the same year a political school named after the hero of the Umbrella War, Hem Chieu, was established in the southwest (Steinberg et al. 1959, 107). That the UIF perceived itself to be connected with the earlier phase of monastic opposition to colonial rule seems clear from its sponsorship of a three-day Khmer Buddhist Conference in February 1951. At this event a play detailing the life of the monk-martyr Hem Chieu was performed, and somewhat later a group calling itself the Achar Hem Chieu Unit was held responsible for the assassination of the governor of Prey Veng in February 1953 (Kiernan 1985, 93–94, 130).

By 1951 the ICP had decided to split into three national parties for Vietnam, Laos, and Cambodia, respectively. The resulting Vietnam Workers' Party (VWP) quickly acknowledged a difficulty in recognizing the communist credentials of the Khmer People's Party (KPP), on the grounds that it was merely the "vanguard party of the nation gathering together all the patriotic and progressive elements of the Khmer population" rather than the "vanguard party of the working class."[6] This seems to suggest that the Vietnamese were disappointed by the Cambodians' less doctrinaire approach, which to some extent remained close to the Buddhist-inspired nationalism of the 1940s. The statement could also point to Vietnamese worries about the ideological purity of a party that admitted monastics. Certainly Vietnamese communists had previously maintained monastic contacts in Cambodia in the hope that they would come up with concrete support for the struggle, but by the time of the split they had become disillusioned. As a Viet Minh Committee for Phnom Penh document intercepted by the French and dated September 11, 1951, peevishly notes, "Contrary to what they promised us, the monks have not yet presented any Cambodian candidates [for the movement]" (quoted in Kiernan 1981, 167).

That other Unnalom-based monks were part of the movement is certain. Prom Samith, for example, seems to have been a member of a small party of monks who accompanied Minh on a preaching tour of monasteries in Kampuchea Krom in November 1951.[7] Their backgrounds ensured that the monasteries of the region became fertile recruiting grounds. In his sermons Minh linked the nationalist cause with the protection of Buddhism. As he put it, "The Cambodian race is of noble origin. It is not afraid of death when it is a question of fighting the enemy, of saving its religion, of liberating its fatherland. The entire race follows the Buddhist doctrine which places death above slavery and religious persecution." He also justified the struggle as one conforming to "the aspirations of the Buddhist religion" (quoted in Kiernan 1985, 93). Minh's insistence on the jeopardy facing Buddhism is a clear extension of Hem Chieu's earlier suspicion of French reforms to the *sangha*. The indirect reference to the need to fight a holy war, however, is new. The preaching tour had some success. An Issarak Buddhist Studies School was founded with an initial intake of thirty students, and a number of senior monks were reconciled as teachers (Kiernan 1985, 93). Just as important, a region with a prior history of millennial and anticolonial manifestations, as the events of 1922 eloquently testify, was being brought to the cause.[8]

By the end of 1952 the UIF claimed to be "boiling over with revolutionary spirit, with love for their country, race and religion." As Kiernan also notes, "Apart from the reference to Buddhism, this could have been a broadcast of 'The Voice of Democratic Kampuchea'" (1985, 75). By the early fifties an Issarak Monks' Association was active in twenty-four monasteries and had more than seven hundred active members in Prey Veng Province. However, it was difficult for monks to become full members of the KPP. As part of the "exploiting class," they had to serve a nine-month probationary period before earning full membership rights (Kiernan 1985, 94). Having said that, it is difficult to doubt that a positive connection existed between segments of the monastic order and the Issarak movement. A senior monk from Wat Mohamontrey, Phnom Penh, for example, is recently reported to have said, "If anyone was going to be killed for being a French spy, and if the monks knew about that, the monks would successfully request the pardon from the Issarak to release that person" (*PPP* 7/22, October 2–15, 1998).

The Cambodian communists of the mid-fifties had generally been pro-Vietnamese and Buddhist, but by the late sixties their perspective had changed significantly. What had happened? In September 1960 the Communist Party of Kampuchea (CPK) was finally established, with Tou Samouth as its secretary and Nuon Chea his deputy. Attendance at its first congress in the railway yards of Phnom Penh included relative newcomers like Ieng Sary and Saloth Sar (later known as Pol Pot). As we have already noted, Tou Samouth had undergone a traditional Buddhist, as opposed to a Franco-Khmer, training and education. Indeed, young party members like Saloth Sar may have been attracted to him for this very reason (Chandler 1999, 43). Tou Samouth's mysterious death in July 1962 had the consequence of leaving the party bereft of any significant figure connected with higher levels of traditional learning and may have been one of the factors that led to the extreme anticlericalism of the Democratic Kampuchea period (1975–1979). It is certainly the case that after Tou's disappearance few senior figures in the party could trace an unbroken lineage back through the old ICP to the events of 1942.[9]

Whatever the nature of post-1962 Cambodian communism, the break with tradition did not come abruptly. While working as acting secretary of the party's Central Committee, Saloth Sar gave a number of seminars in Phnom Penh in late 1962, shortly before escaping into the maquis. Sok Chuon, a Buddhist monk for ten years at the time, remembers the future Pol Pot's speaking persuasively to an audience of fifty—thirty of whom were monks from three monasteries in Phnom Penh—about the "new society." Sok also recalls Saloth Sar's noting that the Buddha had never sold anything (Chandler 1999, 62). Pol Pot claimed to have spent six years in a monastery, two of them as a monk, although most informed commentators have regarded this as something of an exaggeration. The likelihood is that he served a year as a novice, probably around the age of six, at the royalist Wat Botum in Phnom Penh. It seems that his home village of Prek Sbauv, Kompong Thom Province, did not have a monastery, although there was one upriver. Surprisingly, given the poor rural coverage of the order, it belonged to the Thommayut. This, plus the fact that one of his cousins was a favorite of King Monivong's, probably explains his eventual connection with Wat Botum (Chandler 1999, 43).

Saloth Sar's early exposure to Buddhist education had had a positive impact. In his earliest political writings—which date from 1952, when he was a student in Paris—Saloth Sar visualized a reconstituted Cambodia in which a "democratic regime will bring back the Buddhist moralism because our great leader Buddha was the first to have taught (democracy)."[10] Signing himself the "original Khmer" *(khmer daom),* the author also argued that the French-backed Cambodian monarchy was "inimical to Buddhism," for it had placed itself "above religion." By contrast, the Buddha, although the son of a king, had left his family home "[to be a] friend to all men, and to teach people to love one another." Such ideas suggest that, at this period, Saloth Sar shared the same Buddhism-tinged thought universe as Son Ngoc Minh and Tou Samouth.

Somewhat paradoxically for someone later accused of crimes against humanity, Pol Pot came over as a polite and reasonably cultured man. One of his students, for example, remembered him being able to recite Verlaine and Rimbaud by heart (Martin 1994, 108). Yet when he opted for the life of a maquisard, he had no difficulty in renouncing his former life. As Chandler (1999, 6) perceptively comments, Pol Pot had already absorbed the ideals of "disciplined personal transformation, rebirth and enlightenment" from his Buddhist background. His frequent attacks on individualism and—rather more puzzlingly, given subsequent events—his emphasis on kindheartedness may derive from the same source.

Another prominent figure in the CPK, Ta Mok, had also been a monk until he left the order to join the Khmer resistance soon after the Umbrella War disturbances (Thayer 1997, 22).[11] One of the most notorious of all Khmer Rouge commanders, he was born with the name "Oung Choeu" in Pra Keap village, Tram Kak District, Takeo, around 1926. He entered the local monastery around the age of eight, at some stage transferring to Wat Mohamontrey in Phnom Penh. After disrobing, Ta Mok joined the Issaraks. By 1949 he was playing a leading role in the movement.[12] Although Ta Mok had married in the intervening years, in 1954 he appears to have been reordained at Wat Kat Phluk, Kampong Speu Province. There is conflicting evidence on his contacts with organized Buddhism following this event, but Heder (1997, 125) suggests that from there he went to Phnom Penh, where he taught monks and obtained an elementary Pali school degree. It was as a student at the Pali High School that Ta Mok met Pol Pot for the first time, probably in the early 1960s (Kiernan 1996, 87). It is also probably around this time that Ta Mok engaged in heated disputes with some of his fellow monks over the nature of Buddhism. He argued that Buddhist merit-making tended to express itself in socially unproductive forms, such as the construction and enhancement of monastery buildings. In his view, donations would be better used for the building of roads and the provision of other public services (see *PPP* 8/6, March 19–April 1, 1999). It is conceivable that the Buddha would have shared his motivation.

Evidence concerning the early life of Hu Nim, minister of information in Democratic Kampuchea before his execution in July 1977, is instructive. In his forced confession,[13] he recalls that as a small boy he was obliged to live in the local pagoda after his father died. The chief monk brought him up as his own son and provided his first access to education. In the early 1950s he moved to Phnom Penh for further studies, lodging at Wat Unnalom. While there he became involved with "the contemptible Son Ngoc Thanh" (Chandler et al. 1988, 234; see also Chandler 2000, 64–65). Now, Vens. Khiev Chum, Pang Khat, and So Hay were among the Phnom Penh–based recruiting sergeants of Thanh, and Hu Nim's confession suggests that they recruited another senior CPK figure, Chan Chakrei, while he was still a monk attached to the Buddhist Institute (Chandler et al. 1988, 298).[14] There was nothing problematic about this at the time, for Thanh and Minh's Issarak groupings cooperated in the early fifties. However, after the Geneva Agreements on Indochina of 1954, Thanh founded the explicitly rightist Khmer Serei with American support, while around the same time the leftists disbanded, with many prominent members, including the Unnalom monk Prom Samith, decamping to Hanoi. By the 1960s the CPK and the Khmer Serei were vying for influence at the main monasteries in Phnom Penh, but "considerable cross-over between the two movements" remained.[15] Early monastic links with Thanh's grouping, then, were not deemed especially problematic. However, by the beginning of the Democratic Kampuchea period such connections had become highly dangerous.

Despite its early affection for Buddhism and the fact that Cambodian communism had formed a continuum with the Buddhist nationalism of the forties, by the 1960s the party was beginning "to shed its Buddhist mantle" (Keyes 1994, 55). A party document that was probably written as the basis for discussions between Pol Pot and the Vietnamese in Hanoi in June 1965 refers to the approximately 70,000 monks in the country, of whom "c. 60,000 are young and strong." Such monks reportedly had a feudal influence over the people, but "the revolution must understand this problem in depth in order to win over the monks and transform them into an important political force" (quoted in Engelbert and Goscha 1995, 130). The document particularly commends the potential for revolutionary activity among monks with a peasant background. It is difficult to discern whether the Cambodians understood the exercise in an entirely cynical light, but in his written response to the document, Le Duan, the general secretary of the Communist Party of Vietnam, advised, "In Kampuchea, if we are going to build up the [national democratic] front in the villages, then we have to join with religious [forces; otherwise] . . . the bourgeoisie class will use religion in order to draw the peasants away from us. . . . [W]e must think carefully in order to have a correct religious policy" (quoted in Engelbert and Goscha 1995, 130). This seems to reflect concerns about Sihanouk's own manipulation of Buddhism during the Sangkum period. It also needs to be remembered that the Vietnamese had had no real contact with Theravada Buddhism and, in any case, were disillusioned with the supposedly progressive elements in the Cambodian Buddhist order. In this context the recommendation manifests the lack of understanding, the moral insensibility, and the cynicism toward organized Buddhism that came to dominate the subsequent history of the CPK.

Even before the outbreak of the civil war that would end the short-lived Khmer Republic (1970–1975), the CPK was pointing to the economic burden that so many unproductive monks placed on the country. Not only were they leeches upon society, but they also taught the doctrine of karma, which underpinned the belief in "natural inequality" (Hinton 1998, 110) and encouraged the laity to passively accept the status quo. The traditional concept of wisdom had to be redrawn. In the past, a wise man was someone who understood and agreed that karma upholds the social hierarchy. In the future, wisdom would be determined by peasant virtues, such as how much one knew about growing rice. Similar attitudes certainly underlay the French characterization of the Khmer as "lotus-eaters," yet one should not assume that the CPK simply inherited their anticlericalism from European revolutionary sources. An equally vigorous concern over aspects of the monastic life is a recurring theme in the history of Asian cultures. The Zen saying "One day without work, one day without food," for example, expresses a deeply rooted East Asian suspicion of aspects of the religious life.

In the context of the civil war such arguments had an explanatory power. The fact that some monks went over to the side of the communists was further enhanced by Sihanouk's support for the movement as part of a united front against Lon Nol. Indeed, a typical cadre of the time was described as someone who had been a monk for five years, then a low-level official in local government, before becoming a Khmer-language inspector at a pagoda school (Thion 1993, 13–15). Evidence also suggests that monks and ex-monks were particularly successful in recruiting peasants, who seem to have been more convinced by their sermons than by the propagandizing of more explicitly communist cadres. It is possible that without these monastic recruitment officers the communist path to victory would have been much harder to achieve (see Kiernan 1989, 28).

Khmer Republic

Like Sihanouk before him and the Khmer Rouge who followed soon after, Lon Nol dreamed of a revivified Cambodia that would lead the nations of the region into an era of peace and prosperity rivaled only by the civilization of Angkor.

This would entail the creation of a greater Cambodia in which the Khmer minorities in Thailand and Kampuchea Krom would be reunited with Cambodia itself, for "[There] are no more Khmer Krom, Khmer Kandal, Khmer Islam, Khmer Loeu, Lao Khmer or Siamese Khmer. . . . There are only Khmer,"[16] and, as Lon Nol expressed it in a pamphlet, "Neo-Khmèrisme will contribute to prolong the Buddhist era for five thousand years" (Lon Nol 1972). In this connection Lon Nol was anxious to demonstrate that Buddhism was more than a match for Christianity and Islam, so he was not averse to studying their missionary strategies in an attempt to enhance the international standing of Buddhism and its particular association with the Khmer people.[17] This also led him to develop a bizarrely racist ideology. Scholars had for many decades regarded the Mon-Khmer family of languages as crucial to the understanding of Southeast Asian culture, but Lon Nol, by an absurd rearrangement of the term, now came to believe in the messianic mission of a so-called Khmer-Mon race. To this end he established a pseudoscholarly journal and the grandly named Khmer-Mon Institute. Indeed, one of the first delegations to be sent abroad by the new government was headed by the institute's director, the prominent antiroyalist Keng Vannsak (Khing Hoc Dy 1990, 2:72). It went to Burma, apparently to discover the original form of Khmer-Mon dress (Martin 1994, 130).

In late 1970 two factions emerged within the government. One, the Republican group, was linked to the personality and patronage of Prince Sisowath Sirikmatak. The other was associated with Son Ngoc Thanh, who had his base in the Dangrek Mountains along the northern border with Thailand. The Dangrek group appealed to members of the old Democratic Party, but it also gathered support in Buddhist circles. One of its prominent figures, Ven. Khieu Chum, had been a veteran of the Umbrella War and a long-standing associate of Thanh's (see chapter 6). In early March 1971, Khieu Chum chaired a committee designed to write a republican manifesto and bring about a rapprochement between Lon Nol and Son Ngoc Thanh (Corfield 1994, 108).[18] Sirikmatak's government subsequently fell, and Son Ngoc Thanh was appointed prime minister in March the following year.

Khieu Chum appears to have absorbed French attitudes about the "lotus-eating" Cambodians. His concern about their lack of perseverance and their poorly developed work ethic is nicely illustrated by a sermon of the 1950s in which he reworked a traditional poem about weaving to make the weaver start his work early in the morning rather than the "cool afternoon" mentioned in the original (Yang Sam 1987, 43). However, Khieu Chum's more explicitly political views were expressed only in works written after the fall of the monarchy.[19] He also became a frequent speaker on National Radio around this time. The essence of his message was that Cambodia should embrace democratic republicanism because it represented the basic political teaching of the Buddha. Quite apart from the fact that the country had suffered from "thousands of years of absolutism, arbitrariness and tyranny,"[20] Cambodians should reject the monarchy on the grounds that the institution had previously been repudiated by the Buddha when, leaving his family home, he embraced the ascetic life. The regime also pointed to the Buddha's own preference for republican forms of governance, such as that operating among the Vajjians in his own lifetime (see Harris 1999b, 3).

Lon Nol interpreted his battle with the Vietcong and the Khmer Rouge in apocalyptic terms. On May 11, 1970, he declared that "the current war in Cambodia is a religious war" (Corfield 1994, 101), and while recuperating from a mild stroke in Honolulu in 1971, he claimed that he wanted to draw together the Buddhists of Southeast Asia into an anticommunist alliance (Chandler 1991, 212). This desire to strengthen Buddhism both within the country and throughout Asia was given added resonance by the prophetic slogan "If communism comes, Buddhism will be completely eliminated." Lon Nol appears to have seen himself in the role of a Buddhist messiah.[21] The enemy, on the other hand, were atheists and devils *(thmil)*.[22] The attribution effectively deprived the communists of personhood and meant that the normal requirements of Buddhist ethics did not apply. They could be killed without compunction.

Others also suffered as a consequence of the religious war rhetoric. According to provisions of the treaty of August 11, 1863,[23] between Norodom and Napoleon III, Catholics were the only Christians to be tolerated in the Protectorate, yet negativity toward Catholicism was widespread. The murder of the French priest Father Barrea, the pastor of Moat Krasas, in 1867 has already been mentioned (see chapter 5). In the early years of the twentieth century the governor of Battambang had also forbidden Buddhists to use a recently established Catholic hospital (Tauch Chhuong 1994, 35). Much of this negativity appears to have been based on the belief that the church and colonial rule were two sides of the same coin. However, following the Franco-Thai Treaty of April 1907, which ceded the northwestern provinces back to French control, followers of the old Thai governor, Phya Kathathorn, supposedly pillaged the Vietnamese Christian village of Ta Om (Tully 1996, 121–123). The event coincided with an increase in Vietnamese migration to Cambodia. Many of these migrants were Catholic converts who had been encouraged to exploit newly emerging economic opportunities,[24] although their displacement may also have been a way of covering up the lack of progress in missionary work among Cambodians themselves (Khy Phanra 1977, 48). Earlier anti-Vietnamese feeling grew as the popular imagination now forged a link between Catholicism and Vietnam.

By the 1960s, Catholicism was regarded as a "religion of the foreigner" *(sasana barang)*.[25] It had made little effort to integrate itself into Cambodian society. French and Vietnamese were its principal languages, and only a handful of priests were capable of preaching in Khmer. The majority of its adherents lived in so-called Catholic villages on the banks of the Mekong and its tributaries. Almost as soon as Lon Nol seized power, a call to "chop down the Vietnamese" *(kap yuon)* began to spread abroad. Two Catholic churches in Phnom Penh were attacked by mobs on March 13, 1970, and the racial hatred rapidly degenerated into bloodlust. On April 13 around eight hundred Vietnamese men were rounded up and shot dead at Chruy Changvar (Corfield 1994, 68, 96). Arson and rape were also widespread, and the government actively contributed to the mayhem by ordering the closure of all private schools, most of which were Catholic and served pupils of Vietnamese origin. By the time the pogroms had subsided a few months later, only some seven thousand of the original sixty-five thousand Catholics remained in Cambodia. A significant proportion had been killed, and many of the rest had fled to Vietnam. On May 11, 1970, Lon Nol cynically stated, "For the present our Vietnamese brothers will have to return to South Vietnam. . . . Houses abandoned by [them] . . . will be taken care of by their neighbors. . . . We must not do anything that contradicts Buddhism" (as quoted in Caldwell and Tan 1973, 442–443). Ironically, Catholics living in the zones already liberated by the Khmer Rouge were unharmed.[26]

When Cambodia was declared a republic on October 9, 1970, Lon Nol sent a message to the patriarchs of the two monastic orders, assuring them that "the present radical change of political rule is not meant to be prejudicial to Buddhism, which remains the state religion as it has up till now" (*Agence Khmère Presse,* October 9, 1970). Lon Nol also argued that the message of the Buddha was in accord with the Universal Declaration of Human Rights. To emphasize this point, he had the following inscription placed on the republic's monument outside the Royal Palace: "Buddhism teaches us to be honest, to reject selfishness and to promote mutual assistance. Above all, it is a symbol of liberty, equality, fraternity, progress and well being" (Yang Sam 1987, 50).

The regime used pliant monks to counteract communist propaganda in the countryside to very good effect, particularly in the provinces of Pursat, Svay Rieng, and Takeo (Corfield 1994, 93). Yet the *sangha*'s support was not a foregone conclusion. The deep-rooted connection between the *sangha* and the state, traditionally embodied in the person of the king, ensured that many monks were very suspicious about the new turn of events. For obvious reasons, members of the aristocratic and monarchist Thommayut were deeply affected by the fall of Sihanouk. It seems that a significant segment of the order had planned a protest march in Phnom Penh immediately after the coup. The protest was prevented only by the swift intervention of Ven. Huot Tath, superior of the Mahanikay (Yang Sam 1987, 42). However, some monks in Kompong Cham Province did join popular demonstrations for the king's return (Ponchaud 1989, 170). Lon Nol's relations with senior members of the monastic hierarchy were especially problematic. It was only with great difficulty and after consistent pressure that he was able to get a statement condemning the Vietcong "aggressors" from the two patriarchs. However, these two dignitaries refused to give their support to a proposal for a change of name for the Université Bouddhique Preah Sihanoukreach (Meyer 1971, 81).

In late March 1970, China and Vietnam proposed the formation of a National United Front of Kampuchea (FUNK) to bind both Sihanouk and the Communist Party of Kampuchea into the fight to oust Lon Nol. FUNK's political program was accepted at a congress in Peking on May 3, 1970. Among other things, it accused the republican regime of vilifying and distorting the views of "honest intellectuals [and] monks." It also made it clear that the future of the country was linked with the protection and continued prospering of Buddhism, which was to remain the state religion after FUNK had regained control. Other religions—Islam, Catholicism, Protestantism, Cao Dai, and tribal religions specifically named in the program—would also be guaranteed their freedom (Caldwell and Tan 1973, 374, 378). This further polarized the *sangha*. Some monks certainly supported the change in governance, some remained dyed-in-the-wool monarchists, while others had already joined the communists.

As the civil war began to rage, more and more monks displaced by the fighting began to congregate in the monasteries of the main cities. Monasteries in Phnom Penh, in particular, were packed with young men, many of whom were seeking to avoid military service. The overcrowding made it very difficult to engage in traditional monastic pursuits, but educational services were maintained. However, rapidly deteriorating economic conditions meant that there was great pressure to shift the emphasis of the monastic curriculum toward the acquisition of relevant skills. It seems that some of the young monks responsible for these new pressures, such as the demand to have more science in the curriculum so that monastic qualifications would be more in line with those of secular graduates, were working for the communists.

More demonstrations involving monks took place in October 1971. It is difficult to be certain about their political affiliations, but by early 1972 a large swath of monastic opinion was growing uncomfortable about the blatant corruption of the regime. The annual congress of religious dignitaries of both orders, held in January 1972, had passed a motion to the effect that monks should avoid involvement in political matters and that this position should be enshrined in the country's new constitution (Zago 1976b, 113).[27] On the surface, then, it seems odd that both Buddhist patriarchs attended a press conference given by Professor Keo An at the Phnom Penh Law Faculty on February 25, 1972, at which he denounced both Lon Nol and Sirikmatak (Corfield 1994, 126). This may have been an example of political naïveté, for several months later Ven. Huot Tath was striving for impartiality in a letter he wrote to all parties, urging reconciliation (Corfield 1994, 169). In 1973, in a feeble attempt to assuage monastic criticism, the government abolished the title of *samdech* for civilians. Henceforth it was to be a purely monastic title (Martin 1994, 141).

Like most Khmer, Lon Nol retained a strong belief in the efficacy of magic. Some have sought to explain this belief as a function of his ancestry. Certainly his grandfather was a Khmer Krom from Tay Ninh, a region well known for its "mystical ideas" (Corfield 1994, 1). Soon after the coup, Lon Nol called on those trained in the occult arts to use their powers to help defeat the enemy, for the "Mon-Khmer race . . . has always had the magic key to victory in combat" (quoted in Chandler 1991, 205). To protect Phnom Penh, he ordered specially blessed sand to be sprinkled around its perimeter by helicopter (Corfield 1994, 130).

A number of magical squares *(katha)* originally consecrated by an old Mahanikay *sanghareach*[28] were used as a mold for the mass production of many more. These were distributed to government troops. Lon Nol's 1970 decree that soldiers cut their "skin in order to allow the Buddha to enter . . . [their] body and bring strength" is a clear reference to the use of these amulets (Becker 1986, 138).[29] Old monks were also drafted for the production of magical shirts and the like, and the Thai government seems to have cooperated by donating a consignment of red and yellow protective scarves *(kansaeng yantra)* as a form of military aid (Meyer 1971, 90).

Lon Nol suffered a stroke in early 1971 and never ruled effectively again. A superstitious populace—discovering that he had lost the use of his right arm, which he used to sign the order to depose Sihanouk—took this as a bad omen. Much of his time was now spent listening to the military advice of Buddhist holy men who promised supernatural solutions to the conflict. One of these, a monk named Om Mam Prum Mani, claimed to be an incarnation of Jayavarman VII (Chandler 1991, 205). By 1972 Lon Nol is said to have been personally spending around US$20,000 a month on astrological consultations (Corfield 1994, 41).[30]

A number of Buddhist prophecies circulated in the Khmer Republic. One talked of "[a] *bodhi* tree with flat stump, the roots do not grow . . . a poisonous cobra hides quietly at the same place" (quoted in Yang Sam 1987, 51). This example is a clear reference to the elimination of Buddhism, and in retrospect it is easy to identify the cobra with the Khmer Rouge. Kiernan (1976, 374) also mentions a widespread rumor that one of the great heroes of the past, such as Po Kambo or *neak tā* Khleang Moeung, would soon be returning to take part in the war.[31] A millennial tinge may also be discerned in the fact that some Buddhists constructed a wooden palace near Phnom Penh to act as the headquarters of the coming Buddha, Maitreya.

In fact the upsurge in interest in prophecy has its roots a little further back in Cambodian history. The twenty-five hundredth anniversary of the Buddhist religion, Buddha Jayanti, had occurred in 1956–1957, with lavish celebrations held throughout the Buddhist world. Now, the Buddha Jayanti had been widely regarded as a time of crisis in the five-thousand-year-long life of the *dhamma,* because from that point onward, degeneration would quicken. In Cambodia a series of predictions of the Buddha *(Buddh Daṃnāy),*[32] describing the unfolding events at the time, had circulated for at least a century. On the basis of internal evidence, de Bernon (1994, 84) has reckoned the *Buddh Daṃnāy*'s date of composition to be in the mid-1860s.[33] After a rehearsal of the legendary history of Cambodia—which includes an anachronistic reference to the visit of Buddhaghosa around 1072 CE when he is supposed to have secreted a corpus of sacred writings on Phnom Kulen—the text tells of the country's oscillating fortunes. Two and a half millennia after the Buddha, the city of Kaṃbujā was to be totally annihilated by war, the only living survivors being four mendicant monks, four great hermits, and one solitary *achar.* At that time the blood at the *quatre bras* (i.e., Phnom Penh) would rise level with an elephant's belly. However, shortly before this occurred, a bodhisattva called Preah Pād Dhammik—prompted by natural calamities, the spiritual pride of lay Buddhists, and the fact that monks no longer follow the correct rules for wearing their robe and carrying the begging bowl[34]—would enter solitary meditation in a secret place. After the Armageddon, Indra would send Viśvakarman to find Preah Pād Dhammik. Viśvakarman, disguised as a Chinese stranger carrying sacred books on his back, would find him and persuade him to return to the city of Kaṃbujā. Preah Pād Dhammik would order that the hidden texts of Phnom Kulen be retrieved and that the sacred cow *(preah go)* and the Crystal Buddha *(preah kaev),* which had once been taken to Ayutthaya as booty, be restored to Cambodia. Preah Pād Dhammik would then preach to men, gods, and animals; all illness and suffering would disappear; and men would be able to marry fifty wives. Finally he would consecrate two kings, who would both follow the ten royal precepts,[35] to rule over the country. The popularity and influence of the *Buddh Daṃnāy* are demonstrated by the fact that Lon Nol himself drew heavily upon it in his 1970 pamphlet entitled *Chambang Sasana* (The religious war).

Buddhism in the Civil War of 1970–1975

Following the coup, three prominent communists—Khieu Samphan, Hou Youn, and Hu Nim—issued a statement in support of Sihanouk on March 26, 1970. It was addressed "to the Samdech Chiefs of the two Buddhist sects, to venerable monks at all levels, to all our dear countrymen," and pointed out that "monks at all levels . . . are compelled to serve the policy of the reactionaries" (quoted in Caldwell and Tan 1973, 398). A follow-up Declaration of Patriotic Intellectuals—a group that included Khieu Samphan, Son Sen, and Pol Pot—was issued from the liberated zone on September 30, 1971. It stated that monks had previously "enjoyed freedom to exercise their religious rites in peace, freedom to do their studies and *to lead the population toward the road of independence, neutrality and peace*" [italics mine]. The declaration laments that monasteries in the Lon Nol zone have been redeployed as barracks, arms depots, and military posts: "What a pity to see monks being forced to leave their places of worship and the statues of the Buddha. . . . These traitors have even tried to force monks to participate in anti-religious and anti-national elections. . . . They force monks to accompany them in their propaganda activities" (quoted in Caldwell and Tan 1973, 418–419). A particularly vivid example of the latter was the pressure placed on Ven. Huot Tath, patriarch of the Mahanikay, to "excommunicate" Sihanouk for collaboration with the communists.[36]

Although statistics relevant to all areas of recent Cambodian history are remarkably unreliable, it is clear that many monasteries were put out of action or significantly damaged once the civil war erupted. According to one source, 997 monasteries, about a third of the total for the country as a whole, were destroyed from March 1970 to June 1973, with around 70 percent of this figure meeting their fate in 1972.[37] The vandalism has often been uncritically ascribed solely to the communists, a view reinforced by the movement's own sporadic propaganda campaigns. Their self-congratulatory claim that 90 percent of all monasteries, the greatest concentration falling in the eastern and southwestern zones, had been demolished, however, was massively inflated. Another factor not to be forgotten when assessing the situation is that the 310,000 tons of bombs dropped by the Americans in the short period between autumn 1972 and August 1973 (Kiernan 1989, 5) undoubtedly had a major impact on the infrastructure of the provinces close to the border with Vietnam.[38]

Whatever the true figure, both government and opposition troops found monastery compounds to be ideal military bases because they could be easily defended. The Khmer Rouge and the Vietcong also believed that monastic compounds enjoyed another advantage in that a notionally Buddhist government could be expected to respect religious sites. The Lon Nol regime was, after all, supposed to be fighting a holy war, and this must have been one of the reasons why the Khmer Rouge established themselves in the heavily symbolic area around Angkor at an early point in hostilities. However, the communists' assumption that the government would be reluctant to launch attacks on such locations was misplaced. According to Kiernan (1989, 7), U.S. intelligence knew as early as 1970 that many of the "training camps" that the Lon Nol regime had asked the United States to strike by air were functioning monasteries. Certainly, some monasteries must have been used for political meetings, but community gatherings have been one of their traditional functions and no one at this stage could have foreseen the way that events would develop as the decade unfolded.

Wat Sokkharam in Bat Doeung village, some sixteen kilometers from Phnom Penh, had been consecrated by Sihanouk only two years before. It was badly damaged in December 1971 by a napalm attack in which a young monk was killed and two others were injured. The government blamed the outrage on the Vietcong, but when the chief monk was interviewed by Serge Thion shortly after the incident, he attributed responsibility to the forces of Lon Nol.[39] The monk also asserted that the Khmer Rouge taught respect for religious beliefs at evening study sessions held at the monastery. It seems certain that these sessions involved an element of compulsion, yet they were often opened by monks chanting Buddhist verses before the microphone was passed over to officials whose speeches ended with slogans such as "Long live the National Front of Kampuchea presided over by Samdech Norodom Sihanouk" and "Long live the Buddhist religion." At a Front congress in the same year, attended by around 350 chief monks, the abbot of Wat Ang-Pralung claimed that attacks by Lon Nol's planes made it impossible for monks to fulfill their religious duties. He also contrasted the Front soldiers' respect for Buddhism with the profanity and contempt of Lon Nol's forces. The abbot of the Wat Ang Talek, a Thommayut monastery in the Samrong Thong District, confirmed these sentiments, talking of the "yoke of the demon Lon Nol" (Thion 1993, 5–6).

When the rebels liberated rural areas from government control, many monks fled, but there was little uniformity of treatment for those who remained. A 1973 broadcast reported that "in the vast and beautiful liberated zone . . . culture, arts and national traditions are developing splendidly among the large popular masses" (quoted in Edwards 1999, 390).[40] The belief that monks from a peasant background had revolutionary potential meant that they were redefined as "patriotic monks" (Chantou Boua 1991, 230). In June 1973 they were mobilized through the creation of a Patriotic Monks' Association *(preah song snaha cheat),* its members effectively constituting a new ecclesiastical hierarchy. In Komchay Meas District, Prey Veng, for instance, the association claimed a membership of around seven hundred monks from thirty-four monasteries (Kiernan 1985, 345–346). At this stage there was "no ideological commitment to the abolition of Buddhism in the mind of some cadres" (Chantou Boua 1991, 233), but the association established new committees to handle the social, economic, and cultural affairs of the *sangha*. Such committees severely curtailed the time available for more traditional monastic pursuits, such as study and the performance of ritual, and encouraged mutual surveillance. Monks were also expected to become economically active, usually through growing food, the surpluses of which could be supplied to the troops. A special cadre, called a *kank sang*, usually maintained the discipline of monastic work parties (Ponchaud 1978, 148).

Younger monks were selected for reeducation, paramedical battleground duties, and military service, leaving only the odd elderly monk behind in the monastery. Because their disciplinary code precluded the taking of life, some monks abstained from catching crabs and snails in the paddy fields. This placed them at a significant dietary disadvantage over their less observant fellows. Observant monks also had great difficulty in preserving traditional links with the laity, not least because Khmer Rouge propaganda now discouraged villagers from inviting monks to perform rites of one sort or another. In consequence, the economic supports of the monasteries disintegrated, a situation exacerbated by the requirement that all donations to the monastery had to be shared with the local communist authorities. The effect of all of this was to disorient and disaggregate the villagers, for the monastery had traditionally functioned as the prime focus of communal life and shared meaning.

It seems that the rebels' treatment of Buddhism varied from region to region and from official to official. When Thion interviewed Vorn Vet in 1972, the latter halted the conversation to kneel respectfully before some passing monks (Thion 1993, xv).[41] It is also reported that when a very frightened Sihanouk visited Pol Pot in his headquarters in the northern zone in March 1973, monks were assembled for the ex-king to meet and chat with.[42] However, blatant anti-Buddhist sentiment also seems to have made an early appearance around the same time. In late 1972 the contents of a monastic library in Prey Veng Province were burned over a three-day period (Chantou Boua 1991, 230), while Ta Mok made a first call for monks to disrobe and join his army at a meeting of more than three thousand monks in Kompong Chhnang. By July 1973 the Patriotic Monks' Association was calling on each monastery in Kampot and Takeo provinces to supply ten monks each to replenish losses in the army (Kiernan 1985, 346, 377). Many monks took the opportunity to flee across the border to Vietnam. In response, a reeducation center for around two hundred recalcitrant monks was established at Sre Chea near Kampong Trach (Quinn 1976, 14–15).[43]

The southern provinces of Takeo and Kampot seem to have been treated

Cosmologically significant sand mounds *(phnom khsac)*, constructed as part of traditional New Year festivities—Wat Bakong, Prasat Bakong District, Siem Reap Province.

more oppressively than the rest of the country. By early 1973 the observance of traditional ceremonies was being severely restricted. The only public rites now deemed acceptable were the merit making for dead ancestors *(pchum ben)* in September and New Year. The somber tone of *pchum ben* posed few difficulties when set against the background of a continuing war. New Year, on the other hand, had been a time to let one's hair down. Its observance can be rumbustious, sometimes bordering on the orgiastic. Thus it has traditionally acted as a means of releasing social tensions. The local authorities were faced with a dilemma. The transgressive character of the New Year festival meant that it had the potential to unleash unwelcome criticism of the new regime, yet to ban it might store up greater resentment. The answer was to hold it in a seriously emasculated form. Dance was outlawed, all elements of conspicuous consumption were eliminated, and the party determined the songs that could be sung. In any case a slogan that circulated slightly later maintained that there was no need to bother with rituals associated with the old order, for under the new dispensation "every day is a festival" *(thngay na ku bun)* (Locard 1996, 218.)

Even at this reasonably advanced stage of repression, local initiatives could be too enthusiastically implemented and officials were sometimes forced into temporary retreat. In some areas senior monks were stripped of their ecclesiastical titles, and the people were urged to avoid the use of honorific language when addressing them. On other occasions older and less compliant seniors were replaced by younger men. Reports indicate significant popular resistance to these measures, and in light of the backlash the Khmer Rouge took some account of the peasantry's religious sentiments by trying to avoid explicit displays of persecution. Monks were still needed, and we hear, for instance, of banners extolling Buddhism being displayed alongside straightforwardly revolutionary slogans (Thion and Kiernan 1981, 69). Nevertheless, some monks did try to resist the pressure to become involved in political activity. Under such conditions torture and execution are documented, as in the case of a high-ranking monk from Wat Balei Chas, Takeo Province, who is reliably reported to have had his eyeballs gouged out before being killed (Yang Sam 1987, 63).

Communist Victory and the Elimination of Buddhism

Soon after the victory on April 17, 1975,[44] Ieng Sary, the minister of foreign affairs, announced that there would be freedom for all religious groups in the new state. This freedom was subsequently enshrined in Article 20 of the Constitution of Democratic Kampuchea, promulgated on January 5, 1976, which stated: "Every Cambodian has the right to worship according to any religion and the right not to worship according to any religion. Reactionary religion *(sasana pritikriya),* which is detrimental to Democratic Cambodia and the Cambodian people, is absolutely forbidden" (Jennar 1995a, 87–88).

This "freedom" needs to be understood in the context of Asian communist thinking on religious rights.[45] In a speech of December 1975, for instance, Khieu Samphan stated: "Article 20 stipulates that our people have the right to practice whatever religion they like and the right not to practice any religion at all. Also, as stated in our Constitution our stand is to not allow any foreign imperialists to use religion to subvert us" (*FBIS*—Asia and Pacific, January 6, 1976, H-1–9). Most commentators have accepted the hard interpretation, given in Vietnamese propaganda at the time, which referred to Article 20 as a "dead letter" (*Dossier Kampuchea* 1978, 29). However, a softer reading of the article could be held to allow for certain forms of "patriotic" religion. This may explain why, of all the religions that had flourished in Cambodia prior to the Democratic Kampuchea period, only the animism of hill tribes escaped substantial persecution (Etcheson 1984, 151).[46] Naturally, none of the oracular or prophetic functions of any religions would be tolerated. The Constitution certainly terminated

Buddhism's prior status as the religion of the state, although this change need not be interpreted as a total attack on Buddhism's foundational teachings. It could conceivably have held out the possibility of the continued existence of an apotropaic Buddhism divested of all foreign or reactionary components.[47]

This constitutional ambivalence with regard to Buddhism can be illustrated by reference to the funeral rites of Sihanouk's mother that took place in the Royal Palace in September 1975. Although most definitely not a public occasion, the ceremony was presided over by a number of monks who had come over to the Khmer Rouge in the early 1970s and was attended by Khieu Samphan and Son Sen (Ponchaud 1978, 149–150). Nuon Chea's mother also received traditional Buddhist funeral rites at Wat Ka, to the south of Battambang, around the same time (Khun Ken 1994, 86). Indeed, one of the more "popular" revolutionary songs of the Democratic Kampuchea period, "The Red Standard of the Revolution" ("Tung kraham padevat"), focuses in rather repellant detail on the blood sacrificed by the masses. Its first verse includes the refrain "Blood of workers, of peasants, and of intellectuals: / Blood of young men, of monks, and of girls. / The blood swirls away and flows upward, gently into the sky, / Turning into a red, revolutionary flag!" (Locard 1998, 325), indicating that the author, who may have been Pol Pot himself, saw at least some monks as fighting on the right side.[48]

Yet the pressure on institutional Buddhism was significantly raised after the communist victory. The official line was that Buddhism was associated with feudalism, which was one of the three mountains[49] that the revolutionary organization *(angkar padevat)* was determined to uproot. After the communists had taken the Information Ministry on April 17, 1975, Ven. Huot Tath, the Mahanikay *sanghareach,* made a radio broadcast that appealed for a cease-fire and called on commanders to meet with the ousted military High Command, using the words "Now we have peace, put down your guns" (Kiernan 1996, 36–37). Huot Tath then returned to Wat Unnalom, where he was falsely accused of having a wife and children in Paris. Evidence brought before the Vietnamese-backed trial of Pol Pot in 1979 affirmed that Huot Tath was executed at Wat Prang in the old capital of Udong the following day (de Nike et al. 2000, 361, document 2.4.09). It is widely believed that he was crushed by a bulldozer.

Purges of other senior monks occurred almost immediately. Ten of the original twelve members of the influential Tripitaka Commission were identified and executed in the first three days.[50] On April 24 two senior monks from Battambang were flown to Pochentong Airport, having been told that they were to greet Sihanouk. They were executed on arrival, because they had "too much influence over the people" (Ponchaud 1978, 148). Ven. Khieu Chum, a leading figure in the hated Republican regime, was another important target. He was hunted down and killed in Kompong Chhnang Province within the first few weeks (Corfield 1991, 5). The elimination of leading monks continued as the year progressed.[51] This policy was also extended to Khmer Islam. Two of the country's highest Muslim dignitaries, the grand mufti and the *hakkem* of Noor Alihsan mosque, were also executed in July or August, suggesting the regime's even-handed hostility toward all organized religion.

It seems that many ordinary Cham Muslims were told that they could continue to pray privately as long as this did not interfere with their work efficiency. The same general principle may have operated, with some signal exceptions, for the Buddhist laity. Informants told Marston (1997, 92) that they surreptitiously maintained spirit shrines during the Democratic Kampuchea period. However, the frequent movements of population after 1975 severed the link between villagers and their ancestors. In consequence, belief in the whole panoply of autochthonous mythological beings, including the tutelary spirits, or *neak tā,* began to disintegrate. Ponchaud (1989, 168) reports a peasant who came to disbelieve in the power of spirits. "Since they didn't do anything against the Khmer Rouge, I don't trust them anymore."[52] This process was no doubt aided by the propaganda that the spirits were epiphenomena purely related to the old regime. From now on, the revolutionary organization was the only significant power in the land. The message that "Angkar is the master of the water and of the earth" *(angkar mchah teuk, mchah dey)* (Locard 1996, 34) demonstrates a great contrast with activities of the earlier Issarak movement, which tried to gain control over villages by "endowing new Neak Ta" (Ponchaud 1989, 169). Paradoxically, Angkar possesses supernatural capabilities. The oft-repeated slogan "Angkar has the eyes of a pineapple" *(angkar mean phnek mnoah)* seems to point to omniscience, and it may not be too bold to suggest that it manifests some features of a new religion, admittedly one in which the bloodsucking and parasitical monks of an earlier period of development are to be eliminated.

The situation with regard to monks was more complex. Many were evacuated from their home monasteries and forced to walk to a series of distant monasteries, where they were placed on very meager rations and hard labor. Their numbers were greatly increased by those obliged to leave the massively swollen monastic institutions of the capital and other important cities upon their immediate closure following the communist victory.[53] The previous distinction between rural and city monks appears to have further crystallized at this stage. While the former were characterized as "proper and revolutionary," the latter were deemed "imperialists," "April 17 monks" or "new monks."[54] In many cases the "new monks" ended up living side by side with "base monks" of peasant background who had sometimes lived under communist control for a number of years, for monasteries in "base" areas unaffected by large-scale fighting appear to have been in good condition until well after the fall of Phnom Penh.

From this point on, "new monks" were rapidly laicized, and virtually none remained in robes by the beginning of the 1975 rainy season. In any case, they had no means of support, for the laity were no longer allowed to support the *sangha*. Ponchaud (1978, 150) reports that the following chilling order was given in the Battambang area toward the end of 1975: "If any worker secretly takes rice to the bonzes, we shall set him to planting cabbages. If the cabbages are not full-grown in three days, he will dig his own grave." A few monks managed to escape to neighboring countries. Most were set to work, and if they resisted, they were executed just like everyone else. Chantou Boua (1991, 232) notes that residents of a Siem Reap monastery had their biographies investigated for more than a week after the victory of April 17 before being escorted from the premises. They were told, "It is about time other people lived in the monastery." Evidence suggests that disrobing was rarely a voluntary act, even though some monks were almost ironically forced to sign a document certifying that they had "awoken" to their parasitical status.[55]

"Base monks" were treated a little differently. In a speech given to delegates of the Danish Communist Workers' Party who were visiting Cambodia in July 1978, Nuon Chea fleshed out the United Front policy. He distinguished between "rank and file monks . . . [who were] not so reactionary" and higher-ranking *sangha* members. Yet even some monks of the latter sort could be classed with selected big capitalists, civil servants, and government officials as "supplementary forces." That the local Buddhist patriarch approved the call of college students in Battambang to surrender the city to FUNK and allow Sihanouk to return shortly before the fall of Phnom Penh (Corfield 1994, 219) indicates that some senior monastics, assuming they had any awareness of the nature of the United Front policy, were not especially hostile to the communists' intentions. In addition, many ordinary monks had, both before and after liberation, become convinced that the CPK would "defend the country and religion" against foreign aggression. They "held aloft our banner even if they did not like communism" (Nuon Chea 2001, 12).[56]

On April 24, 1975, a three-day Special National Congress was held in the capital. Among those attending, Phnom Penh Radio announced "20 representatives of the Buddhist clergy" (quoted in Kiernan 1996, 54). One must assume that these were base monks. In some zones such monks were allowed to observe the traditional three-month retreat *(vassa)* that ends in October. It is customary to end *vassa* with a ceremony called *kathen*, in which laypeople offer new robes to chosen monks as a means of making merit. Rather intriguingly, we find isolated examples of an "inverted" *kathen* ceremony at the end of *vassa*

1975, when selected base monks were presented with revolutionary garb—black trousers, black shirt, and a traditional Khmer scarf *(krama)*—by communist officials, after which they were "invited" to leave the monastic order.[57] Doubtless, few refused.

In the period between October and December 1975 almost all monasteries still remaining active in the country were closed. A party document, dated September 1975 and entitled *About the Control and Application of Political Leadership in Accumulating Forces for the National Front and Democracy of the Party,* stated: "90 to 95 percent of the monks have disappeared, in the sense that the majority of monks have abandoned religion. Monasteries, which were the pillars for monks, are largely abandoned. The foundation pillars of Buddhism are abandoned . . . in future they will dissolve further" (quoted in Chantou Boua 1991, 235). The postvictory persecution of Buddhism should be seen as part of a wider program to control all aspects of daily existence in line with the revolutionaries' goals "to push the people to be happy" (Kiernan 1996, 328). The persecution appears to have unfolded in four stages. In the first phase, members of the ecclesiastical hierarchy and monks closely associated with the Lon Nol regime were rounded up and almost immediately executed. Next, the defrocking of "new monks" was largely accomplished by July 1975. This was followed several months later by the laicization of base monks and, finally, by the full elimination of institutional Buddhism. Much has been made of the formative influence that study in France had on some members of the CPK's inner circle. One might expect that the extreme anticlericalism revealed in these measures may, in part, have been imbibed from the French socialist tradition.

All of this smacks of a well-coordinated policy, yet initial appearances can be deceptive. At a meeting on May 20, 1975, Pol Pot announced an eight-point program, the fourth element of which was to "defrock all Buddhist monks and put them to work growing rice" (Kiernan 1996, 55). One member of the audience asserts that Pol Pot actually proposed a more extreme line, to the effect that monks "had to be wiped out *(lup bombat)*" (Kiernan 1996, 57), but given that the witness was Heng Samrin, the head of the future Vietnamese-backed Peoples' Republic of Kampuchea (PRK) and an influential figure in the overthrow of the Khmer Rouge, we should regard such evidence with some caution. Similarly, Khieu Samphan's reported remark that "if we are faithful to the people, it does not matter what we do to the Buddhist monks"[58] need not imply any policy of mass extermination.

Martin (1994, 183) is probably correct in her belief that despite the significant losses sustained by the population, of which disrobed monastics formed a part, there was no policy for their systematic liquidation in Democratic Kampuchea. Nevertheless, uncooperative monks might be accused of being enemy agents and summarily executed. During the trial in absentia of Pol Pot, held at Phnom Penh in August 1979, Ven. Tep Vong, a pro-Vietnamese monk from Wat Bo, Siem Reap, produced evidence that the Khmer Rouge had executed fifty-seven monks, including three of his own nephews, in the Chan Sar Subdistrict (de Nike et al. 2000, 149, document 2.1.2.03). Another trial document tells of the persecution, eventual disrobing, and narrow escape from death of Ven. Sin Um of Wat Ratanamuni, Prey Veng Province, even though he had "supported Pol Pot and Ieng Sary during the resistance against the Americans and Lon Nol" (de Nike et al. 2000, 362, document 2.4.09). Estimates made in 1980 suggest that about 63 percent of monks died or were executed by the Pol Pot regime, but these bald figures shed little light on the factors underlying the deaths. In most cases we do not know whether their end was a direct consequence of their previous monastic status.

Nevertheless, all observers agree that, by the end of the period, the number of monks in the country was negligible. One trustworthy source (Kiernan 1990, 39) observes that "of a total of 2,680 Buddhist monks from 8 of Cambodia's 3,000 monasteries surveyed by Chantou Boua, only 70 monks were found to have survived in 1979," while Keyes (1994, 60) claims a figure of 100, the majority in Vietnamese exile. Official sources give a much lower figure of 12 monks to have remained in robes until the end of the Democratic Kampuchea period.[59]

There does not seem to have been a consensus among the revolutionaries on what to do with Buddhism. Some argued in favor of the retention of money, schools, and religion, and reports were emerging as late as mid-1976 from the eastern zone that Buddhism was still being permitted to flourish.[60] It is also known that individual monks were protected from time to time, particularly if they were relatives of important cadres (Kiernan 1996, 60–61, 205, 338). The case of the base monk Ven. Srey Ith (b. 1907), the *chau adhikar* of Wat Kork Kak, Kandal, is instructive here. Ignoring the warnings of ex-students to leave his home monastery, he was forced to disrobe after *vassa* 1975. However, his age and status were recognized by local officials, and he was assigned light duties in the agricultural commune to which he was attached. After curing the sick child of a senior cadre by using traditional healing techniques, he was allowed to live for a time as a hermit on a nearby hill. While there, he was brought alms food by sympathetic revolutionaries.[61] Another monk, Ven. Las Lay (b. 1914), currently a senior member of the Mahanikay hierarchy, had been ordained at Wat Sbeng, Khum Thieu, Kandal Province, at the age of twelve and moved to Phnom Penh the following year, where he subsequently came under the influence of Ven. Chuon Nath.[62] Ven. Las Lay remained in robes for two months following the evacuation of Phnom Penh. However, after his forced return to the lay life, he managed to maintain his devotions unobtrusively by chanting quietly to himself. There are a number of parallels between his account and that of Ven. Srey Ith. Former students in the Khmer Rouge, for example, gave occasional donations of food to Ven. Las Lay. He also claims to have been appointed a "president of funerals," in which role he was obliged to perform Buddhist death rites for senior cadres and their relatives. It seems that the apotropaic dimension of religion could not be entirely extinguished by the new state, for it is known that other ex-monks, especially those believed to possess magical powers, secretly continued to perform protective rituals for the sick, the malnourished, the bereaved, and the terrified.[63]

Evidence that defrocked monks often attempted to live according to Buddhist precepts is quite widespread, although doing so was clearly far from easy. One monastic survivor told Hinton (1997, 119) that he fell into sin by working in the fields, where he inevitably killed living creatures. Ex-monks were also forced to marry. However, a variety of stratagems could be employed to avoid this. Ven. Las Lay, for example, successfully resisted the pressure by feigning illness. Ven. Oum Som, one of the two survivors from the Tripitaka Commission, had been sent from Phnom Penh to Kompong Cham Province, where he grew vegetables and outwardly acquiesced in the view that, as a monk, he had plowed the fields on the backs of the people. He also claims to have avoided forced marriage. In this and other ways he remained true to his monastic vocation. Of course, it is virtually impossible to corroborate such claims. There seems little reason not to take them at face value, although their frequency, and the fact that they would become crucial in the reestablishment of monastic seniority following the reintroduction of institutional Buddhism after the demise of Democratic Kampuchea, may raise the occasional doubt.

Once monasteries had been emptied, they could be put to other purposes. Some were dismantled to provide building materials for civil engineering projects. Others became local economic bureaus or torture and execution facilities.[64] They were also used to house pigs. The oft-repeated assertion that Buddhist palm-leaf manuscripts were used for rolling tobacco is rather obvious propaganda, for the resulting cigarette would have been virtually impossible to smoke.[65] Nevertheless, sacred texts were burned and thrown into rivers, while funerary monuments and Buddha images were smashed and recycled. A slogan of the time advised, "If you demolish a statue of the Buddha, you will gain a sack of cement" *(komtech preah muey ang chomnenh simang muey bau)* (Locard 1996, 152). Two celebrated and powerful Buddha statues from the Siem Reap region—Preah Ang Chek and Preah Ang Chom—are supposed to have been destroyed, along with several highly venerated images at Angkor Thom and Angkor Wat.[66] Yet the extent of iconoclasm in Democratic Kampuchea (DK) remains to be established, particularly in light of conflicting reports. Becker

(1979), one of the few Western visitors to the country during DK, for instance, reported that when she visited Angkor toward the end of the period, she could detect no major damage to the temples beyond that caused by water seepage, fungal growth, and the like. We should also bear in mind that, on its own, iconoclasm need not be a sign of absolute hostility to all aspects of religion, as a multitude of examples from the history of Christian lands demonstrate.

Vandalism of monastic premises certainly occurred on a large scale during Democratic Kampuchea, yet the full extent of the practice is rather difficult to determine. The widely held belief that almost all monasteries were destroyed after 1975 is difficult to accept, not least because much available evidence is problematic. To give one example, an official publication of the successor regime, the People's Republic of Kampuchea, maintained that in Phnom Penh alone forty-seven monasteries had been ruined. However, Vickery (1988, 71) notes that "most of the city's old wats survived [Democratic Kampuchea] intact except for minor damage and deterioration," and some people have asserted that only twenty-six monasteries had existed in the first place.[67] It is clear that the purpose of such propaganda was to blacken the name of the Khmer Rouge, not to establish the facts of the case.

Many more monasteries than had been supposed survived the period in fair condition. An intriguing report in the *Phnom Penh Post* (May 7–20, 1993, 20), although credulous in tone, seems to convey this impression. It tells the story of the miraculous salvation of Wat Phnom Sia, between Kampot and Kep. According to local inhabitants, when Khmer Rouge forces came to blow it up, huge snakes appeared from the temple mound and killed them. Subsequent units were too frightened to repeat the actions of their comrades, so the monastery remained intact. Of course, it is quite possible that superstition did flourish among the revolutionaries, but the account is more likely a fanciful attempt to explain something that was, given the general lack of good information, regarded as an anomaly. It should also be borne in mind that, although the Khmer Rouge years had a very deleterious impact, some evidence points to continuing damage to monasteries after the January 1979 liberation by Vietnam. A good example here is Wat Keo Preah Phloeung in Phnom Penh, which was leveled in 1979 so that the site could be redeveloped for the housing of officials.[68]

Internalization of Buddhist Symbolism and Language

Prophecies of the demise of Buddhism that had circulated in the republican period seemed to be coming true. By 1978, Female Comrade Yun Yat, the minister of culture, information, and propaganda, told a Yugoslav reporter that

"Buddhism is dead and the ground has been cleared for the foundations of a new revolutionary culture" (Stanic 1978). However, the same reporter claimed that an ex-monk who was present at the time rather courageously took issue with her on the grounds that, for him at least, Buddhism and communism were essentially compatible. His fate is unknown, but the story suggests that a generalized Buddhist essence may in some way have been subsumed into Cambodian communism. As Ponchaud (1989, 172–173) has suggested, Buddhist modernism was built on the assertion that the Buddha's teachings were based on scientific and rational grounds. If one accepted this premise, obstacles to the accommodation of the doctrinal and practical resources of Buddhism to the socialist world picture might be substantially reduced.

During the civil war the morality of the monks had been criticized by the Khmer Rouge, who began to observe a lengthy list of moral rules, or Angkar commandments *(angkarviney)*, loosely based on the ten precepts of the ordained monk. The *angkarviney* were partly designed to prove that the revolutionaries were more worthy of the laity's respect than the *sangha* was.[69] Ascetic attitudes may also be found in some of the revolutionary slogans of the time. "Physical beauty is an obstacle to the will to struggle" *(somphoah la'a: chie uhpesah ney chhanteah prayut)* and "Comrade, don't touch women" *(mit min trou pahpoal nieri: phet laoey)* (Locard 1996, 219–220), for instance, easily cohere with the Buddhist monastic worldview. Revolutionary asceticism was a feature of the Constitution of Democratic Kampuchea, which compared the "cleanliness" of the new order with the "obscenity" of the imperialist past (see Edwards 1999, 391), while Khieu Samphan's statement to the Third National Congress of December 1975—"There are no thieves, drunkards, hooligans, or prostitutes in our country. . . . Movies, magazines which used to spread the corrupt, perverted culture exist no more" (*FBIS*—Asia and Pacific, January 6, 1975, H-1–9)—might arguably have been uttered by a Buddhist monk. Indeed, Hinton (2002, 63, 69) sees Angkar's desire to purify society as a mirror to the rule of righteous Buddhist kings of previous epochs.

Of particular relevance here is the dual emphasis placed on self-reliance *(ekareach mcahkar)*[70] and renunciation *(leah bang)*. The population were regularly exhorted to renounce both worldly goods and control over their personal destiny, the aim being to systematically uproot all emotional ties and strike at the heart of the old society. The notion of heating *(tapas)* oneself to eliminate impurities, so well attested in mainstream Buddhist literature, was particularly widespread. Hinton (2002, 84) points to the terrifying ubiquity of the metaphor of tempering iron *(luat daik)*. Those who were deemed insufficiently malleable had to be hammered into shape. If they resisted, they were reheated through self-criticism and hammered again. As is the case in other revolutionary settings, the emphasis was on "taming" the individual to serve the organization (Hinton 1997, 20), for the Khmer Rouge required not active heroism but the renunciation of self. Ith Sarin, for instance, describes weekly criticism and self-criticism sessions in which personnel were expected to root out individualist tendencies, even those related to eating and drinking. Yet this had been a traditional concern of monks, as is indicated by the prominent place given to such matters in the Vinaya. In a sense, the regime "both initiated sociopolitical transformations that undermined traditional constraints on violence and incorporated pre-existing cultural models into their genocidal ideology" (Hinton 1998, 96). One of the charges made against those not prepared to become involved in executions during the period was that they were "unable to cut off their heart" (Hinton 1998, 95, 113). In other words, their emotional responses were not sufficiently disciplined, a concept conceivably related to Buddhist notions of mental training.

The most appropriate means to achieve self-control was through a life of sexual abstinence. If this proved impractical, Angkar provided a narrowly regulated context in which sexual relations might be pursued: hence the frequent references to forced marriage in the Democratic Kampuchea period. Naturally, polygamy was also forbidden (Carney 1977, 11, 47). Attempts to deconstruct the family are another common feature in the reports of survivors. From now on, Angkar would be both mother and father. As a revolutionary song of the time explained, Angkar has "loving-kindness, the loving-kindness of someone great without measure" (Hinton 2002, 70, quoting Marston 1994, 110).[71]

Nuon Chea (2001) endorsed this "monastic/ascetic ethic" in the previously mentioned speech, when he complained that many cadres were reluctant to drop everything, particularly their families, and flee to another part of the country when the situation demanded. Laurence Picq (1989, 48)—who, by virtue of being married to the CPK cadre Suong Sikhoeun, was one of the only Westerners to have survived the period—also describes how even husbands and wives of high-ranking individuals were separated and forced to live a virtual monastic existence. Elsewhere, Pin Yathay (1980, 227) has noted that one of the consequences of this enforced lifestyle was that many people experienced an almost complete extinction of sexual desire. Although an emphasis on ascetic denial seems to have been present in comparable movements, such as the Chinese Cultural Revolution, this crypto-monastic arrangement appears to have been a distinctive feature of the Khmer Rouge experiment. It may be going too far to assert that the Cambodian revolutionaries saw themselves as forming another religion based on Buddhism but with the advantage of class analysis, as

Salter (2000, 295) suggests, but there can be little doubt that internalization of aspects of an older religiously inspired thought universe was pervasive during the period.

Examples of a tendency to reconfigure and reemploy Buddhist symbolism and modes of thought, all the while against a background of extreme harassment of Buddhist institutions, are quite common throughout the period. The language of the wheel, an ancient symbol of the Buddha's teaching and of the power of the righteous Buddhist monarch *(cakravartin),* for instance, gained new currency in the slogan "The wheel of revolution . . . never stops and . . . will crush all who place themselves in its path." Some revolutionary slogans were reworkings of *cpāp'*[72] and proverbial literature (Locard 1996, 3–4, 236), the very formulae learned by young monks as part of their "practical canon" of training.[73] This is clear in the expression "Imperialist heart, the mouth speaks only of Angkar" *(chet chie chakrapoat, moat chie angkar)*[74]—a reworking of the more traditional "Heart of Devadatta, mouth of a deity *(chit chie tevatoat, moat chie tevoda)* (Locard 1996, 169–170)—which could more loosely be translated as "Sweet words mask an evil heart." The *Reamker* also appears to be the source of some slogans. "I am truly born from a furrow traced by the plow" *(bokul khnhom kaoet chenh pi: tchrolong neangkoal sotsat)* (Locard 1996, 195) is an edifyingly agrarian reworking of the Sītā birth narrative.[75] Finally, one wonders whether the denouement of the popular tale *Tum Teav* has any relevance to the atrocities committed under Pol Pot. In the story the incident in which Ârchoun and seven generations of his relatives are buried up to their necks and their heads severed by a plow is highly reminiscent of the practice of "cutting off the family line" *(phtach pouch)* characteristic of the "disproportionate revenge" exacted during Democratic Kampuchea (Hinton 1997, 233).[76]

In daily conversation, use of the word "I" *(kñom)* was discouraged (Marston 1997, 168–169),[77] and bourgeois affectations of the form "thank you," "please," and "sorry" were deemed unnecessary, for there was no further need to express indebtedness (Marston 1997, 171). Similar rejection of customary language was also a feature of the Chinese Cultural Revolution, and this may have been the influence here. However, the fact that from the philosophical perspective Buddhism repudiates the concept of an abiding self, while in terms of practice Theravada monks must refrain from enunciating thanks on being given alms food, may also be germane. After the fall of the Khmer Rouge the belief was widespread that the terminology employed in the regime's official documentation was not standard Khmer but some special, almost arcane and priestly language incomprehensible to the average person. Scholarly research into the documents of the interrogation and execution facility at Tuol Sleng, S-21, confirms this to some extent. According to Heder (1991, 20), they are written in "a peculiar ar-got that resulted from the attempts of Khmer speakers of Pali and Vietnamese to render into Khmer the vocabulary and syntax of Vietnamese communist phraseology." Heder notes, "The resulting jumble of Pali and Khmer neologisms and fractured syntax is at times unintelligible to even native speakers of Khmer."

In the crucial area of party dogma, the term "*paṭiccasamuppāda*"—usually rendered as "dependent origination," the central concept of Buddhist thought—was employed to translate "dialectical materialism" into Khmer (Communist Party of Kampuchea Central Committee, 1976).[78] Elsewhere, the three groups that made up the country's population are compared to the structure of a *stūpa,* in which the progressive masses constitute the base, the core organization the bell, and the party membership the tip (Communist Party of Kampuchea Central Committee, 1978). A former cadre, interviewed in 1979, had grumbled that "Pol Pot and the others were very good at making theory in terms of the 10–point elements, the 8—this, the 6—that, and all the rest of it, but when it came to the basic question of how to end the war they didn't have an answer" (quoted in Chandler 1999, 179). There is a striking parallel here between Marxism and Buddhism, for both could be construed as intellectual disciplines absorbed in the construction of scholastic lists.

In his December 1975 speech to the National Congress, Khieu Samphan stated, "Our people are working collectively to dismantle the old field embankments and replace them with new high, tall, and straight structures, forming a great checkerboard network throughout the country" (*FBIS*—Asia and Pacific, January 6, 1975, H-1–9).[79] On one level this is merely a depiction of rational and scientific agrarian reform. However, one must bear in mind that this repatterning fits well with traditional Buddhist cosmological speculation. The statement hints at a Buddhist-inspired re-creation of the country as a pure land with the "empty" or phantom city of Phnom Penh at its heart. An obvious objection to the thesis is that this vision of an ideal world arranged in a checkerboard fashion is a feature of Mahayanist texts, like the *Sukhāvatīvyūha Sūtras,* and entirely inappropriate in the Cambodian Theravada context. In addition, it is inconceivable that CPK leaders would have been familiar with these sources. But it is known that Mahayanist elements have been present in the unreformed segments of the Cambodian Buddhist *sangha.* The best modern example of "pure land" influence is in the consecration and demarcation of a *vihāra,* the quintessential Buddhist sacred space. In this traditional rite, eight stone boundary *(sīmā)* markers, or *nimitta,* are dropped into specially dug pits, which are indicated by the intersections in a checkerboard arrangement made of bamboo poles laid on the ground. It seems that these pits are activated by a few drops of human blood, an act that points to the archaic and sacrificial origin of the practice (Giteau 1969b, 44).[80] The connection between blood sacrifice and reconfiguration of the environment is highly relevant to the Democratic Kampuchea context, and it is not beyond the bounds of possibility that deeply rooted patterns were at work at a subliminal level.

This attempt at repatterning the world also coheres well with the notion of "starting from zero" *(cap pdaem bi son)*. The Cambodian revolutionaries' desire to return the country to "year zero" is certainly somewhat odd, for orthodox Marxist analysis sees the ideal state as the culmination of linear history, not a cyclic return to the most archaic stage of production. Heder (1997, 107) has argued that the post-1975 events were an example of Habermas' "romantic socialism," in which nostalgic images of the peasant universe are dominant. But the question still remains open as to the source of that romantic ideal. I would continue to press the case for a proper consideration of the indigenous cultural factors that may have influenced the worldview of the Khmer Rouge. Among these factors is likely to be the Buddhist-tinged "belief that Cambodians could build their collective future, but rooted in a cyclical notion of time" (Salter 2000, 284). A further insight into the paradox of the vision may be obtained by consideration of the word "*kasang,*" usually translated as "to build." In Democratic Kampuchea the term was often employed in the context of "building up socialism." However, Marston (1994, 113–114) has shown that "*kasang*" actually had a dual meaning. It signifies "to build up" but can also represent the opposite, "to tear down."[81] It could be argued that this is entirely consistent with the traditional Buddhist understanding of history as an endless cycle of coming into being followed by dissolution.

Chandler (1999, 76–77) has suggested that the time spent in the maquis before gaining control of the country gave Pol Pot and his fellow revolutionaries an almost magical or mystical power of the sort obtained by the ascetic heroes of the *Reamker* and the early Buddhist tradition.[82] This early sojourn in the forest, then, replicated the ancient model of kingship in which a period of renunciation in the uncivilized realm is the ideal preparation for eventual appearance on the political and ritual stage.[83] Indeed, in 1977 Pol Pot claimed that his work with tribal peoples in the forests of the northeast some fifteen years previously had built up the invincible force that prefigured final victory (Quinn 1982, 31). These experiences undoubtedly fed the perception of some Cambodian communists that they were capable of reshaping the world on a massive scale.

With the collapse of Democratic Kampuchea the leaders withdrew once more. Deprived of external support, the rump of extreme Cambodian communism fell back again on a cultural inheritance linked to heroic Buddhist-inspired rebellions of the past. From the late 1980s, Pol Pot lived at a forest headquarters, Office 87, a compound strongly resembling a Buddhist monastery or forest hermitage. He also talked of pure party members as being "ordained," and teaching sessions in which the world was characterized as caught in a titanic clash between the forces of good and evil were delivered in a "monastic style," with primacy given to oral presentation. Many of his listeners reported being strongly impressed by what they had heard (Chandler 1999, 175–177). Moreover, in 1978 Pol Pot had said that he aimed to live with a "Buddhist calm mind" (Stanic 1978). In some respects, then, his career may be read as a warped epitome of the mythical and ascetical ideals that underscored Cambodian culture for many centuries before the opening of the modern epoch.

In a book describing his own imprisonment and interrogation by the Khmer Rouge in late 1971, Bizot (2000, 161–164) records a conversation in which he attempted to persuade his inquisitor, Duch,[84] that even at that early period the discipline and practice of the movement had clear parallels with Buddhism in terms of their renouncing of worldly goods, family, and children and the following of a specific discipline *(viney)*. Initiation into both organizations also involves a ceremony in which the candidate receives a new name and a set number of clothing items; seven pieces in the case of a monk, six[85] in the case of a soldier. Both maintain distinctions between fully initiated members and those undergoing apprenticeship, and parallels may also be found even in the way they intone their respective litanies, all the way down to the incorporation of similar trills at the end of each stanza. Unsurprisingly, Duch was entirely unconvinced. For this committed communist, Buddhism was obviously the opium of the people. It had contributed to a brutalization of the peasantry, whereas Angkar wished to glorify it. For Duch, Bizot was suffering from intellectual delirium. Nevertheless, Duch did agree that the Cambodian people needed to rediscover the source of their morals.

There has been no shortage of scholarly analysis of the factors that contributed to the unique form of communism that culminated in the extreme violence and dislocation of the Democratic Kampuchea period. The Chinese Cultural Revolution is a highly significant element in this regard. Both Pol Pot and Ieng Sary admitted as much at the time.[86] Both movements enhanced the role of the young as part of an attack on vested interests and the concept of "expertise." Both manifested hostility toward individual, as opposed to collective, incentives, and both indulged in a high degree of rural romanticism (Quinn 1976, 180–183). Mao had, for instance, urged millions of city dwellers to join rural communes to maximize production through the *xiafang* movement. But here is an important difference: coercion may have been used in China, but violence and terror as a means of achieving rapid transition to a "pure" society were not deployed there to the extent used by the Khmer Rouge.

The cities were never emptied as they were in Cambodia, and although the idea had been vaguely contemplated, money was not abolished during the Cultural Revolution.[87]

These differences imply that a simple line of inheritance is not sufficient to explain the Cambodian situation. In addressing this difficulty, some commentators have argued that a basically pure Maoist lineage was contaminated by adventitious factors, like the brutalization *(déraillement)* of the populace induced by the long years of bloody conflict prior to victory on April 17, 1975, or the personal neuroses and sexual impotence of major figures in the communist movement. While some of these accounts are more convincing than others, most are premised on the notion that the Khmer Rouge represented a form of degenerate Maoism. Some have been more catholic in their quest for influences. Karl Jackson (1989, 250), for example, allows that the intellectual roots of Khmer communism "included Maoism, European Marxism, Fanonism, perhaps Stalinism, and certainly Khmer nationalism." This multiple genealogy is a definite step forward, although it is still focused largely on influences extraneous to Khmer history and cultural traditions. Of course, I do not wish to claim that dramatic social and political change cannot be precipitated solely by foreign influences, but one would expect a careful examination and dismissal of relevant indigenous factors before such a conclusion was reached. With the exception of one or two vague hints in the literature,[88] it is not clear to me that these considerations have formed a significant part of the scholarly project to understand Cambodia at this crucial point in its history.

It is a commonplace that Buddhism, its monastic segment in particular, has been cynically exploited by successful movements of Asian communism. I do not wish to deny this. However, it is only a part of the picture. There has been a reluctance, particularly among Western scholars, to accept Buddhism as a localizable "total fact." What I mean by this is that when we look at Buddhism, we are apt to see only its philosophical and scholastic superstructure.[89] Now, in its Asian heartlands, intellectual endeavor has always tended to be part of a specialized and restricted domain, but Buddhism has also operated on a far wider level to sustain and inform the cultures with which it forms a whole. It has achieved this by the provision of educational and welfare facilities, as well as through more direct involvement in the apparatus of state. Buddhists are not, and never have been, people outside history. Buddhism has never been entirely otherworldly or, in Hegel's characterization, a religion of "Being-within-itself." Such notions are premised on the modern conception of a separation between church and state, yet they have been influential in the discounting of the tradition's political dimension. This is surprising, given that Buddhist monks and ex-monks have actually been significant figures in the exercise of political power in various parts of Asia, for only they had the mobility, education, and moral authority to create effective countrywide organizations during the premodern period.[90]

In the last couple of chapters we have seen how, in the twentieth century, Cambodian monks were enormously influential in the establishment of organized anticolonialism. Many more were involved in building up the Communist Party of Kampuchea. Thus they were direct contributors to social and political change, even though this practice would eventually undermine their traditional authority. Nevertheless, the terrible recent history of Cambodia demonstrates that Buddhism can survive even when its institutional forms have been destroyed. Its apotropaic rituals possess an enduring power for suffering humanity, while its symbolism and language have the protean ability to adapt in even the most extreme circumstances. This aspect of Buddhism would ultimately ensure its future reestablishment.

8

Cambodian Buddhism after the Khmer Rouge

Buddhism in the Early People's Republic of Kampuchea

In May 1978, Heng Samrin gave a speech in Cambodia's eastern zone revealing the existence of a dissident grouping within the Khmer Rouge. He called on "all patriotic forces regardless of political and religious tendencies," including "Buddhist monks and nuns," to join a united front to help "topple the reactionary and nepotistic Pol Pot–Ieng Sary gang" (Steve Heder, in *PPP* 8/6, March 19–April 1, 1999). A United Front for National Salvation of Kampuchea was formed on December 2, 1978. Heng Samrin became president of its fourteen-person Central Committee, which included Long Sim—described as "a revolutionary monk for over 50 years"—acting as representative for the *sangha* (Vickery 1986, 161).[1] With the aid of Vietnamese troops the United Front quickly liberated most of the country. It is said that when the soldiers arrived in a village, they dismantled the hated communal kitchen and brought "in a few monks to reassure the people" (Kiernan 1996, 442). These early acts in the overthrow of the Khmer Rouge led to the establishment of a Vietnamese-backed People's Republic of Kampuchea (PRK) in January 1979.

The Heng Samrin government gradually reversed some of the most extreme antireligious policies of the previous regime. A partial restoration of Buddhism was one of its first acts on coming to power. The fourth element of its eleven-point program addressed "the right to freedom of opinion, association, and belief." However, this element was intended to apply only in a restricted sense to Buddhism and Khmer Islam. Christianity was not accorded such freedoms. As if to emphasize the changed circumstances, as well as to gain useful propaganda, a delegation of the communist-sponsored Asian Buddhists' Conference for Peace made an official visit to Cambodia in April 1979,[2] and a party representing the Buddhist Association for the National Salvation of Kampuchea attended the Fifth Congress of the Asian Buddhists' Conference for Peace in Ulan Bator in June of the same year. The conference delegation's speech bitterly complained that "Chinese big nation hegemonic expansionism imposed on Kampuchea an extremely brutal regime which brought to our nation a genocide never before seen in history" (de Nike et al. 2000, 146–147, document 2.1.2.02). The speech is replete with revolutionary jargon and entirely void of any significant reference to Buddhist practice or doctrine, because, in the earliest phase of the PRK, religion was manipulated largely for cosmetic and propaganda reasons. For all intents and purposes the new state continued the previous regime's suppression of Buddhism, for this was obviously in line with the socialist emphasis on rationality, science, and the dignity of work.

Despite an initial feeling of euphoria, particularly given the mass trauma associated with the recent past, popular opinion soon turned against the Vietnamese-backed regime. This was not surprising, given Vietnam's status as Cambodia's traditional enemy. It was therefore essential that additional support be found for the regime in order to bolster its waning legitimacy. The two strongest institutions in the country had always been the *sangha* and the monarchy, but the regime could hardly play the royal card, for Norodom Sihanouk was already looking to form an opposition group—eventually called the Coalition Government of Democratic Kampuchea—with the Khmer Rouge and Son Sann's Khmer People's National Liberation Front (KPNLF).[3] With only the monastic order to fall back on, Buddhism was partially restored around August 1979. The PRK's early policy toward Buddhism needs to be read in this light.[4]

Monastic ordination in the aftermath of Democratic Kampuchea proved difficult for a number of reasons. On the practical level it was impossible to assemble the necessary quorum of fully ordained monks to perform the valid rite. Nevertheless, there is good reason to believe that some monks were unofficially reestablished quite quickly, for some thirty-nine had signed a report, dated June 13, 1975, used in evidence at the PRK's August 1979 trial in absentia of Pol Pot and Ieng Sary. The text makes it clear that sixty-eight monks, including many of the signatories, were already residing at Wat Sansam Kosal, Phsar Doeum Thkao District, Phnom Penh.[5] Other ex-monks took to shaving their head and wearing white. Such individuals began to form a core of organized Buddhism, their services being sought for the performance of ceremonies to commemorate the dead, for as Ernest Gellner has pointed out, "Marxism has nothing to say to personal tragedy and bereavement."

Another major constraint was the authorities' desire to keep a tight reign on extragovernmental activity. On September 19, 1979, seven "carefully chosen" former monks, all with between twenty and sixty years of former service, were reordained with government approval at Wat Unnalom.[6] The Theravadin monks from Vietnam—headed by Thich Bou Chon, adviser to the Central Commission of Vietnamese Theravada Buddhism—who performed the ordination rite comprised a mixture of Khmer who had fled to Vietnam during the DK period plus some ethnic Khmer from Kampuchea Krom (Keyes 1994b, 60n36). The reordainees included Vens. Koeut Vay, Sovanna Chot Prak Dith, Idanthero Non Nget,[7] and Dhammasatha Ken Vong (Yang Sam 1987, 80). The youngest member, Ven. Tep Vong (b. 1930), claimed that he had been imprisoned and sentenced to four years of forced labor at the beginning of the DK period (Danois 1980, 73). He had also given evidence, during the show trial of Pol Pot the previous month, that the Khmer Rouge had executed fifty-seven monks, including three of his own nephews.[8] It is clear that the seven were held in high regard by the new party apparatus, and most went on to assume high-profile roles at the interface between church and state. The scholar-monk Ven. Koeut Vay (d. 1994), for instance, had been an original member of the Salvation Front (Ros Chantrabot 2000, 20) and was soon to become the "preceptor of Cambodia." Yet it has been difficult for these monks to break free from the implications of this linkage with the Vietnamese. Their enemies have sometimes described them as "Vietnamese monks in Khmer robes."[9]

The PRK subsequently articulated the view that, from Pol Pot's assumption of power, "authentic cadres and party members were progressively discarded" ("Provattesa songkhep robos pak," quoted in Frings 1997, 829), and the organization fell under the influence of an opportunistic clique composed of Pol Pot, Ieng Sary, and Khieu Samphan alone. Frings (1997, 837) has suggested that the reason other significant individuals, such as Nuon Chea, were not specifically condemned was that there was little evidence that they had maintained contact with foreign states. In particular, they were not regarded as lackeys of the "Beijing expansionists" by the pro-Vietnamese government. The argument is persuasive, but another interpretation is possible. As the PRK developed, many of its leaders moved slowly in a more positively Buddhist direction. Perhaps they saw themselves as preserving unique features of the revolutionary movement that had became submerged with the disappearance of Tou Samouth in 1962. We have already seen that he had been an important link between the communists and higher levels of Buddhist traditional learning (see chapter 7). With the ousting of Pol Pot, this connection, one that had never been entirely uprooted during Democratic Kampuchea, might be gradually revived.

Monks and Monasteries

According to a PRK policy statement published in a circular of August 19, 1979, monks were to have the same rights and duties as all other persons. They should possess identity cards and respect government regulations (Vickery 1986, 161).[10] They were not permitted to engage in mendicancy and, in contravention of the norms of monastic discipline *(vinaya),* were also expected to engage in agricultural labor. As "state employees" they were expected to cultivate vegetables in the grounds of the monasteries for their own consumption. The authorities clearly preferred that they cultivate the soil, thereby avoiding the cultivation of potentially disruptive mental states. However, as things began to relax, monks were allowed out of their monasteries for one hour every morning for alms collection, and older members of the laity were permitted to visit the local pagoda in the evenings after the day's work had been completed. Even so, alms giving was discouraged. The laity were expected to focus their limited resources on more explicitly social benefits (Löschmann 1991, 18–19, 21).

Management committees were set up for individual monasteries at this time. They consisted of a majority of lay members who represented the secular authorities. In this way the government was able to outmaneuver uncooperative senior monks (W. Collins 1998a, 52). Lay members also ensured that a proportion of donations to the monastery was redirected to the building of hospitals, roads, and schools. The few foreign observers to visit during the period report that portraits of Marx and Ho Chi Minh were prominently displayed alongside Buddha images in the few functioning *wats* (Luciolli 1988, 187).

A report prepared for the August 1979 trial of Pol Pot had maintained that "several principal temples of our 26 pagodas in Phnom Penh were sacked" during Democratic Kampuchea (de Nike et al. 2000, 145, document 2.1.2.01).[11] So the repair of all of the country's pagodas was incorporated into the Salvation Front's program. Work proceeded slowly. The reestablishment of pagodas was closely supervised, and new foundations could not be started willy-nilly. However, by 1981 some were being rebuilt, and a number of *kathen* ceremonies had taken place, presumably against a background of growing affluence. Although the state did not allocate funds for such undertakings (they were largely financed by local communities), sympathetic officials sometimes helped *wat* building committees acquire inexpensive materials (Vickery 1986, 162–163). There is also some evidence of the pruning of religious structures that had survived DK intact. Wealthy urban areas, for instance, had sometimes accommodated several closely grouped monasteries, but even by the mid-1980s only one of these monasteries had generally been granted permission to function. Many of the rest, particularly in the Phnom Penh area, were used as military barracks, offices, housing, and the like, although this type of use need not necessarily be regarded as a restriction on the freedom of religion, for, given the economic devastation of the time, the local resources to support more than one monastery must have been severely restricted.

Provincial ordination commissions were established early on, and prospective monks were obliged to make formal applications, including a curriculum vitae, to the nearest office. Although the state recognized traditional ordination practices, the receipt of Buddhist teachings from other countries was not permitted (Vickery 1986, 161). A reduction of the quorum from ten to five monks for a higher ordination was also introduced. This was perfectly valid from the *vinaya* perspective. However, the requirement that no male under the age of fifty could ordain, a measure ostensibly designed to maximize the forces of production, was not.[12] Temporary ordinations were also forbidden, although the authorities appear to have actively encouraged the ordination of handicapped men on the grounds that they were not economically active and could best be cared for in a monastic setting. As time went on, ordination became somewhat easier, although local authorities still retained the right of veto.

From April to June 1981 a national gathering of 400 monks in Phnom Penh celebrated the revival of Buddhism and the victory of January 7. However, it is difficult to be certain about the rate of growth of monasticism in the early PRK period. In an interview with the *Toronto Globe and Mail* in September 1981, Ven. Tep Vong claimed 3,000 monks, and 700 pagodas under construction, nationwide. However, a scholarly estimate in the same year concluded that 500 monks had been reordained and 1,500 had entered the novitiate (Keyes 1994b, 61). A year later, Cambodian officials computed a total of 2,311 monks in 1,821 monasteries (Yang Sam 1987, 81),[13] an overall decrease of around 60,000 monks since the Khmer Rouge seized power.[14] This averages out to less than 2 monks per monastery, a figure well below the limit of 4 imposed by the government. There were some exceptions to this rule, particularly in Phnom Penh. The 20 monks residing at Wat Unnalom in 1980 were complemented by a further 8 the following year. Indeed, a total of 170 monks officially occupied monasteries in the capital during 1981.

The Fourth Congress of the party in June 1981 resolved that "the United Front for the National Salvation of Kampuchea must be constantly enlarged and developed and must have a political line acceptable to each social layer, in particular the monks, intellectuals, the ethnic minorities." In September of the same year Ven. Tep Vong was "elected" head of a unified monastic order. He did not adopt the traditional title of *samdech sanghareach* (His Excellency, king of the *sangha*), arguing that it would have been inappropriate in a socialist

(left) Heavily damaged pagoda (unidentified)—early 1980s. Courtesy of Documentation Center of Cambodia.

(below) Ruined monastic library—Wat Krapuchaet, Kandal Province, early 1980s. Courtesy of Documentation Center of Cambodia.

Traditional mural of the Buddha after being attacked by Devadatta. Less traditionally, he is tended by named Western patrons—Wat Kompong Thom, Kompong Thom Province. Courtesy of Caroline Nixon.

setting. Instead he was referred to as president *(prathean)*. Administrative posts were also created at the provincial and village levels, with village presidents effectively acting as pre-1975 *achars* (see Vickery 1986, 162, and Gyallay-Pap and Tranet 1990, 367). The unification of the Cambodian *sangha* was unprecedented. It dissolved the boundaries between the pre-1970s royalist and pro-Thai Thommayut and the larger Mahanikay monastic fraternities *(nikāya)* and seems to have been modeled on the situation in Vietnam, where Theravada and Mahayana Buddhism had been unified in the early 1960s. Indeed, a senior monastic source stated that after unification "our monks are neither Mahanikay nor Thommayut but Nationalist monks" (Yang Sam 1987, 86).[15] Nevertheless, it

Mural of Khmer Rouge hell—Wat Kompong Thom, Kompong Thom Province. Courtesy of Caroline Nixon.

seems that the practice of the unified order was oriented around Mahanikay interpretations of monastic discipline *(vinaya)*.[16]

The politicization of the monastic order was now far more explicit than had been the case under any other Cambodian regime. Pen Sovan, the secretary-general of the Kampuchean People's Revolutionary Party (KPRP), said: "As far as monks are concerned, our Front has a well-defined political line: to respect the traditions, mores and customs of our people. All monks who have direct relations with the people are members of the Front" (quoted in Kiernan 1982, 181). It appears that three monks served on the party's Central Committee (Thion 1983, 317). Others were among the 148 candidates who contested the PRK elections of May 1, 1981 (Steve Heder, in *PPP* 7/11, June 5–18, 1998). Tep Vong also occupied a number of purely political posts, including that of vice president of the Khmer National Assembly and vice president of the Central Committee of the Khmer United Front for National Construction and Defense (KUFNCD), an organization formed to represent and control nonparty groups (Yang Sam 1987, 80). This paradoxical position no doubt informed his public utterances. As an example, he had argued that some types of political violence might be condoned from the Buddhist perspective, specifically citing the activities of the Buddhist-inspired Issaraks of the 1950s (Löschmann 1991, 24).

In 1982 Heng Samrin, now general secretary of the KPRP, addressed the First National Buddhist Monks Congress, at which he extolled Cambodian Buddhism as a religion in harmony with democratic principles. As such, it would "last forever." He also praised the positive contribution of Buddhists to society, particularly those with a nationalist outlook such as Achar Mean (Son Ngoc Minh) and Ven. Hem Chieu (*FBIS*—Asia and Pacific, June 2, 1982, 16).[17] At the Second Congress of 1984 these themes were developed. Heng Samrin reminded his audience that they must be prepared to fight to protect the state against its enemies, for the existence of the state was the necessary condition for the flourishing of Buddhism itself.[18] Intriguingly, he characterized these enemies—no doubt he was thinking of the Khmer Rouge—as the hordes of Māra, the Buddhist embodiment of evil. Furthermore, monks should be particularly vigilant with regard to their fellows who may be using the ordained state for acts of subversion. They should also "completely discard unhealthy beliefs" (Keyes 1994b, 62). These congresses also aimed to establish good relations with the *sangha* in Vietnam and Laos. In addition, Tep Vong had made visits to the Soviet Union and to Mongolia, where he was able to observe and learn about church-state relations (Try 1991, 359).[19] Cambodian Buddhism was beginning to engage with a wider Buddhist world, even though this activity was largely restricted to the communist bloc.

In due course an official document, entitled "Buddhism and the Fatherland," defined the correct relationship between religion and state (Löschmann 1991, 25n20). The government also laid down eight conditions for the proper regulation of the *sangha*, namely:

1. to learn the significance of the political line
2. to educate the laity with regard to party ideas
3. to model themselves on the Buddha and fight the enemy
4. to preserve and cultivate the patriotic and revolutionary spirit exemplified by monks like Ven. Hem Chieu[20] and Achar Mean
5. to preserve the cultural heritage
6. to promote and improve production among the people so that their living standards may be enhanced
7. to assist in building social service establishments
8. to carry out all of the above to achieve victory (Yang Sam 1987, 85)

It is important to read such exhortations in the correct light. Although the government was committed to strong levels of regulation, the weakness of its bureaucratic systems meant that there was ample opportunity to subvert official policy. The regulation of ordination and the resulting cap on monastic numbers, for instance, could be partially circumvented by the establishment of unofficial *wats*. In rural areas young monks seem to have circulated in significant numbers, even though their ordinations had not been registered. I have also interviewed senior *sangha* members who claim to have secretly taught Pali long before the study of Buddhist literature was officially tolerated toward the end of the 1980s.

Only modest numbers of Khmer had escaped the country before April 1975, but, with the establishment of DK, escape became significantly more difficult. Creation of the PRK eased the freedom of movement in Cambodia, and the numbers attempting to cross into Thailand grew dramatically. The question of how many were actually fleeing political repression has been hotly debated, but the flow became so great that several refugee camps were established along the border. In most of these camps, monks who had been defrocked in early DK could resume their previous functions, and as the camps became more established, young men and women, many of whom had lost family members, were attracted to the religious life to the extent that monasteries were eventually constructed.[21] The camp Khao I Dang, for example, had a large Mahanikay pagoda, Wat Pothirot, with between forty and eighty monks and novices (Guthrie-Highbee 1992, 54–55). It was regarded as an important resource in the refugees' resistance to the Christian missionary activity that often follows in the wake of human disasters.[22]

The internal organization of the camps was controlled by Cambodian political factions variously opposed to what they regarded as the Vietnamization of the country. Monastic affiliations were colored by the situation. Site B contained pro-Sihanouk monks, the monks at Site 8 were pro–Khmer Rouge,[23] and Site 2,[24] which was temporarily the second-largest Khmer "city" in the world and the fourth-largest concentration of people in Thailand, contained supporters of Son Sann. Ponchaud (1989, 171n7) reports that a pagoda without any formally ordained monks was established at Sakeo, a camp originally housing DK military and their camp followers. It subsequently became a center of opposition to the Khmer Rouge and, for a time, had to be protected every night by several hundred men armed with bamboo spears. However, by this time the Khmer Rouge had begun a shift in their position on Buddhism. Ieng Sary admitted to various "political errors" made during DK, including the suppression of religion (Willmott 1981, 217n22),[25] and a draft political program of August 1979 had declared an apparent commitment to "freedom of belief and religion." Indeed, when the California-based monk Ven. Bel Long visited another Khmer Rouge border camp in early 1980s, he was given a warm welcome by Khieu Samphan (Yang Sam 1987, 91).

Thaw in Official Attitudes toward Buddhism

Löschmann (1991, 17) has argued that the Buddhist *sangha* was particularly accommodating during the early PRK because it had no landholdings prior to the Democratic Kampuchea period and monasteries did not need to engage in potentially acrimonious legal disputes to regain control once the country's internal circumstances had normalized. This seems unlikely, for, as was noted in chapter 3, monastic landholding was a reality in prerevolutionary Cambodia, although at a lower level than in other Theravada countries such as Sri Lanka. The problem for the *sangha* was rather different. In the first place, most of those with a good understanding of the issue were outside the country or dead, but, rather more obviously, high levels of surveillance and control ensured that the monastic order remained well behaved.

As the new decade unfolded, a government-sponsored mass ordination of fifteen hundred monks took place in Phnom Penh (Kiernan 1982, 173, 177, 181), and various restrictions on monk ordination were lifted in mid-1988. In July, Phnom Penh Radio began to start each day with a broadcast of a Buddhist service from various city monasteries.[26] The establishment of a new State of Cambodia (SOC) in April 1989 had been precipitated by a gradual Vietnamese military withdrawal.[27] Its new constitution restored Buddhism as the state religion (Try 1991, 17n21).[28] Prime Minister Hun Sen (b. 1951) also apologized for earlier government "mistakes" toward religion, and asked to be pardoned, in a series of talks around the country.[29] He and other leaders attended a ceremony at the Buddha bone relic *(preah sakya moni chedi)* next to the Phnom Penh railway station and engaged in other acts of conspicuous Buddhist piety, such as the construction of an ossuary shrine to those who died in DK, replete with explicit Buddhist cosmological motifs, at the killing field of Choeung Ek on the outskirts of Phnom Penh.[30] A tax on temple-monasteries was also abolished around this time, and the structure of Buddhist primary and secondary education, including Pali schools, reemerged in the early 1990s.[31] It is estimated that the number of monks in the period 1985–1989 was about 7,250, but by 1990 the figure had risen to around 16,400, of whom 6,500 were novices (Keyes 1994b, 63). Much of this growth, including the greatly enhanced program of monastery reconstruction, was actually being financed by individuals within the Khmer diaspora, but the administration's newfound enthusiasm for all things Buddhist seems to have enhanced Hun Sen's popularity. It also undermined some of the Buddhist support for political groups opposed to the government (Chandler 1990, 62).

The Vietnamese finally withdrew from Cambodia in September 1989, and in mid-October 1991, a few days before signing the Paris Peace Accord, the KPRP changed its name to the Cambodian People's Party (CPP). In the process it renounced "authentic Marxist-Leninism" and its history of revolutionary struggle. It embraced the "free market" and elected a new party hierarchy.[32] In a speech delivered to the Extraordinary Party Congress of mid-October, Hun Sen made it clear that "the CPP . . . had no previous history of revolutionary struggle" (quoted in Frings 1994b, 357). This opened the way to establishing a very different genealogy, and six months later the party's newspaper, *Pracheachon*, was declaring that the CPP was the "little brother of the Sangkum Reastr Niyum Party," the Cambodian experiment with anticommunist Buddhist socialism led by Sihanouk from 1955.[33] This astonishing about-turn must have led to some consternation in the ranks, for as late as 1987 the party's official line was that Buddhist socialism was a sham designed to maintain "the prerogatives of the exploiting class" and "nothing more than a capitalist regime distinguished as socialist in order to build capitalism" (Frings 1994b, 360).[34]

The New Political Platform of the CPP stated: "The citizens' honour, dignity and life must be protected by laws. The death penalty is abolished. Buddhism is the state religion with the Tripitaka as basis of laws. All religious activities are allowed in the country. The traditions, customs and cultural heritage of the nation must be preserved and glorified, as well as the traditions of all the nationalities living in the Cambodian national community."[35] The scene was now set for the restoration of the monarchy as an indispensable pillar of the state, something that would have been inconceivable a few years earlier.[36] In November 1991, Sihanouk returned to the country from long-term residence in China and resumed the traditional function of supreme patron of the *sangha*.[37] The following month he invested *sanghareachs* for each of the two pre-1975 monastic fraternities. Ven. Tep Vong took control of the Mahanikay, while Ven. Bour Kry, a prominent figure from the Cambodian community in Paris, headed up the Thommayut. Official restoration of both ecclesiastical hierarchies followed in February 1992.[38] For the first time since the mid-1970s both *nikāyas* enjoyed theoretical equivalence, but the peace settlement had also stimulated the return of many refugees from Thailand and other neighboring countries. Included in their number were monks, some of whom had remained in robes throughout the 1970s and 1980s. Their return to Cambodia would, in due course, raise a number of uncomfortable questions about the seniority of the newly appointed ecclesiastical hierarchy.

Senior members of the *sangha* (2000): *(right)*, Ven. Bour Kry; *(below)*, Ven. Tep Vong; *(opposite, top)*, Ven. Non Nget; *(opposite, bottom)*, Ven. Las Lay.

1993 Elections

The United Nations–sponsored elections in May 1993 arose out of the Paris Peace Accord and were conducted under the principle of universal adult suffrage. As Bektimirova (2002, 65) has noted, the international community was guilty of a degree of cultural insensitivity in reaching this decision, for it meant that monks voted for the first time in Cambodia's history. Many senior figures, however, felt that the *sangha* should stand apart from the political process. Ven. Non Nget told me that he and Ven. Bour Kry both made unsuccessful presentations to Yasushi Akashi, a special representative of the UN secretary-general, to try to resolve the problem,[39] and there is reasonable evidence that some senior monks dissuaded younger colleagues from voting when the time came. Having said that, the elections clearly provided a context in which those who did vote were able to give concrete expression to long-held social and political affiliations. The imposition of universal suffrage, then, contributed to a further politicization and fragmentation of the *sangha,* a process that has been a feature of Cambodian religious life since the beginning of the modern period, persisting down to the present.

The Buddhist Liberal Democratic Party (BLDP), led by Son Sann, was one of the many parties formed to fight the election. Representing the anticommunist Khmer People's National Liberation Front (KPNLF), it had origins in the refugee camps along the Thai border (Somboon Suksamran 1993, 144).[40] In 1984 Son Sann had founded a Khmer Buddhist Research Center at Rithisen—under the guidance of Ven. Pin Sem,[41] the *chau adhikar* of the Rithisen camp *wat*—which by 1989 had become the largest functioning Cambodian Buddhist monastery in the world, with around two hundred monks and novices (Gyallay-Pap and Tranet 1990, 369). The research center aimed to revive and preserve Buddhist traditions, scriptures, and scholarship and sought to keep exiled *sangha* members in communication with their fellows. Its first publication argued for a more socially engaged Buddhism in which monks should leave the security of their monasteries and expand "their knowledge in political and social questions and . . . exercise influence in regard to motivating the population for the liberation of their country from foreign domination and the Marxist-Leninist ideology" (Son Soubert et al. 1986, 157).[42] The BLDP was clearly conceived as a means for realizing this goal.

In the end, the BLDP won only ten seats in the Constituent Assembly, but it was the third-largest party after the CPP and FUNCINPEC[43] (a royalist party led by Sihanouk's eldest son, Prince Norodom Ranariddh), which had fifty-one and fifty-eight seats, respectively. Intriguingly, the CPP had discouraged the populace from voting for other parties, on the grounds that those parties would erase all of the CPP's recent achievements, such as the restoration of monasteries (Edwards 1996, 58n25), and there is evidence that the police wrote reports on the political meetings of non-CPP parties held in the monasteries of Phnom Penh (Marston 1997, 360). Not everything ran according to CPP plans, however. Thompson (1999, 243) tells an interesting story of a local *achar* from Wat Kien Svay Kuong, Kandal, who was arrested by local officials on suspicion of supporting FUNCINPEC. At this monastery the Brahmanical deity Hanumān *(kamhaeng)* is venerated as a tutelary spirit *(neak tā)*, and one night during his incarceration Hanumān is said to have wrecked the local CPP offices. The *achar* was released almost immediately.

As a result of protracted haggling, FUNCINPEC was obliged to form a coalition government with the CPP, along with some minor BLDP representation.[44] Son Sann was appointed chairman of the Constituent Assembly, and he also supervised the drafting of the September 24, 1993, Constitution, which restored Sihanouk to the throne.[45] However, the BLDP was soon riven by a variety of disputes. In July 1995 its Ieng Mouly faction[46] separated from Son Sann and his son Son Soubert, stating that the father was too old, too weak, and too "racially prejudiced and paranoid," particularly with regard to Vietnam, to lead the party. In September of the same year, Son Sann's house was struck with a grenade, and some of his supporters, both lay and monastic, were violently attacked by unknown assailants at Wat Mohamontrey, Phnom Penh (*PPP* 4/15, July 28–August 10, 1995, 5; 4/20, October 6–19, 1995, 1–3). Subsequently, Ieng Mouly reached an accommodation with Hun Sen and was appointed minister of information. Son Sann retired from active politics in January 1997 and died in Paris in December 2000.

According to the September 1993 Constitution, the motto of the Kingdom of Cambodia is "Nation, Religion, King" (Article 4).[47] Buddhism was also established as the state religion (Article 43). It has been argued that, by renewing the old association of Theravada Buddhism and *khmèritude*, the drafters were able to underline the sharp cultural boundary between Cambodia and Vietnam, the latter being Communists, Catholics, or Mahayanists (Martin 1994, 260). Article 43 also ensures that "Khmer citizens of either sex shall have the right to freedom of belief." However, "freedom of religious belief and worship shall be guaranteed by the state on the condition that such freedom does not affect other religious beliefs or violate public order and security." There are echoes of PRK and DK thinking on the need for strong controls here. One can only speculate that the CPP, given its previous history, was the most likely group to have argued for the inclusion of such restrictions. Another section of the Constitution that is relevant from a Buddhist perspective is Article 13, which charges that "within a period of not more than seven days [of the death of the previous king], the new King . . . shall be chosen by the Royal Council of the Throne," comprising six persons, including the two *sanghareachs*.[48]

The Ministry of Cults and Religious Affairs was reestablished in 1992, taking over responsibility for religious policy from the Khmer United Front for National Construction and Defense (KUFNCD) (T. Huxley 1987, 169).[49] Hean Vanniroth, a FUNCINPEC member, became its first secretary of state. Its main aims were to reestablish the ecclesiastical structures that existed before 1970, to develop and consolidate monk education,[50] and to reestablish the Buddhist Institute and reissue its previous publications. Article 68 of the Constitution had in fact asserted that the "State shall disseminate and develop the Pali schools and the Buddhist Institute." The institute itself restarted in June 1992 and has been funded by ongoing grants from two non-Khmer nongovernmental organizations (NGOs)—the Heinrich Böll Foundation (HBF) and the Japanese Sotoshu Relief Committee (JSRC).[51] The institute's quarterly journal, *Kambuja Suriya,* resumed publication in 1994. Originally based in Wat Unnalom, the Buddhist Institute now has a purpose-built center in Phnom Penh funded by the Japanese Rissho Koseikai Fund for Peace in commemoration of the ninetieth year of the movement's founder, Nikkyo Niwano.

Virtually the entire library of the original Buddhist Institute, comprising around 30,000 titles and 4,000 documents, has disappeared, although whether this occurred as a deliberate and concerted act of vandalism or was simply due to foraging for paper has not been established. Indeed, some informed sources believe that some of the institute's holdings may still exist at a forgotten location. De Bernon (1997, 44n33), for instance, recalls the odd fact that the library was still intact when it was visited by someone from the Ministry of Education in the early months of 1979. The JSRC has been heavily involved in republishing materials relating to Buddhism and Khmer culture.[52] Original publications have been brought from Japanese libraries for this purpose. In June 1995 the JSRC presented the king with 1,200 copies of the complete 110-volume set of the Khmer Tripitaka for distribution to monasteries and libraries (de Bernon 1998a, 880). It is difficult to assess how these are used, but my own observations suggest that the volumes are often housed in glass cabinets at the rear of a *vihāra,* where they become cult objects. The low level of study of Pali texts is partly a consequence of the lack of educational attainment in the *sangha* as a whole, but it also demonstrates the reemergence of traditionalist suspicion of nonvernacular religious writing.

Since July 1991 the École Française d'Extrême-Orient (EFEO) has sponsored research into the identification and conservation of surviving Buddhist manuscripts, under the auspices of the Fonds pour l'Édition des Manuscrits du Cambodge (FEMC). It has been estimated that 95 percent of the literary patrimony of Cambodia inscribed on palm leaves or traditional paper was destroyed in the holocaust (de Bernon 1998a, 873). Initial reports suggested that manuscripts had survived in quantity in only four Phnom Penh monasteries—Wat Neak Voan, Wat Sansam Kosal, Wat Chak Angre Kraom, and Wat Stung Meanchey (de Bernon 1992, 245). But there have been some notable surprises. A library at Wat Thmei, Kang Meas, Kompong Cham Province, was discovered in the late 1990s. It appears that in 1975 the *chau adhikar* distributed texts to pious villagers, who were urged to hide them until things died down. Ven. Ken Vong (d. 1994), the *chau adhikar* of Wat Saravan in Phnom Penh and one of the original seven monks reordained in September 1979, also managed to make a collection of around 3,400 manuscripts after 1979. It now forms the largest collection in the country and is held in a library that bears his name in his old monastery.[53] It is now administered and managed by EFEO. The EFEO's current work in Cambodia, then, represents a reversal of the policy of the school in the pre-Independence period. At that time the school was keen to promote Buddhist modernism through its sponsorship of Pali scholarship and the like. Now, largely as a result of Bizot's groundbreaking work, it is heavily engaged in retrieving and evaluating the resources of Buddhist traditionalism.

Emergence of Recent Sangha Groups

Mahanikay Modernists

As we have already seen, the Mahanikay had grown in strength and influence during the colonial period as a result of the activities of monks such as Vens. Chuon Nath and Huot That. Their reformed *sangha*, the Thommakay, had been especially vehement in its criticism of the "corrupt practices" of the traditionalists. Ven. Mahaghosananda is an heir to the modernism of Chuon Nath. Born Va Yav in Takeo Province around 1922,[54] he became a monk at the age of fourteen. Having studied at the Buddhist University in Phnom Penh, he traveled to India to work for a doctorate at the newly established Buddhist University of Nalanda. While there, he seems to have come under the influence of Nichidatsu Fujii, who founded the Japanese peace-oriented Buddhist sect Nipponzan Myohoji and was himself involved with the work of Gandhi. In 1965 Mahaghosananda moved to a forest hermitage in southern Thailand under the tutelage of the insight meditation *(vipassanā)* master Ajahn Dhammadharo, remaining there for eleven years. In 1978 he made his way to the Cambodian refugee camps on the Thai border that were growing rapidly as Democratic Kampuchea began to collapse. In this new context he helped establish temples for the spiritual, educational, and cultural uplift of the people. In cooperation with Peter Pond, a Christian social activist, he formed the Inter-Religious Mission for Peace in Cambodia in 1980. One of the aims of the organization was to identify, support, and reordain surviving Cambodian Buddhist monks. To aid this process, Mahaghosananda helped found more than thirty temples in Canada and the United States in these early years. He also worked as a consultant to the United Nations Economic and Social Council. In 1981 he stated, "We must find the courage to leave the traditional temple and enter the temple of the teeming human experience that is filled with suffering. . . . [I]t is important to remember that we carry our temple with us always. We are the temple" (quoted in Hansen 1988, 61). In consequence of these and other utterances, his standing in the Cambodian exile community began to grow, and he was elected *samdech* by a small gathering of monks and laity in Paris in 1988.[55]

As conditions in Cambodia improved after the creation of the SOC in April 1989, Mahaghosananda took up residence at Wat Sampeou Meas, Phnom Penh,[56] but he first came to general prominence as the leader of a peace march *(dhammayietra)* that began on April 13, 1992, in which about 350 monks, nuns, and lay Buddhists escorted approximately 100 refugees from the camps back to their villages against a background of official opposition, for neither the Thai nor the Cambodian government would give permission for the marchers to cross the border.[57] However, by the time the marchers arrived in Phnom Penh, the numbers had swollen significantly, to the extent that the event was covered by some sections of the international media. In recognition of Mahaghosananda's enhanced status, Sihanouk conferred the title "Leader of Religion and Peace" *(samdech song santipeap)* on him later the same year.[58] Such was his celebrity that some early followers came to believe that he was the salvific figure "come from the west" mentioned in nineteenth-century prophetic works such as the *Buddh Daṃnāy*. To his credit, Mahaghosananda quickly disabused them of this notion.

It seems that Ven. Tep Vong had been involved in the early stages of organization of the first Dhammayietra, although he subsequently withdrew his support. The suspicion remains that he had been warned off by the government.[59] Nevertheless, annual Dhammayietra have become a regular feature of Cambodian life. Originally they were organized by the Dhammayietra Center for Peace and Reconciliation (CPR), based at Wat Sampeou Meas, but as doubts about the financial probity of some senior staff began to surface at the end of the 1990s, attempts were made to decentralize the movement.[60] The April 2000 march through Banteay Meanchey Province to Sisophon, for instance, was organized at the local level.[61]

The CPR had originally been established at Taprya, on the Thai-Cambodian border close to the Site 2 refugee camp. Its founders were an ex-Jesuit, Bob Maat; Liz Bernstein; and the Paris-based Mahanikay monk Ven. Yos Hut. They then co-opted Mahaghosananda, and the Dhammayietra movement was formed. It would not be inaccurate, then, to suggest that the first march was largely organized by foreigners. Indeed, many of the early marches were led by chanting Japanese Nipponzan Myohoji monks, and as late as 1997 the US$27,000 necessary for the organization of the sixth Dhammayietra came mainly from "Christian and ecumenical foreign NGOs, International Organizations, and King Sihanouk" (Yukiko Yonekura 1999, 86–87). The movement is theoretically interreligious and has tried to involve Cambodia's other religious and ethnic groupings, even though only Buddhists and Christians have actually participated in the marches. It also claims that Buddhism itself has a history of such marches, pointing slightly disingenuously to the example of the Buddha himself, who walked every day to collect alms and preach (Yukiko Yonekura 1999, 90). Mahaghosananda (1992, 70) has also written, "During his lifetime, the Buddha lobbied for peace and human rights."[62]

Most marches have focused on specific issues, many of which have not been welcomed by the Cambodian authorities. The fourth Dhammayietra in 1995 was intended to raise awareness of the issues surrounding land mines. The marchers crossed into Vietnam where, despite initial reluctance, they were received by high-level government and Buddhist officials (Yukiko Yonekura 1999, 84). The 1996 event highlighted the adverse impact of large-scale deforestation, and a sixth march in 1997, co-organized by the Campaign to Reduce Violence for Peace,[63] entered the Khmer Rouge strongholds of the northwest. On reaching Pailin, the marchers were greeted by Ieng Sary, Y Chhien, the town's mayor, and other important Khmer Rouge defectors (*Cambodia Daily*, April 21, 1997). The seventh walk started on July 19, 1998, at Wat Prey Lavia in Mahaghosananda's home province of Takeo, ending at the Royal Palace on July 24. On July 23 the walkers stopped at the Center for Culture and Vipassana in Prek Ho, near Takhmau, run by Professor Chheng Pon, a former actor and minister of culture and information (1981–1990) during PRK/SOC. A figure active in the effort to reestablish Khmer art, culture, and religion following their virtual disappearance during Democratic Kampuchea, Chheng Pon was also the National Election Committee chairman for the 1998 elections (*PPP* 7/15, July 24–30, 1998). He has been much reviled by those who oppose the results, and it may be that the organizers of the march wished to enhance Chheng Pon's credibility once more.[64] Other more localized marches have been organized against prostitution in Phnom Penh's Toul Kok red-light district and in support of stranded Vietnamese fishing families, a pariah group in contemporary Cambodia (*PPP* 3/5, March 11–24, 1994, 1; 3/7, April 8–21, 1994, 4).

Since problems associated with gun attacks on the 1994 Dhammayietra, marchers have been trained in ways of dealing with fear through Buddhist meditation. The training particularly focuses on the cultivation of the divine abidings *(brahmavihāra)*, with specific emphasis on the development of compassion *(karunā)*. Walking meditations involving the practice of mindfulness are also recommended (Moser-Puangsuwan n.d., 3).[65] The movement claims to be entirely nonpartisan. It also tries to weed out undisciplined monks, many of whom have been ordained for a relatively short time and may have entered the order only to avoid military conscription or to gain some kind of economic or educational advantage. The movement's commitment to the Buddhist Middle Way means that all explicitly political banners, military uniforms, and weapons are forbidden on the march, although it is reliably reported that several monks carried pictures of the nationalist hero Ven. Hem Chieu in 1998 (*PPP* 7/22, October 2–15, 1998).

Ven. Yos Hut is another reformed Mahanikay activist with close connections to Mahaghosananda.[66] A senior monk at Wat Langka, Phnom Penh, he is also the president of the Fondation Bouddhique Khmère, with offices in Cambodia and France. One of the foundation's projects was the construction of a hospital (begun in 1996) in Kampong Trabek, Prey Veng Province. Yos Hut is also planning a forest monastery, with associated educational and development-oriented features, on some hundred hectares of land acquired in the same region. Recently some hostility between the local authorities of Kampong Trabek District and monks associated with this work has crystallized in the attempt to defrock Ven. Khot Khon, the abbot of Wat Beng Bury, for supposed sexual misconduct and involvement in politics. The charge seems to have arisen after the visits of several high-profile FUNCINPEC officials, including Prince Sisowath Satha, to the monastery (*PPP* 9/12, June 9–22, 2000). The chief monk of Kampong Trabek District has subsequently attempted to solve the dispute by suggesting that Khot Khon either return to the lay life or move to another monastery. This intervention suggests a level of government (i.e., CPP) opposition to aspects of the engaged Buddhist agenda, particularly when they are linked with the activities of opposition parties, and shows that more generalized political interference in the internal administration of the *sangha* is not simply a feature of the past.

Engaged Buddhism in Cambodia received more general support from a massive influx of foreign NGOs in the lead-up to the 1993 elections. The activities of the German-based Konrad Adenauer Foundation (KAF) and its funding of a socially engaged "development-oriented Buddhism" are particularly instructive. Between 1994 and 1997, for example, the Buddhism for Development (BFD) organization, based at Wat Anlongvil, Battambang Province, received around $750,000 from the KAF.[67] The BFD was founded in April 1990, growing out of attempts by Son Sann and Ven. Pin Sem to revive Khmer Buddhist culture at the Rithisen refugee camp on the Thai border, which had also been funded by the KAF (see Guthrie-Highbee 1992, 54–55). In the field it concentrates on the training of Buddhist monks in rural development work, the establishment of rice and money banks and of tree nurseries, and compost-making activities. It has also held a series of annual national seminars on Buddhism and the development of Khmer society. One of the BFD's senior activists, Heng Monychenda, has written a number of books, including *Preahbat Dhammik* (1996), that aim to give Buddhist-based moral guidance to Cambodian politicians.[68] Another NGO, the Deutsche Gesellschaft für Technische Zusammenarbeit (GTZ) has, since February 1995, worked mainly through local *wat* communities in Srok Stung, Kampong Thom Province, to encourage community development.[69] It has also helped to redevelop the pilgrimage site at Phnom Santuk (*PPP* 10/21, October 12–25, 2001). The GTZ seeks to regenerate the moral influence of Buddhism in contemporary society. It argues that laypeople have always engaged in pagoda-related activities as a form of merit making. The challenge, then, is to extend the range of traditional merit-making actions to include things like tree planting, pond digging, and bridge and road building so that the laity will become involved as a form of self-interest motivated by Buddhist principles.[70]

Environmental concerns have gained much attention in recent years, so the KAF also supports the Santi Sena movement based at Wat Prey Chlak, Svay Rieng, which works on forest preservation and similar activities. The leader of Santi Sena is Ven. Nhim Kim Teng,[71] a close associate of Ven. Yos Hut's. Both monks have been involved in the Monk Environmental Education Program (MEEP), funded by the United Nations Development Programme and based around a consortium of twelve local NGOs.[72] More formally, an Inter-Ministerial Steering Committee for Environmental Education, drawing on the resources of the Ministry of Cults and Religious Affairs and a variety of Buddhist associations, has produced an environmental manual for primary teachers. Rather more surprisingly, Ta Mok, generally regarded as the most brutal of the surviving Khmer Rouge leaders, is known to have expressed typically idiosyncratic environmentalist views: "Whoever destroys the forest is not allowed to be a leader. . . . Whoever blows up and shoots fish are *yuon* [a derogatory term for the Vietnamese] and have their throats cut. . . . Whoever burns the forest, if arrested, has to be burned alive."[73]

The KAF has a Protestant Christian ethos, so it is hardly surprising that it and other NGOs active in the region harbor some doubts about traditional forms of Cambodian Buddhism that, from the Protestant perspective, appear excessively quietistic, ritualistic, and wrapped in superstition. One of the more paradoxical aspects of this attitude is that it parallels that which justified the kinds of reform of Buddhism that were forced through during the PRK period. The funds that such NGOs can make available to institutional Buddhism—which is only now reemerging after many decades of stagnation, neglect, and persecution—are considerable, particularly given that the government itself is strapped for cash. Yet this external funding may have a distorting effect on the development of Buddhism in Cambodia, quite comparable to that induced by official control of the *sangha* during the colonial and PRK periods. To put the matter simply, external financial support is given exclusively to forms of Buddhism moving in a socially engaged, modernist direction. Here is a clear example of what Charles Taylor (1989) terms "the affirmation of ordinary life," a potentially momentous move away from "the supposedly higher activities of contemplation" in favor of ordinary living and production.[74] From what we know about the history of Buddhism in Cambodia, it is only a matter of time before the traditionalists will react to what they regard as a foreign-financed and potentially unpatriotic segment within the monastic order, and this could be quite damaging to the immediate prospects of a Buddhist revival in the country.

Nevertheless, support for engaged Buddhism has been given by the king himself, who has described the work of the BFD and similar groups as "an important contribution to the revival of the concept of 'Buddhist Socialism' which . . . [he] encouraged during the historic Sangkum Reastr Niyum period" of the 1950s and 1960s (*Buddhism and the Development of Khmer Society* 1996, 50). It is in this context that we should interpret Ven. Mahaghosananda's appointment as Sihanouk's special representative for the protection of the environment in 1994.[75] The post is an entirely novel creation, having formed no part of the pre-1975 monastic hierarchy. However, given government opposition to some aspects of Mahanikay activism, it is tempting to regard the construction of such extraecclesiastical roles as an attempt by the king to construct an alternative, non-CPP-controlled Buddhist hierarchy.[76] Having said that, most reformed Mahanikay monks have managed to steer clear of explicit political favoritism. When the king sent a letter to the Dhammayietra organizing committee, asking them to call off the 1994 walk for fear of violence, for example, Mahaghosananda ignored the advice (Yukiko Yonekura 1999, 85). For Mahaghosananda and his supporters, meaningful change in Cambodia can be successfully achieved only through radical transformation of individual minds. The arena of explicit social engagement makes no sense unless it is premised on such an assumption. Such "mysticism" (Hughes 2000) sits well with the desire to keep the movement entirely nonpartisan. It also tends in the direction of a complete separation of church and state. As another prominent engaged monk, Ven. Hok Sovann, has argued, the *sangha* will lose the people's respect if it is seen to be involved in "politics instead of practicing the traditional monk's discipline."[77] Yet, ironically, as leading Mahanikay modernists have tried to avoid the murky waters of domestic politics, they have gradually been drawn into other perilous alliances. Therefore they must strive to avoid the charge that they have become nothing much more than servants of the international community.

Thommayut

The monastic order in Cambodia has been divided into two fraternities *(nikāya)* since 1855, when King Ang Duang imported the newly formed Thommayut *(dhammayutika nikāya)* from Thailand through the agency of Mahā Pan, a Khmer monk belonging to King Mongkut's spiritual lineage. Norodom subsequently established Wat Botum Vaddey—adjacent to the new Royal Palace in Phnom Penh—as the headquarters of the new order, and Pan was installed as its first Cambodian *sanghareach*. In nineteenth-century Thailand the introduction of the new order took place without opposition, but this was not the case in Cambodia, where skirmishes occurred with some regularity (Bizot 1976, 9). This resistance may have had something to do with the French, who regarded the Mahanikay, particularly those from its reformed wing, as exercising a beneficial influence on the populace and a positive attitude toward the Protectorate. Thommayut monks, on the other hand, were thought to be politically suspect because of their supposed allegiance to the Thai court (Forest 1980, 143).[78] A largely urban phenomenon, the Thommayut has always been much smaller in terms of its numbers and its geographical spread.[79]

The Thommayut was aristocratic in orientation, and its connections to Thailand put it into a doubly difficult relationship with the communists, who regarded even the most innocent of contacts with foreign states as treasonable acts (Chantou Boua 1991, 229).[80] Additionally, the Khmer Rouge seem to have favored rural monks over those based in the cities. Given all this, there is good reason to suppose, although there is no reliable quantitative evidence in support, that Thommayut monks suffered greater persecution during Democratic Kampuchea than did their Mahanikay fellows. Official resistance to the Thommayut continued after institutional Buddhism was reestablished in the early PRK period. We have already noted that official recognition had been given in 1981 to a unified *sangha* that ostensibly dissolved the differences between the two established orders but, in fact, privileged prior Mahanikay practice. Many prominent figures of the time argued that this arrangement would help eliminate the elitist, unpatriotic, and monarchical influences of the Thommayut. It was only in December 1991 that the two orders were re-created after Sihanouk appointed Ven. Tep Vong and Ven. Bour Kry as patriarchs of the Mahanikay and the Thommayut, respectively.

Ven. Bour Kry is originally from Battambang, where he had been the second assistant to the chief monk of Wat Bopharam, the regional headquarters of the Thommayut. Before promotion to the position of *chau adhikar* of a monastery close to the Thai border, he had been secretary to the *mekun* of Battambang Province (Ang and Tan 1992, 292). Like many of the reformed Mahanikay figures already discussed, Bour Kry spent the DK and PRK periods as part of the Cambodian diaspora. When Phnom Penh fell in April 1975, the only Cambodian monk in Paris had been Ven. Yos Hut, who was there for postgraduate studies. In due course he was joined by a number of refugees, including Bour Kry, who had escaped via Thailand. A house in Vincennes, to the southeast of the city, was subsequently bought, and Wat Khemararam was established in its garden. Personal and political differences soon began to affect the exile community.[81] Martin (1994, 251) notes that in the late 1980s the Khmer New Year was celebrated on successive Sundays by three separate politically oriented factions—FUNCINPEC, KPNLF, and neutrals, each with its monastic supporters. It was only a matter of time before the other monks, including Yos Hut himself, formed alternative centers in and around Paris. This left Bour Kry at Wat Khemararam.

It was around this time that Sihanouk favored Bour Kry with a number of ceremonial titles in recognition of the fact that one of his sons had spent time as a temporary monk under Bour Kry's tutelage.[82] Given Bour Kry's Thommayut affiliation, it is hardly surprising that he was both closer to the royal family and rather more traditional in his observance of *vinaya* than other Cambodian monks in France. Only Wat Khemararam was properly delimited by *sīmā* markers, for instance. But Bour Kry also had a reputation as an astrologer, and, despite opposition from more traditionally minded Khmer, he encouraged women to take a more active role in ceremonies.[83] He also seems to have encouraged his supporters to make financial contributions to FUNCINPEC (Kalab 1994, 69).

Today at Wat Botum, the symbolic center of the order and home of the *sanghareach*, Thommayut monks are greatly outnumbered and are physically isolated, in a separate section of the compound, from members of the Mahanikay.[84] The situation reflects the relatively short history of the newly formed order, for all monks at Wat Botum had been part of a unified order before 1991, and after that time most reverted to the Mahanikay. But since the reestablishment of a full Thommayut hierarchy, some influential posts have been occupied by prominent pro-government Mahanikay monks. It could be argued that they are well placed to feed intelligence to the relevant authorities. The second figure in the hierarchy, the *mongol tepeachar (maṅgaladevācārya)*, for example, was until quite recently Ven. Oum Som (1918–2000), the Mahanikay chief monk of Wat Mohamontrey, Phnom Penh.[85] The continued manipulation of monastic management committees through the incorporation of pro-CPP placemen has also had a significant stifling impact on dissent.[86] The role of Hun Sen's father, as chairman of the Wat Botum committee, is an excellent example.[87] He is not the ideal figure to bring about reconciliation between the Mahanikay and the Thommayut factions at the divided monastery. Official suspicion of monarchical and pro-FUNCINPEC organizations and individuals clearly persists, and although members of the Thommayut are once more permitted to go to Thailand for higher ordination *(upasampadā)*, they are distrusted for much the same reasons as they were in the colonial and communist periods.

Thommayut monks do not appear to possess the developmentalist and reformist interests of their modernist Mahanikay counterparts. This may simply be because the Mahanikay is overwhelmingly the largest order. It is also more rural than the Thommayut. However, senior Thommayut figures have been invited to events sponsored by foreign NGOs, but they have shown some reluctance to attend. This reluctance can be explained in a number of ways. The order's strict observance of monastic discipline, such as the prohibition on handling money and digging the soil, may be a factor. Another possibility is that the Thommayut hierarchy is concerned about the adverse impact that the receipt of international funds might have on the traditions of Cambodian Buddhism. Given their greater contact with Thailand, they are likely to be more aware of this as a potentially divisive issue. A final possibility is that the feuding noted during the exile in Paris has not been entirely healed.

Certainly, the Thommayut are not entirely unconcerned with wider social questions, a fact underlined by a well-publicized disagreement between Bour Kry and Tep Vong.[88] Following a conference for monks organized by the National AIDS Authority in May 2000, the two *sanghareachs* appeared to be at loggerheads about how best to respond to the HIV/AIDS problem. Tep Vong's view was that the scale of the problem had been greatly inflated by Cambodia's enemies in order to discredit the political leadership of the CPP. He also argued that the right course of action was a crackdown on brothels and prostitutes. He also regarded AIDS as a karmic punishment, so monks need not take any role in comforting the sick.[89] Bour Kry, on the other hand, has argued that monks should minister "moral support to the sick, so they can die peacefully—even though they have committed a bad thing" (*PPP* 9/12, June 9–22, 2000). Nevertheless, he is unconvinced that monks should be disseminating a safe-sex message to the general population, because this would involve use of language incompatible with their monastic vocation. Unlike the reformed Mahanikay, who have actively engaged in AIDS education, and the Mahanikay hierarchy, who tend to view the epidemic as a foreign and ideological threat, the Thommayut seem to be steering a middle course.

Explicit Politics

The power-sharing arrangement between the CPP and FUNCINPEC that was imposed as a result of the May 1993 elections was never likely to last. In July 1997, violent conflict between armed factions of the two parties broke out and concluded to the advantage of the former. After the event, Ven. Oum Som is reported to have told *sangha* members that FUNCINPEC was in league with the Khmer Rouge and should be "sent out of the city." Despite concerns about the CPP's organization, a further election in July 1998 produced a result in favor of the CPP.[90] Angered by the election outcome, Sam Rainsy Party supporters organized a rally at the Olympic Stadium, Phnom Penh, on August 22.[91] Six days later, monks led a candlelight procession, and another rally, including a significant number of monks, was held on the following day. After a while the crowd of perhaps as many as sixteen thousand moved off in the direction of the National Assembly, where speeches were made. Some speeches, including at least one by a young monk, expressed strong anti-Vietnamese sentiments (*PPP* 7/19, September 4–17, 1998).[92]

According to unconfirmed reports, another young monk was severely injured and subsequently disappeared outside the Hotel Cambodiana on September 7, 1997, where Sam Rainsy was staying after a grenade attack on Hun Sen's compound. Around three hundred monks—some holding posters denouncing Hun Sen, others carrying wreaths for monks missing from previous demonstrations—were in the vanguard of a march through central Phnom Penh the next day. One of the leaders, Ven. Chin Channa, used a megaphone to remind listeners of the example of Ven. Hem Chieu, the anticolonialist monk of the early 1940s.[93] Having been photographed by a pro-government newspaper in an earlier demonstration, he was branded a dangerous activist, and wanted posters appeared in Phnom Penh monasteries. He was spirited out of the city by international human rights activists. The aim of the September 8 event had been to claim the body and hold a funeral service for the monk reportedly killed the day before. They had also intended to "beg violence" from the authorities—in other words, to draw any aggression down upon themselves and thereby defuse a potentially dangerous situation.[94] Indeed, when charged by police, most fled, but one monk sat in the lotus position and offered up a greeting with palms held together *(sompeah)*, receiving a blow to the neck with an electric prod for his troubles. Lack of experience in organizing demonstrations, combined with possible infiltration by agents provocateurs, seems to have led the event to spiral out of control (*PPP* 8/19, October 2–15, 1999).

On September 9 two monks were reported as having been shot by police outside the U.S. Embassy, where they had gone to gain support for an end to the post-election violence. One of them, twenty-one-year-old Cheng Sokly, subsequently had an AK-47 bullet removed from his body and survived. He reported witnessing the shooting of another monk in the back of the leg. A young male body with head injuries was retrieved downriver at Peam Chor, Prey Veng Province, on September 11. It had a shaved head and eyebrows but curiously had been hastily dressed in a police uniform (*Cambodia Daily*, October 17, 1998). The demonstrations gradually died down, and on September 16 a UN human rights envoy named Thomas Hammarberg declared that sixteen bodies, "including two in saffron robes," had been found since the beginning of the troubles.

The question naturally arises whether it is legitimate for Buddhist monks to participate in such potentially violent events. One young monk told me, "If the government wants to keep Buddhist monks from getting involved in politics, they should not allow monks to vote. But we do vote." Ou Bun Long, a prominent member of the Khmer Buddhist Society (KBS)[95] and a spokesman for the Sam Rainsy Party, also claimed that the monks' actions were not a technical violation of monastic discipline *(vinaya)*, and a number of senior *sangha* members also seem to have agreed, in private, that the events might be justified from the Buddhist perspective. But they were almost immediately condemned by those thought to be close to the ruling party. Ven. Oum Som, for instance, appeared on national television on September 10 to say, "Monks from the provinces and pagodas of the city have attended illegal demonstrations with civilians. This is against the rules of Buddhism."[96] There is certainly some justification in the criticism, since this was during the three-month rainy season retreat *(vassa)*, a time when monks should be secluded within their monasteries. However, Oum Som also accused three monks of causing their own injuries through fear and ill discipline, a charge repeated by an Interior Ministry spokesman who also claimed that some of the monks involved in demonstrations were not "real monks."[97]

Throughout this period there seems to have been genuine anxiety among some members of the Phnom Penh *sangha* who feared that they were under police surveillance. Twelve monks are reported as having barricaded themselves

Police officers attacking young monks near Central Market, Phnom Penh—September 8, 1998. Courtesy of Heng Sinith and Documentation Center of Cambodia.

into a room at the top of one of the buildings at Wat Unnalom, and there were repeated rumors that monks had disappeared (*PPP* 7/20, September 12–17, 1998).[98] I am reliably informed that Ven. Tep Vong called in members of Hun Sen's bodyguard unit, as well as military police officers who were supplied by municipal governor Chea Sophara and used electric cattle prods and small arms to flush out dissidents within the monastery. "Unnalom monks know how to run!" was a much repeated maxim at the time. Unsurprisingly, relations between Tep Vong and monk activists have deteriorated significantly over the last few years, to the extent that the Mahanikay *sanghareach* is variously accused of corruption, rudeness, simony, nepotism, philistinism, and lack of patriotism by his young opponents.[99]

Given the heightened tension, very few laypeople attended city monasteries during the annual fortnight of offerings to the ancestors *(pchum ben),* which began on September 20, 1998. The lack of attendance is verified in a letter that the king is reported to have written to Hun Sen, asking him to authorize the free movement of monks during the ceremonies. Around 50 percent of Phnom Penh–based monks attempted to leave their monasteries for the country immediately after the troubles, although a significant number were ordered off trains and turned back at road checkpoints (*Cambodia Daily,* September 17, 1998; *PPP* 7/22, October 2–15, 1998). Despite the government's partial success in preventing the spread of monastic disaffection, it seems likely that a fairly wide circle of young *sangha* members were radicalized across much of the country in the next few months. Attempts to mark the first anniversary of the September 1998 demonstrations with a ceremony at Wat Unnalom were frustrated by a formal *sangha* declaration issued by Tep Vong and calling for the arrest of the organizers. However, the event did eventually take place at Wat Botum after Bour Kry gave the necessary permissions.

Sam Rainsy appears to have had an ongoing involvement with anti-CPP elements within the *sangha.* He had been a temporary Thommayut monk at Wat Botum for three weeks toward the end of 1996 and rejoined the order for a spell in January 2001 after the death of his mother. He appears to enjoy good relations with Bour Kry (*PPP* 5/24, November 29–December 12, 1996, 3).[100] Members of his party erected various memorial *stūpas* for sixteen victims of a grenade attack on one of their demonstrations on March 30, 1997, yet each has been dismantled, ostensibly because they infringed planning regulations. The last of these was constructed on May 16, 2000. It contained some of the victims' ashes and a Buddha image. It seems that a policeman charged with its destruction refused to carry out the order and was demoted. Bour Kry's announcement that destroying the structure was equivalent to destroying the Buddhist religion may have had some bearing on his decision (*PPP* 9/11, May

26–June 8, 2000). On October 23, 2000, Sam Rainsy began a hunger strike at the memorial site to protest corruption in the distribution of supplies to flood victims, but after two days he was forced to withdraw to Wat Unnalom so that the authorities could prepare for the November water festival and the forthcoming state visit of the Chinese president Jiang Zemin (*PPP* 9/22, October 27–November 9, 2000). He remained there for a further three days but seems to have received minimal support.[101] One might also add that there was little hope of success once he had been transferred to a monastery controlled by such a prominent supporter of the CPP as Tep Vong.

Many returning to the towns after the Democratic Kampuchea period had found their homes destroyed or occupied by others. Urban monasteries were often the only places left for them to live. But the problem of laypeople dwelling in monastic premises has not gone away and is still acute in Phnom Penh. Clearly the problem is greatly magnified when the squatters are not Khmer. Fighting between monks and Vietnamese occupants of Wat Chak Angre Leu, to the south of the city, flared up in May 2000 after the *chau adhikar,* Ven. Keo Bun, threatened self-immolation if the squatters did not leave. He asserted that the Vietnamese insult Buddhism in a variety of stereotypical ways (*PPP* 9/7, March 31–April 13, 2000). They are supposed to have been running a karaoke, a brothel, and a church on the monastery grounds. After their eviction the Student Committee for Democracy began to construct a statue of Ven. Chuon Nath at the monastery, with the king apparently making a US$1,000 donation toward the cost of its construction.[102] There is some reason to suppose a link between those involved in the September 1998 events and members of the Student Committee for Democracy. It is more difficult to be certain whether a connection with Sam Rainsy also exists.[103]

We have already noted Tep Vong's strong defense of the karma doctrine in the context of AIDS. This viewpoint also has its political dimension. In a speech over the 2000 New Year period, Sam Rainsy appealed for his supporters to stop having faith in karma, on the grounds that the doctrine is traditionally interpreted on an individualistic basis. He argued that if people habitually envision suffering as a result of their own actions, this tends to undermine the responsibilities of corporate organizations. This in turn leads to poor governance, corruption, and associated social ills. There are echoes of the communist critique of Buddhism here, yet it is also a fairly explicit attack on the actual government. Prominent CPP members perceived it as such, and some have accused Sam Rainsy of treason by attacking the state religion. Whether the charge could ever be made to stick, there seems little doubt that Sam Rainsy is keen to challenge the governing party's dependence on a carefully choreographed form of institutional Buddhism.[104]

Unreformed Mahanikay

In chapter 3 we saw that an esoteric tradition of Theravada Buddhist practice has existed in Cambodia for many centuries. Adepts of these ancient rites *(boran)*[105] distinguish themselves from their reformed coreligionists in a variety of ways, most especially in the latter's reliance on a series of "nonorthodox" ritual and meditative techniques. The *boran* movement began to reestablish itself once more around the beginning of 1989, as the state control of religion diminished and the country was rapidly moving away from doctrinaire communism toward the warm embrace of the free market. Before 1970 the esoteric tradition had flourished in the provinces of Siem Reap and Kompong Cham. A significant representative from the earlier part of the century, Ven. Mony Ung Choeum, the chief monk of Kompong Cham, appears to have had a number of run-ins with Ven. Chuon Nath, for example (Marston 2000, 3).

One of the most active figures currently involved in reestablishing *boran* practice today is Ven. Daung Phang, originally the chief monk of Kroch Chmar District, Kompong Cham Province. He is said to have the power of prophecy and is adept at various magical practices. In addition, Daung Phang is closely associated with Hun Sen, who also comes from Kroch Chmar.[106] Having already held a number of annual traditional monastic rites of probation *(parivāsa)* in Kompong Cham, he organized a similar event at his new monastery, Wat Prek Barang, Kompong Luong, in February 1997. Unlike normal Theravada usage, which envisages *parivāsa* as a period of suspension and penitence for an individual monk who has infringed certain rules of discipline, in the unreformed Mahanikay of Cambodia *parivāsa* refers to a collective rite of purification through the performance of various ascetic practices. The 1997 event seems to have provoked considerable opposition from modernizers. Indeed, when Ven. Daung Phang held a repeat of the rite the following year at Wat Champuskaek, he was sternly rebuked by Ven. Non Nget,[107] the dispute becoming so heated that unsuccessful attempts to adjudicate were made by the Ministry of Cults and Religious Affairs. Either in an attempt to reach a compromise or perhaps as a way of opening up a breach between himself and Non Nget, Tep Vong was a major participant in similar *parivāsa* rituals in 1999 and 2000. The latter was a rather grand affair within the precincts of Angkor Thom—an event clearly designed expressly to establish a connection between the traditionalists and the ancient Angkorian state (de Bernon 2000, 475–476).

The previously mentioned Wat Champuskaek, some ten kilometers south of Phnom Penh on the eastern bank of the Bassac River, is another center for the traditionalists.[108] Its *chau adhikar*, Ven. Om Lim Heng (b. 1964), seems to act as another quasi-official chaplain to Hun Sen, who lives in nearby Takhmau.

His photograph, prominently displayed in a rather magnificent thousand-Buddha hall within the monastery compound, shows him with a medal, conferred by Hun Sen, hanging from his monastic robes.[109] Yet another monk with putative magical powers, Om Lim Heng specializes in mass water sprinkling. Indeed, so many people can gather at the monastery during peak times that he is obliged to use a power hose to accomplish this task. A particular specialism is his protective lustration of expensive motorcars. Given the high incidence of auto theft and general lawlessness in the country, this is particularly appreciated by his followers. Wat Champuskaek must be one of the wealthiest religious establishments in the land. It has benefited from a resurgence of conspicuous merit making by the newly mega-rich, mostly high-ranking politicians and members of the military who seem to have appropriated large amounts of state property and land when the communist era came to an end.[110] The inauguration of its ceremony hall on March 18, 2000, was a particularly lavish occasion. Hun Sen contributed US$110,000 to the *wat*'s US$600,000 building program. Other major donors included Hok Lundy, the head of the police; Cham Prasith, the minister of commerce; and Moeung Samphan, a three-star general and the father-in-law of Hun Sen's eldest daughter (*PPP* 9/6, March 17–30, 2000).

As Evans (1993, 133) has noted, the rapaciousness associated with many modern forms of Southeast Asian governance, whether they be monarchical, military dictatorships, or socialist, has meant that the only safe and—because it may be viewed as a means of expunging previous misdeeds—emotionally satisfying means of channeling surplus wealth is through the sponsorship of religious rituals.[111] *Boran* monasteries in Cambodia appear to prosper disproportionately in this sort of climate. Wat Samraung Andeth, near Phnom Penh, is another example. The magical powers of its *chau adhikar*, Ven. Roth Saroeun, attract many donations from politicians and businessmen keen to advance their careers through contact with his special powers.[112] The success of his entrepreneurial magic means that the monastery has become a refuge for large numbers of orphans and poor students from the provinces who can be assured of basic food supplies and lodging.[113] Clearly, such wealth distribution has been an important feature of institutional Buddhism throughout its history.

A widely acknowledged characteristic of Buddhist modernist spiritual practice throughout the Theravada world is its emphasis on insight meditation *(vipassanā)*. This involves the development of clear insight into the rising and falling of physical and mental phenomena. It is thought that by simply applying the three marks of impermanence, suffering, and not-self to these states, one will eventually see all things as they truly are. Perhaps most important for our purposes is that the practice does not require the cultivation of highly concentrated states of mind. Bare awareness is quite sufficient. Now, the *boran* movement in Cambodia refers to the modernists as "adepts of *vipassanā.*" Ven. Daung Phang has also asserted that *vipassanā* practice is "foreign" and "different from the traditional Khmer *kammaṭṭhan,*" which he teaches. The conclusion is quite clear. Modernist influences come from outside the country, whereas traditional practices are an expression of true *khmèritude.* The reformed segment of the *sangha,* it seems, has been seduced into following an alien and unpatriotic path.

In a study of the role of Buddhist ideals in the Burmese political context, Houtman (1999, 307–308) has found that *vipassanā* practices are preferred by members of the National League for Democracy (NLD) as a means of coping with the psychological stresses of imprisonment and repression.[114] The military, on the other hand, is inclined toward a more magical, concentration-oriented practice *(samatha),* "since it permits power over [the external world] *loka.*" The crux of Houtman's position is that mental culture is not just about private psychological spaces. Initiatory practices of the highly concentrated *samatha*-type are certainly about the cultivation of a hierarchy of interior states, but such states reflect and endorse the traditional hierarchical and nondemocratic forms of social organization favored by the current regime.[115] Insight meditation *(vipassanā),* on the other hand, places its emphasis on bare awareness, analytic (as opposed to synthetic) reasoning, and the dissolution of hierarchy. It leads to a suspicion of traditional power structures and is therefore more in tune with the democratic ideals of the NLD. There are clear parallels here between the Burmese and Cambodian religio-political contexts. The unreformed Mahanikay in Cambodia is also patronized by a nondemocratic kleptocracy that is fascinated and charged through its contact with those believed to be skilled magical manipulators of power. Their reformed counterparts, on the other hand, adhere to forms of mental culture that sustain liberal political norms and rely on the support of modernizing forces both within the country and farther afield.

Cambodian Buddhism reemerged quite gradually after the darkness of the Pol Pot years. Throughout the 1980s it suffered from heavy-handed ideological manipulation, while its institutional growth was significantly curtailed by the new regime. However, it did manage to occupy a niche that was protected, to some extent, from the worst excesses of government interference, and, with the great easing of restrictions following the withdrawal of Vietnam from the country at the end of the decade, it was well positioned to regain some of its prerevolutionary forms and functions. This process accelerated significantly in the lead-up to the 1993 elections, a few short years in which the spotlight of the international community's concerns played concentratedly on Cambodia, although we should bear in mind that all efforts to revivify Buddhism were massively vitiated by the very high proportion of educated monks who lost their lives during the Democratic Kampuchea period. The aftereffects of those events have cast their shadow down to the present day.

Evans' study (1993, 133) of the forms of Buddhism that have developed in the two very different economies of Thailand and Laos is also instructive. In the former country, rationalist forms that place an emphasis on individual salvation have emerged in large numbers. In Laos, on the other hand, economic stagnation and socialist control of the *sangha* have signally failed to produce any significant forms of Buddhist modernism. The situation in Cambodia is probably midway between those in Laos and Thailand. Over a relatively short space of time the country has shifted from a uniquely extreme and nationalistic communism to a strange amalgam of authoritarianism and free-market influences. As a result, religious groups covering the entire range of the spectrum from modernism to traditionalism have emerged. They may be differentially arranged across a series of parallel continua, each reflecting some dimension of this basic polarity.

Modernism of both the Mahanikay and the Thommayut varieties is largely associated with leading figures who were out of the country during the DK and PRK periods. Among the traditionalists, we find individuals who either survived DK in a disrobed state in Cambodia itself or escaped to Vietnam, subsequently rising to positions of influence during the PRK. The traditionalists also tend to adopt a strongly patriotic line, although in this they are outtrumped by many younger members of the *sangha* who appear to be the most harshly anti-Vietnamese. The Thommayut clearly has difficulties in reconciling its links to Thailand with the national interest, and its growth has suffered accordingly. Mahanikay modernists, by contrast, are the most relaxed about the encroachment of globalization.

Looked at from a different perspective, modernist groups have suffered suspicion, sporadically developing into outright persecution, from the ruling party. In the case of the young monks, this has been especially severe. Both the Mahanikay hierarchy and the unreformed segment of the order have specific relations to the CPP, although the latter appears to be less doctrinaire than the former group of older "revolutionary monks" who, over the last two decades, have sought to advance the party line through the reconstruction of a carefully choreographed form of state Buddhism. The *boran* movement appears less interested in fighting the battles of the past and generally further removed from the paraphernalia of the state. It has, however, benefited significantly through allying itself with wealthy ex-communists and the mushrooming business sector.

Conclusion

Buddhism has had an active presence in Khmer population zones for approximately one and a half millennia. During that time it has manifested a variety of differing forms, while its influence has ebbed and flowed both among members of the ruling elite and in the wider population. It was an important ingredient in the religious life of the earliest significant polity in the area, Funan, which flourished from the fifth to the mid-sixth century CE, and some evidence suggests that its influence penetrated to the highest levels of the state. Contact with India seems to have played some as-yet-unspecified role in the establishment of a Buddhist presence in the region. The same may be said concerning early intercourse with Dvāravatī, although the evidence is rather slender. We know with rather more certainty that a number of Funan-based monks helped promote certain texts, ideas, and practices in China during a crucial moment in its early engagement with Buddhism, but it is difficult to be certain about the precise sectarian affiliations of these early interpreters of the teachings of the Buddha. Epigraphical, archaeological, and associated sources tend to point in the direction of the Mahayana, although the odd occurrence of Pali inscriptions could conceivably indicate that non-Mahayanist elements were also present in Cambodia at a fairly early period.

Following a waning of Buddhism's fortunes in the successor Zhenla period (550–802), Mahayanist influences magnified at specific points in the history of Angkor (802–1431), possibly as a consequence of bursts of missionary activity emanating from India. But Buddhism, despite sporadic evidence of royal patronage, must be regarded as the poor relation of a variety of more dominant Brahmanical cults during most of the Angkorian period. At some points it left little impact on the historical record, and even when it was able to exercise a lively presence, this was largely through the evolution of Hindu-Buddhist syncretisms. A significant exception to this rule can be found during the reign of the last great king of Angkor, Jayavarman VII (1181–c. 1220). Under his patronage, tantric Mahayana concepts permeated the ritual life of the state, while the ancient Indian notion of righteous Buddhist kingship appears to have given shape to some aspects of the policy that Jayavarman used to govern his empire.

A short but focused period of muscular opposition to the rites of the ancien régime toward the end of the Angkorian period put an end to much of Jayavarman VII's legacy. The symbiosis of Mahayana Buddhism with the ritual of state, so visibly expressed in that king's massive architectural projects, did not survive the changed economic, political, and environmental circumstances. The same holds true for Brahmanism. But the influence of Theravada traditions, perhaps imported from neighboring states, began to increase. By the immediate post-Angkorian period they had achieved dominance, a situation that has continued to the present without significant deviation.

The Buddhism of post-Angkorian Cambodia preserves some interesting and distinctive ideas and practices sometimes at odds with the "purified" or reformed Theravada represented today in many regions of South and Southeast Asia. Such "unorthodox" and baroquely esoteric elements were first brought to scholarly attention by the work of François Bizot. They are sometimes said to constitute a subgenre designated by the term "tantric Theravada." The origin of the tradition is still the subject of debate. Esoteric elements may have been present in the Theravada of neighboring geographical regions before it became established in Cambodia, but we do know that tantric notions, both Buddhist and Brahmanical, were widespread during the Angkorian period. It is not inconceivable that they percolated into the Theravada tradition after it had established its dominance in Cambodia.

It seems that the new religious dispensation was less oriented to the demands of an elaborate and centralized state. Neither did it require large-scale temple construction or the territorial expansion that made that possible. Such changes were not a radical break with the past, for Theravada Buddhism, once it had anchored itself in Cambodian soil, possessed a remarkable facility for assimilation and accretion. Despite the shift in religious regime, certain key preoccupations and dichotomies were preserved. Theravada cult activity, for instance, owes a significant debt to quite archaic ways of understanding reality, while basic structural and sociological features of the tradition largely persisted down to the present, particularly in the field of monastic economy.

The cult of kingship was preserved from the earlier period, but somewhat shorn of its Brahmanical and tantric garb. The ideal monarch was no longer considered an embodiment of divine power, although there is some evidence that he may have become associated with the future Buddha, Maitreya. But he was now primarily the protector of the monastic order, the visible and institutional expression of the Buddha's powerful insight into the true nature of reality. Theravada doctrine considers protection of Buddhism to be the indispensable prerequisite for any properly functioning state. By ruling in accord with these insights, then, a righteous king ensures the uninterrupted continuation of both the physical and the moral order *(dhamma)*—indeed, of the entire cosmos. The physical layout and symbolism of the successor capitals of the middle period of Cambodian history, such as Longvek and Udong, also replicated important elements of Angkorian pattern. Contrary to the popular idea that ancient temple complexes had been abandoned after the fall of Angkor, many important sites remained in use, although now they were rededicated to the Theravada cult. Angkor Wat, for example, was remodeled so that it could serve as a beacon of the new faith. So successful was this reappropriation that, in time, Angkor Wat became an important magnet, drawing Buddhist pilgrims from as far away as Japan. Clearly, post-Angkorian and Buddhist Cambodia retained a high profile in the wider region.

Despite the oscillating influences of both Thailand and Vietnam on Cambodia after the fall of Angkor, Theravada Buddhism subsisted in a relatively steady state with no major shocks or shifts to the established religious order for several hundred years. Even Rāmādhipatī I's unique and unexpected conversion to Islam in the mid-seventeenth century appears to have had little long-term impact. This situation of gentle stagnation continued until the latter half of the nineteenth century, the Cambodian "middle ages" coming to an end with Ang Duang's introduction of Thai courtly and religious culture after his coronation in 1847. Duang's reign marked an end to Vietnamese interference and brought about a kind of Theravada renaissance best represented by the importation of the reformist Thommayut from Bangkok. The imposition of the French "protection" in the reign of the next king, Norodom, also led to many reforms in political organization, together with a removal of the court to a newly constructed capital at Phnom Penh.

Although the policies and interests of Duang and the colonial power were unconnected and arose from vastly differing motivations, both regimes appear to have contributed to an increase in tension within the monastic order. But while Duang shared the reformist and Pali-oriented outlook of Mongkut, the king of Thailand, the French seem to have been especially suspicious of the political aspects of the monastic order founded on these insights, and they did much to frustrate its activities. As the twentieth century unfolded, splits between those who claimed to follow the new teachings *(thor thmei),* based on a modernist concern to rediscover a pure form of Buddhism free from the accretions of the past, and adherents of the old teachings *(thor cah)*, who jealously guarded what they regarded as a unique cultural and religious heritage from attack by hostile external forces, came strongly to the surface. However, the structure of tension between the two camps became increasingly complex with time. The French intervention in Buddhist education is particularly relevant here, as are the obstacles the authorities put in the way of Thommayut expansion. A consequence of the latter was that the battleground for the fight between the two parties became largely confined to the Mahanikay. Modernists within the Mahanikay clearly benefited from French support, and their triumph is most adequately illustrated by the career of Ven. Chuon Nath. But monastic traditionalism, although marginalized, survived into the 1970s. The political upheavals of this period would, in time, lead to an almost total elimination of the monastic sector. But the old tensions were set to break out again once institutional Buddhism reached a critical mass a little over a decade after its reestablishment following the defeat of the Khmer Rouge.

The Buddhist contribution to an emerging sense of nationhood is a major theme in the modern history of Cambodia. A number of late nineteenth and early twentieth century insurrections appear to have had a Buddhist element, and some, though by no means all, were motivated by anticolonialist sentiment. The situation was naturally viewed with deep concern by the colonial authorities. The emergence of the Vietnamese new religion, Cao Dai, in the early years of the twentieth century seems to have reinforced these fears. Its activities also gained the attention of senior members of the Cambodian ecclesiastical hierarchy, who, on the one hand, were obliged to condemn it while, on the other, viewing it as a model for a new and more challenging relation with the French. The first real manifestation of organized anticolonialism in Cambodia finally materialized in 1942, when a monk-led demonstration challenged various reforms that were being imposed on the Khmer people. In a crucial sense the event opened the floodgates, and it may not be too bold to assert that the country moved toward independence on a breaking wave of Buddhist activism and martyrdom that had its seeds in the late nineteenth century.

In the early years of independent Cambodia, Sihanouk abdicated the throne to found his People's Socialist Community (Sangkum Reastr Niyum), a movement of Buddhist socialism. Its failure, particularly when taken alongside the ex-king's undoubted personal foibles, led critics to view the entire project as a cynical and insufficiently considered exercise in political narcissism, but in fact it did mirror parallel developments in other regions of Theravada Southeast Asia. However, Sihanouk was overthrown in 1970, and Cambodia slid quite rapidly into disorder and violence. The prince had quite explicitly manipulated Buddhism for his own political ends during the Sangkum period, but in this he had not been unique. The French had got there before him, and it is unsurprising that the process was replicated by various political groups in the civil war that consumed the first half of the decade.

The process of disintegration culminated in the fall of Phnom Penh to extreme nationalistic communists in April 1975. The resulting state of Democratic Kampuchea lasted only until the end of 1978, when it was toppled by a fraternal invasion of Vietnamese communists. It took some time for the outside world to wake up to the devastation and horror of the Democratic Kampuchea period, but the regime has subsequently achieved great notoriety. What is perhaps less widely appreciated is that the Buddhist-inspired nationalist movement of earlier decades had been a fertile seedbed for the germination of Khmer communism. Only once the movement had grown and developed did some of its leading members seek to break their links with the past by shedding all prior connections. It is against this background that we should seek to understand the communists' vehement anticlericalism, which led inexorably to the elimination of institutional Buddhism. Yet even at the height of the Democratic Kampuchea period, subliminal Buddhist influences remained and affected Khmer Rouge behavior and ideology.

The gradual reemergence and recovery of organized Buddhism after the darkness of the Pol Pot years were slow, in part because of its ideological manipulation by the new Vietnamese-backed government but also because of the very high proportion of educated monks who had lost their lives under the Khmer Rouge. Nevertheless, the monastic order's importance in conferring legitimacy on the regime was recognized by the new authorities, and this helped the order gain a toehold within the political system that prevailed in the early years of the 1980s. Great changes following the breakup of the Soviet Union and the withdrawal of Vietnam from the country at the end of that decade, combined with the impact that preparations for the internationally monitored 1993 elections brought in their wake, meant that the *sangha* was now able to restore its prerevolutionary institutional forms, even though the situation had become somewhat more complicated by the thoroughgoing politicization of the ecclesiastical hierarchy in the immediate post-DK period. Influential monks who had survived from the 1970s, admittedly little more than a handful, also felt unconstrained when it came to reigniting old controversies, especially those loosely clustered around the twin poles of modernism and traditionalism. Current factionalism within the monastic order needs be read in this light.

No form of Buddhism came so close to total extinction as that in Cambodia during the late 1970s, and given the recent histories of religious persecution in other regions of East and central Asia, that is saying quite a lot. Since that nadir, Khmer Buddhism has gradually learned to adapt and prosper as socialist controls were first gradually relaxed and then finally disappeared. In fact, adaptation to a great variety of political contexts—be they colonial, monarchical, socialist, republican, or doctrinaire Marxist—has been a marked feature of its history over the last century and a half. On the evidence of this short survey, it may be no exaggeration to assert that an accommodating spirit has been an intrinsic feature of Cambodian Buddhism since its inception. The visible presence of the *sangha* and its unique significance as the only institution able to operate effectively and with high levels of mass support throughout the whole of the country have ensured that almost all governments have felt the need to cultivate the Buddhist sector, whatever their political philosophy. There is little reason to assume that this situation will change in the near future.

Appendix A

Cambodian Inscriptions Discussed in the Book

Pre-Angkorian and Angkorian Periods

Inscription no.[a]	*Location*	*Date*	*Language (S/K/P)*[b]
K. 7	Prasat Pram Loveng, Thap Muoi, Plaine des Joncs	6th century *Śaka*[c]	K
K. 40	Wat Bati, Takeo	5th century *Śaka*	S
K. 45	Phnom Trotung, Kampot	890 CE	S
K. 49	Wat Prei Val, Ba Phnom, Prey Veng	664 CE	S
K. 53	Kdei Ang, Prey Veng	667 CE	S
K. 75	Wat Preah Nippean, Kompong Speu	1628 CE	K
K. 82	Wat Nokor, Kompong Cham	1566 CE	K/P
K. 111	Wat Sithor, Kompong Cham	968 CE	S
K. 132	Anlung Prang, Sambor, Kratie	692, 708 CE	S
K. 144	Prasat Kombot, Kompong Thom	12th–13th century *Śaka*	K
K. 157	Wat Kdei Car, Kompong Thom	953 CE	S/K
K. 161	Preah Khan, Kompong Svay	1002 CE	S
K. 163	Ampil Rolum, Kompong Thom	6th–7th century *Śaka*	K
K. 166	Wat Srei Toul, Kompong Thom	17th century CE	K
K. 177	Preah Theat Khvao, Kompong Thom	Mid-15th century *Śaka*	K/P
K. 214	Phnom Banteay Nan, Battambang	982 CE	S/K
K. 225	Thmar Puok, Battambang	989 CE	S
K. 235	Sdok Kak Thom, Prachinburi (Thailand)	1052 CE	S/K
K. 244	Prasat Ta Keam, Siem Reap	791 CE	S
K. 254	Trapan Don On, Siem Reap	1129 CE	S/K
K. 266–268	Bat Chum, Siem Reap	953, 960 CE	S/K
K. 273	Ta Prohm, Siem Reap	1186 CE	S

continued

Inscription no.[a]	*Location*	*Date*	*Language (S/K/P)*[b]
K. 290	Tep Pranam, Siem Reap	Late 9th century CE, with Khmer additions of 1005–1015	S/K
K. 294	Bayon, Angkor	12th century *Śaka*	K
K. 300	Angkor Wat, northeast corner of surrounding ditch	After 1327 CE?	S
K. 339	Prasat Kok, Siem Reap	10th century *Śaka*	S
K. 359	Veal Kantal, Stung Treng	7th century CE	S
K. 368	Sai Fong, Vieng Chan (Laos)	1186 CE	S
K. 388	Hin K'on, Nakhon Ratchasima (Thailand)	6th century *Śaka*	S/K
K. 397	Phimai, Nakhon Ratchasima (Thailand)	1110, 1113 CE	K
K. 410	Lopburi, Ayutthaya (Thailand)	1022, 1025 CE	K
K. 417	Prasat Chikreng, Siem Reap	970 CE	S
K. 485	Phimeanakas, Siem Reap	12th century *Śaka*	S
K. 495	Ban Bung Ke, Ubon (Thailand)	886 CE	S
K. 505	Khau Rang, Prachinburi (Thailand)	639 CE	S/K
K. 538	Phum Ta Tru, Siem Reap	978 CE	S/K
K. 600	Angkor Borei, Takeo	611 CE	K
K. 604	Sambor Prei Kuk, Kompong Thom	627 CE	S
K. 701	Prasat Komnap, Siem Reap	9th century *Śaka*	S
K. 754	Kok Svay Chek, Siem Reap	1308 CE	K/P
K. 755	Wat Chnah, Prei Krabas, Takeo	6th century *Śaka*	K
K. 806	Pre Rup, Angkor	961 CE	S
K. 809	Prasat Kandol Dom, Siem Reap	c. 885 CE	S/K
K. 820	Tuol Preah Theat, Kompong Speu	7th century *Śaka*	S/P
K. 908	Preah Khan, Siem Reap	1191 CE	S
K. 953	Phimai, Nakhon Ratchasima (Thailand)	1041 CE	S/K
K. 1000	Phimai, Nakhon Ratchasima (Thailand)	8th century CE	S
K. 1012	Phnom Kbal Spean, Phnom Kulen	11th century CE	S

[a]The K. numbers are a standardized system of designating Cambodia inscriptions. For further details, see Cœdès 1966.

[b]S = Sanskrit; K = Khmer; P = Pali.

[c]1 *Śaka* = 79 CE.

Appendix B

Evidence Chart Based on Materials Discussed in Chapter 1

POLITY	*Date*	*Evidence of Buddhist activity*	*Sources*	*General observations*
Funan (to c. 550)	5th–7th CE	Buddha images in Mekong Delta area—imported and locally produced. Iconography suggests presence of Śrāvakayāna. Mahayana influences also present, though less evident	Extant statuary	Existence of Śrāvakayāna and Mahayana Buddhism as background to Brahmanical state cult. Some evidence for Funan as center of Buddhist learning and scholarship
	480–510	Buddhist monks from Funan active in Middle Kingdom	Chinese sources	
	c. 514–c. 550	Rudravarman sends Buddhist cult objects to Chinese emperor		
	546	Paramārtha, an important Indian Mahayanist, leaves Funan after extended stay for China		
	Mid-6th CE	Possible existence of monastic Buddhism in royal circles	K. 40	
Zhenla (550 to 802)	7th CE	Possible state persecution of Buddhism early in century	Chinese sources	Buddhist decline in early period followed by modest reemergence of both Śrāvakayāna and Mahayana, probably in royal circles
		Invocation to Buddha, Maitreya, and Avalokiteśvara	K. 163	
		Possible existence of Theravada-like practices	K. 388, K. 755, and K. 505	
		Institution of monastic slavery	K. 163 and K. 505	
	664	Possible existence of monastic Buddhism in royal circles	K. 49	
	708	Image of Prajñāpāramitā established	K. 132	
	761	Early Khmer use of Pali	Prachinburi inscription	
	791	Image of Lokeśvara established	K. 244	
	886	Buddhism in the Mun valley	K. 495	
	Late 9th	Yaśovarman I establishes Brahmanical and Buddhist monasteries	K. 290	
		Evidence of Brahmanical/Buddhist syncretism in Yaśovarman I's reign	K. 290 and K. 701	

Angkor (802 to 1431)	From mid-10th	Explosion of Buddhist imagery	Carvings, statuary, etc.	
	960	Buddha, Avalokiteśvara, Prajñāpāramitā triad installed at Angkor + some tantric imagery	K. 266 + Bat Chum	
	961		K. 806	
	968		K. 111	
	1020s	Possible existence of Mahayanist philosophical concepts	K. 410	Background presence of Buddhism until c. 10th century, after which Mahayanist and Tantric tendencies spread
	1066	Mahayana philosophy, and supporting Indic texts, circulate	Sab Bāk inscription	
	1108	Mahayana and Śrāvakayāna monks in Lopburi area	K. 394	
	Early 12th	Tantric ideas in Khmer domains	Beng Mealea and Banteay Samre	Mahayana becomes state ideology under Jayavarman VII; Brahmanical and Mahayanist influences waning as Angkorian civilization begins its decline
	1181–c. 1220	Tantric ideas and imagery at Phimai. Mahayanist temples appear at Angkor	Abundant archaeology and epigraphy	
	c. 1243–1295	Jayavarman VII emerges as Buddhist monarch. Many Mahayanist structures built. Evidence of highly symbolic ordering of realm in line with Buddhist cosmological teachings		Growth and survival of Śrāvakayāna Buddhism into the post-Angkorian period
	1296–1297	Possible contacts with Mahayanist scholiasts fleeing Muslim persecution in north India	Circumstantial	
	13th-14th	Possible Buddhist (Theravada?) contacts with Burma, Ceylon	Burmese and Ceylonese sources	
		Anti-Buddhist backlash under Jayavarman VIII	Buddhist imagery vandalized	
		Probable existence of Śrāvakayāna (Theravada?) monks at Angkor	Zhou Daguan	
		Śrāvakayāna temple constructed at Angkor	Preah Palilay	

Appendix C

Ecclesiastical Hierarchies in the Two Cambodian Buddhist Orders

Mahanikay

Leader of the Order

Samdech Preah Mahā Sumedhādhipatī Sanghanāyaka Gaṇamahānikāya (His Holiness, the Most Learned of All, Supreme Leader of the Monks of the Great Group)

Rājāgaṇa of the First Class

Preah Dhammalikhita
Preah Bodhivaṃsā
Preah Vanarata

Rājāgaṇa of the Second Class

Preah Mahāvimaladhamma
Preah Buddhaghosācariya
Preah Dhammaghosācariya
Preah Ghosadhamma
Preah Sāsanāmunī
Preah Munīkosala

Rājāgaṇa of the Third Class

Preah Sirisammativaṃsā
Preah Buddhavaṃsā
Preah Sākyavaṃsā
Preah Upālivaṃsā

Preah Ñāṇavaṃsā
Preah Sumedhavaṃsā

Rājāgaṇa of the Fourth Class

Preah Dhammavipassanā
Preah Samādhidhamma
Preah Ñāṇakosala
Preah Sirisangāmunī
Preah Sirivisuddhi
Preah Dhammavaṃsā
Preah Ñāṇasaṃvara
Preah Vinayasaṃvara
Preah Indamunī
Preah Devamunī
Preah Vinayamunī
Preah Debsatthā
Preah Sīlasaṃvara
Preah Gambhirathera
Preah Ariyamaggaññāṇa
Preah Vibhaddaññāṇa
Preah Pavarasatthā
Preah Dhammavisuddhivaṃsā
Preah Ñāṇavisuddhivaṃsā
Preah Piṭakadhamma

Thommayut

Leader of the Order

Samdech Preah Sudhammādhipatī Sanghanāyaka Gaṇadhammayutikanikāya (His Holiness, the Most Righteous of All, Supreme Leader of the Monks of the Righteous Group)

Rājāgaṇa of the First Class

Preah Mangaladebācariya
Preah Buddhācariya

Rājāgaṇa of the Second Class

Preah Mahābrahmamunī
Preah Dhammottama
Preah Ariyakassapa

Rājāgaṇa of the Third Class

Preah Ariyavaṃsā
Preah Dhammakavivaṃsā
Preah Ñāṇaraṇsi
Preah Mahāviravaṃsācariya

Rājāgaṇa of the Fourth Class

Preah Padumavaṃsā
Preah Dhammamunī
Preah Vajiramedhā
Preah Ariyamunī
Preah Devamolī
Preah Dhammathera
Preah Amarābhirakkhita
Preah Mahārājadhamma
Preah Ratanamunī
Preah Dhammatrayalokācariya
Preah Dhammavarottama
Preah Ñāṇaviriya

After Chuon Nath 1976, 42–43.

Abbreviations

A.	*Aṅguttaranikāya*
ASEMI	*Asie du Sud-Est et Monde Insulindien*
BEFEO	*Bulletin de l'École Française d'Extrême-Orient*
BSEI	*Bulletin de la Société des Études Indochinoises*
BSOAS	*Bulletin of the School of Oriental and African Studies*
Cv.	*Cūḷavaṃsa*
DhA.	*Dhammapadaṭṭhakathā*
FBIS	*Foreign Broadcast Information Service*
IMA	"Inscriptions modernes d'Angkor"
J.	*Jātaka*
JSEAS	*Journal of Southeast Asian Studies*
JSS	*Journal of the Siam Society*
K.	Cambodian inscription
Khp.	*Khuddakapāṭha*
M.	*Majjhimanikāya*
PPP	*Phnom Penh Post*
S.	*Saṃyuttanikāya*
Sn.	*Suttanipāta*
Sp.	*Samantapāsādikā*
T.	Taishō shinshū daizōkyō
Vin.	*Vinayapiṭaka*
Vism.	*Visuddhimagga*

Acronyms

BFD	Buddhism for Development
BLDP	Buddhist Liberal Democratic Party
CEDORECK	Centre de Documentation et de Recherche sur la Civilisation Khmère
CPK	Communist Party of Kampuchea
DK	Democratic Kampuchea
EFEO	École française d'Extrême-Orient
FEMC	Fonds pour l'Édition des Manuscrits du Cambodge
FUNCINPEC	Front Uni National pour un Cambodge Indépendent, Neutre, Pacifique, et Coopératif
FUNK	National United Front of Kampuchea
GTZ	Gesellschaft für Technische Zusammenarbeit
HBF	Heinrich Böll Foundation
ICP	Indochinese Communist Party
JSRC	Japanese Sotoshu Relief Committee
KAF	Konrad Adenauer Foundation
KBS	Khmer Buddhist Society
KPNLF	Khmer People's National Liberation Front
KPP	Khmer People's Party
KPRP	Kampuchean People's Revolutionary Party
KUFNCD	Khmer United Front for National Construction and Defense
MEEP	Monk Environmental Education Program
NLD	National League for Democracy
NLF	National Liberation Front
PRC	People's Republic of China
PRK	People's Republic of Kampuchea
SOC	State of Cambodia
UIF	Unified Issarak Front (= Samakhum Khmer Issarak)
VWP	Vietnam Workers' Party
WCRP	World Conference of Religion and Peace
WFB	World Fellowship of Buddhists

Notes

Unless otherwise noted, all translations of quotations are mine.

1. Buddhism in Cambodia

1. Associated with figures like Doudart de Lagrée, Harmand, Aymonier, Barth, Bergaigne, Senart, and Lévi, culminating in Cœdès.

2. For a comprehensive list of Cambodian inscriptions discussed in this book, see appendices A and B.

3. For an exception, see Jacob 1979 and 1993b.

4. Only three Sanskrit inscriptions have been definitively attributed to the Funan period. Vickery (1998n47) holds that this is insufficient evidence to argue for the presence of an Indian population in the region.

5. Meaning "armor, defense, coat of mail, etc.," i.e., the idea of protection. Often found at the end of names of members of the Indian warrior class *(kṣatriya)*.

6. Skilling (pers. comm.) observes that this association can be established only by circular arguments.

7. For a detailed discussion, see Dupont 1955, 189–210. For illustrations, see Tranet 1998.

8. For a recent contesting of received wisdom on the topic, see Dowling 1999.

9. Discussed in detail by Vickery (1998, 53–56).

10. For a good survey of Chinese sources relevant to the study of Cambodian history, see Yang Baoyun 1994.

11. These two monks are also called Saṅghavarman (= Sien k'ie p'o lo) and Mandrasena (= Man t'o lo sien), respectively. The latter stayed until c. 520 CE.

12. Saṅghapāla cooperated with Mandra on a translation of the *Ratnamegha sūtra* (T. 659) and also rendered the *Saptaśtikā prajñāpāramitā* (T. 233) into Chinese. His other

works, preserved in the Chinese canon, are Taisho 314, 358, 430, 468, 984, 1016, 1491, 1648, and 2043. Mandra's rather poor Chinese translations also include the *Ratnamegha sūtra* (T. 658) and the *Saptaśtikā prajñāpāramitā* (T. 232).

13. For a more detailed discussion, see Skilling 1994a.

14. The embassy of 517 CE seems to have incorporated a Buddhist monk named Dharmapāla (= Tang-pao-lao). In 519 CE, gifts to the Chinese emperor included a white Indian sandalwood image of the Buddha (Majumdar 1953, 34).

15. See Paul 1984, 14–15, or Pachow 1958, 14, for further details.

16. Vickery (1998, 136–137) believes it to be later, perhaps from the ninth century.

17. Possibly the son of Kulaprabhāvatī, the author of K. 40.

18. Later inscriptional evidence confirms the presence of the Bhāgavata, or Pāñcarātra, sect in Funan. K. 806 (dated to 961), for instance, appears to attest their presence through explicit reference to the Pāñcarātra doctrine of the four emanations of Viṣṇu *(caturvyūha)* (Bhattacharya 1955a, 113).

19. These are in what art historians term the Phnom Da style A. Dowling (1999) has suggested a somewhat later date.

20. Vickery 1998, 48, quoting from Kozlova, Sedov, and Churin 1968.

21. Bronze images of Avalokiteśvara from Ak Yom are a little earlier and could be the earliest extant explicitly Mahayana pieces of art in Southeast Asia (Nandana Chutiwongs 1984, 377–378).

22. Some scholars have regarded this as a conscious imitation of the Pallava temple of Panamalai; see Longhurst 1930, 7–8. Girard-Geslan (1997, 159), on the other hand, suggests a Calukya influence.

23. For full details of the site, see Tranet 1997.

24. This is the earliest dated reference to a Buddhist "work of merit" *(puṇya)* in the inscriptional record (Vickery 1998, 106).

25. Discovered by Robert Dalet and now in the Musée Guimet, no. 18,891. The inscription renders this famous passage: "*ye dhammā hetuprabhavā teṣam hetuṃ tathāgato avaca / tesañ ca yo nirodho evaṃvādī mahāsamano*" (Whatever phenomena arise from a cause, of these the Tathāgata has told their cause, / And that which is their cessation, the Great Contemplative has such a doctrine) (*Vin.* i.40). The formula occurs quite frequently in the inscriptional record of Southeast Asia. For detailed coverage, see Skilling 1999.

26. It has generally been regarded as pre-Angkorian, although Vickery (1998, 252) believes it to be later.

27. It is difficult to find a precise English equivalent for this term. The term "serf" or "bondsman" may be more appropriate. The provision of staff to maintain a religious structure and its properties was common in India and Southeast Asia until modern times. The issue of monastic slavery in Buddhist Cambodia is discussed in chapter 3.

28. Another probable seventh-century text [K. 755]—found on the pedestal of a seated Buddha image at Wat Chnah, Prei Krabas, Takeo—also mentions the donation of *kñuṃ vihāra*.

29. For consideration of the cult of Avalokiteśvara in Theravada Sri Lanka, see Holt 1991.

30. His realm is assumed by many to have been in southern Sumatra.

31. See Briggs 1951 in this connection.

32. Probably not the island with the same name. Vickery (1998, 29) has suggested that it is a reference to Champa.

33. Evidence suggests that the priestly office was transmitted down the female line, and many prominent Brahmanical families may have been related to the royal blood.

34. A Sanskritized form of the old Khmer *"kamrateṅ jagat ta rāja."* On the *devarāja* cult, see Kulke 1978, Kulke 1993, and Vickery 1998, 423–425.

35. The mundane character of the concept is underlined in the Sdok Kak Thom inscription [K. 235, v. 82] by the term *"kamrateṅ phdai karoṃ,"* i.e., "lord of the lower plane."

36. Khmer portion vv. 69–78.

37. A common feature of Angkorian kingship. The thirteenth-century Chinese visitor to Angkor, Zhou Daguan, confirms that Khmer kings, at least during his time, were buried in a funerary temple (Cœdès 1968a, 215). The temple housed an image of Śiva's mount *(vāhana),* the bull Nandin; hence the name "Preah Ko," which means "sacred bull."

38. See the Sanskrit/Khmer inscription [K. 809] from Prasat Kandol Dom, Siem Reap Province.

39. *Nāga*-balustrades—most famously found at later structures, like Angkor Wat and the entrances to Angkor Thom—occur at the Bakong for the first time. The *nāga* symbolically links the earthly realm to the heavens, so these structures emphasize that anyone entering the temple has passed from one sphere into another.

40. The term *"baray"* probably derives from the Sanskrit *"pārājana,"* meaning "vast."

41. Preah Ko and Bakong, e.g. Intriguingly, the inscriptional record contains no mention of the distribution of irrigation water to fields, although the digging of *barays* is mentioned. Angkor maintained a complex canal system, but no channels for distribution of water to surrounding fields have been discovered. In the late thirteenth century, however, Zhou Daguan described a near-perfect system of floodwater-retreat agriculture, which is the same system as that practiced today (Stott 1992, 52). Van Liere (1982, 46) examined the various dams on the Siem Reap River, flowing down from Phnom Kulen, but concluded that their total capacity could never have irrigated more than four thousand hectares, assuming this was ever their purpose.

42. A unique feature of the inscriptions discovered at some of these sites is that they are digraphic; i.e., they contain text in the usual Pallava-derived Khmer characters alongside writing in a Nagari-derived script from northern India.

43. Temple administration was much the same whether it was a Brahmanical or Buddhist foundation. Internal administration was handled by a *kulapati,* who was also responsible for the accommodation of pilgrims. In addition, there might be a high func-

tionary called the professor *(adhyāpaka),* who was also responsible for education and learning. Both Ta Prohm and Preah Khan of Angkor were led by an *adhyāpaka.* According to the Tep Pranam inscription [K. 290], the head of the Saugatāśrama was a *kulapati-adhyāpaka.* Bhattacharya's study of temple administration at Angkor concludes that although there were some parallels to the situation in large contemporary temples in southern India, it is also clear that the two systems of administration must have evolved in quite different ways (Bhattacharya 1955b, 198).

44. Filliozat's methodology is largely based on the monumental work on Borobudur by Paul Mus (1935). As such, it tends to regard the structure as representing a unified conception. In fact, the Bakheng underwent a series of structural changes in the course of its useful life.

45. Vickery's discussion here owes a good deal to Alkire's research (1972) into old Micronesian navigational techniques, which are thought to have depended on the use of a "square theoretical compass."

46. A colossal Buddha image lying on its right side in *parinirvāṇa* was eventually constructed on the Bakheng's summit, completely transforming earlier structures in the process. B.-P. Groslier (1985–1986b, 13) describes it as "maladroit peut-être mais énorme."

47. Kavīndrārimathana is also mentioned in a Khmer addition to the Tep Pranam stele [K. 290], dating from the period 1005–1015 CE.

48. Vv. 1–3, 25–27, 65–67.

49. For a detailed discussion, see chapter 4.

50. Another Buddhist temple, Prasat Lak Nan, was also established nearby around the same period.

51. V. 275.

52. This methodology has been less successful for pre-Angkorian Buddhist materials, for fairly obvious reasons.

53. For detailed treatment of K. 214, see Kern 1906.

54. The text is inscribed on a miniature temple, just over a meter in height, with sculpted representations of some of these divinities sitting in its six niches. It might seem strange that Indra is included in the list, but the evidence suggests that he was co-opted by Buddhism relatively early in its history. A later inscription at the Bayon [K. 294] does refer to Indra as a "servant of the Buddha" (Pou 1995, 147). Another contemporary inscription at Prasat Kok [K. 339] invokes the triple jewel and talks about the restorations conducted at the site, most notably to an earlier image of the Buddha.

55. It is unclear whether the reference to expulsion means expulsion from the *sangha.* If it did, this would be the first reference in the Cambodian historical record to a king's interference in the discipline of the Buddhist order. Bizot (1988b, 111–112) points to some of the difficulties in the precise understanding of the text.

56. See Chirapat Prapandvidya 1990. Udayādityavarman II (r. 1050–1066) is specifically mentioned in the Khmer part of the text.

57. See chapter 4 below.

58. Preah Pithu is actually a complex of five temples. Only Temple X is Buddhist.

It possesses a frieze of buddhas inside the shrine and a Buddhist lintel. Probably dating from the fourteenth century, Temple X is surrounded by leaf-shaped *sīmā* markers typical of the Theravada (Giteau 1975, 16).

59. The Buddhist scenes at Phimai contain little traditional *Jātaka* and life-of-the-Buddha material.

60. This figure, as the temple's central supramundane "deity," is clearly the Buddha (Jacques 1985, 275). Another figure of Trailokyavijaya has been tentatively identified at the eleventh-century Buddhist temple of Phnom Banon near Battambang (Snellgrove 2000, 450). Trailokyavijaya is generally regarded as a powerful protector of Buddhism in the tantric tradition, particularly in the Japanese Shingon school (Woodward 2001, 252).

61. See Cœdès (1913b). Beng Mealea contains one of the earliest carved images of the earth goddess, Nang Thorani. Others, also dating from the twelfth century, are found at Ta Prohm at Angkor and Ta Prohm of Bati.

62. The present Khmer names of Angkorian monuments often bear little relation to the original names that are still attested by the inscriptional record. "Ta Prohm" is a modern name, meaning "grandfather Brahma." Its inscriptional designation was "Rājavihāra," meaning "the king's monastery." For detailed coverage, see Pou 1990.

63. The name "Preah Khan" (lit., "Holy Sword") is modern. The temple is called Jayaśrī in the inscription.

64. Another modern name, "Neak Pean" probably means "coiled snakes." The coiled-snake motif occurs in the sanctuary of Neak Pean and may represent the *nāgas* Nanda and Upananda. Alternatively, "Neak Pean" may be a version of "*nirpean*" = "*nirvāṇa.*" The inscriptions refer to the temple as Rājyaśrī.

65. Some scholars have thought that Jayavarman VII suffered from leprosy and was, in fact, the Leper King so widely mentioned in Cambodian myth and legend. Some have also argued that Neak Pean's association with Avalokiteśvara suggests that the structure was a place of healing, given that in medieval India the deity was thought to have the power to cure leprosy (Nandana Chutiwongs 1984, 319–320). For a fuller discussion of the Leper King, see Chandler 1976a and note 5 in chapter 2 below.

66. See Boulbet and Dagens 1973, 9–10.

67. Boisselier (1965, 81–82) believes that they both make reference to the *Kāraṇḍavyūha sūtra.*

68. See Mallmann 1948.

69. For a detailed treatment of the scenes, see Nandana Chutiwongs 1984, 321–323. Unfortunately, at least one of these has been removed in its entirety by professional thieves in recent years.

70. From the Pali "*bejayant,*" the name of Indra's palace. For Mabbett (1997, 352), the Bayon represents "a dynamo of royal charisma . . . plugged into a great bank of batteries of spiritual power" in which the center feeds on the religious potencies of the periphery.

71. Prasat Preah Stung at Preah Khan of Kompong Svay seems to have been the first structure to use similar face towers.

72. The historian Tāranātha, for instance, states that *mahantas* and *pandits* from Odantapuri fled to Pagan, Pegu, and Kamboja (almost certainly Cambodia) at the beginning of the thirteenth century.

73. One of the hospital edicts [K. 368, v. xiv] compares the activities of warriors and healers, since both get rid of the kingdom's ills. Preah Khan also had a hospital within its precincts. Most of the hospital edicts are rather similar; they refer to their royal foundation and lay down rules for the organization of the facility. For a list of sites, see Majumdar 1953, 493–494.

74. The Bat Chum inscriptions [K. 266–268, quoted in detail by Snellgrove (2000, 459)] ascribed such sanctity to the Siem Reap River that "with the exception of the sacrificial priest, no-one may bathe in the waters coming from this *tīrtha,* born at the summit of the holy mountain of Mahendra [*A.* 21]." A mid-eleventh-century inscription at Phnom Kbal Spean [K. 1012] characterized it as the "torrent of Rudra, river of Śiva, this Gaṅgā" (Jacques 1999, 361).

75. We should not be too simplistic. Brahmanism was not neglected during Jayavarman VII's reign. His Brahmanical chaplain *(purohita)* appears to have come from Burma (Cœdès 1968a, 173). Nevertheless, his Bayon inscription does state, "the mountain of Śiva in the Himalayas has been uprooted . . . new kings must have recourse to me" (quoted in Kulke 1993, 374).

76. Inscription of Preah Khan, Angkor [K. 908, dated 1191].

77. "Palilay" is a form of the Pali "Pārileyya," the name of the elephant, as well as of the forest area in which the scene is set. For a detailed treatment of its iconography, see Boisselier 1966, 99–105, 127–176, 299.

78. It opens with an invocation to the *trikāya,* Buddha, and Lokeśvara.

79. Woodward (2001, 251) suggests that a "turn to Theravada Buddhism" may have taken place toward the end of Jayavarman's reign. One assumes that Woodward has these events at the back of his mind, for he supplies no hard evidence to back up his contention.

80. See Ilangasinha 1998, 195. A number of authors have also noted the great similarities between the Satmahalprāsāda and Wat Kukut at Lamphun, Thailand (Silva 1988, 102–106).

81. An interesting bronze finial in the Bayon style from the first half of the thirteenth century shows Viṣṇu standing above an unmistakable figure of the earth goddess, Nang Thorani. The iconography is unique and puzzling. Despite the lack of obvious evidence on the object itself, the only reasonable interpretation is that it replaced an original Buddha figure during the period (Lerner and Kossak 1991, 159–160). If this is the case, Boisselier's thesis will need to be modified, since the finished product is not Śaivite nor does it look as if it originally had a tantric significance.

82. Chandler (1996, 72) draws parallels between Zhou's term "*zhugu*" and the Thai "*chao ku*"—a respectful form of address for a monk. Zhou Daguan was puzzled by the way palm-leaf strips "are covered with black characters, but as no brush or ink is used, their manner of writing is a mystery"—a fairly clear reference to the form of writing that continued in Cambodia to the end of the nineteenth century. He also reports that

the Cambodian king slept at the top of a golden tower, the Phimeanakas, where he nightly united with a nine-headed *nāga* protector appearing in the form of a beautiful woman before rejoining his wives and concubines.

83. Quoted from Pelliot 1951, 411–420.

84. See Cœdès 1936. As we shall see in due course, this pattern is also followed by a number of middle-period Cambodian kings.

85. The Khmer portion of the inscription tells how the king also sponsored the construction of a Buddha image called Śrīndramahādeva. It is exceedingly rare to find any royal figure described as "god-king" *(devarāja)* in the inscriptional record. Śrīndrajayavarman has this unique distinction in K. 144, a Khmer inscription consisting of a eulogy to a *kuṭi* at Prasat Kombot constructed by the king's guru.

2. The Middle Period and the Emergence of the Theravada

1. In contrast, Saveros Pou (1979, 333) has suggested, although without any especially convincing evidence, that Theravada Buddhism took over smoothly from prior Mahayana traditions because both had been religions of the people.

2. *Jinakalamali* 92–93, quoted in Sirisena 1978, 105.

3. The key caste-related terms "*jāti*" and "*varṇa*" certainly do occur in the inscriptional record, but they provide scant evidence for any caste-based system of social organization in ancient Cambodia. In the Khmer context the term "*jāti*" simply implies "birth or origin" with no specific Indic connotation, and the term for the four castes *("caturvarṇa")* is rare. Pou (1998, 127) regards usage of the latter as purely rhetorical. For a detailed treatment of the evidence for an Indic caste system in ancient Cambodia, see Mabbett 1977.

4. A good example of the latter is the *Baṅsāvatār prades kambujā,* redacted in 1941 by Ven Hās' Suk, chief monk *(mekun)* of Kandal Province (Mak Phœun 1981, 10). Monivong's chronicle is another example. It never quotes the king's direct speech or the substance of ministerial discussions, although the king is represented twice by indirect speech. One of these instances is related to the consecration of a Buddhist monastery in 1935, where he warns monks against schismatic activity. Only three of his many royal decrees appear in the text, and all concern reforms of the Buddhist order.

5. According to one of the chronicles, Preah Thong came to the throne in 267 BCE (Mak Phœun 1984, 38–41). The story of Preah Thong has circulated in many forms (see Gaudes 1993; and for South Indian Pallava parallels, Cœdès 1911). In one version he arrives in the region from a foreign land and falls in love with a serpent princess *(nāgī).* They marry, but in due course his *nāga* father-in-law warns Preah Thong not to build a tower with four faces at his new capital. Preah Thong ignores the advice, and a murderous conflict between the two ultimately leads to the father-in-law's death. As a result of contact with the poisons emitted by the dying *nāga*-king, Preah Thong contracts leprosy and is obliged to abandon his capital, which is subsequently ruled over by mon-

keys. He is eventually cured by the holy waters of the Siem Reap River and returns to occupy the throne once more.

This rendering of the story clearly identifies Preah Thong with the equally legendary Khmer Leper King *(sdach kanlong)*. Interestingly, a series of South Indian and Sri Lankan traditions seems to talk of the visit of a leprous Khmer king to their region. For instance, an image of Lokeśvara sculpted on a rock in the Weligama region of Sri Lanka is said to represent this figure, who is supposed to have been cured of his affliction nearby. A bronze Khmer image of Lokeśvara, found in the same area and now in the Colombo Museum, is also held to represent this Leper King, according to local tradition (Goloubew 1925, 510).

6. These are now popularly supposed to be housed at Prasat Preah Theat Khvao, some way to the east of the central Angkor complex, in Kompong Thom Province (Thompson 1999, 100).

7. The chronicles, intriguingly, claim that he took the throne at Angkor Thom in 1 CE (Mak Phœun 1984, 59–60).

8. On one occasion Kaetumāla returned to heaven in Indra's chariot, and Dāv Vaṅs Ascāry recovered him only after spending seven days ensuring that everyone in his kingdom was following the Buddhist precepts.

9. Viśvakarman (Pali Vissakamma) is the creator of the earth and sky in the Rg Veda (x.81), an incomparable artist and artisan in the *Mahābhārata* (e.g., i.2592), and the divine architect who also fashioned the golden wheel of the *cakravartin* in Vālmīki's *Rāmāyaṇa*. In the Theravadin *Vessantara Jātaka*, Viśvakarman is sent by Indra to construct a forest hermitage and a perfect pleasure ground in which all uncivilized or rustic values are banished, and savage nature and the sources of supernatural evil are tamed. In his Buddhist reformulation, Viśvakarman is preeminently a civilizing deity and the propagator of Buddhist culture (Dolias 1990, 123). Hence his association with the construction of Angkor Wat, the ultimate expression of Cambodian Buddhist culture, at least in its post-Angkorian form.

10. According to the early seventeenth-century *Poem of Angkor Wat*, Angkor is the earthly counterpart of Vejayanta, the heavenly palace of Indra. From that time on, the palace was protected by the sacred bull *(preah go)* (Pou 1987–1988, 340). The poem exists in a number of forms, one of which appears to have been redacted by Mahā Pan, the first *sanghareach* of the Thommayut (Khing Hoc Dy 1990, 123).

11. Not to be confused with the Buddha's attendant of the same name.

12. A date of 656 CE is given in the texts.

13. In 1195 CE, according to the chronicle. The Lao had the Emerald Buddha in their possession for only a short time before it was lost, this time to the Thai. The Khmer version of events is largely corroborated in the Thai version of the story. In the *Chronicle of the Emerald Buddha*, for example, we hear that a vessel dispatched to the King Anuruddha (r. 1044–1077) of Pagan from his counterpart in Ceylon, carrying both the Emerald Buddha statue and the Tripitaka, ran aground at Angkor Thom before continuing to its rightful destination (Notton 1933, 24–25).

14. A Pali text still extant in Cambodia, the *Mahāratanabimbavaṁsa* (Epoch of the

Great Jewel Image), maintains that the Emerald Buddha was made by Nāgasena from a Cambodian emerald *(marakata)* (Saddhatissa n.d., 88). Another legend, more or less dismissed by Woodward (1997, 507), suggests that the Emerald Buddha was carved from a jewel used in an oath of allegiance conducted by Sūryavarman I around 1011 CE. Also see Lingat 1934, 37.

15. The Sutta collection had been on the boat in the previous story.

16. *Kaev preah phloeung* is deposited at Wat Kaev Preah Phloeung. Mak Phœun (1995, 95n59) suggests that this monastery was named after one of its famous chief monks, Kaev Preah Phloeung, who is supposed to have assassinated King Cau Bañā An around 1600.

17. For a Khmer-language account of the various legends told to pilgrims during visits to Angkor Wat, see Mar Bo 1969.

18. The northernmost tower has an image of the Buddha in *bhūmisparśamudrā* very similar to that at Preah Palilay (Gosling 1991, 13–14).

19. Another tradition includes the Crystal Buddha *(preah kaev)* in the haul. There is a current belief that both holy objects are still secretly guarded in Bangkok. If a Khmer could gain access and splash soy sauce or vinegar on them, Cambodia would regain its greatness (F. Smith 1989, 39). Also see Chandler 1996, 85–86.

20. Also see Giteau 1975, 86.

21. Northeastern Thailand still has a fairly strong, though poor and traditional, Khmer community. Many able Khmer monks from the area become chief monks of important monasteries in Bangkok, for competent young Thai are increasingly secularized and tend to enter more profitable professions.

22. Completed under his successor (Notton 1933, 4). Mongkut's famous son, Prince Damrong Rajanubhab, described a pilgrimage to the sacred site in his book *Nirat Nakhon Wat* (Journey to Angkor).

23. Those mentioned in the chronicles include Wat Preah Cetiya Parbata, more commonly known as Wat Phnom; Wat Koh; Wat Langka (originally to the north of the *phnom*); Wat Buddhaghosa; and Wat Khbap Tā Yang, now known as Botum Vadi. Thompson (2000, 254) suggests that the arrangement of Bañā Yāt's *stūpa* mirrored the fourfold configuration of Buddha images also found at Longvek and Wat Nokor a little later. This may indicate the presence of the cult of Maitreya at the site. See below.

24. The reign of Paramarāja II (Cau Bañā Cand) was 1516–1566. Khin Sok (1988) gives the reign as 1529–1567.

25. "Laṅvaek" can mean "crossroad" in Khmer, i.e., the place traditionally associated in Indic thought with a *cakravartin*. Thompson (2000, 256n12) suggests that the word is cognate with "*catumukh.*" See note 47 below.

26. The original stone feet of this image are still housed in the sanctuary, although the current image of bronze appears to have been cast by Udong-based kings in the nineteenth century.

27. Aṭṭhārasa. King Sisowath and *sanghareach* Tieng restored Wat Attharasa in 1911 (Marquis 1932, 480). According to current popular belief, the now severely damaged Preah Put Attaroes blocks an entrance to the center of the earth and is still a source of

great power. It can, for instance, assist in obtaining U.S. visas. A belief also circulates that the secret tunnel was used by anticolonialist Buddhist hermits as a hiding place during the pre-Independence period (*PPP* 10/13, June 22–July 5, 2001).

28. Mak Phœun (1995, 190n193) reports that twenty-three statues were arranged in front of these images in two rows. The first row contained the twelve principal disciples of the Buddha; the second, the eleven kings who were supposed to have been in attendance at the Buddha's death.

29. Also see Lunet de Lajonquière 1902, 1:217, and Ros Nol 1997.

30. Also see Giteau 1975, 24, 50, 78. Intriguingly, Preah Ang Thom lies on its "inauspicious" left side, contrary to the norm that a buddha should lie down on the right.

Brahmanical rock carving in Cambodia goes back much earlier, as attested by the various works at Phnom Kulen and Kbal Spean. See Boulbet and Dagens 1973.

31. Various legends concerning Khleang Moeung, each with a specific geographical focus, circulate in Cambodia. According to one, he was actually a Pear tribal named Nup who managed to raise the phantom army through the intervention of the tribe's guardian spirit (Porée-Maspero 1961b, 395).

32. Exactly the same thing is supposed to have happened to *preah khan* after Sihanouk was deposed in April 1970. The importance of sacred swords as part of the regalia of kingly power is illustrated by the fact that both Thai and Cambodian kings, and even usurpers like Po Kambo (see chapter 6), have endeavored to obtain a sacred saber supposed, in legend, to have been in the possession of the Jarai King of Fire. The Jarai are a tribal people living in the northeastern borderlands of Cambodia. See Hickey 1982b, 130, and Leclère 1903.

33. Also see Jacob 1986a, 117, and Giteau 1975, 79.

34. These inscriptions are designated "IMA," from the French "Inscriptions modernes d'Angkor."

35. Also see Giteau 1975, 34.

36. For a detailed consideration of the identity of the author of IMA3, see Mak Phœun 1995, 41–45.

37. The IMAs seem to recognize a plurality of *sanghareachs*. A total of eight are mentioned in IMA37, vv. 29–30 (Lewitz 1974, 314), while the traditional Codes Cambodgiens talk of five *mahāsaṅgharājas*, plus two assistants, who counsel the king on custom, law, and religion (Leclère 1898, 1:61). The situation seems to have been much the same in the Thai Sukhothai and Ayutthaya periods. However, we cannot assume that the title meant the same then as it came to mean in the modern period (Vickery 1973, 67n48).

38. B.-P. Groslier (1985–1986, 21) has suggested that a Tibetan monk's pilgrimage account (MacDonald 1970), previously thought to have been to Rangoon, was actually to Angkor.

39. Lit., "thousand Buddhas."

40. The Buddha spent a total of nineteen rainy seasons in residence at Jetavana, which had been donated by an important lay disciple named Anāthapiṇḍaka. A plan of the Jetavana monastery—made by Shimano Kenryo, a seventeenth-century traveler

from Nagasaki—is a fair representation of Angkor Wat (Yoshiaki Ishizawa 1998, 75). It is now in the Shokokan, the municipal museum of Mito. Also see Péri 1923, 119.

41. In his lengthy poem *Nirieh Nokor Wat* (Un pélerinage à Angkor en 1909, *Kampuchea Surya*, 1934—quoted in Edwards 1999, 201), Ind laments that his fellow Khmer have been reduced to coolie status by French custodians anxious to return the structure to its "original" state.

42. According to a manual of monastery architecture written in 1954, important Buddha images need be protected only in a simple open-sided shed. It is not necessary to construct a *vihāra* for the purpose (Giteau 1971a, 126).

43. Another important structure at Srei Santhor that dates from the same period is Vihear Suor. Hun Sen and his wife top the list of donors in its recent renovation (Thompson 1999, 79).

44. Other *stūpas* in the vicinity house relics of the royal family. One of these is popularly supposed to emit a strong radiance as a presage of important events. Nearby are the strongly venerated *stūpas* of the legendary king Baksei Chamkrong and his general Meun Ek (Thompson 1999, 83).

45. Other early images are found at Beng Mealea, Ta Prohm of Angkor, and Ta Prohm of Bati (Giteau 1967, 136–137).

46. On the architectural history of the *stūpa* in Cambodia, see Marchal 1954. Thompson (1999, 55–56) has argued that both Preah Palilay and the Bayon represent the fusion of a *stūpa* and a tower *(prasat)*. She also notes that the Khmer term "*prang*" may nowadays mean either a *prasat* or a *stūpa*.

47. Thompson (1999, 226–227; 2000, 255–256) notes that the designation "*catumukh*" (lit., "four faces") for the point in Phnom Penh where the Sap and the Mekong rivers meet and split once more may be interpreted in this way. Thus it represents the ritual space where mundane and supramundane forces come together, i.e., where a revivified Khmer kingship and the hope for the messianic age merge.

48. These slaves were possibly Thai captives who had previously made difficulties for the king.

49. Probably equivalent to the rank of *sanghareach*.

50. As late as 1944, Sambok was an important ceremonial site. It was referred to as the "spirit of the Preah Khan sacred sword" *(neak tā preah ang preah khan)* and was associated with the contact between the Khmer kingship and the Jarai Kings of Fire and of Water (Hickey 1982b, 141).

51. Uttung Meanchey = Udong the Victorious. Because of the large number of *wats* in the area, the region around Udong is sometimes called the "region of a hundred pagodas."

52. Synopses of the seven books of the Abhidhamma.

53. Udong has remained a center for ascetic practice down to the present. Interestingly, it has also been a magnet for Muslim renunciants. See Baccot 1968.

54. On his literary work, see Leang 1966.

55. Subsequently known as Wat Preah Sugandh Mean Bon. According to Mak

Phœun and Po Dharma (1984, 287, 290), Cau Bañā Tū had been a monk at Wat Preah Put Leay Leak, in Babaur, prior to assuming the throne.

56. A story concerning Preah Sugandh Mean Bonn interestingly explains the origin of Cambodia's sizable Chinese community toward the end of the nineteenth century, when the chronicles were largely redacted. A Chinese ruler has been suffering from pains in the head. His trusted astrologer tells him that he was a dog living in Cambodia in a previous life and should send ambassadors to consult the learned monk. They visit king Cau Bañā Tū and are conducted to the *senghareach*'s residence, where he confirms the astrologer's suspicions. The dog had intelligently and loyally served a chief monk called Mahadhatu. Indeed, the merit generated in this manner had contributed to his present favorable rebirth. However, Mahadhatu had buried the dog at the foot of the eastern slope of Phnom Preah Reach Trop, where the roots of bamboo were now penetrating the dog's skull—hence the Chinese king's discomfort. The dog's corpse is subsequently disinterred at the predicted spot, a funerary monument is erected at the site, and the Chinese king is cured. As a result Preah Sugandh Mean Bonn appears to have built up a special relationship with the Chinese, who began to establish roots in Cambodia (Mak Phœun 1981, 160–161). For detailed coverage of the Chinese community in Cambodia, see Willmott 1970.

57. Possibly Cham as well (Manguin 1985, 11).

58. According to Jesuit sources, this king vacillated between Islam and Christianity before making his choice. This vacillation seems to indicate that the decision may have had more to do with geopolitical factors than with specifically religious issues.

59. Another chronicle has him falling in love with a Muslim girl from Khleang Sbek village near Udong (Mak Phœun 1990, 62). For information about the Cham, see note 81 below.

60. Even today the graves of Muslim saints are revered, and ceremonies—particularly those associated with spirits, witches, werewolves, and so on—are attended by Buddhist neighbors who regard Cambodian Muslims as masters of the magic arts. Vickery (1984, 181) relates how women from Phnom Penh crossed to the Muslim village of Chrui Changvar to "get predictions of the future, love potions for husbands and lovers, and noxious prescriptions for rivals."

61. He died in captivity in Hue around 1659 CE.

62. When the French first arrived in Cambodia, they were struck by the amity that appeared to exist between Muslims and Buddhists. Pavie (1901, 1:28–29, quoted in Mak Phœun 1990, 52), for instance, observed, "Un peuple musulman et un peuple bouddhiste unis en des relations presque fraternelles. . . . Les fêtes religieuses, les fêtes périodiques du people et des villages étaient toujours pour eux des prétextes à réunions amicales."

63. Also see Leclère 1898, 2:295–296, and Mak Phœun 1995, 394.

64. Skilling (2001b, 58–59) demonstrates that the inscription's author had a sound knowledge of Buddhist textual traditions. The inscription mentions both Nāgasena and Milinda, characters from the *Milindapañha,* and a number of *Jātaka* stories. The text also refers to an apocryphal *Jātaka,* the *Lokaneyyappakaraṇa,* which was rendered into verse by the Cambodian court poet Nong in 1794 CE.

65. Nong may have presided over the previously mentioned commission to revise the Buddhist canon.

66. It is difficult to be certain of the historicity of some of these assertions.

67. A number of high-ranking Khmer officials had also joined the movement. They were subsequently tried and executed.

68. From *The Recommendations of Tā Mās (Rīoengpandanṁ Tā Ms);* quoted in Hansen 1999, 20.

69. The Vietnamese appear to have had a heavily fortified base at Wat Preah Vihear Samna (Giteau 1975, 227). Leclère (1914, 434–440) reports that bricks from the demolished fort in Phnom Penh were also transported to Udong to fuel Duang's "mania for construction."

70. Previously named Wat Kraing Punlei.

71. Previously called Wat Rajadhipesa.

72. Yang Sam (1990, 82–83) has suggested that this division of patriarchal labor reflects the traditional distinction between village-dwelling and forest-dwelling monks, but this seems unlikely. On the precolonial appanages, see Leclère 1894a, 179–182.

73. *Kākāti Jātaka* (no. 327), a story about the seduction and kidnapping of a king's principal wife by a supernatural being, and *Sussondī Jātaka* (no. 360), a work on a similar theme. For a Khmer-language appreciation of Duang's literary endeavors, see Leang 1965.

74. Hon Bunlong (c. 1750–1805). See Khing Hoc Dy 1990, 188, and Osipov 2000, 6.

75. Vickery (1982, 85) has suggested that there may have been more than one individual called Nong.

76. A Pali version, the *Lokaneyyappakaraṇa,* is a "Treatise on Secular Discipline" that circulated quite freely in post-Angkorian Southeast Asia. Jaini (1986) ascribes the text he edited in the National Museum of Bangkok to an unknown fifteenth-century monk living near Chiang Mai.

77. *Jātaka* no. 484.

78. The anti-opium crusade eventually took on an anti-French flavor. The theme is taken up in Ind's famous collection of stories, *Gatilok* (1859–1925), particularly in the tale of the "Oknya who smoked opium who used his influence to harm inhabitants of the region" (v. 2, 41–46; see Hansen 1999, 46, 60–61). Ang Duang was the first Cambodian monarch to raise taxes on opium and alcohol (Forest 1980, 215). On the connection between the opium trade and French colonialism, see Descours-Gatin 1992.

79. In this context Chandler's suggestion (1983, 119) that Duang's humility at the end of his life was a reaction to his sense of failure as a king seems a little harsh.

80. In true Buddhist kingly fashion, Duang sponsored a national rain-making ceremony in the month of *srap* (July–August) in 1859. This is noteworthy, for the usual time of the year for such rites is the month of *vissakh* (April–May). It seems that the ceremony was delayed because of the king's absence in Kampot (Chandler 1976b, 170n3).

81. The Jahed (from the Arabic "*zahid*" = anchorite, recluse, etc.) are also known as Kom Jumat (Friday group) on the grounds that, unlike the vast majority of Muslims, they have Friday at midday as their only specified time for prayer. The group are

mainly centered around Udong but are also found in some parts of Pursat and Battambang provinces.

Tauch (1994, 108) asserts that the Muslims of Battambang were Sufis. The Thai governor of the province in the late nineteenth century seems to have treated them well and was fascinated by their magical skills. For a detailed discussion of Islam in Cambodia, see Ner 1941 and W. Collins 1998b.

The two other Islamic groups are the Cham and the Chvea. The Cham claim descent from Ali Hanafiah, who is said to have brought Islam to Champa. The scholarly consensus is that the Cham bani (from the Arabic *"beni"* = sons [of the prophet]) of Phanrang, Phan-ri, and other Cham villages in Binh-thuan Province, Vietnam (Durand 1903, 54), had come into contact with Persian or India Sh'ia elements at an early stage in their development. The village of Reka Po Pram, Tbong Khmum, Kompong Cham Province, still has the grave of Kai Po Behim (Ibrahim), who is supposed to have led one Cham group from their homeland to Cambodia. Both the Jahed and the Cham acknowledge a strong Cham heritage. However, Jahed identity is bound up with a sense of Cham history and culture, whereas the Cham are more attached to the Cham religion, i.e., Islam.

The Chvea (Khmer pronunciation of "Cham Jva" = Java) have a Malay-Indonesian heritage. They declare an ancestral connection with Pattani in the upper Malay Peninsula, interestingly an area with a vulnerable Muslim minority since Thailand brought the region under Buddhist domination. The Chvea do not speak Cham, and they communicate with the other Muslim grouping only with great difficulty. They are commonly referred to as Khmer Islam, although this term is also now widely used to designate all Cambodian Muslims. Both Cham and Chvea pray five times daily and would generally be considered orthodox, unlike the Jahed.

In the first French census of the country in 1874, around 25,500 Muslims, accounting for 3 percent of the overall population of Cambodia, were recorded. Baccot (1968, 17) gives the following figures: 58,684 for 1921 and 73,469 for 1937.

82. San, a blind Muslim saint, lived at the Ta San mosque during Norodom's reign. He seems to have been revered by Muslims and Buddhists alike. Indeed, the queen mother regularly paid him her respects. The ending of a cholera outbreak in 1874 is ascribed to San's miraculous intervention (Cabaton 1906, 46).

83. Khin Hoc Dy believes that this was done in imitation of one of the Buddha's principal disciples, Mahā Moggallāna, whose body, according to Cambodian tradition but not canonical sources, was fed to birds of prey by heretics. Similar funerary practices were already widespread in Funan, as Chinese witnesses testify (Pelliot 1903, 270). They are also well attested in medieval and modern Tibet.

3. Theravada Buddhism in Cambodia

1. Excerpt from a royal chronicle, quoted in Chandler 1983, 118–119.

2. According to Steinberg et al. (1959, 52–53), there are thirteen distinct tribal groups

in the country as a whole. However, only five—Rhade, Jarai, Stieng, Kui, and Pear—have been sufficiently distinguished by scholarship. The Rhade, mainly located in the Darlac sector of Vietnam but also found overlapping into Stung Treng, and the Jarai have been designated Indonesian in racial type. They speak Cham dialects.

3. Naturally, the montagnards reject the designation.

4. The connection between governance and food also applied in Thailand, where the king was said to "eat the royal treasure" and where governors, on taking office, started to "eat the town" *(kin muang)* (Bunnag 1977, 22).

5. *"Bon,"* the Khmer word normally translated as "merit," also denotes "dignity or rank." Conversely, *"samsak,"* meaning "power or rank," possesses a moral connotation (Edwards 1999, 99).

6. The Thai king Rama I had copies made for his own coronation in 1785. The regalia disappeared from the Royal Palace in Phnom Penh after the coup of March 18, 1970, and have not been seen again. For a photograph of the collection taken before it went missing, see Jeldres and Chaijitvanit 1999, 77. The principal items in the regalia are a sword *(preah khan)*; the victory spear *(preah lompeng chey)* supposed to have been owned by the gardener-regicide Ta Trasak Pha'em, a legendary ruler of the late Angkorian period; and a dagger *(kris)* given to the Muslim king of Cambodia, Rāmādhipatī I (r. 1642–1658), by a Malay princess. King Norodom believed that the sword had been made by Viśvakarman (Aymonier 1883, 173). Piat (quoted in Hickey 1982b, 128) was told by court Brahmins *(baku)* that *preah khan* was one of four sacred swords associated with "vassals that protect the kingdom at the four cardinal points"—a possible reference to the four great protector kings *(cātummahārājikadeva)* of the Buddhist tradition.

7. Other gifts from this same source were held to have mysterious powers. A tunic sent by the two kings to the royal court was employed in rain-making rites. After addressing the five protectors of the kingdom, the king sprinkled the tunic with water while four priests squatted, imitating the call of the frog (Hickey 1982b, 139).

8. Court etiquette at Udong was quite restricting for the king, who, for instance, always ate alone. The cutting of his hair was particularly troublesome, for the barber wore special rings on his fingers designed so that they would not discharge the royal power. Southeast Asian kings were also expected to maintain extensive harems as a sign of their magical potency. In Cambodia the practice continued into the modern period. For example, Ang Duang had thirty-two direct male and thirty-four direct female descendants; Norodom, fifty-three male and sixty-six female; and Sisowath, seventy-one male and eighty female (*PPP* 8/7, April 2–12, 1999).

9. Chandler 1975b, 347–348. Geertz' term "theatre state" seems appropriate in this context.

10. This could reflect a conscious borrowing from the Hindu caste system. Its foundational document, the *Puruṣasūkta* (Rg Veda x.90), uses precisely the same image to outline the origins of the four great castes or estates *(varṇa)*.

11. This is indirect evidence that senior Buddhist monks in the premodern period came from high-ranking family backgrounds.

12. Court Brahmins are a feature of other Theravada states in Southeast Asia. They

officiate at various state rituals regarded as contrary to the discipline *(vinaya)* of Buddhist monks. The five Brahmanical deities *(pañcaksetr)* traditionally associated with the *bakus'* rituals at the Royal Palace at Phnom Penh are variously listed, but the list always includes Īsūr (Śiva), Nārāy (Viṣṇu), and Umā/Candī. However, it never contains Indra or Brahmā, for they are widely regarded as Buddhist deities. Indeed, neither occupies a prominent place in the pre-Buddhist pantheon of Cambodia.

13. The parallels represent my modification of a schema given by Try (1991, 54). The four chief ministers are "congruent with the guardian deities of the four cardinal points" (Solomon 1970, 11), i.e., the *cātummahārājikadeva.* When grouped around the king on formal occasions, clad in their "strikingly colored uniforms," they constituted a *maṇḍala* (Chandler 1983, 112, 114).

14. The Wat Prek Kuy chronicle imagines the country as a walled city with five gates, at Sambaur, Kompong Svay, Pursat, Kampot, and Chaudoc (Chandler 1973, 29). Each *dey* was the sphere of a royal delegate *(sdach trañ)* who, despite his purely ceremonial function, had a higher rank than officials given the more arduous task of actually administering the region.

15. During an annual ritual called *tāṃṅ tu,* provincial delegations brought various natural curiosities, such as fossils, monstrous roots, and bizarrely shaped stones to the Silver Pagoda in Phnom Penh. Ang Chouléan (1986, 204) has described this as a recapitulation of the Angkorian rite.

16. The Kreung hill tribe of Ratanakiri have recently been troubled by the logging activities of a Taiwanese timber company, which has been exploiting forests where the ancestors are supposed to dwell. The village chief is reported as having said, "The forest gods are very angry. . . . We have heard the sound of screaming and the beating of drums from the forest that show their anger. . . . Four people in our village have died since the logging started, because the forest gods are angry" (*PPP* 8/17, August 20–2 September 1999). The cutting down of a fig tree outside the National Assembly to facilitate the state visit of Chinese premier Jiang Zemin in November 2000 was also held to be the cause of a number of otherwise unexplained deaths. Cambodian secretary general Chan Ven arranged a Buddhist exorcism on April 1–2, 2001 (*PPP* 10/18 April 13–26, 2001).

17. The bill was paid by Prince Ranariddh in gratitude for the *neak tā*'s help in his electoral successes of 1993. Many of Pursat's electoral candidates, plus some national leaders such as Prince Ranariddh and Sam Rainsy, also visited the statue in the run-up to the 1998 elections (*PPP* 7/17, July 24–30, 1998).

18. A corruption of "*siddhi-svāsti,*" one of the opening words of many magical treatises and a term suggesting supernatural power and success.

19. We know that Umā Mahiṣāsuramardinī was a popular subject for Cambodian sculptors over a long historical period. Vickery (1998, 154) notes that although the name is not specifically mentioned in pre-Angkorian sources, a female buffalo-slayer did appear in the iconographical record quite frequently, particularly in the south of the country.

20. Try (1991, 288) asserts that a human sacrifice to *neak tā* Me Sar, sponsored by

Governor Dekcor, took place at Ba Phnom as late as 1884. It seems that the *neak tā* Krol of Kompong Thom may have received human sacrifices until 1904 (Bonnefoy 1991, 2:923).

21. The monks also recited prayers at neighboring sites associated with *neak tā* Kraham Ka (red neck), *neak tā* Sap Than (everyplace), and *neak tā* Tuol Chhnean (fishing basket mound).

22. Thboung Khmum and Kompong Svay, two of the five regions in which a royal delegate *(sdach trañ)* had his seat (Porée-Maspero 1962–1969, 1:246–248). Only the *sdach trañ* and the king himself had the power and authority to order capital punishment (Chandler 1974, 215n39).

23. The ritual sacrifice of buffalo, often involving liquor-drinking female priestesses, is still practiced in some parts of northern Thailand. Vickery (1998, 142n11) witnessed one of these rituals taking place against the backdrop of a large portrait of the Buddha. A number of *neak tā* were offered animal sacrifices until quite recently. *Neak tā* Mno of Wat Vihear Suor received both a crocodile and a monkey, while *neak tā* Tenon of Kandal Stieng had a monkey (Porée-Maspero 1954, 635).

24. The connection with agriculture is clearly very important. Ebihara (1968, 426) noticed that *neak tā* were sometimes encouraged to help prevent crabs from cutting the stalks of rice seedlings.

25. According to tradition, the propitiation of *neak tā* Khleang Moeung once involved the sacrifice of a male buffalo in each province of the kingdom.

26. The word "*boramei*" *(pāramī)* is clearly related to the Buddhist idea of the perfections (Ang Chouléan 1988, 37). The *boramei* are also mobile. Bizot (1994a, 110–111) describes a consecration rite by which a *boramei* may be transferred from an old to a new image.

27. The earth goddess is also mentioned in the *Rāmakerti* (v. 397). Variations on this story are also found in two Burmese texts, the *Tathāgata-Udāna-Dīpanī* I, 199, and the *Samantacakkudīpanī* I, 205–207 (both cited by Duroiselle 1921–1922, 146). The author of the last text concludes that the legend, given that it is not attested in canonical sources, is a "popular fancy." He underlines his view by citing the example of the seventeenth-century monk Tripitakalankara, who, given the unorthodox nature of the image, caused it to be erased from the wall of a cave.

28. In Laos she is also the goddess of the soil, responsible for fertility and harvests. Her area of responsibility overlaps somewhat with that of the *phībān* (Laotian equivalents of the *neak tā*), although the *phībān* are geographically more specific and functionally less well-defined (Condominas 1975, 258).

29. Vickery (1984, 4) describes a spirit temple between Battambang and the Tonle Sap, the foundations of which contained the body of a pregnant woman who had been buried alive. This may have been a fairly common procedure in the region, for Tauch Chhuong (1994, 24–25) also tells of a dike constructed in the late nineteenth century in the same area. Interred within it was a boat containing a ritually murdered pregnant woman. There seems to have been a taboo against pregnant women's crossing dikes connecting with special shrines. It is probable that the woman was killed because

of the power generated by her death and, more importantly, by that of her unborn child. On the protective qualities of a desiccated human fetus *(goan krak)*, see below in the text.

30. The altars of oracles *(snang)* are invariably furnished with images of the Buddha and the future Buddha, Maitreya *(preah si ar maikrey)*. They may also hold additional items, such as phallic stones, a photo of Preah Ko, a statue of Nang Thorani, and so on.

31. Wat Vihear Suor was recently restored by Sihanouk and Hun Sen (Bertrand 1998, 1119, and *PPP* 11/01, January 4–17, 2002). Today it houses a famous shrine to the *boramei* Yay Tep, who occupies a small Buddha image standing midway between the two sanctuaries (Bizot 1994a, 121). Many *snang* associate themselves with the royal cult once again at this location.

32. These are housed in the Ho Preah Athi chapel to the right of the throne in the Throne Hall (Jeldres 1999, 68).

33. In the past, such monks performed nocturnal meditations in wild places, particularly the forest, in order to make contact with various spirits. These practices gave them great power and charisma. The laity consulted them on many matters, both great and small. As an example of the latter, some *loak dhutang* were believed to be able to divine winning lottery numbers (Ang Chouléan 1988, 39).

34. There is a popular belief that many *pret* had once lived as monastery boys *(kmeng vat)* (Ang Chouléan 1986, 197).

35. Thompson (1996, 15) mentions a monk's performance of a *hau braling* ceremony in order to reintegrate the *braling* of a man who had returned home from seventeen years of forced exile in France.

36. A yantra designed to exorcise spirits contains the written text, "Please give the heartwood of the Abhidhamma, the one that is the greatest, . . . to come and take away the anger" (Eisenbruch 1992, 305).

37. The convention appears to be that *gru* use yellow pigments for the construction of Buddhist-based yantra and red pigments for yantras related to Brahmanism (Eisenbruch 1992, 293).

38. On the *dhmap'*, see Ebihara 1968, 436, and Ang Chouléan 1986, 256. When most other *gru* enter a Buddhist monastery, they put their healing powers on hold and accept the role of an *achar*.

39. The word derives from the Pali term "*gāthā*," meaning "verse or stanza."

40. Menstrual blood is sometimes used in love potions. Blood from a first period may be saved and used as a medicine for birth complications.

41. For example, *Kpuon moel jatā rās nis gāthā yanta dāṃs buos* (Book [allowing] a preview of the destiny [of men] and [containing] diverse magical formulae), MS 466, Bibliothèque de l'Institut Bouddhique, Phnom Penh, quoted in Khin Sok 1982, 117.

42. Metal *katha* are often wound around a knotted cotton thread and employed as a waist belt.

43. Soldiers and the police are particularly attracted to the magical protective power of *katha*. In combat one may be carried in the mouth or secured in the hair. It is also

quite common for soldiers to wear a belt or collar *(kse katha)* consisting of seven or twelve separate amulets.

44. The disregard for this ordinance is underlined by the fact that on January 20, 1941, a monk called Sip wrote to the king, suggesting that all of the kingdom's monks be ordered to prepare *kansaeng yantra* for soldiers going to the front (Ang Chouléan 1986, 68n159).

45. In de Bernon's interesting study (1998c), Kong Seng Huoen is described as having been initiated, while he was a monk, by three separate religious masters in Battambang Province. Women are not tattooed, although Chean Rithy Men (2002, 226–227) describes an unusual example of this taking place in the Khmer diaspora in the United States. A good account of the use of tattoos in Thailand may be found in Terwiel 1994, 69–79.

46. Tannenbaum's study (1987) of tattoos among the Theravadin Shan in Maehongson Province, Thailand, also shows that they are not regarded as decoration. In her view, they are primarily medicaments. Those who have tattoos must observe the five lay Buddhist precepts and various food restrictions to ensure their apotropaic effectiveness. The most spectacular tattoos are those designed to "close off the body" and make a person impervious to weapons. However, the powerful five-buddha tattoo causes others to like or fear the bearer. It may not be worn by women and must be received on a special raised platform while dressed in white and observing the eight precepts. The ink used is red and contains the exfoliated skin of a monk. This is the reason that its bearer is treated with such respect. He is dressed in a monk's skin.

47. I am grateful to Judy Ledgerwood (pers. comm.) for pointing this out to me.

48. It is possible that the use of *goan krak* is not unrelated to the mystical embryology of the initiatory Buddhist path that is discussed in more detail in chapter 4. These practices involve the religious practitioner's attempt to create an embryo of the Buddha within his or her own body. Also see Guthrie-Highbee 1992, 50.

49. Among the many hilltop monasteries, almost always built on or alongside Brahmanical ruins, Leclère (1899, 441) mentions Wat Anh-Chey on the right bank of the Mekong between Kompong Cham and Krouchmar, and Wat Prasath-Andeth in Kompong Svay District of Kompong Thom Province.

50. Intriguingly, Preah Ang Thom lies on its left side, yet the Buddha is supposed to have died lying on his auspicious right side. It is difficult to know why this should be so. The shape of the boulder would certainly have allowed the more usual form of representation.

51. Also see Dalet 1934, 796. The presiding protector deity of Phnom Santuk is *neak tā* Kraham Ka, who once lived as Decho Borara'a Thipadei Meas, a feudal lord of Kompong Thom (Ros Nol 1997).

52. At the time, Sihanouk's Sangkum government had been insistent that everyone should engage in productive work so that they were not parasites. The ascetics' lifestyles should, perhaps, be read in this light.

53. They were used as execution and disposal sites during the Pol Pot period, and piles of human remains may still be seen there today. It is reported that many skulls have recently been stolen for magical purposes (*PPP* 10/15, July 20–August 2, 2001).

54. This tradition is discussed in further detail in chapter 4.

55. Another cluster of religiously significant caves may be found at Phnom Trotung, also in Kampot Province. An inscription [K. 45] dating to the reign of Yaśovarman was found there, and the caves were sites of considerable pilgrimage activity in the past. When Lunet de Lajonquière (1902–1911, 1:48) visited at the end of the nineteenth century, they had been completely abandoned. In the interior of the cave is a fairly ruined brick structure (about three meters square) on a laterite foundation. It is built around a stalagmite with a broken stalactite overhead (Bruguier 1998a, 1998b).

56. For a detailed treatment of the reestablishment of the cult at Phnom Baset, see Ang Chouléan 1993, 198–200. A certain amount of xenophobic hostility has emerged recently after a Chinese temple, Kong So Em, was built on the summit (*PPP* 10/12, June 8–21, 2001).

57. Wat Chaudotes seems to have been founded by the mother and the aunt of King Ang Duang in 1865 (Marquis 1932, 479).

58. In this connection B.-P. Groslier (1985–1986a, 68) has asserted that the monastery is an obvious variation on the bachelors' houses so typical of Oceanic civilizations.

59. This had been the case at Wat Tep Pranam, Udong, where some old bronze Buddha images were uncovered during demolition work in the early 1970s (Giteau 1971b).

60. The remains of the poor tend to be stored in small communal urns within the *vihāra,* often close to the northeast corner of the altar base.

61. For a general discussion of the relationship between monastic asceticism and fecundity in Southeast Asian Buddhism, see Harris 2000b, 149–154.

62. Ang Chouléan (1987–1990, 13–14) describes the ritual performed at Wat Prèk Ampil for a *bray* named "the lady" *(jaṃdāv)* that inhabits the monastery's canoe, or holy vehicle *(preah dīnāṃṅ).*

63. In royal monasteries the *indrakhīla* is dropped into position by the king (Giteau 1969b, 48).

64. Particularly elaborate ceremonies may involve as many as nine *achars.*

65. According to tradition, the Buddha authorized offerings to the *nāga* Kroṅ Bali when a Buddha image is dedicated or when *sīmā*-root stones are buried (Giteau 1969b, 25–26). This minor deity appears to be a Cambodian transformation of the demon king Bali, an Indian mythological figure defeated by the god Viṣṇu. For more detailed treatment of the cult of Kroṅ Bali, see Porée-Maspero 1961a and Martel 1975, 239–240.

66. The majority of such stones were once supplied by craftsmen based in the village of Padhay, to the north of the Great Lake on the road from Phnom Penh to Skun.

67. Despite the thoughtless destruction of many older monastic structures, *sloek sema* often remain undamaged and abandoned in an ignored corner of more modern monasteries. King Monivong (1927–1940) seems to have been so concerned by this that he ordered unused markers in the province of Pursat to be collected and deposited safely at Prasat Bakan (Giteau 1975, 17).

68. The text has been translated and studied by Giteau (1971a).

69. Obviously, her schema must by treated with some caution. Tauch Chhuong (1994, 56) has noted that Chinese brick makers and bricklayers generally built monasteries in the Battambang region at the end of the nineteenth century. It seems possible that they followed some set architectural and iconometrical standard, but we do not know this for certain. For more detailed information of the furnishing and structure of specific monasteries, see Dalet 1936 and Carbonnel 1973. Martel (1975, 227–254) also provides an excellent account of the physical, organizational, and cultic structures of Wat Lovea, near Angkor.

70. It was reputedly made from a *koki* tree *(Hopea odorata)* by a senior monk called Jai.

71. Other traditions associate the monastery with the defeat of Kan by Paramarāja II (Cau Bañā Cand, r. 1516–1566) (Giteau 1975, 181–182).

72. Some legends also associate the relic with the great Theravadin exegete Buddhaghosa. It seems that Unnalom had originally been called Wat Sarikathat. The relic was moved to Wat Prang, Udong, in 1909 (Cœdès 1918, 17n3).

73. Skilling (1992, 111) has pointed out that this "gesture of dispelling fear" is found throughout the Buddhist world and is clearly associated with the protective qualities of the Buddha. Curiously, both images had feminized names, "*preah nang cek*" and "*preah nang cam,*" probably because they had been homologized with a local *boramei vat*. Their photos may be found on the cover of Bizot 1994b. David Chandler (pers. comm.) is not sure that they are Buddha images at all.

74. Giteau (1975, 197–198) feels that there is something simian in these images. She also sees parallels with the iconography of Kubera, the Vedic god of wealth.

75. Scenes from the *Temiya Jātaka* and the *Sirī Jātaka,* both of which are very popular in Cambodia, occur on the panels.

76. Royal monasteries could sometimes be identified by their external iconography, such as the Holy Sword *(preah khan)* incorporated into the pediment. Actually, it is rare for any nineteenth-century pediment to contain specifically Buddhist scenes, and the Buddha himself never appears. This was probably because it was important to protect such images from the elements. Much more common on the external walls are painted or bas-relief scenes from the *Rāmakerti* (Giteau 1975, 227, 257–258).

77. Like the *Rāmakerti,* the story of Preah Chinavong involves battles between kingly heroes of the settled land and *yakkha* kings of the forest (Thierry 1982, 130). Other *Jātakas* of local composition include the *Rathasena Jātaka* and the *Bimbābilāp*. The former recounts the adventures of the bodhisattva when, as the son of one of twelve sisters, he was imprisoned in a forest. The latter gives an account of the accusations and confessions of the Buddha's ex-wife.

78. For a good recent study of monastery paintings from the late nineteenth and early twentieth centuries, see Nafilyan and Nafilyan 1997.

79. The *vihāra* had been used as a prison during Democratic Kampuchea. When I visited in 1997, the lower parts of the interior murals had been destroyed by damp and by accumulated rubbish, but many marvelous scenes in the upper register were largely intact. They were, however, deteriorating because of a leaking roof.

80. San Sarin (1975, 5n4) points out that monasteries well into the 1970s, particularly those that housed large numbers of monastery boys, were important places for the acquisition of artisan skills such as carpentry, painting, masonry, and so on.

81. He may previously have been taught painting by a monk called Tā Yuos (Bizot 1989, 62).

82. One of the problems with Jacques' approach to the question is that it is based on known Indian customs. We do not know whether these customs applied in the Angkorian context.

83. Long lists of slave names are attested in the record. Names such as "hating injustice" *(saap anyāya)* or "made to be loved" *(jāpi sralañ)* appear to indicate that some must have been treated favorably. Others, like "stinking" *(sa-uy)* or "sullen" *(sgih)*, convey a rather different impression (Jacob 1993b, 310). It is also noteworthy that the ancient inscriptions frequently employ high-status Sanskrit names when referring to individual slaves (Jacques 1970, 25).

84. This offense included the killing of a monk for theft and arson at a monastery. It was not entirely uncommon for monasteries to be pillaged. Kampot Province seems to have been particularly prone to the threat. In August 1918, for example, the monks of Wat Ansong, Ba Phnom, Prey Veng, were driven out of their monastery by bandits who made it their stronghold for a short period (Forest 1980, 347, 379).

85. It seems that paid labor at a monastery, on the odd occasions that it happened, could be anything up to double the rate paid elsewhere (Ebihara 1968, 302).

86. *Cpāp' tumnien pi boran* states that all monastic property is ultimately owned by the Buddha (Leclère 1898, 1:172).

87. The practice has continued down to the present period. Choan and Sarin (1970, 130) record that in the late 1960s a pious layman donated a house in Phnom Penh, inherited from his mother, to Wat Tep Pranam in Udong. When Kalab (1968, 521) studied a village in Kompong Cham in the 1960s, she discovered that although the majority (83 percent) of the land was privately owned, often by absentee landlords, 1 percent was the property of the king and 1 percent was owned by the monastery. Only monastery land was considered inalienable.

88. Not all *don chi* are old. Try (1991, 186–187), for instance, noted an upsurge in religious vocation among young widows sometime after the end of the Democratic Kampuchea period. For a detailed discussion of the origin, role, and discipline of the Theravada nuns' order, see Wijayaratna 1991.

89. When Sihanouk was ordained for three months on July 31, 1947, the ordination was of this type. He had previously made a vow to his spiritual director that if his life was saved during the short Japanese occupation of Cambodia, he would become a monk

90. For more detailed discussion of the various kinds of ordination, see Bizot 1976, 6, and Try 1991, 167–168.

91. Bizot (1976, 40–41) has pointed to interesting parallels between monastic

seclusion and female rites of passage. The rite of entering into the shade *(cul mlap)*, for example, is associated with the onset of menstruation. The girl must observe a dark seclusion during which meat and fish are avoided and men may not be seen. Ebihara (1968, 459) notes that *cul mlap* had been rarely practiced for forty years or so by the time she did her fieldwork.

92. Manuscripts describing the *hau braling nag* ceremony are fairly common throughout Cambodia, even today (Thompson 1996, 12n43).

93. Quoted in Thompson 1996, 20n71.

94. Quoted in Rhum 1994, 153.

95. It was once customary to refer to a monk who had returned to the lay life as *pandit* or *antit* (lit., "scholar") (San Sarin 1975, 5).

96. Promulgated August 24, 1924; see *Royaume du Cambodge* 1924, 40.

97. The fifteenth-century case of Ven. Nhem, who had been accused of striking and killing a royal slave, is instructive in this connection (*Cpāp' tumnien pi boran;* Leclère 1898, 1:164–165).

98. A significant proportion of contemporary *achars* appear to have been monks forcibly defrocked during the Democratic Kampuchea period (W. Collins 1998a, 21). To confuse matters somewhat, graduates of the Pali school in Phnom Penh are also awarded the title "*achar.*" As a consequence they are permitted to carry a special fan (Bizot 1976, 13–14).

99. See Pou 1987–1988, 342; 1995, 158.

100. For a detailed depiction of the roles of the four *achars* attached to a monastery near Siem Reap, see Martel 1975, 234–237.

101. The term can have quite negative connotations. It may, for example, be used for a pimp or a smuggler.

102. For a general discussion of seasonal rituals, see Harris 2000b, 139–149. On September 27, 1910, Governor Nhek of Choeung Prey wrote a letter to the *résident* describing the lavish Buddhist rain-making ceremonies he had personally sponsored two weeks previously on a nearby mountain (Forest 1980, 106).

103. Or *kathen*—an annual ritual at the end of the rainy season in which robes are offered to the *sangha.*

104. In March 1899, for example, 5,000 piastres was spent on fireworks, musical entertainments, and offerings to monks during the eight-day cremation rite for the deceased *chau adhikar* of Wat Dey Dos, Kompong Cham (Forest 1980, 338n4).

105. *Gihipaṭipatti* (System for lay devotees) contains the principal texts used in the lay liturgy. It was originally printed in 1926 in an edition compiled by Chuon Nath, Huot That, and Oum Sou and subsequently went through a number of new editions.

106. Ebihara (1966, 177–178) also cites evidence that the first lay precept is the most strongly observed. She describes the situation of a man who, during a period of internal conflict in the mid-1940s, killed some people and was too scared to return to his home village for fear of social ostracism. Unfortunately, she does not explain the full circumstances of his crime.

4. Literary and Cult Traditions

1. *Kram brah raj krit samghari,* for instance, contains regulations concerning the relations between monks and private individuals (Khing Hoc Dy 1990, 1:64).

2. Known as the fifty *Jātakas (ha seup jati).*

3. Usually of *Corypha lecomtei*, a plant common to the area north of the Cardamom Mountains. Leaves of the sugar palm *(Borassus flabellifer),* or *tnot,* may also be used.

4. The best treatment of traditional manuscript production is given in Ly Vou Ong 1967. Also see Becchetti 1994, 56.

5. Monié (1965) gives a good account of the cremation of Ven. Cap Bau, an eighty-four-year-old chief monk at Wat Svay, Siem Reap, in February 1963. Fabrice (1932) describes a similar rite for a centenarian monk from Angkor Wat.

6. In the early 1990s the École Française d'Extrême-Orient (EFEO) began to systematically research how much Cambodian literature had survived the upheavals of the previous two decades. It came up with the following breakdown by genre: 90 percent religious texts, 3 percent literature, 3 percent traditional medicine, 3 percent magical formulae and divination, and 1 percent law (de Bernon 1998a, 874–875).

7. G. Groslier (1921, 7) asserts that this attitude toward texts is very old in Cambodia, given that even in the Angkorian period they were sometimes stored in buildings surrounded by water.

8. The Cambodian royal chronicles indicate that the *Sattapakaraṇa,* a synopsis of the seven books of the Abhidhamma, was generally recited during the obsequies for medieval Cambodian kings.

9. See Iv Tuot 1930. Many works at the impressive library of Wat Po Veal at Battambang were recopied around 1920 and lodged at the EFEO library in Hanoi.

10. The *Maṅgalatthadīpanī* was written by Srimaṅgala in Chiang Mai around 1524 CE. The text is a commentary on the twelve verses of the *Maṅgalasutta* [*Kph.* no. 5 = *Sn.* 258–269] (von Hinüber 1996, 179). Such anthologies became very popular in the medieval period, even to some extent eclipsing the canonical texts from which they were drawn.

11. On coming to power, Rama I had many of these monks defrocked or, in some cases, executed (Bizot 1988b, 94; 1976, 5–6).

12. The Thai script was also regarded as newfangled (having been invented by King Ramkhamhaeng in 1283) and problematic for the rendering of Pali, which, like Khmer, is not a tonal language (Yang Sam 1998, 251).

13. The term "Mahānikāy" does not appear in chronicles or inscriptions and came into being only at this time (Bizot 1988b, 103).

14. See chapter 2 above.

15. Another version of the text, copied in Thailand in 1836, was placed in the Royal Library, Phnom Penh, by S. Karpelès in the 1920s (Filliozat 2000, 452).

16. Sāriputta, Ānanda, Mogallāna, Koṇḍañña, Gavampati, Upāli, Kassapa, and Rāhula.

17. On *siddhi-gāthā,* see Skilling 1992, 129–137.

18. The *maṇḍala* appears unprecedented in Pali literature. However, a description of eight monks seated in a circle for *paritta* is found at *Dha.* xii.8. The Burmese also have a ceremony that utilizes a similar *maṇḍala* arrangement of Buddha disciples. See Htin Aung 1962, 8. Jaini (1965, 79) asserts that this is the only Pali text in which Rāma is so glorified.

19. At that time Wat Unnalom was the powerhouse of Pali canon–based orthodoxy in Cambodia. Given the setting, it is predictable that a prominent modernist, presumably Ven. Chuon Nath, would characterize a potentially problematic text like the *Mahādibbamanta* in this way. See chapter 5 below.

20. For a detailed inventory, see Pou and Haksrea 1981.

21. Thierry (1968, 174) suggests that all *cpāp'* have the Indian *Nītiśāstra* corpus as their remote inspiration.

22. As has already been noted in chapter 2, the hero of the text, Dhanañjay kumār, appears to be based on Mahosadha, the central figure of the *Mahāummagga Jātaka.*

23. Possibly the five dreams of the Buddha, *A.* iii.240.

24. Probably a collection of protective *(rakṣā)* texts, or *parittas*. See Skilling 1994b, 2:66.

25. Two known *Cpāp'* give specific counsel to Chinese and Sino-Khmers, respectively, and Khing Hoc Dy (1990, 1:77n176) has suggested that the strong odor of utilitarianism pervading the genre reveals some Confucian influence.

26. Chandler 1984, 276. All subsequent verse numbers are references to the French translations of Pou 1988 and Pou and Jenner 1975, 1976, 1977, 1978, 1979, and 1981.

27. This seems to be a clear reference to the *Parābhavasutta* of the *Sutta Nipāta* (vv. 91–115), where mention is made of *itthīdhutto, surādhutto,* and *akkhadhutto,* i.e., degeneracy connected to women, alcohol, and gambling.

28. Another version of *Cpāp' Srī* was compiled by King Ang Duang. See Pou and Haksrea 1981, 476n68.

29. Buddhist monks also wrote treatises, such as the *Kram Rajanitisastr* (Book of royal jurisprudence), for the proper guidance of Cambodian kings during the medieval period. For a more detailed study of this material, see Malay Khem and Ly Theam Teng in the Khmer Literature section of *Le Cambodge Nouveau,* 1971–1974.

30. Its reference to "five good flavors of fruit" (vv. 48–49) seems to have an origin in the *Jātakas* (Pou and Jenner 1978, 368).

31. Pou and Jenner 1978, 392.

32. See chapter 2 above.

33. Pou and Jenner 1981, 168–169.

34. For a detailed treatment of the evidence, see Filliozat 1983 and Bizot 1989, 27.

35. With a very few other sites, such as Wat Kampong Tralach Leu and Wat Bo, Siem Reap, these are the sole remnants of Cambodian mural painting to have survived the vandalism of the period. Unfortunately, they are heavily splashed with recently applied whitewash.

36. The Thai *Ramakien* shares most of the Buddhist preoccupations previously mentioned in connection with the *Reamker*. As Prince Dhaninivat (1963, 24) observed

of the famous version of the epic story by Rama I (r. 1782–1809), it was written "to the glory of the Master's [= Buddha's] teachings."

37. This Buddhist reworking is also hardly surprising, given that similar things were happening in India itself. The canonical *Dasaratha Jātaka* (no. 461—*J.* iv.123–130), for instance, is a brief nod in the direction of the *Rāmāyaṇa.* At the end of the *Jātaka* the bodhisattva declares that he was once Rāma.

38. On this rite, see Sem 1967. Bizot (1989, 29) also mentions the celebrated *lkhon khol* of Wat Svay Andet.

39. The *Adhyātmarāmāyaṇa,* an appendix to the *Brahmāṇḍa Purāṇa,* and Śaṅkara's *Ātmabodha,* are both texts that interpret the *Rāmāyaṇa* in this manner (Bizot 1989, 42).

40. See Bauer 1989. Throughout all of Indochina, at least until very recent times, the *upasampadā* ceremony has been based on a Mon prototype. Even though the Ceylonese Mahavihāra tradition established itself in Burma in the twelfth century, and in Thailand in the fifteenth, it did not modify the criteria of validity received from the Mon. Bizot argues that matters of doctrine were never quite so important to the Southeast Asian mind-set as the correct performance of valid ordination rites.

41. See Skilling 1992. Cousins believes that these derive "from the Canon itself."

42. Among the various potential influences mentioned in Bizot's many writings are the *Upaniṣads,* Vedic initiations, animist ritual, Mahayana Buddhism, Tantrism, and the religious thought universe of the Angkorian civilization.

43. See chapter 1 above.

44. For example, *Vism.* 115–116. In his commentary, Dhammapāla connects these secret texts with the three basic teachings of "emptiness, . . . taking rebirth, and [the law of] conditionality" (Cousins 1997, 193).

45. The term "*yogāvacara*" is known to the canonical compilers and is a common term in the Abhidhamma. However, in Cambodia and in other parts of Southeast Asia it is used in a more specific sense. The *yogāvacara* is someone skilled in esoteric techniques and may, but need not, be ordained.

46. We have already seen that this is the only section of the tripartite canonical collection that was well represented in monastic libraries before the emergence of the reform movement. The Abhidhamma's connection with death and transformation is also well attested. The oral repetition of these works is particularly powerful and meritorious, particularly the final work, the *Mahāpaṭṭhāna.* Each is connected with a day of the week and with a particular part of the body. When someone dies, the work relevant to the day of death and the organ of cause should be recited so that demerit may be counteracted.

47. A similar opposition has been described by la Vallée Poussin (1937) in his treatment of the relationship between Musīla and Nārada.

48. Cousins (1997, 195) calls the techniques "tantro-kabbalistic." This actually gives a good flavor of the domain that involves a theory of correspondences, as well as letter, sound, and number mysticism, all wrapped up in a ritual context.

49. Loose translation of Bizot 1992, 33.

50. See Bizot 1980, 247–248. The term "Mahā Paṭṭān" appears to be a reference to,

and personification of, the seventh and final volume of the Abhidhamma Pitaka, the *Paṭṭhāna.*

51. I am grateful to Judy Ledgerwood (pers. comm.) for pointing this out to me. The entrance to the cave was certainly very narrow, but the exclusion of pregnant women appears to have been principally related to the dangers they represent in the ritual environment.

52. The first Thursday after the start of *vassa* is a recommended time.

53. The *Cūlavaṃsa* mentions that a sect of *paṅsukūlikas* once existed in Sri Lanka, but they seem to have died out.

54. When people are ill, they are taken to the local monastery, where, assuming the position of the dead, they are covered with a piece of cloth or a monastic robe. The officiating monk then recites the *Bojjaṅga* and *Dhammacakkapavatana Suttas,* meditates on impure *(asubha)* things, and finally recites the *paṅsukūl* formulae to eliminate the malady. A similar rite may be performed to extend a person's life. Such a ceremony is mentioned in a modern inscription at Angkor Wat, dated 1671 CE (Lewitz 1973b, 209).

55. The 1860 funeral rites of Ang Duang are instructive in this regard (see chapter 2 above). It was also not uncommon for someone to donate his or her mortal remains to a monastery, where the body, sometimes housed in a latticed shrine surrounded by concentric enclosures, became a meditational object.

56. Rites of this type are designated by the term *"pak spaek,"* meaning "to peel off the skin" (Bizot 1981a, 75).

57. This seems problematic since there are five of these. A stronger correspondence would have been with the five aggregates *(khandha).*

58. Nāṅ Cittakumārā and Nāṅ Cittakumārī respectively represent the mind *(citta)* and mental factors *(cetasika)* (Bizot 1976, 119). As such, they also denote the psychophysical being in the intermediate state between two existences.

59. The *indriyas* are the sense faculties.

60. The letters need not have an esoteric significance. A modernist like Chuon Nath, in his *Khmer Dictionary* (1938), draws parallels between the three letters and the triple jewel, while Cousins (1997, 199) points out that in Thailand the three letters are also derived from the opening stanza of Mongkut's *Verses Invoking the Power of the Triple Gem (Rattanattayappabhāvūbhiyācanagāthā).*

61. In some of his later writings Bizot (e.g., 1992, 29) sees parallels between this initiatory body and the Mahayana doctrine of the embryo of the Tathāgata *(tathāgatagarbha).*

62. The late but canonical *Apadāna,* for instance, has much to say on the subject. Very similar teachings have been given new and popular currency in modern Thailand through the "Vijja Dhammakaya approach" of Ven. Sot (Chao Khun Phra Mongkol-Thepmuni, 1884–1959), the late Mahanikay abbot of Wat Paknam Bhasicharoen, Thonburi. For his life and teachings, see Magness n.d. A recent doctoral thesis by Mettanando Bhikkhu (1999) has shown that the teachings do not originate with the founder of the modern movement, for he himself drew on earlier sources. In particular, attention is drawn to the writings of Kai Thuean (1733–1832), a forest-dwelling

monk *(āraññavāsī)* from near Ayutthaya who was appointed patriarch *(saṅgharāja)* by Rama II in 1820.

63. For example, *M.* ii.17.

64. In a related text the descent of the breath to different parts of the body is associated with visualizations of achievements on the path through stream-entry, once-returner, and never-returner status all the way to the final realization of *nirvāṇa* (Bizot 1980, 247–248).

65. The use of the term *"a ra ham"* in this way is quite widespread in the Theravada. The following correspondences with the triple jewel *(triratna)* and the Tripitaka are found, for instance, in the commentary on the famous pre-Buddhaghosa *Vimuttimagga,* which may originally have had some connection with the nonorthodox Abhayagirivihāra (von Hinüber 1996, 126):

a = Buddha and Sutta pitaka
ra = Saṅgha and Vinaya pitaka
ham = Dhamma and Abhidhamma pitaka

66. It is possible that some of the metaphors found their way into more exoteric materials. *Cpāp' Kūn Cau,* a didactic treatise on moral behavior, for instance, teaches that "if your boat is smashed, if your junk is ripped apart, even in remote Lanka, you will always be able to return home" (v. 30). See Pou and Jenner 1977.

67. The text is discussed briefly by Leclère 1899, 42–43. For a more detailed treatment, see Bizot 1980, 225–226.

68. Bizot and von Hinüber suggest a possible Sāṃkhyā influence on the text.

69. The *Dhajaggasutta* in its various forms is highly regarded throughout the Buddhist world as an excellent means of dispelling fear. It is included in many collections of *parittas.* See Skilling 1994b for a detailed treatment.

70. The *Braḥ Dhammaviṅsuṅ*'s account of combining sound and a dry substance to create the boy springs to mind here.

71. Bizot identifies and illustrates eight basic types: image of the Buddha *(preah buddha' nimitta);* horse footprints *(choṅ seh);* net *(saṃṇāñ);* leap *(lot);* lattice of Naray, i.e., Viṣṇu *(nārāyṇ' kralā');* separated segment *(peṅ bhā);* ladder of crystal *(janṇḍor kev);* and circular *(vaṅ')* (Bizot and von Hinüber 1994, 56–84).

5. Cambodian Buddhism under Colonial Rule

1. *Ratchakitchanubeksa,* quoted in Yang Sam 1998, 253. Before the reforms, Battambang city had twenty-two monasteries. By 1906 this number represented around 15 percent of the monasteries in the province as a whole. Many of the monasteries had been built by members of the Thai aristocracy. Wat Damrei Sar, for example, had been financed by Chhum, the Thai governor (1892–1907).

2. Governor Chhum is said to have learned fencing and boxing from a monk at Wat Snoeng. Tauch Chhuong (1994, 122) tells an amusing story of monks from Wat

Sampau, near Battambang, who, when they were required to take meals at Chhum's residence, experienced great difficulty in averting their gazes from the women who served them naked from the waist up.

3. This Udong monastery may have subsequently been renamed Wat Sugandh Mean Bon in honor of Mahā Pan (San Sarin 1975, 18–19). There is some confusion over the precise date of the establishment of the Thommayut in Cambodia. Some sources give 1854, others 1864. For a short discussion of the issue, see Hansen 1999, 80n35.

4. Interestingly, no Thommayut monasteries were established in the Thai-controlled provinces of Battambang, Siem Reap, and Sisophon before they were ceded back to Cambodia in 1907. In Laos the Thommayut had also been imported from Thailand at approximately the same period. However, it established itself only in the south of the country, with a couple of additional temples in Vientiane. Perhaps surprisingly, no Thommayut monasteries ever existed in Luang Prabang, the royal capital.

5. The staff was once part of the monk's equipment. Interestingly, it is the only item specifically rejected by the Thommayut. The objection to its use appears to stem from reforms introduced by the fifteenth-century Thai monk Dhammagambhīra, who had been exposed to the teachings of the Mahāvihāra in Ceylon (Bizot 1988b, 36, 135).

6. For a more detailed description of the differing ways in which the two fraternities wear their monastic robes in Thailand, see Bizot 1993, 81–82. The discussion also applies to the Cambodian context.

7. This technique is termed *sutr rah* (Brunet 1967, 202).

8. Mahā Pan was a native of Battambang but had left his home to take up the monastic life in Bangkok at the age of twelve. He seems to have been ordained in 1849 (Try 1991, 15–16), first in the Mahanikay Wat Saket but a little later at the Thommayut Wat Bowonnivet. Before attaining high ecclesiastical office, Pan had distinguished himself as an early editor of the Cambodian royal chronicle. In this connection he seems to have been the first person to append legendary and prophetic materials to the beginning of the chronicle text, probably drawing both on the oral tradition and on various historical sources that were already circulating in Thailand (Cœdès 1918, 19–20).

9. As late as 1941, King Sihanouk was obliged to intervene in a dispute over the correct way of wearing the robe. He ordered the Committee for the Coordination of Religious Affairs to ban the Thommayut practice of putting the rolled end of the robe over the shoulder (Yang Sam 1987, 18–19).

10. It has been reissued a number of times in Cambodia.

11. There is some confusion in the secondary literature about when precisely Mahā Pan attained this position. French scholars, such as Martini, tend to place the event in 1864, i.e., after the Protectorate had been established. In my view it is more likely that he was first appointed in 1855 and that the ceremony of foundation at Wat Botum around 1866 merely underlined this status.

12. Thompson and Adloff (1955, 189) express the suspicion crisply when they note that, from the French perspective, the Thai were "chronically responsive to appeals from Khmer dissidents." For more evidence of French ill will toward the Thommayut, see Collard 1925, 54.

13. Some evidence suggests that Thommayut lay supporters have been wealthier than their Mahanikay counterparts. For further discussion, see Ebihara 1968, 381. The Thommayut order is also predominantly urban and tended to set up its monasteries in areas occupied by the French (Edwards 1999, 276).

14. There is some lack of clarity in the sources regarding the number of monks in the delegation. Bou Norin (1957) mentions three, but the number five is also mentioned. The precise date of the embassy is also a little uncertain.

15. The Marammavansa and the Upalivansa orders are mentioned in the Khmer sources.

16. Preah Rattanak Sarak. See Meyer 1969.

17. Bou Norin (1957) gives the following list: Samdech Preah Sukunthea Sanghareachea thipadey paññasīlo "Pan," Samdech Preah Mangkol tepeacarya Bhaddagu "Iem," Samdech Preah Mongkol tepeacarya paññadīpo "Suk," and Samdech Preah Sudhammāthipadey Buddhanāgo "Ung Srey."

18. On his life and death, cf. Flaugergues 1914a and 1914c.

19. For a discussion of some of the difficulties entailed by this term, see Crosby 2000.

20. The Portuguese estimate of around one-third of the male population living as monks at the end of the sixteenth century (see B.-P. Groslier 1958, 160) must be regarded as wildly inflated.

21. The vast crowds that congregated to witness its opening ceremonies in late 1902 seem to have given the *résident supérieur* considerable cause for concern (Tully 1996, 27–28).

22. However, Sihanouk stayed there for the rainy-season retreat *(vassa)* that began on July 31, 1947.

23. Monks from both the Thommayut and the Mahanikay also gather to recite Buddhist texts during the cremation rites of a Cambodian king, another important state ceremony. A hundred monks from each order, for instance, recited the *Sattapakaraṇa,* a synopsis of the seven books of the Abhidhamma, during Sisowath's funeral in 1928.

24. The statue is now housed in the Silver Pagoda. Surprisingly, it was not damaged during the Republican and Democratic Kampuchea periods. If Thompson's thesis (1999; 2000) is correct, the image indicates a largely unbroken tradition, dating from soon after the fall of Angkor and the introduction of Theravada Buddhism into Cambodia, which reinforced links between kingship and the Buddha of the future. King Ang Chan is said to have dedicated a similar image when his father, Prince Ong, died in the middle of the sixteenth century (Moura 1883, 2:45).

25. Sisowath did subsequently enter Wat Bowonnivet, the Thommayut headquarters in Bangkok, in 1864. Edwards (1999, 263) states that Norodom had also been a monk at Wat Bowonnivet.

26. When Ebihara was doing anthropological fieldwork in 1959–1960, the village of Svay possessed two Buddhist monasteries, Wat Prerung and Wat Svay. The former belonged to the Mahanikay, while the latter was Thommayut. It appears that a head monk of Wat Svay had "converted" to the Thommayut at the end of the nineteenth

century. Other monks in the monastery did likewise, but some had left to take up residence at nearby Mahanikay monasteries. It seems that there had rarely been tension between the two monasteries, although their natural rivalry could occasionally be exacerbated by economic conditions. To give one example, both monasteries normally held annual postharvest celebrations. However, following the poor harvest of 1959, village resources were insufficient to fund both rituals. The festivities, such as they were, would have to be consolidated and held at only one of the monasteries, but because no agreement could be reached, the festival was eventually canceled (Ebihara 1966, 188; 1968, 378).

27. See Steinberg et al. 1959, 70–71, and Kiernan 1985, 3–4.

28. Martel (1975, 228, 235–236) mentions that in the 1950s the Mahanikay Wat Lovea, near Angkor, switched affiliation from traditionalist *(boran)* to modernist *(samay)*, to the great consternation of the villagers. Traditional ceremonies were frowned on, and as a result fewer ordinations occurred and the monastery went into decline. In the eyes of most villagers, the tarnishing of the previously elaborate ceremonial life of the monastery meant that their significance in the locality was mysteriously diminished. Certainly, lower attendances entailed a consequent loss of income for the village.

29. On these grounds Edwards (1999, 309) classes him as a traditionalist. In 1942, Lvi Em Vadhipañño had written a modern Khmer gloss on the *Abhidhammattha-vibhāvanī,* an important handbook on the Abhidhamma (Bizot 1989, 20).

30. The title of *sanghareach* was not bestowed on Ven. Ker Ouk, because he came from the *vipassanādhura* branch of the *sangha,* not the more scholarly *ganthadura.* Thus he was not proficient in Pali (Olivier de Bernon, pers. comm.).

31. Em resigned his posts as both director of the École Supérieure de Pali and president of the Tripitaka Commission immediately after Hem Chieu's arrest by the authorities in 1942.

32. According to San Sarin (1998, 128), Chuon Nath was at this time a firm supporter of the official attempt to romanize the Cambodian language. Ven. Hem Chieu was just as firmly opposed.

33. For a brief biography see, Leang Hap An 1970a.

34. Huot Tath took over the leadership of the Mahanikay in 1969, following Chuon Nath's death, and was executed by the Khmer Rouge in April 1975.

Evans (1993, 133) contrasts the forms of Buddhism that have emerged in the two very different economies of Thailand and Laos over the last forty years. In the buoyant economy of the former, reformist movements, which place a strong emphasis on the notion of individual salvation, have emerged in large numbers. In Laos, on the other hand, economic stagnation, combined with a strong socialist control of the monastic order, has signally inhibited development in a modernist direction. Nevertheless, Laos did have an equivalent to Chuon Nath in the person of Nhouy Abhay, who directed a small-scale "renaissance of Lao Buddhism" in the 1960s (Zago 1976a, 123).

35. Purusakara (1954, 29) specifically identifies the Thommakay with these successors of Thong.

36. In his memoir of Chuon Nath, Huot Tath refers to this sojourn as a period of

"awakening." The two monks may have been sent to Hanoi in an attempt to defuse the dispute raging between traditionalists and modernists.

37. Published to coincide with Chuon Nath's cremation in 1970.

38. They seem to have criticized the custom of prohibiting *vassa* observance for novices as unsupported by *vinaya*.

39. When Sihanouk granted an honorary doctorate in Khmer literature to Chuon Nath on May 28, 1967, he referred to these events in his accompanying speech.

40. Ven. Dhammalikhit Uk Chea appears to have been particularly vocal.

41. Quoted without attribution by Keyes 1994b, 47. Also mentioned, without a date, by Martini (1955b, 418n1).

42. The first official work to roll off the press was the program for the festivities connected with the inauguration of the Silver Pagoda in 1902 (Khing Hoc Dy 1990, 2:4n9). One of the problems with the first printed works in Khmer produced in the colonial period was that they had actually been printed in Saigon. This made them even more unattractive to traditionalists (Marston 1997, 18). Reading was a minority pursuit for the Khmer well into the modern period. Even by the late 1960s the majority of Cambodia's reading public were ethnic Chinese and Vietnamese (Piat 1975).

43. These issues recurred several decades later when the French tried to romanize the Cambodian written script.

44. The popularity of the work is indicated in a letter of July 30, 1925, written by Suzanne Karpèles to the *résident supérieur*. She states that, of all the works in the Royal Library, it is the "book in greatest demand" (quoted in Hansen 1999, 83).

45. Finot (1927) gives a 1914 date for the commencement of the project.

46. Ind (1859–1925) wrote a number of works, including the famous *Gatilok* (a collection of 112 folk tales), *Subhasit cpāp' srī*, and *Nirieh Nokor Wat* (A pilgrimage to Angkor Wat), a lengthy poem written after he had been part of Sisowath's entourage during a visit to the sacred site in September 1909 (see Edwards 1999, 201). He also translated a Thai version of the royal chronicles into Khmer (Khing Hoc Dy 1985; 1990, 2:10). A laicized monk from Wat Unnalom, Phnom Penh, he received the title of Oknya Suttantaprījā shortly before the creation of the Dictionary Commission (Hansen 1999, 7). The missionary priest Sindulphe-Joseph Tandart studied Khmer with Achar Ind while composing his two-volume dictionary (Tandart 1910).

It seems that two of the religious dignitaries appointed to the commission—Ven. Thom Suos, chief of the Thommayut monastery of Prea Youravong, Phnom Penh, and Ven. Chan of Wat Unnalom—had no day-to-day involvement in the proceedings (Cœdès 1938, 316–317).

47. Ind had already introduced some of these changes in a grammar primer for use in schools. It was criticized by some Thommayut monks and members of the royal circle who had once been students of Mahā Pan. The latter had implemented previous orthographical reforms that were now felt to be under threat (Hansen 1999, 105).

48. Other monks selected included Prea Amra Kerakhet Phuong of the Thommayut and Prea Samu Moha Banha Sim of the Mahanikay.

49. It is often referred to simply as the *Dictionnaire Chuon Nath*.

50. In due course a list of some three thousand new words was published serially in *Kambuja Surya* (Jacob 1986a, 122).

51. See his *Principes de Creation des Mots Nouveaux* (1966). Keng Vannsak was a French-trained scholar and a prominent antimonarchical nationalist. His views were widely supported by many in the emerging modernized intelligentsia, particularly teachers and students in secular schools. As a result, Keng Vannsak was imprisoned by Sihanouk in 1954 and again in 1968. Although never a member of the Communist Party of Kampuchea, Keng Vannsak could be regarded as the spiritual father of the communist cell within the Cambodian Students' Association in Paris. He did, for instance, make his flat available for meetings. Peter Gyallay-Pap (pers. comm.) describes him as "Cambodia's intellectual guru of linguistic nationalism." Also see Marston 1997, 20.

52. For a detailed account of the vicissitudes of the project, see Leang Hap An 1970b.

53. As an example, Achar Ind criticizes the cult of various Brahmanical deities such as the sacred cow *(preah go)* and grandmother Daeb *(yāy daeb)*, arguing that "since we are lay followers of the religion of the Buddha it is not right to venerate [these statues]." See *Gatilok*, vol. 3, pp. 39–43 (quoted in Hansen 1999, 89–90).

54. One of five *suttas* contained in the *Khuddakapāṭha*, itself one of the fifteen books in the *Khuddaka Nikāya*. The scholarly consensus is that the *Khuddakapāṭha* is a relatively late work.

55. The only reference I have been able to find to this declaration is in a mimeographed publication by the Khmer Buddhist Society in Cambodia (n.d.). The seven duties were as follows: maintaining the pagoda, taking care of the pagoda's donated property, learning the concept of leadership and the monks' rules, managing care for children living in the pagoda, working with lay supporters, communicating with the committee of official monks, and helping the government wherever possible.

56. These were the *Gihipatipatti* for the laity, the previously mentioned *Samaneravinay* for novices, and the *Bhikkhupadimok* for monks.

57. Principal of Dhammaduta College, Rangoon.

58. Ven. Chuon Nath's *chedi* contains the ashes of many other individuals, since it is possible to rent a space there for a relative whose future chances of a favorable rebirth are believed to be enhanced by proximity to the saintly *sanghareach*. It also acts as a safe and a meritorious repository for fragments of sacred writings, statues, etc., that are housed there once their useful life is over.

59. Subsequently modified on May 26, 1948.

60. This arrangement was bound to cause some difficulties when the monastic hierarchy was reestablished in the 1980s, following the almost total elimination of institutional Buddhism during the Democratic Kampuchea period. The matter is discussed in more detail in chapter 8.

61. It seems that originally such meetings had occurred at the provincial level.

62. For a full breakdown of the hierarchies of both orders as they stood in 1960, see appendix C. Also see Martini 1955b, 416–424, and Meas-Yang 1978, 39–41.

63. *Anukun* rank at the level of the *thananukrama*, which is immediately below the fourth class of *rājāgaṇa*.

64. Some scholars have argued that the French deliberately restricted education for Cambodians in order to achieve and maintain power in the colony. Clayton (1995, 1) shows that the lack of Cambodian educational participation stemmed as much from Cambodian resistance as it did from French planning.

65. Worries that other European powers would muscle in on the act were never far from the surface. In his 1901 inaugural address as president of the newly formed EFEO, Louis Finot warned that if the French neglected the cultural heritage of Indochina, the topic would be studied "by orientalists from rival empires" (Edwards 1999, 184).

66. A committee to revise *wat* school education was first set up in 1904. It included French officials, Khmer palace dignitaries, and one monk, Ven. Sakyavong from Wat Unnalom. It seems that Thommayut monks were unwilling to cooperate with the French's tampering with traditional matters (Edwards 1999, 278).

67. However, religious education was not conceived as forming a part of the official curriculum (Edwards 1999, 327). For the full text of the decree, see Bilodeau 1955, 63. Also see Russier 1913, 410. Article 4 made provision for the periodic lay inspection of the schools, with inspectors being appointed by the administration.

68. This problem was not confined to Buddhist Cambodia. When Rama I's edition of the *Three Worlds (Traibhūmi)* document, an important Theravada cosmological treatise, was first published commercially in Thailand in 1913, the preface noted that, "When the *Traibhūmi,* composed by sages in ancient times . . . , is compared with the writings of geography today, [we can see that] investigations in the arts and other branches of knowledge have progressed much farther. For these reasons some statements contained in the *Traibhūmi* tend to be not quite correct." In other words, the conflict between traditional Asian and modern Western understandings of the world was resolved by an appeal to modernism. For further discussion of the way in which the issue was tackled in Thailand and Japan, see Harris 2000a, 123–125.

69. Subsequently amended by a royal ordinance of April 11, 1912.

70. For his thoughts on the subject, see Manipoud 1935.

71. These figures are supplied by Bilodeau (1955, 21–22). Edwards (1999, 329) gives the figure of 53 renovated schools in 1931. Bezançon's statistics (1992, 21, 25) are largely in line with Edwards'.

72. Wat Po Veal, Battambang, became the site of an École de Pali on November 17, 1933 (Filliozat 2000, 459n44).

73. Many such schools were sponsored, at very little cost, and taught both traditional and modern subjects. By the 1960s around half of the renovated schools still taught at least three levels of Pali (Gyallay-Pap and Tranet 1990, 363). By the time that the Khmer Rouge came to power in 1975, more than 10,000 *bhikkhus* and novices were studying in these schools.

74. The commission was originally associated with the work of palace minister Thiounn (c. 1865–1941), the son of a businessman from Kompong Chhnang. He entered French administrative service in 1883, rising to high office as the fortunes of the more traditional members of Cambodian high society waned with the increase in French

influence. As such, Thiounn is an excellent example of the newly emerging secular intelligentsia *(neak cheh doeng).* He collected and recorded traditional tales and poems and was also responsible for vernacular versions of the ten final *Jātakas* and of the *Paṭhamasambodhi,* which were published in the 1927 edition of *Kambuja Surya.* The commission was created in 1934 and directed by Éveline Porée-Maspero from 1943 to 1950. Her magisterial three-volume *Étude sur les rites agraires des Cambodgiens* (1962–1969) draws heavily on material collected by the commission. Also of note in this connection is the earlier *Mœurs et Coutumes des Khmèrs* (1938), by Guy Porée and Éveline Maspero.

75. As part of this phenomenon, Louis Finot had been prompted by Chuon Nath and Huot Tath to write *Le Bouddhisme, son origine, son evolution,* whose Khmer translation was published in 1929.

76. The controversy over the South Vietnamese Cao Dai movement is discussed in chapter 6.

6. Buddhism and Cambodian Nationalism

1. Po Kambo claimed to be the grandson of King Ang Chan II (r. 1794–1835). A royal pedigree has generally been necessary to gain support for most large-scale activities in Cambodia. In reality Po Kambo was a montagnard. There was some disagreement among contemporary observers over his precise affiliation. Some held that he was a Rhade; others, a Jarai.

2. Ven. Prak from Tay Ninh is said to have commanded one of the rebel groups. He was killed in action during the insurrection.

3. The causes of the rebellion are not clear-cut. There seems to have been an anti-Catholic element in the revolt, given that a French priest named Father Barrea, the pastor of Moat Krasas, was beheaded by the rebels immediately after celebrating Mass on January 9, 1867, despite earlier warnings that he should leave the area (Ponchaud 1990, 80). There may also have been an anti-Vietnamese element, in that colonial policy had encouraged substantial numbers of Vietnamese to relocate to Cambodia. Memories of previous ill treatment by the Vietnamese were still fresh in the minds of many Khmer.

4. The head was publicly exhibited in Phnom Penh the following day (Moura 1889, 2:167–169).

5. Oknya Suttantaprījā Ind was a prominent member of the Dictionary Commission; see chapter 5. He became a *bhikkhu* at twenty years of age, studying in Bangkok for seven years. He subsequently worked as a scribe for King Sisowath for ten years (Tauch Chhuong 1994, 13–14, 98; Yang Sam 1998, 256).

6. There also appear to have been a number of localized uprisings around the time that the northwest provinces were returned to Cambodia by Thailand in 1907 (Forest 1980, 51). Under such conditions monasteries often served as a place of sanctuary for those sought by the authorities, whether they were Thai or Khmer.

7. See Forest 1980, 398–440. Forest bases his account on the analysis of an official

dossier entitled *Complot contre la Sûreté Extérieure de l'État organizé dans la province de Takeo* (1898).

8. In 1925 an ex-monk in Stung Treng managed to stir up a rebellious following through the intervention of "a golden frog with a human voice" (Chandler 1996, 148).

9. Soon after the overthrow of Sihanouk in 1970, Lon Nol issued a decree recommending that soldiers cut their skin "in order to allow the Buddha to enter . . . [their] body and bring strength" (Becker 1986, 138). This is a reference to the ancient apotropaic practice of inserting thin metal strips inscribed with Buddhas or other auspicious symbols under the skin. In the 1980s, Khmer People's National Liberation Front (KPNLF) troops also commonly sported tattoos for protective purposes (*PPP* 4/18, September 8–21, 1995, 20). For a solid survey of the use of tattoos in the Cambodian context, see de Bernon 1998a. A good account of the use of tattoos in Thailand may be found in Terwiel 1994, 69–79.

10. For a full account and analysis of the incident, see Chandler 1982a.

11. Shortly after the incident, a royal decree was issued changing the name of the village to Direchan (lit., "bestial") and ordering the performance of expiatory Buddhist ceremonies on the anniversary of the *résident*'s death for a further ten years.

12. The character of the troublesome Buddhist monk begins to make its appearance in the French exotic literature of the early part of the twentieth century (Edwards 1999, 290–291). The connection also explains why the main streets of Phnom Penh were named after such figures during the People's Republic of Kampuchea period (1979–1989).

13. *Gatilok* v. 10, p. 27, and v. 1, p. 78, quoted in Hansen 1999, 29 and 212.

14. *Summary of Annotated Party History*, translated in Karl Jackson 1989, 251–268.

15. A variety of spirits are prominent in the Cao Dai pantheon, including the T'ang poet Li Po (aka Ly Thai Bach), but the highest of all is His Excellency the Grandfather Immortal (Cao-Dai Tien-Ong). The millennial character of the movement is conveyed by the fact that it is also known as the Great Way of the Three Epochs of Salvation (Dai-Dao Tam-Ky Pho-Do). Its adherents believe that the third and final world epoch is about to dawn. During the first epoch both Amitabha Buddha and the first Chinese emperor mediated between the earthly and heavenly realms. These were superseded by Śākyamuni Buddha, Confucius, Lao Tzu, and Jesus in the following era, but in the coming age the Cao Dai spirit, also known as the Jade Emperor of Supreme Being, will guide the world to spiritual maturity (R. Smith 1970b, 578–579).

16. A few kilometers northeast of Tay Ninh town is the holy mountain Phnom Choeung Bak-deng (aka Nui Ba-den). This had been a Khmer sacred site long before the arrival of the Vietnamese (Malleret 1941, 170).

17. In 1901 around 45 percent of the province's population were Khmer (Brocheux 1972, 447).

18. When a Cao Dai temple was dedicated in Phnom Penh in 1937, once more virtually all followers were Vietnamese (Kiernan 1985, 6). In the 1950s and 1960s there were around seventy thousand adherents in Cambodia. The leader of Cao Dai in Vietnam seems to have fled to Cambodia in the 1960s, where he was granted political asylum. Reestablished in Cambodia in 1985, Cao Dai currently has about two thousand devo-

tees, with headquarters in a small compound next to the Intercontinental Hotel (*PPP* 9/7, March 31–April 13, 2000).

19. In early editions of this important periodical, articles appeared as a single undifferentiated group. However, by 1943 the journal contained two sections: one devoted to articles on literature, the other focusing on religion. Chigas (2000a, 138–139) has suggested that the ordering of material so that the literary part of the publication preceded the religious part possibly symbolized a shift in priorities among Phnom Penh's intelligentsia. In 1951 the ordering of the two sections was reversed.

Another early Buddhist periodical, *Ganthamālā* (Garland of books), was established by royal ordinance in April 1924. Its first edition, which did not appear until 1927, contained a translation and commentary by Ven. Huot Tath on the *Sigālovāda Sutta,* the Buddha's most important sermon to the laity.

20. "Nagara Vatta" means "temple city" but is also a play on "Angkor Wat." This is often incorrectly referred to as the first Khmer-language newspaper. In fact, it was preceded by *Kambuja Surya* in 1927 and by *Srok Khmer* (Cambodian nation) a few months later. Interestingly, the banner head of *Srok Khmer* depicted the three central towers of Angkor Wat and may have been, in part, a model for *Nagara Vatta.* However, what differentiates *Nagara Vatta* from the other two is its greater interest in "political" questions. At its peak it had a circulation figure of about five thousand.

21. A good example is Khim Tit's *Qu'est-ce que le bouddhisme?* (1969).

22. Ebihara (1968, 548) describes this in her doctoral thesis. However, during her stay in a Cambodian village in 1959–1960 (admittedly some two decades later), she never saw a monk behaving in a like manner. In her words, "While several monks at the local temples are impressively intelligent and well-informed, they do not appear to be significant sources of secular news and information for the community."

23. The negativity is not really surprising, given that Cao Dai had originally been quite hostile to what it saw as the "heretical" establishment of the Buddhist Institute (Khy Phanra 1975, 331).

24. The original example for the romanization and rationalization of a non-Roman script language had recently been given by Turkey, in 1928.

25. In some ways it is odd that it was this measure, among so many others, that provoked outrage, particularly given the widespread acceptance of an earlier proposal to romanize Vietnamese in neighboring Cochinchina.

26. For a hagiography of Hem Chieu, see Kong 1972. His ashes were returned to Phnom Penh in July 1972, the thirtieth anniversary of his arrest, by order of Lon Nol.

A history of the KPRP/CPP (Kampuchean People's Revolutionary Party/Cambodian People's Party) written in 1991 by Chey Saphon recognizes the important role played by Achar Hem Chieu in the revolutionary struggle. It also asserts that he was the leader of the Association of the Black Star *(samakom phkay khmau)* (Frings 1994a, 10–11). However, this occult anti-French and anti-Japanese movement with supposed links to the Issaraks and the Democratic Party seems to have come to light only in 1947, four years after his death. Chandler (1991, 32) is of the view that it may never have existed.

27. Only laypersons may come before a secular court. The extrajudicial status of the *sangha* is underscored by the fact that a monk may not witness a legal document or be a witness in court. Neither can he make a formal complaint if injured, attacked, or robbed (Steinberg et al. 1959, 67).

28. It has sometimes been claimed that the demonstration was sponsored by the Japanese. A Japanese airplane is also said to have flown over the demonstration as a gesture of support. More broadly, the French scholar Malleret (1946–1947, 32) maintained that it was no secret that the Japanese were attempting to organize Indochinese Buddhism for their own benefit. The general period is covered in some detail in Chandler 1986.

29. Karpelès' retirement in 1941 probably also "contributed to the uncoupling of the *sangha* and the French administration" (Edwards 1999, 340).

30. He served as a captain in the Imperial Japanese Army from 1943 (Thach Bunroeun 1993, 81).

31. Edwards (1999, 343) names Khim Tit as the intermediary in these communications.

32. Another of their coconspirators, Bunchan Mul, was also released at this time. He subsequently became minister of cults and religious affairs under Lon Nol. His story is told in his *Kuk Niyobay* (Political prison) of 1971, partially translated in Kiernan and Chantou Boua 1982, 114–126.

33. For some information on the period of Thanh's career, see Christian 1952a.

34. One of the major Democratic figures, Sim Var, had been closely associated with *Nagara Vatta* (Corfield 1994, 10–11).

35. The Liberals were "frankly royalist and Buddhist" (Thompson and Adloff 1955, 178), and Norindeth appears to have gained the support of "great landowners and provincial monks" (Martin 1994, 53).

36. Exactly the same provision later found its way into the constitution of Democratic Kampuchea. It is entirely possible that the idea of Buddhism as a state religion was consciously imported from Thailand. It has sometimes been surmised that King Chulalongkorn—who established Buddhism as the state religion of Thailand, particularly through the administration of the Sangha Act of 1902--had been impressed by this model of church-state relations following his first visit to Europe in 1897.

37. Narada had arrived from Vietnam, where he had donated three similar relics to the Theravadins, the Mahayanists, and the Cao Daiists of that country. He had previously been in Phnom Penh in 1939, when he planted a cutting of the *bodhi* tree on the grounds of the École Supérieure de Pali.

38. This could be the same relic that is now housed in the Silver Pagoda (Jeldres and Chaijitvanit 1999, 43). There is some confusion in the various contemporary accounts. According to Chum Ngoeun (1996, 17), Lvi Em visited Sri Lanka in 1956, bringing back a Buddha relic that was subsequently deposited in the Silver Pagoda.

39. Other prominent members were Keo Tak, Dap Chhuon, Prince Norodom Chantarangsey, Chanto-Tres, and Leav Keo-Moni (Kiernan 1981, 165).

40. In the elections of September 9, 1951, his Victorious North East Party managed to win four seats (Lee 1976, 231).

41. On these two images, see chapter 3. They are supposed to have helped him in a near miraculous escape from Siem Reap to Phnom Kulen after he turned against the government. Dap Chhuon had been told by an astrologer that this course of action was doomed to failure. He was indeed killed, but not before dispatching his unfortunate adviser (Meyer 1971, 87).

42. The concept seems to have survived until the reign of Norodom, whose person was considered so charged with sacrality that when he once fell from his carriage in Phnom Penh, no native Cambodian felt able to assist him. Cf. Moura 1883, 1:226.

43. Try (1991, 81–82) asserts that almost immediately after Sihanouk came to the throne, some monks were publicly critical of his cozy relationship with the French. In this connection, Try recounts an interesting story of how a monk wielding an umbrella broke the nose of the *résident supérieur*'s director of cabinet. The story is told in more detail in Norodom Sihanouk 1981, 75.

44. On the clear parallels here with Laos, see Evans 1998, 90–91.

45. Samdech Preah Mongkol Tepeachar Keo Uch (1889–1968) was *chau adhikar* of Wat Botum and second in the Thommayut hierarchy at the time of his death. He was said to have possessed an exceptional memory, had a store of knowledge about the history of Cambodia in the nineteenth century, and spoke Thai, Lao, and Vietnamese fluently. His example shows that erudition and a cosmopolitan nature were not the exclusive preserve of Mahanikay modernizers. See Meyer 1969, 24.

46. See Zago 1976a, 111, and Schecter 1967, 67. Ebihara (1968, 381) appears to indicate that Sihanouk stayed at Wat Svay on this occasion. Preah Vihear was seized by the Khmer Rouge in July 1993. When Ta Mok visited in the rainy season of 1997, he said, "This is a very good temple. . . . The Khmer people cannot build temples like this anymore. . . . We have to protect the temple and not allow the *yuon* [i.e., the Vietnamese] to capture it" (*PPP* 7/7, April 10–23, 1998).

47. A very similar version of the story is also known in Burma.

48. See Spiro 1966, Ebihara 1966, and Pfanner and Ingersoll 1961–1962, for instance. It is rare to find literature that argues for the compatibility of Buddhism and capitalism. One exception is Martellaro and Choroenthaitawee 1987.

49. Rock Edict XII.

50. When Sihanouk tried to explain Buddhist socialism to Mao Zedong in the early 1960s, the latter is reported as responding, "Socialism is very complicated" (Chandler 1991, 87).

51. Sihanouk acknowledged this influence in an interview in which he placed particular emphasis on the support given him by Zhou Enlai when they first met at Bandung (Martin 1994, 77).

52. In the early to mid-1940s, Em had also been director of the Association pour la Formation Morale, Intellectuelle, et Physique des Cambodgiens de Cochinchine (Malleret 1946–1947, 20).

53. He had written the national anthem *(nokareach)* in 1941 with the words:

May heaven protect our King
And give him happiness and glory;
May he reign over our hearts and our destinies.
He who—heir to the builder Monarchs—
Governs the proud and old kingdom.

The temples sleep in the forest,
Recalling the grandeur of the Moha Nokar [= Angkor].
The Khmer race is as eternal as the rocks.
Let us have confidence in the faith of Kampuchea,
The Empire that defies the years.

Songs rise in the pagodas
To the glory of the holy Buddhist faith.
Let us be faithful to the creed of our ancestors
So that Heaven may reward us
Of the old Khmer country, of the Moha Nokar.

54. Even quite recently, Sihanouk has sought to remind his people of the high ideals of the Sangkum period. After a speech made to Wat Committee members from Kompong Thom in October 1997, he named Chuon Nath and Huot Tath as great supporters of the movement. He then handed out copies of a book on the Sangkum Reastr Niyum.

55. Secular education underwent "khmerization" in 1967, and committees were set up to invent appropriate neologisms for translation purposes. A good number of committee members were monks. Needless to say, many neologisms were derived from Pali (Martin 1994, 73).

56. Chau Seng's educational reforms focused on the khmerization of the curriculum (Ayres 2000, 43–45). By the early 1960s, Chau Seng was also rector of the Université Bouddhique in Phnom Penh. In 1967 he was editor of the leftist newspaper *La Nouvelle Dépêche* (Quinn 1982, 40), amid some suspicion that he was a prominent Communist Party functionary. He eventually completed a doctoral thesis, "Éducation et développement au Cambodge" (1970). See also Népote 1974, 767, 776. Sihanouk told Willmott (1981, 227n57) that Chau Seng was not a communist but had lived as an agricultural worker during the Democratic Kampuchea, dying in 1978 shortly before the Vietnamese invasion.

57. Called the Écoles Élémentaires de Pali before Independence.

58. During this period the Ministry of Cults and Religious Affairs had responsibility for regulating the *sangha* in a variety of ways. It reviewed applications for the construction of new monasteries and insisted that such developments should provide educational facilities to elementary school level. In 1962 it was combined with the Ministry for the Interior. The joint ministry became responsible for Buddhist education, which was not, therefore, controlled by the Ministry of National Education (Try 1991, 64–65).

59. Its director was Ven. Pon Sompheach Dhammārāma.

60. Ing Thuong High School, for example, directed by Ven. Iv Tuot. A native of Battambang, Iv Tuot became *chau adhikar* of Wat Po Veal in 1921 and remained there for the rest of his life. He is the author of the Khmer-language *Historique de la pagode de Povéal (Battambang)* (1930). For a photo of Iv Tuot, see Purusakara 1954, 26.

61. For a good breakdown of the state funding of education in the Sangkum period, particularly as it applied to higher education, see Fergusson and Le Masson 1997.

62. Steinberg (1959, 255) asserts that the association may also have been involved with more explicitly political matters.

63. The girls lodged at the women's hermitage at Wat Phnom Sampau, a little distance from Battambang town (Bareau 1969, 15).

64. Ministry of Cults and Religious Affairs statistics, quoted in Try 1991, 148. The numbers do not differentiate between novices and fully ordained monks.

65. From a peak of 1,615 in 1960, the number had fallen sharply by the middle of the decade.

66. Also see Somboon Suksamran 1993, 138.

67. Broadcast on Phnom Penh Radio, May 19, 1968 (*FBIS*—Asia Pacific, May 20, 1968, H1–2). Steve Heder (1979b, 22n86) has noted that the Thai marshal Sarit Thanrat, who personally supervised summary executions of political opponents around the same time, also seems to have acknowledged the karmic consequences of his acts.

68. Iv Tuot had also been the teacher of the prominent lay Buddhist nationalist Nhok Them (1903–1974), author of *The Rose of Pailin (Kulap pailin)* (1943). At an early age Nhok Them had studied in Thailand, returning to Cambodia in 1930, where he created a center for the study of Buddhism. As a reward for his efforts he was appointed to the Tripitaka Commission. Disrobing in 1938, he subsequently became secretary general of the Buddhist Institute, with particular responsibility for disseminating Buddhist teachings in Kampuchea Krom and Laos (Khing Hoc Dy 1990, 2:55).

69. Monks were not eligible to vote or hold political office. Nor could they give evidence in court or witness a legal document (see Leclère 1890, 32–33). This point is made succinctly in an official publication of the period (Ministre de l'Information 1962, 21). This situation changed, despite the opposition of a number of senior monks, in the lead-up to the 1993 elections.

70. *Tum Teav* is a traditional story committed to literary form by the poet Sânthor Mok (1834–1908) at the beginning of the twentieth century. Mok was born in Udong and educated at Wat Kuk, where he mixed with members of the royal family. A monk between 1845 and 1858, he subsequently married and joined Norodom's court in Phnom Penh, finally becoming minister of finance (Khing Hoc Dy 1981; Collard 1925, 29–39). *Tum Teav*'s popularity is underlined by the fact that a verse version written by Ven Som (1852–1932), *chau adhikar* of Wat Kompeauv, Sithor Kandal, Prey Veng Province, is also well known (Khing Hoc Dy 1990, 2:7–8). For a translation and study, see Chigas 2000a. *Tum Teav* was also read as an antiroyalist text in the People's Republic of Kampuchea (PRK) period.

71. Tum does not disrobe according to the correct ceremony, and Teav also vio-

lates her "entering into the shade" *(cul mlap)*, a ritual associated with the onset of menstruation. Thus the lovers have both dishonored established customs.

72. Sihanouk also used a medium to contact the spirit of Princess Nucheat Khatr Vorpheak—a distant nineteenth-century relative who was said to have miraculously survived being eaten by a crocodile—so that she might offer him advice on foreign policy.

73. In fact, the new head of state, Lon Nol, suppressed the festival on that occasion, the first time that it had failed to happen for many years (Meyer 1971, 86). After Sihanouk was ousted, Zhou Enlai provided him with quarters on Anti-Imperialist Street, Beijing (Chandler 1990, 59).

74. Early plans to overthrow Sihanouk took place at a meeting held at Wat Ha, Kompong Kantuot, Kandal (Corfield 1994, 53).

75. "Déclaration de M. Boun Chan Mol, président de la délegation cambodgienne à la Conférence mondiale des leaders bouddhistes à Seoul (République de Corée)," *Agence Khmère Presse,* November 2, 1970, 10.

7. Liberation

1. Sometimes wrongly assumed to have been an alias of Son Ngoc Minh.

2. Official repression meant that the ICP was weak in most regions of Vietnam. One exception was eastern Cochinchina.

3. Samakhum Khmer Issarak. Like so many Khmer terms, "*issarak*" derives from a Pali word, in this case "*issara,*" meaning "lord, master, chief."

4. There has been some confusion about Minh's identity. He was not Son Ngoc Thanh's brother, as some have maintained, nor should he be confused with Sieu Heng, a practitioner of traditional medicine who came over to the communist cause in 1944. The name is clearly a nom de guerre, formed by combining "Son Ngoc Thanh" and "Ho Chi Minh" (see Becker 1986, 63). Minh's true name may have been Pham Van Hua (Lamant 1987, 93, 95). He seems to have been born in Kampuchea Krom.

5. A photograph of the monks attending the meeting may be found in Christian 1952b.

6. VWP telegram of June 1952, quoted in Heder 1979b, 2. It also seems that the Vietnamese, drawing on Lenin's *Left-Wing Communism: An Infantile Disorder,* classed the Cambodian revolution as infantile. See Nuon Chea 2001.

7. Prom Samith and Nuon Chea, who eventually became deputy secretary of the Communist Party of Kampuchea (CPK), were among the select group of the "best and brightest" Khmer revolutionaries to relocate to northern Vietnam following the Geneva Agreements of 1954 (Engelbert and Goscha 1995, 47). Nuon Chea returned to Cambodia soon afterward.

8. The crucial role of the Khmer Krom Buddhists in the Vietnamese liberation movement is illustrated by the example of Huynh Cuong. He was secretary of the Cochinchina Khmer Buddhist Association from 1943 and graduated from the Buddhist Institute in 1945. Later he worked as an inspector of Pali schools in the western Mekong

Delta before gaining election to the National Liberation Front (NLF) Central Committee in 1962 (Kiernan 1985, 24).

9. Nuon Chea and Sao Phim were important exceptions (David Chandler, pers. comm.).

10. "Monarchy or Democracy," in *Khmer Nissit* (Cambodian student) (1952), translated into French in Thion and Kiernan 1981, 357–361. Khieu Samphan, a fellow Paris-based student and an important member of the CPK, was still calling Cambodia a "Buddhist country" in 1959 (Thion and Kiernan 1981, 103).

11. Ta Mok was also known as Chhit Chhoeun, Eang Eng, and Nguon Kang. I have arrived at the date of 1942 for Ta Mok's departure from the order by extrapolating from information volunteered in an interview reported by Thayer (1997).

12. He seems to have commanded groups in both Kung Pisey District of Kampong Speu and his home district of Tram Kak.

13. Chandler (2000, 89) notes that autobiographical writing was rare and had a low literary status before Democratic Kampuchea, when the self-critical life story *(pravatt'rup)* became a key element in the work of the secret prison S-21.

14. Also known as Prom Sambot, he was arrested in May 1975 and presumably executed.

15. Steve Heder, pers. comm., October 2001. Heder also claims that Son Sen was connected to the Buddhist Institute around this period. Son Sen had been a student in Paris with Pol Pot and went on to become vice premier and minister of defense in Democratic Kampuchea. He and many of his extended family were executed on Pol Pot's orders in June 1997.

16. *Khmer Satiranaroat* (Khmer Republic) 1/5, September 14, 1974, 3, quoted in Edwards 1999, 389.

17. "Discours du Marechal Lon Nol a l'ouverture de l'Assemblée Nationale," *Agence Khmère Presse,* September 15, 1972.

18. Bunchan Mul also seems to have been involved. Also see Ros Chantrabot 1993, 40.

19. For a list of his principal writings, which include *Buddhasasana prajadhipateyy sadharanarath* (Buddhism, democracy, republic) and *Prajadhipateyy cas dum* (Ancient democracy), see Zago 1976b, 115n34. Khieu Chum's activities were not always helpful to the Lon Nol government. In 1973, for example, he and Ven. Pang Khat, another Umbrella War wager in 1942, encouraged student protest against certain aspects of the regime, apparently unaware that the Khmer Rouge had infiltrated some of the student groups involved. Ven. Huot Tath, the Mahanikay *sanghareach,* was forced to issue him with a reprimand (Corfield 1991, 5).

20. Manifesto of the Committee of Intellectuals for the Support of the Salvation Government, March 18, 1970, quoted in Edwards 1999, 387.

21. Lon Nol's younger brother, Lon Non, was another key player in the Khmer Republic. He believed himself to be a reincarnation of Akineth, an ascetic magician in the *Reamker* (Corfield 1994, 113).

22. The term derives from the ethnonym "Tamil." It seems to have entered Khmer

as a result of contact with Sri Lanka, probably via Thailand, and reflects the racial antipathies of some Sri Lankan missionary monks. On the role of Buddhist nationalism in the conflict between Sinhalese and Tamils in Sri Lanka, see Tambiah 1992, 123–128.

23. Articles 13 and 15.

24. Economic and industrial activity in the largely Vietnamese *quartier catholique* of Phnom Penh grew particularly rapidly after World War I (Tully 1996, 259).

25. This was still the case after the fall of the Khmer Rouge. In 1982 Chea Sim, chairman of the National Assembly, reportedly said that "the Christian religion [by virtue of its foreignness] has no place in the People's Republic of Kampuchea" (quoted in "Religion in Kampuchea," *Religion in Communist Lands* 16 [1988], 170).

26. For a detailed treatment of the events, see Ponchaud 1990, 135–141.

27. The 1972 Constitution (Article II, Part 2) affirmed Buddhism as the state religion.

28. Meyer (1971) seems to suggest that this was Chuon Nath. Given Chuon Nath's views on magic, this is rather unlikely.

29. In the 1980s, KPNLF troops also commonly sported tattoos for apotropaic purposes (*PPP* 4/18, September 8–21, 1995, 20).

30. Not everyone benefited from Lon Nol's indulgences. Fifty-five of the 100–odd people held under arrest in Queen Kossamak's house in March 1973 were astrologers who had rather unwisely predicted the overthrow of Lon Nol before April had ended (Lee 1976, 455).

31. I am grateful to Youk Chhang for supplying me with the third name.

32. See *Put Tumniay* (1952) and *Put Tumniay* (1970). For a French translation of *Buddh Daṃnāy,* see de Bernon 1998c.

33. It was probably written by one of the parties vying for power following the death of King Ang Duang.

34. It is clear that the author of the *Buddh Daṃnāy* was sympathetic to the Thommayut.

35. Interestingly the ten royal precepts listed in the text are not the same as those found in orthodox Pali sources. The first, for instance, obliges a king not to convert to a non-Buddhist religion (de Bernon 1998c, 52).

36. See Norodom Sihanouk 1970, 16. It is not clear to me that the term "excommunicate" holds any precise meaning in the Theravada tradition. Sihanouk seems to agree that it is incompatible with Buddhist tradition, yet, later in the same address, he calls on Huot Tath to "excommunicate" the Lon Noliens.

37. The precise nature of the destruction is difficult to determine. A small proportion were effectively demolished; many more were damaged but repairable.

38. According to Youk Chhang (pers. comm.), at least 539,129 tons of bombs were dropped on Cambodia throughout the total period of conflict.

39. Thion had been allowed to visit selected CPK zones, and all of his interviews were thoroughly vetted by the party (David Chandler, pers. comm.).

40. Edwards suggests that the report, far from being cynical United Front propaganda, may have reflected the actual feelings of more liberal elements within the revolutionary movement.

41. Vorn Vet was also known as Sok Thouk. In October 1975 he was the minister in charge of industry, fisheries, and railways, and he eventually rose to the rank of deputy prime minister. He was executed in 1978.

42. Chandler (1999, 99) thinks that they may have been soldiers in disguise. This seems odd to me. Sihanouk had spent two short periods in robes and, as the constitutional protector of Buddhism, could be expected to be able to identify someone masquerading as a monk.

43. Ponchaud has argued that, unlike Chinese and Vietnamese communists, the Khmer Rouge did not really engage with the concept of "reeducation." They preferred self-criticism, and if this did not work, there was always straightforward torture, confession, and extermination. Ponchaud links this to differences in prior religious outlook. For the Chinese and the Vietnamese, Confucianism, with its insistence on moral reformation, provides a logic for reeducation. Buddhism, on the other hand, emphasizes the doctrine of karma and the possibility of future suffering in hell. For Ponchaud, both of these ideas contribute to a Khmer tendency toward violent and exemplary punishment, in the hope that this might mitigate future torments. After hearing many reports from refugees, he concluded that "one cannot help observing a certain complicity between the executioner and his victims, each of them accepting the tragic rules of the game by which they were governed" (Ponchaud, 1990, 236).

44. This was the twenty-fifth anniversary of the foundation of the Unified Issarak Front. Chillingly—although perhaps not surprisingly, given the Khmer penchant for gambling—many people "wagered on the number, day, and hour that rockets would be fired on Phnom Penh" (Martin 1994, 127).

45. The 1954 Chinese Constitution, for example, states that "every citizen of the People's Republic of China (PRC) shall have freedom of religious belief," but the starting point here is that the majority should be free not to believe. Freedom of belief, then, is a minority right, and minorities are not expected to interfere in the rights of the majority. In the PRC, the term "religion" is interpreted in the strict sense of ritual, doctrine, and belief. As such, its prophetic role is most definitely ruled out (Yu 1987, 373), and anything of this sort comes under the legal heading of "counterreligious activity."

46. From the late 1960s both Pol Pot and Ieng Sary had employed tribal bodyguards from the Jarai and Tampuon peoples. They were regarded as particularly faithful to the revolution (Kiernan 1996, 302).

The first Khmer Rouge attacks on the Cham Muslim minority occurred around 1972 in the southwestern zone by order of Ta Mok. Women were forced to cut their hair short in the Khmer style, the traditional sarong was banned, and restrictions were placed on religious activities. Nevertheless, policy toward the Cham was not always hostile; rather it depended on local conditions and the outlook of regional cadres. However, by mid-1978 the massacre of Cham, even those who obediently followed all the restrictions placed on them by the authorities, arguably "constituted a campaign of racial extermination." In a pioneering study of the issue, Kiernan (1988, 17, 30) concludes, "It seems inescapable that over one-third of the Chams, about 90,000 people, perished at the hands of the Pol Pot regime." Also see Osman 2002.

47. The communists described Buddhism as a foreign religion with origins in Thailand (Ponchaud 1990, 234). This is interesting because only the royalist Thommayut is of purely Thai origin.

48. Of course, the song could have been composed well before 1975.

49. The others were imperialism and reactionary capitalism.

50. Of the twelve, only Ven. Oum Som and Ven. Heng Leang Hor survived Democratic Kampuchea.

51. Ven. Phul Tes, the Thommayut *sanghareach,* had died of ill health several months before and, in the chaos, had not been replaced.

52. For detailed discussions of the cult of the *neak tā,* see Forest 1992 and Ang Chouléan 1986. Judy Ledgerwood (pers. comm.) points out that such reports need to be weighed against other stories in which the Khmer Rouge unsuccessfully tried to take action against the *neak tā*—explosives used to blow up their houses did not work, the cadres got sick, and so on.

53. Chantou Boua's informants told her that by 1975 the number of monks at Wat Unnalom, the headquarters of the Mahanikay in Phnom Penh, had grown from three hundred to one thousand as they fled to the city from liberated zones (Chantou Boua 1991, 230).

54. A parallel dichotomy is found in the postrevolutionary division of society into two "castes" or "nonsocial classes": "base people" *(neak mulethan),* peasants associated with the liberated areas long before final victory, and "new people," mainly urbanites who came under CPK rule after April 17, 1975. It may not be too far-fetched to suggest that the arrangement had its basis in the "insufficiency ethic" (first articulated by Weber), which traditionally expresses itself in Buddhist cultures as an equivalent asymmetry between the religious aspirations of the religious and those of the laity. Given that the Thai-inspired Thommayut was almost exclusively urban, it could be that the authorities wished to distinguish between Mahanikay and Thommayut monks in this manner.

55. See Chantou Boua 1991, 235. Keyes (1994b, 70n27) believes that there are significant parallels in the ways temples were destroyed and monks defrocked in Yunnan during the Chinese Cultural Revolution.

56. Today Nuon Chea claims to be a devout Buddhist layman (*PPP* 10/15, July 20–August 2, 2001).

57. Ven. Non Nget, interview with the author, November 19, 1999.

58. Quoted in Norodom Sihanouk 1980, 49.

59. This statistic is from the Center for Advanced Studies and the Ministry of Cults and Religious Affairs, published in *Cambodia Report* 2(2) (March–April 1996), 23.

60. Kratie Province in the east of the country is regarded as the safest place to have lived during the Democratic Kampuchea (DK) period. Chantou Boua (1991, 235) also interviewed one monk who claimed to have remained in robes until January 1977. However, when the DK army began its attempted recovery of Kampuchea Krom in March 1978, monks from approximately twenty pagodas were kidnapped, forcibly disrobed, and transported to Cambodia (Kiernan 1996, 426).

61. Ven. Srey Ith, interview with the author, February 13, 2001. I have heard other

stories of similar figures surviving in this way. Ven. Koeut Vay is supposed to have lived on a hill in southern Kompong Thom Province, clad in a white cloth that hid his monastic robes. Koeut Vay subsequently became a member of the National Salvation Front, alongside Tep Vong, in December 1978 (Ros Chantrabot 2000, 20). A scholar-monk, he died in 1994.

Shapiro-Phim (2002, 188–189 recounts the stories of two individuals who performed ritual dance with the tacit support of local Khmer Rouge officials. In one case the dancer was secretly supplied with food as a consequence.

The need to physically retain one's robes is a feature of other stories. I have also heard that some ex-monks cut up their robes to make revolutionary clothes that were then dyed black. By so doing, they were able to retain a symbolic and magical connection with the Buddha's protective power.

62. Ven. Las Lay, interview with the author, February 14, 2001. Las Lay is Samdech Dhammalikhit.

63. Dith Pran was punished for secretly gathering rice in autumn 1975. Beaten and tied to a tree for two days, he expected execution. After being unexpectedly released, he shaved his head in a traditional expression of Buddhist piety, telling the Khmer Rouge that this was a cure for migraine. He has also talked of secret devotions, including lighting candles for the dead, throughout the period (Mahaghosananda 1992, x-xi). Shapiro-Phim (2002, 188) mentions a similar case of ritual head shaving.

64. In September 1980, Wat Ampe Phnom near Kampong Speu was discovered to have been one such center. Mass graves, indicating in excess of five thousand deaths, were discovered nearby, and a torture room with skeletons and implements of torture was found in a compartment under the temple's floor. The pagoda on Phnom Bros, close to Kompong Cham town, was also used as an execution center in the DK period (Hinton 1997, 27–28).

65. I am grateful to Olivier de Bernon (pers. comm.) for pointing this obvious fact out to me. It is known, however, that fragments of ancient texts were sometimes used as medicaments, which were occasionally administered by smoking (Hansen 1999, 75).

66. Evidence of Ven. Tep Vong to the trial of Pol Pot in August 1979; de Nike et al. 2000, 149, document 2.1.2.03. There are some discrepancies in the records of vandalism offered at the trial, however. Youk Chang (pers. comm.) claims that Preah Ang Chek and Preah Ang Chom were thrown into a pond. A 1972 photograph of the two deities adorns the front cover of Bizot 1994b.

67. This issue deserves detailed research. To date, no independent scrutiny of the pattern of monastery destruction in Cambodia has been conducted. On the number twenty-six, see de Nike et al. 2000, 145, document 2.1.2.01.

68. One also hears frequent rumors that sacred writings and precious Buddha images from Wat Unnalom were taken off to Ho Chi Minh City following the defeat of the Khmer Rouge. Such rumors may, of course, be motivated by little more than anti-Vietnamese sentiment.

69. This strategy was also employed by the Mongolian Communist Party in the late 1920s. See Sarkisyanz 1958, 626.

These precepts, both negative and positive, are listed in Yang Sam 1987, 70. A list of fifteen are discussed by Ith Sarin (quoted in Kiernan 1976, 376). Ith Sarin, an inspector of primary education who spent time in the maquis as a candidate party member throughout most of 1972, lists them as follows:

1. be modest and simple to the people
2. don't take bribes
3. beg pardon of the people for any wrongs
4. behave in a refined unobtrusive manner following the traditions of the people
5. don't go beyond bounds of propriety with women
6. don't drink
7. don't gamble
8. don't touch money, property of the people, or of Angkar
9. have a burning rage towards the enemy
10. engage in manual work
11. work well with colleagues
12. constructively conduct criticism and self-criticism sessions
13. don't depend on others, foreigners in particular, to make the revolution
14. maintain the image of mastery of the task at hand
15. realize that though the task may be difficult, the struggle will be victorious (Carney 1977, 50–51, quoting from Ith Sarin 1973)

70. As in the slogan, "All people must rely only on themselves" *(khluen ti poeng khluen)* (Locard 1996, 56).

71. Loving-kindness *(mettā)* is, of course, a key Buddhist virtue.

72. *Cpāp'* are traditional didactic poems on moral themes. Mainly composed by monks, they are part of the basic curriculum of monastic education. See chapter 4.

73. On the contrast between the "practical" or "ritual" canon and the "formal canon" in the context of Buddhist monastic education in Sri Lanka, see Blackburn 1999.

74. It is worth noting that the meaning of the term "*chakrapoat*" has migrated a good deal in modern Khmer. Traditionally it meant a righteous Buddhist king (= Pali *cakkavatti*). Since the Democratic Kampuchea period, it has connoted "imperial."

75. It is also perhaps no coincidence that the revolutionary saying "We strive to become our own masters step by step" (quoted in Chandler et al. 1988, 96) is surprisingly similar to the message taught by the famous Cambodian monk-activist Mahaghosananda in the 1990s. See chapter 8 below.

76. The practice of burying an offender in earth up to his neck for a period of time is also attested in Thai traditional law texts. See Richardson 1874.

77. The fact that the leaders of the regime remained unidentified for far longer than security considerations required may be connected to the idea of self-abnegation.

78. Other examples of Khmer Rouge terminology that reveals appropriation of traditional Buddhist terms include "*marga*" = "policy line" (original meaning = "path"), "*mitt*" = "comrade" (original meaning = "friend"), "*vaṇṇḥ*" = "social class" (original

meaning = "caste"). For more detailed discussion, see Carney 1977, 65–66, and Marston 1997, 163.

79. Ebihara (2002, 96) says that she was shocked to see the extent of these new fields when she returned to the countryside for the first time well after the end of the DK period.

80. For a stimulating discussion of the connection between Buddhist sacred space and sacrificial ritual in the Thai context, see Wright 1990. The radical reorganization of space is evoked by Allman (1982, 9). On revisiting a resort that he remembered from the pre–Pol Pot era, he reports, "I had expected Kep, like the rest of Cambodia, much changed from the last time I had seen it, but not even all the reports and personal accounts of what the Khmer Rouge had done to their country provided adequate preparation for Kep. *The horrible thing about Kep was, quite simply, that it no longer existed at all*" (italics mine).

81. In some contexts, "*kasang*" could be a word that instilled great fear, for it was sometimes used as a euphemism for "to kill" (Marston 1994, 115–116). Here is an example of the regime's "diabolical sweetness," i.e., saying one thing but meaning another.

82. Morris (1999, 71–72) describes the Khmer Rouge ideology as "hyperMaoist," in the sense that its adherents seemed to be trying to "outdo Mao Zedong." This hyper-Maoism is characterized by an emphasis on the primacy of the human will and ideological purity over material factors such as technology. Such belief led to highly unrealistic, almost magical assessments of their prospects in battle against their main enemy, the Vietnamese. Despite massive imbalances in manpower and equipment, they held that they could inflict thirty times as many losses on the enemy as they would themselves receive in the border conflict of 1978 (Morris 1999, 104). Chandler (1999, 164) is also inclined to interpret Pol Pot's apparent invisibility in the 1980s as an example of this power.

83. In common with most cultures of the region, the Cambodians contrast the world of settled, rice-growing existence *(sre)* with the wilderness (*prei;* lit., "forest") beyond. Norodom Sihanouk's assertion (1980, 155) that "the most fanatic Khmer Rouge soldiers were from the mountain and forest regions" combines the primordial fear of wilderness with terror of the Khmer Rouge, whose executions tended to be administered at night, a time traditionally connected with danger, disorder, lack of civilization, and violence.

84. Duch (aka Kang Kek Ieu, Ta Pin, Hong Pen) was educated at the Lycée Sisowath, where in 1959 he came in second in the country's national baccalaureate examinations. He subsequently became chief of the Khmer Rouge S-21 security facility at Tuol Sleng, where around sixteen thousand persons perished. He admitted this involvement after being baptized as an evangelical Christian in the Sangke River, Battambang, on January 6, 1996, by Cambodian-born pastor Christopher LaPel. Pastor LaPel says that he first met Duch in 1995 when the latter attended a two-week Christian leadership seminar in Chamkar Samrong village. Subsequently, Duch went on to establish a church in his village of Ruluoh, Svay Check District. Until recently, he had been working for at least two nongovernmental organizations (NGOs)—American

Refugee Committee and the Christian-based World Vision, both of which were impressed by his commitment and efficiency (*PPP* 8/9, April 30–May 13, 1999). He is now in prison awaiting trial for his crimes. For a good biography of Duch, see Chandler 2000, 20–23.

85. Consisting of trousers, shirt, cap, scarf *(krama)*, sandals, and bag.

86. While on a visit to China, Pol Pot said that "Comrade Mao Tse-tung's works and the experience of the Chinese [cultural] revolution played an important role at that time" (*FBIS*—People's Republic of China 1, October 3, 1977, A-20–21). Some internal sources referred to the Cambodian revolution as a "Super Great Leap Forward."

87. That policy was implemented in Democratic Kampuchea. It is tempting to interpret it as a radicalization of the tenth Buddhist monastic precept, which forbids the handling of gold and silver. Money was reintroduced by the PRK on March 25, 1980 (Kiernan 1982, 173). For a detailed treatment of the social, economic, and political consequences of the early stages of Vietnamese occupation, see Heder 1980.

88. The most recent and explicit is the following claim by Hinton (2002, 71): "The actions and ideology of the DK regime seem to draw heavily on pre-existing forms of cultural knowledge. . . . The Khmer Rouge leaders were also inspired by traditional conceptions of purity, particularly the idea of the universal monarch who, because of his moral superiority and enlightenment, is able to purify society by bringing order and coherence."

89. To employ a phrase recently coined by S. Collins (1998, 571), the study of Buddhism can too easily degenerate into a survey of the "Varieties of Buddhist Opium."

90. For a detailed consideration of Buddhism as an ingredient in political change in Asia over the last century, see Harris 1999c.

8. Cambodian Buddhism after the Khmer Rouge

1. He is called Ven. Long Sim by Kiernan (1982, 169). Both Heng Samrin and Chea Sim, another important member of the front, had past monastic connections (Löschmann 1991, 21n11, 24).

2. This is mentioned in a letter by Ven. Wipulasara Thera, a Sri Lankan monk who had been a member of the delegation and the general secretary of the World Buddhist Sangha Council, in response to some criticisms of Michael Vickery (*PPP* 3/18, September 9–22, 1994, 8–9).

3. The KPNLF was formed at Sokh Sann, Thailand, on October 9, 1979, by Son Sann and his two sons, Son Soubert and Son Monir. Son Sann (1911–2000) was a devout lay Buddhist who became convinced that the troubles of the Khmer people were the result of their non-Buddhist conduct. He was in the first cabinet to be formed after the September 1946 elections. As an "extremist element" in the Democrat Party, he was sometimes hostile to the king (Thompson and Adloff 1955, 186). However he was the president of the National Assembly in 1952, the first governor of Cambodia's National Bank (1955–1968), and the prime minister (1967–1968). Son Sann was rapidly mar-

ginalized by Lon Nol and placed under house arrest. He left for Paris in June 1970, where he unsuccessfully sought to bring about a resolution of the civil war. He had conceived the possibility of a "third force" in Cambodian politics and seems to have gained the support of the Mahanikay *senghareach,* Ven. Huot Tath, but Sihanouk subsequently accused Son Sann of being "a dreamer, not a man of action" (quoted in Corfield 1994, 136). Chandler (1990, 58) asserts that Sihanouk appreciated Son Sann's political skills yet "shied away from the older man's Buddhist moralizing, and his austere personal style."

4. Try (1991, 39) describes the PRK's attitude toward Buddhism as a "mariage idéologique bouddhico-marxiste."

5. The report was reviewed by a committee of Phnom Penh monks and authenticated by Le Khech Thoms Nol Moni, a Buddhist clergy representative (de Nike et al. 2000, 145, document 2.1.2.01).

6. It seems that some of the candidates, e.g., Koeut Vay, had disrobed a little earlier. The ordination ceremony *(pabbajjā upasampadā)* was of the traditional *okāsa* type (Bizot 1988b, 121).

7. Non Nget had been a base monk at Wat Prey Chnor, Takeo, and claims to have retained his vows (this is usually a veiled reference to forced marriage) throughout DK, despite being forced to defrock at the end of *vassa* 1975.

8. De Nike et al. 2000, 149, document 2.1.2.03. Also see *FBIS*—Asia and Pacific 21, August 1979, quoted in Yang Sam 1987, 69.

9. Or as "Khmer bodies with Vietnamese minds" *(khluon khmaer kuor kbal yuon);* see Hinton 2002, 90. The matter is clearly sensitive. When Michael Vickery (1986, 196n9) questioned Mme. Peou Lida, who was vice president of the PRK Salvation Front and also responsible for religious affairs, she denied any explicit Vietnamese involvement in the reordinations. Nevertheless, opponents refer to Tep Vong as a "false monk" and "a Communist . . . [who] has always been devoted to the Vietminh" (Martin 1994, 237). A commonly heard complaint from young monks today is that Tep Vong spends too much time in Vietnam.

10. One source asserts that monks were expected to pay higher taxes than most other workers (Keston College staff 1988, 169).

11. The report had been reviewed by a committee of Phnom Penh monks and authenticated by Le Khech Thoms Nol Moni, the Buddhist clergy representative.

12. This restriction was not lifted until 1988.

13. Keyes (1994b, 61n39) claims that the meeting took place in Siem Reap in 1980.

14. DeVoss' claim (1980, 62) that "of 80,000 Cambodian monks, 50,000 were murdered—often beaten to death—during the three years of Pol Pot's savage rule" must be treated with considerable caution.

15. There are parallels here with the situation in Laos following the revolution of 1975. The new head of the Unified Sangha Organization in Laos was also termed president *(prathean),* not the more customary "*phra sangkarat.*" However, Evans (1990) has shown that the vast majority of Lao peasants, who were entirely acculturated to habits of deference, paid little or no attention to these language reforms. Given that such per-

sons constituted a linguistic majority, it was only a question of time before the official terminology had been eroded and old patterns of usage were reestablished. The same general principle holds good for Cambodia.

16. As Keyes (1994b, 64) has noted, "It appears that the modernist approach to Buddhism first championed by the Thommakay faction of the Mahanikay order may be the most favored in the PRK."

17. It is interesting that Hem Chieu was generally referred to by the title "*achar*" in the PRK period. An *achar* is technically a senior lay Buddhist rather than a monk. Yet Hem Chieu did rise to public prominence after he had been defrocked and sent to jail, so the lay designation does make some sense. Recasting monastic heroes in this way would certainly have been more attractive to the communist authorities. Frings (1997, 813) makes the point that early heroes of the anticolonial struggle, e.g., Achar Sua (1864–1866), were given their honorary title well after the event and often by communists who, one would have thought, would have been keen to avoid the unwelcome associations the title evokes. Forest (1992, 88) confirms the association of *achars* and "mouvements de contestation."

18. Vickery (1994, 110) has observed that adherence to a pure Marxist ideology may have been pretty minimal, even at the beginning of PRK. As the years progressed, Heng Samrin's "'Marxism-Leninism' was hardly more than the strong state ideology that animates several Southeast Asian capitalist regimes."

19. A limited number of young monks were sent for further training to Nepal, India, and Sri Lanka in the early 1980s.

20. It seems that the PRK authorities blamed Sihanouk for the arrest and forcible defrocking of Hem Chieu (Frings 1997, 818).

21. By the late 1980s–early 1990s there were some fourteen *wats* in the various border camps, housing more than four hundred monks (Peter Gyallay-Pap, pers. comm.).

22. Smith-Hefner (1999, 24, 32) notes that the vast majority of aid agencies working in the camps were Christian. Indeed, many of the refugees who eventually settled in America "attended Christian services in the early resettlement period." Nevertheless, very few ultimately rejected their Khmer Buddhist heritage.

23. In the mid-1980s, Site 8, the Khmer Rouge "show camp," had an active pagoda (Keston College staff members 1989, 338).

24. Including the camps Rithisen and Nong Samet.

25. Ven. Mahaghosananda (1992, 68) says that in 1981 he was asked by a Khmer Rouge leader to establish a temple at the border. He also asserts that his movement was supported by the Khmer Rouge (*Cambodia Daily,* March 18, 1997). Subsequently, he and his followers organized their 1997 event in the Khmer Rouge strongholds of the northwest. The marchers were greeted by Ieng Sary, Y Chhien (mayor of Pailin), and other important ex–Khmer Rouge on their arrival in Pailin (*Cambodia Daily,* April 21, 1997). More recently, Ieng Sary sponsored a Buddhist ceremony in Pailin in which he and his wife, Ieng Thirith, received monastic blessings on the third anniversary of his defection to the government (*PPP* 8/17, August 20–September 2, 1999). The consensus among both professional Cambodia-watchers and the ordinary citizens of the country

is that the whole thing smacks of cynicism. Nowadays Ieng Sary and his wife make a point of visiting the funerary monument of his father and other family members at Wat Svay Poper, one of the capital's few functioning Thommayut monasteries, whenever he visits Phnom Penh.

More recently, Buddhist leaders have adopted a conciliatory approach to the past excesses of Khmer Rouge leaders; Ven. Tep Vong, for instance, has likened Ieng Sary to Angulimala, the murderous brigand of canonical Buddhism who was converted by the Buddha (*PPP* 6/6, March 21–April 3, 1997, 17). This is quite a change from Tep Vong's view as recorded in the proceedings of Pol Pot's trial, where he said that the Khmer Rouge crimes meant that, from the Buddhist perspective, the perpetrators should be considered to have "lost their human nature." As such "these savage beasts should be turned upside down like bats, with their legs in the air above their heads, and once they have fallen they will be condemned to hell" (de Nike et al. 2000, 152, document 2.1.2.03). The supreme patriarch's change of heart appears to mirror the government's changing political line.

26. Kalab (1994, 67) claims that the broadcasts alternated between Mahanikay and Thommayut. This seems strange, given that the two orders were not officially reestablished until 1991.

27. The withdrawal of Vietnamese troops was, in no small part, an economic consequence of the breakup of the Soviet Union.

28. See the official journal *Pracheachon* for May 11, 1989.

29. Most notably in Kampot in February 1989 (Ponchaud 1990, 205–206). Another source (Keston College staff members 1989, 337) places this improvised speech in January. It was delivered to around two hundred monks and old people at Wat Chum Kriel, Kampot. After the 1993 elections, Hun Sen was frequently seen personally sponsoring village works of one sort or another. Indeed, he even wrote songs inspired by these events that were broadcast on the radio. One of the more popular, "The Life of a Pagoda Boy," tells the story of his life as a pagoda boy at Wat Neak Von, Phnom Penh, in the mid-1960s. It appears that he fled Phnom Penh in 1968 when his mentor, a monk from Wat Tuol Kork, was arrested following the Samlaut uprising (Jennar 1995b, 206).

30. More recently there has been some controversy about what to do with the bones, many of which are now badly decayed, of those slaughtered in the killing fields. Sihanouk has suggested that they be given a Buddhist "burial," whereas the Cambodian People's Party (CPP) wants to keep them as a reminder of genocide and as a focus of a National Day of Hate (*PPP* 7/15, July 24–30, 1998). The Day of Hate was first instituted on May 20, 1983, but was suspended in 1993. However, during New Year and *pchum ben,* monks still perform a ceremony for the dead of Democratic Kampuchea at Tuol Sleng (*PPP* 8/8, April 13–19, 1999).

31. By 1990, twenty-six Pali schools, based on the 1950s–1970s model, had opened (Löschmann 1991, 22).

32. Vickery (1994, 109) is skeptical about how far PRK cadres could be regarded as Marxist-Leninists in the first place. He says, "I never met anyone who had a clear idea of what Marxism-Leninism is, or who cared."

33. *Pracheachon,* no. 1061, May 24, 1992. The editorial adds that Sihanouk had endorsed this view "with the brightness of a bodhisattva." Shortly after this, the CPP claimed to be the "rightful heir *(neak bondo ven troeum trouv)* of the line of the People's Socialist Community *(sangkum reastr niyum)*" (*Pracheachon,* no. 1091, June 27, 1992).

34. Judy Ledgerwood (pers. comm.) suggests that the shift may not have been so astonishing after all. By this time, hardly anyone gave a damn about Marxism or any other political ideology.

35. *Kampuchea,* no. 623, October 21, 1991, 3–4, quoted in Frings 1994b, 363.

36. Although accomplished only in July 1993, the reversion of most major Phnom Penh streets to their Sihanouk-era names—e.g., Son Ngoc Minh to Monivong, Tou Samouth to Norodom, Po Kambo to Prince Monireth, and Kampuchea-Vietnam to Kampuchea Krom—clearly reflects the changed thinking.

37. According to a story circulating at the time, when the urn at the Independence Monument was opened for cleaning just before the return of Sihanouk, three black owls emerged—a bad omen relating to the past (Thion 1993, 197).

38. The title of "*samdech*" was reintroduced for a senior monk around this time, although it had already been conferred on Son Sann (1911–2000), a political ally of Sihanouk's, and would later be offered to the leaders of the CPP and FUNCINPEC (Front Uni National pour un Cambodge Indépendent, Neutre, Pacifique, et Coopératif) (Marston 1997, 176).

39. Ven. Non Nget, interview with the author, November 18, 1999. Interestingly, a former monk, Kuoch Kileng (1971), had unsuccessfully agitated for the right of monks to vote in elections in 1971 (Yang Sam 1987, 41).

40. Kalab (1994, 70) reports that PRK soldiers defecting to the KPNLF on the Thai border were required to be ordained temporarily so that they could be taught "traditional values and morality" before joining their new army units.

41. Despite their political differences, Pin Sem is Ven. Tep Vong's nephew.

42. Thach Bunroeun, a Khmer Krom and a doctoral candidate at the University of Hawai'i, also envisaged rekindling the country's Theravada Buddhist heritage. Inspired by the example of Sulak Sivaraksa in Thailand, he proposed the creation of a Khmer International Relations Institute, which would act as a locus for Khmer expatriots and local people to solve a dazzling array of social and political problems on the basis of Buddhist insights. The institute would use monks to introduce "Western democracy" to the people. Intriguingly, his thesis also called for the reestablishment of the Khmer-Mon Institute of the Lon Nol era (1993, 331). Thach Bunroeun did eventually establish the Preah Sihanouk Raj Academy in late 1993. It collapsed amid bitter infighting in March 1996.

43. See note 38 above.

44. The three ministerial posts of the coalition government were youth and sport; rural development; and relations with Parliament (*PPP* 2/14, July 2–15, 1993, 3).

45. For a detailed discussion of this document, see Gaillard 1994. Jennar (1995a, 5) has warned that we should be careful in our treatment of all recent Cambodian constitutions, for they are "at best, a declaration of intentions." Many of their provisions

are nothing more than a window onto the "principal preoccupations of the ruling class, including the image of the country they hoped to offer to the outside world."

46. Ieng Mouly was born in Prey Veng into a politically active family. His father had been a member of the pre-1955 Democratic Party. Corfield (1991, 26) describes Ieng Mouly rather nonspecifically as a "Buddhist activist."

47. The equivalent Thai slogan, "Chat, Satsana, Phramahakasat," was created by Rama VI (Vajiravudh; r. 1910–1935). Wyatt (1984, 229) refers to it as a "trinitarian mystery."

48. By comparison, on the death of Norodom in 1904, a similar council comprised the *résident supérieure,* five ministers, the chief of the palace Brahmins, and the two *sanghareachs* (Forest 1982, 62–63).

49. Since its reestablishment, the Ministry of Cults and Religious Affairs has always been led by FUNCINPEC officials.

50. See Hean Sokhom 1996. The Buddhist University was reestablished in 1997 with a variety of Khmer and Sri Lankan staff, taking its first cohort of about forty students from the Buddhist High School, which had itself formally reopened in May 1993.

51. The HBF is linked with the German party Alliance 90/The Greens. It also sponsors the Nuns and Laywomen's Association of Cambodia, inaugurated in 1995, which is concerned with the moral and development-oriented education of women and children.

The JSRC began its work in the late 1970s in Bangkok, where it reprinted a wide variety of Khmer literature for circulation in the refugee camps on the border (Khing Hoc Dy 1994, 30). It seems that the JSRC had been stung into taking a role in this humanitarian crisis after a number of criticisms in the *Asahi Shinbun,* a leading Japanese newspaper. The paper noted that although Christian agencies had been involved almost from the beginning, the Japanese seemed to be doing nothing for their Asian and Buddhist brothers and sisters (Ian Reader, pers. comm., December 12, 1999). The JSRC is partially sponsored by the Japanese Committee of the World Conference of Religion and Peace (WCRP) (Löschmann 1997, 100). Another Japanese lay Buddhist organization, Soka Gakkai, was involved in distributing used radios in the lead-up to the 1993 elections (Marston 1997, 303).

52. The first Buddhist publication to appear after the Democratic Kampuchea period was a version of the *Dhammapada,* published by the Khmer *sangha* in California in 1990 under the guidance of Ven. Mahaghosananda.

53. The National Library only has 800 manuscripts.

54. He may be somewhat older, a fact supported by differing dates of birth given in published sources. It seems that his sponsor, Ven. Chuon Nath, may have claimed that Mahaghosananda was a little younger so that he would meet the entry requirement when he enrolled for his doctorate in India.

55. Possibly Hok Sovann's Paris-based Annual World Conference of Khmer Monks (Peter Gyallay-Pap, pers. comm.). Mahaghosananda regarded the position as provisional, stating that he would resign when conditions in Cambodia returned to normality and a fully valid ecclesiastical hierarchy had been established (Mahaghosananda 1992, 15–16).

56. Since 1999 his permanent home, partly because of failing health, is Wat Kary Vong Bupharam, Leverett, Massachusetts.

57. Buddhist nuns are very prominent in the movement. On the seventh Dhammayietra in July 1998, nuns outnumbered monks by 80 to 26.

58. *Marching in the Buddha's Steps, Cambodia Daily* special supplement, May 1998, 6.

59. Bob Maat, interview with the author, February 11, 2001.

60. Mahaghosananda was awarded the fifteenth Niwano Peace Prize in 1998. The cash involved, amounting to 20 million yen, was used to finance various Cambodian NGOs, although there have subsequently been some claims of misappropriation.

61. *Coalition for Peace and Reconciliation Newsletter,* January 2001. The event was also supported by the Ministry of Cults and Religious Affairs.

62. Ponleu Khmer, a coalition of Cambodian human rights and development NGOs, also has connections with the Mahaghosananda circle. In addition, some Buddhist monks have received training as disseminators of human rights by the Cambodian League for the Promotion and Defense of Human Rights, an organization with links to the European Union and the French government (*PPP* 1/6, September 25, 1992, 8).

63. A consortium of local NGOs facilitated by Westerners and some Khmer-Americans (Peter Gyallay-Pap, pers. comm., October 12, 1999).

64. Sam Rainsy, for instance, regards Chheng Pon as a CPP supporter.

65. There are clear parallels here with the activities of other engaged Buddhist leaders in Asia, e.g., A. T. Ariyaratne in Sri Lanka. See Bond 1996, esp. 136–138.

66. When the Khmer Rouge took control of Cambodia, Yos Hut was pursuing postgraduate studies in Paris. After a spell in Australia he worked for the United Nations Border Relief Operation on the Thai border until 1990 (Kalab 1994, 62–63). My own interviews with Yos Hut (November 30, 1997, and November 20, 1999) indicate that he is well integrated into the NGO community.

67. Peter Schier, permanent representative of KAF in Cambodia, interview with the author, December 11, 1997.

68. Heng Monychenda, originally a monk at Wat Prasatsiri, Monychenda, disrobed in 1997 after a brief period as a graduate student at Harvard.

69. Also see the GTZ publication by Ros Nol (1995).

70. Another example of an NGO that is working through the monastic order is Partage, a French organization. It was organized in Cambodia in 1995 as Dhammic Solidarity (Samakithor), a European Union–funded community development project in Battambang Province.

71. Concerns about a lack of financial transparency at the Dhammayietra Center for Peace and Reconciliation (CPR) have already been noted. Similar doubts have occasionally surfaced in connection with Santi Sena.

72. A seminar designed to launch the MEEP was held at the Buddhist Institute in November 1997. A white paper and other elements of the proceedings of the seminar were subsequently published as Gyallay-Pap and Bottomley 1998.

73. *Khmer Rouge Papers for 7 December 1997*, quoted in *PPP* 7/10, May 22–June 4, 1998.

74. See esp. chapter 13 of Taylor 1989.

75. At about the same time, the king conferred the title "International Patriarch" on Mahaghosananda (David Channer, pers. comm., October 5, 1997).

76. Ven. Tep Vong is closely associated with Chea Sim, the chairman of the CPP and the president of the National Assembly. According to one of my informants, Chea Sim made a donation of robes and 120 million riels to Wat Unnalom monks during the *kathen* ceremony at the end of the 1996 rainy season. Having received this on behalf of the *sangha*, Tep Vong allegedly transferred it back to another CPP member on Chea Sim's behalf. Naturally this angered and alienated many younger monks. Chea Sim has also contributed funds toward the rebuilding of Wat Po Ampil in Takeo Province. This may explain why it was the target of a grenade attack that killed one person on March 26, 1998 (*PPP* 7/7, April 10–23, 1998).

77. Letter to *PPP* 2/17, August 13–26, 1993, 6. This is a surprising statement, given Hok Sovann's own political activism. While living in a refugee camp in Thailand, Hok Sovann (1983) wrote an indictment of the Khmer Rouge's treatment of Buddhism (Yang Sam 1987, 55). I have been unable to consult this work. He also broadcast anticommunist sermons weekly on the Voice of America through much of the 1980s and early 1990s and tried to discourage overseas Khmer from returning home.

78. For a discussion of official disapproval of the Thommayut's links with Thailand, see chapter 5 above.

79. A 1959 inventory found that 1,725 of the country's monasteries were affiliated with the Mahanikay, but only 106 were associated with the Thommayut (Chuon Nath 1976, 41). In the mid-1990s around 3 percent of the monastic population belonged to the Thommayut. Statistics are from the Center for Advanced Studies and the Ministry of Cults and Religious Affairs, published in *Cambodia Report* 2(2) (March–April 1996), 23.

80. Also see Ponchaud 1990, 234, on the Khmer Rouge's claim that Buddhism is a foreign religion.

81. Smith-Hefner (1999, 25–26) reports similar disputes in the fledgling Khmer monastic community in Massachusetts. One clash focused on a monk who was widely believed to have been a past member of the Khmer Rouge.

82. Kalab (1994, 61) claims that Bour Kry possessed a ceremonial fan embroidered with the words "Head of all monks in France."

83. Although a modernist, Ven. Bour Kry does not condemn popular religion (Ang Chouléan 1986, 331).

84. Ordinations into the Thommayut seem to have gathered pace since the early 1990s. Reportedly, 150 monks were ordained in early July 1992 alone (*PPP* 1/2, July 24, 1992, 6). In November 1999, Ven Non Nget supplied me with the following (very high) figures for Wat Botum: Mahanikay— c. 600, Thommayut— c. 200.

85. He was also the inspector general of Buddhist education and the director of the Buddhist University. Born into a Kompong Cham farming background in 1918, Oum

Som became a monk at the age of sixteen. He became a member of the Tripitaka Commission in 1956 and was also part of the team that worked with Chuon Nath on the fifth edition of the *Khmer Dictionary*. As such, he had been a member of the Thommakay group. Oum Som was also one of the seven monks to be reordained in September 1979. His critics sometimes accused him of being a "communist monk." As we shall see shortly, he was a prominent critic of the young monks' demonstrations in 1998. His role as inspector is now in the hands of Ven. Non Nget.

86. The imposition of CPP appointees appears to be more prevalent in Phnom Penh than in country districts, where elders are in a better position to block unwelcome interference.

87. Apparently, he had been a monk at Wat Unnalom, where he was close to Ven. Chuon Nath. He disrobed around 1945 to join the anti-French resistance (Mehta and Mehta 1999, 15, 22–23).

88. Feuding between Tep Vong and Bour Kry seems to have been ongoing since at least 1998 (*PPP* 7/22, October 2–15, 1998).

89. A 2002 visit to AIDS projects run by monks in Thailand has shifted Tep Vong's view somewhat. As a result, Ven. Van Saveth of the Mahanikay Wat Norea in Battambang has been asked by the Ministry of Cults and Religious Affairs to expand his own AIDS project. It looks as though substantial amounts of foreign aid will pass through monks like him in the near future (*PPP* 11/8, April 12–25, 2002).

90. In the lead-up to the election, the CPP had been claiming encouraging levels of support among both Buddhist and Cham communities (*PPP* 7/11, June 5–18, 1998).

91. Sam Rainsy was the FUNCINPEC finance minister until late 1994, when, following an unsuccessful campaign against corruption, he left to found his own party.

92. Although it is fairly commonplace for Khmer to express extreme anti-Vietnamese sentiments, I have nevertheless been struck by the number of times such sentiments have cropped up in conversations with young monks. They are, in part, a coded criticism of Hun Sen because of alleged connections with Vietnam.

93. Born in 1975 near Sisophon, Chin Channa became a novice monk at Wat Tik Thlar, in his home village, in June 1991. He was inspired by a visit of Mahaghosananda to the *wat* on the first Dhammayietra in April 1992. Shortly after this event, he continued his education by learning Pali in Mongol-Borey before attending Wat Damrei Sar in Battambang. He came to Wat Unnalom in February 1998 to enroll at the Buddhist University and disrobed in late 2001.

94. Some reports suggest that the idea for the September 8 event may have emerged among some monks connected with the Campaign to Reduce Violence for Peace.

95. The KBS was founded by Khmer-Americans in the early 1990s and funded partly by USAID, the U.S. Agency for International Development. Ou Bun Long is its former director.

96. I have it on good authority that Oum Som was forced into this condemnation against his will.

97. When I interviewed Ven. Non Nget (b. 1924), the leader of the Mahanikay seg-

ment at Wat Botum and a significant supporter of Hun Sen's on November 18, 1999, he repeated these charges and added that some monks had also used slingshots against the police.

98. Estimates given to me by leaders of the young monks are significantly higher. Interviews I conducted in autumn 1998 confirmed the widely held view that between five and seventeen monks permanently disappeared around this time.

99. Smith-Hefner (1999, 28) reports that Tep Vong is not universally admired in the Khmer-American diaspora. One of her interviewees expressed the view that if Tep Vong visited their temple, he would not be entertained, on the grounds that he is both ill educated and untrustworthy.

100. I interviewed him at Wat Botum on February 6, 2001, while he was still in robes.

101. Olivier de Bernon (pers. comm.) believes that Sam Rainsy recognized that this Gandhian "*mode d'expression*" was inappropriate in contemporary Cambodia.

102. Ven. Chuon Nath's iconic status has increased of late. In October 1999 a three-day seminar in Phnom Penh, designed to celebrate the thirtieth anniversary of Chuon Nath's death, was sponsored by the Buddhist Institute, the Ministry of Cults and Religious Affairs, and CEDORECK (Centre de Documentation et de Recherche sur la Civilisation Khmère). Formed in Paris in June 1977, CEDORECK prepared a manifesto, *Pour une société khmère meilleure,* condemning the Khmer Rouge and recognizing that positive elements of traditional Khmer society needed to be grafted onto equally positive elements of Western culture in order to build a sustainable future (Martin 1994, 203). Nouth Narang, CEDORECK's founder and a CPP representative, was also the president of the organizing committee of the October 1999 event.

103. Ven. Yos Hut told me that he believed that some Sam Rainsy Party members had taken robes with a specific intention to infiltrate the *sangha* (interview with the author, November 19, 1999). I think that this is unlikely and do not wish to assert that young monks support Sam Rainsy in any particularly explicit manner. A more likely explanation is that implicit politicization occurs through regular discussion of grievances with the many poor students who also live in and around urban monasteries.

104. Letter from Bora Touch, in *PPP* 9/18, September 1–14, 2000.

105. The Thai equivalent "*burana*" has the sense of "reconstruct, rehabilitate, repair, or restore" and is often used in the context of rebuilding temples and the like. Its companion term, "Vatthana(kan)," on the other hand, invokes growth or increase. Rhum (1996, 350–351) has pointed out that in premodern Thailand, to say that something was "traditional" simply meant that it formed part of a class of things deemed "good." Nowadays, when it is necessary to legitimate something by reference to its fit with the internal workings of society, the term "traditional" is used. The term "modernity," on the other hand, tends to validate by reference to external factors.

106. A rumor circulates to the effect that Ven. Daung Phang has a direct phone line to Hun Sen (Marston 2000, 8).

107. Ven. Non Nget's official position in the Mahanikay hierarchy is *samdech preah bodhivong.* He is therefore one of the three *samdech sangh* in the *rājāgaṇa* of the first

class immediately below Tep Vong. Non Nget appears more hostile to the political affiliations of the *boran* movement than to its ideals and practices, a point reinforced by his own claim to possess supernatural abilities. He also admitted to having both Thai and Khmer teachers in the past, although "the Khmer have more magical powers" (interview with the author, November 18, 1999).

Disputes between traditionalists and modernists can occur within the same monastery. The current situation at Wat Bo, Siem Reap, where Ven. Pin Sem is *chau adhikar,* is a case in point. Likewise, in Kompong Cham there is evidence that the laity will feed only monks who champion its own particular viewpoint (Marston 2000, 4).

108. Evidence offered to the 1978 trial of Pol Pot indicated that Wat Champuskaek was an important detention and execution center (de Nike et al. 2000, 278–286, document 2.3.7.01/02/03/04).

109. Despite his relative youth, Ven. Om Lim Heng has a senior position in the national hierarchy of the Mahanikay (*rājāgaṇa* of the second class). Although I have not been able to confirm this, it is widely rumored that he bought the position from Ven. Tep Vong.

110. According to recent statistics released by the Ministry of Cults and Religious Affairs, US$6 million is spent every year during *kathen.* With 3,612 monasteries in Cambodia, this averages out at about US$2,000 each (*PPP* 7/23, October 16–29, 1998).

111. Large religious donations by the notoriously corrupt, perhaps as a means of expunging previous misdeeds, are likely to have been a feature of all periods of Cambodian history.

112. Roth Saroeun spent some of the DK period in Kampuchea Krom.

113. When I interviewed Roth Saroeun on November 16, 1999, he assured me that it was necessary to generate income equivalent to 150 kilograms of rice per day to supply the 350 monks, 150 nuns, 100 orphans, and an unspecified number of students living at the monastery. When I visited him again in February 2001, he was in America, where he has many supporters within the Khmer community.

114. P. Jackson (1989) has also noticed that Thai *vipassanā* traditions both deny traditional cosmology and point to the possibility of a nonsupernaturalistic *nibbāna* realized in democratic modes of thinking and behavior.

115. According to Houtman (1999, 333n6, 335), two prominent Burmese figures in the anticolonialist movements of the 1930s—Saya San, a healer and an author of a number of works on "worldly knowledge," and the alchemist Thakhin Kodawhmaing, a great supporter of Aung San's—both drew on Buddhist *samatha* currents. Currently another magician-monk, the Thamanya Sayadaw, also represents a considerable source of power beyond government control. His icon is commonly seen in almost all taxis, and he attracts a significant income from the many pilgrims who visit him. These resources are used to support many of the destitute who congregate at his mountain retreat.

Glossary

abhayamudrā: An iconographical hand gesture *(mudrā)* denoting "absence of fear."

Abhidhamma: The third and final "basket" of the Tripitaka. A collection of seven Pali books that attempt a systematization of Buddhist doctrine against the background of meditational practice.

achar: A lay Buddhist specialist. He may also be involved in the administrative, educational, and moral life of a *wat.*

arhat: Literally, a "worthy one." A Buddhist saint who, like the Buddha, has achieved the final goal of awakening.

Avalokiteśvara: An important Buddhist divinity associated with the quality of compassion.

baku: A Brahmanical priest. In Cambodia he was preoccupied with various rituals of kingship.

baray: A large man-made lake or tank of water.

bhikkhu (Sanskrit: *bhikṣu*): A fully ordained male member of the *sangha.* A Buddhist monk.

bhikkhuṇī: A fully ordained female member of the *sangha.* A Buddhist nun.

bhūmisparśamudrā: The "earth touching" gesture. In Buddhist iconography it recalls the time when the Buddha called on the earth goddess to witness his liberality in previous existences.

bodhisattva: An important term with multiple meanings. In Theravada Buddhism it generally refers to the Buddha's lives prior to his enlightenment.

Brahmanism: The dominant Sanskrit-based and priestly strand within the Indian Hindu tradition.

Brahmā: A major Brahmanical deity associated with the power of creation.

Brahmin: A Hindu priest and a member of the purest of the four classical castes *(varṇa).*

buddhapāda: The footprint of the Buddha. An important devotional device in Theravada Buddhism.

cakravartin: "Wheel-turner." A Buddhist ruler, either mythological or historical, who governs his realm righteously and in harmony with the teachings of a Buddha *(dhamma).*

chau adhikar: The chief monk of a *wat.*

chedi (Sanskrit: *caitya*): A funerary monument. Sometimes used as an alternative for "*stūpa.*"

dhamma (Sanskrit: *dharma*): An important and multivalent Pali term. In this book it denotes the Buddha's teachings. It is one of the three jewels *(triratna).*

dhammarāja: A king who rules in accordance with the Buddha's teachings.

Dhammayutika Nikaya: *See* Thommayut.

dhutaṅga: A set of thirteen ascetic practices, such as living in a cemetery, that monks may adopt if so moved.

gopura: The gateway, often quite elaborate, of a Brahmanical temple.

Harihara: A Brahmanical deity, representing a fusion of the qualities of Śiva and Viṣṇu.

Jātaka: A class of Buddhist writings dealing with the previous lives of the Buddha.

karma: "Action" is the primary meaning of the term. The law of karma is an expression of the Buddhist belief that all intentional actions, whether positive or negative, have future consequences.

kathen (Sanskrit: *kaṭhina*): Robe cloth supplied by the laity to monks at a ceremony of the same name, marking the end of *vassa.*

kot (Sanskrit: *kuṭi*): A monastic hut or communal dwelling place for monks.

Kṛṣṇa: An important Brahmanical deity, of rustic origin, associated with the concept of love.

liṅga: A phallic iconographical device representing the Brahmanical deity Śiva; hence the alternative form, "Śivaliṅga."

Mahanikay: The "great group." The name now given to that segment of the Thai and Cambodian *sangha* largely unaffected by the great currents of nineteenth-century Buddhist reform.

Mahayana: The "great vehicle." With the Theravada, one of the two major forms of Buddhism to have survived from the early historical period. It was once important in Cambodia and still flourishes in North and East Asia.

mahāsaṅgharāja. See *sanghareach.*

maṇḍala: A symbolic circular diagram, often conceived as a cosmogram, used in Buddhist meditation. It is especially associated with tantric practice.

mantra: Sacred sounds, often used in a ritual or meditational context, believed to possess supernatural and transformational powers.

Meru: A vast mountain that, according to Buddhist cosmology, stands at the center of our world system.

nāga: A class of mythological snake beings associated with water and the underworld.

neak tā: A Cambodian ancestral or tutelary deity.

nirvāṇa: The goal of Buddhist practice. A state in which the fire of desire has been extinguished and all suffering is ended.

Pali: An ancient Indian language, closely related to Sanskrit, used for the composition of the Theravada canonical corpus.

pāramitā: A spiritual perfection.

parinirvāṇa: The final passing away of a buddha who, because he has uprooted all desire, will never be born again. According to legend, the Buddha was lying on his right side when this occurred.

paritta: A series of short Pali texts chanted for protection or blessing.

Prajñāpāramitā: A female Buddhist divinity regarded as "mother of all the buddhas." Also a corpus of Mahayana writings dealing with the "perfection of wisdom."

prasat: A Brahmanical temple.

prateyekabuddha: A class of buddhas who remain in solitude without teaching the *dhamma.*

puṇya: A meritorious action resulting in some positive future state, either in this life or the next.

Śaiva: Adjectival form of "Śiva."

Śākyamuni: Literally, "the sage of the Śākyas." An epithet of the Buddha.

Śiva: A major Brahmanical god associated with destruction, transgression, and disorder. A Dionysian deity, Śiva is often represented iconographically by the *liṅga.*

Śivaliṅga. See *liṅga.*

Śrāvakayāna: Literally, "the vehicle of the hearers." A term used mainly in Mahayanist works to describe all those Buddhists, including members of the Theravada, who do not follow the Mahayana path.

sangha: In its widest sense, the Buddhist community. More specifically, the order of monks and nuns.

sanghareach (Pali: *saṅgharāja*): "King of the *sangha*"—a title for the highest monk in a Buddhist ecclesiastical hierarchy. Sometimes rendered as "supreme patriarch." The titles "*mahāsaṅgharāja*" (great king of the *sangha*) and "*saṅghanayaka*" (leader of the *sangha*) are effectively synonymous.

saṅghanayaka. See *sanghareach.*

Sanskrit: An important classical Indian language used in the composition of most Brahmanical and some (mainly Mahayana) Buddhist sacred writings.

sīmā: A boundary delineating Buddhist monastic territory.

stūpa: A distinctively shaped Buddhist architectural structure designed to house relics or other sacred objects.

Tantra: An esoteric Brahmanical or Buddhist text. Also refers to a species of secret rituals, often involving mantras, *maṇḍalas,* and characteristic body postures *(mudrā),* transmitted by a spiritual master to his disciple in oral form.

Theravada: Literally, "the path of the elders." A school of Buddhism that dominates the South and Southeast Asian cultural sphere. Its teachings, embodied in the Pali canon (Tripitaka), are sometimes considered more conservative than those encountered in the Mahayana.

Thommayut: An aristocratic and reformist order within the Thai and Cambodian

Buddhist *sangha*. Founded in the nineteenth century by Rama IV, king of Thailand, it sought to return monastic practice to its original purity.

Tripitaka: Literally, "the three baskets." The tripartite corpus of Theravada sacred writings in Pali constituted by the Buddha's rules for monastic discipline (Vinaya), his sermons (Sutta), and the Abhidhamma.

triratna: The "three jewels," i.e., the Buddha, the Dhamma, and the Sangha. Also known as the three refuges, they are regarded as having central significance in all forms of Buddhism.

upasampadā: Higher ordination. The ritual through which one becomes a *bhikkhu.*

uṣṇīṣa: A fleshy protuberance on the head of a Buddha. One of the thirty-two marks of a superman.

Vaiṣṇava: Adjectival form of Viṣṇu.

vajra: A thunderbolt. Often employed in a Buddhist context as a symbol for sudden spiritual transformation.

varṇa: Any one of the four great divisions or castes of ancient Indian society.

vassa: The annual three-month-rains retreat, usually lasting from July until October.

vihāra: A Buddhist monastery, although in Cambodia the term is often restricted to the monastery's central shrine hall.

Vinaya: Rules of Buddhist monastic discipline constituting the first great division of the Pali Tripitaka.

Viṣṇu: A major Brahmanical god tasked with maintaining universal order. An Apollonian deity who is venerated in a variety of differing forms.

wat: A Buddhist monastery. The Southeast Asian equivalent of the Pali *vihāra.*

yantra: A symbolic geometrical device, often containing Pali or Sanskrit letters, used in esoteric and specifically tantric forms of Buddhism. It is believed to possess protective and initiatory qualities.

Yogācāra: A major school of Mahayana Buddhist philosophy. Originating in India around the fourth century CE, it has primarily been interested in psychological and epistemological issues.

yogāvacara: "One who practices yoga." More specifically, a term used for an initiate of the esoteric or tantric tradition within Theravada Buddhism.

Khmer Word List

achar kar អាចារ្យការ
achar thom អាចារ្យធំ
achar vat អាចារ្យវត្ត
achar yogi អាចារ្យយោគី
aeng phloeung អាំងភ្លើង
angkar padevat អង្គការបដិវត្តន៍
angkarviney អង្គការវិនយ
anukun អនុគុណ
anusamvacchara-mahasannipat
អនុសំវច្ឆរមហាសន្និបាត
arak អារក្ខ
assath អាសាធ

baku បគូរ
baky vappadharm ពាក្យវប្បធម៌
bālāt-kun បាល័តគុណ
bhikkhu ភិក្ខុ
bidhi sak ពិធីសាក់
bon pgah បុណ្យផ្កា
boramei vat បារមីវត្ត
boran បុរាណ
braling ព្រលឹង
bray ព្រាយ
bray pallangk ព្រាយបល្ល័ង្ក
bray preah pāramī ព្រាយព្រះបារមី
buak thor cah ពួកធម៌ចាស់
buak thor thmei ពួកធម៌ថ្មី

cah srok ចាស់ស្រុក
cah thom ចាស់ធំ
cap pdaem bi son ចាប់ផ្តើមពីសូន្យ
chāk mahāpaṅsukūl ឆាកមហាបង្សុកូល
chau adhikar ចៅអធិការ
chauvay khet ចៅហ្វាយខេត្ត
chedi ចេតិយ
ches ជេស្ឋ
cpāp' ច្បាប់
crieng ច្រៀង
cul mlap ចូលម្លប់

danlap ដន្លាប់
dey ដី
dey preah ដីព្រះ
dhmap' ធ្មប់
don chi ដូនជី
dvar meas ទ្វារមាស

ekareach mcahkar ឯករាជម្ចាស់ការ

gambhir គម្ពីរ
gamtaeng kralā កំម្តែងក្រឡា
garbh preah mata គភ៌ព្រះមាតា
goan krak កូនក្រក
gru គ្រូ
gru sot គ្រូសូត្រ

hau braling ហៅព្រលឹង
hau braling nag ហៅព្រលឹងនាគ
hora ហោរ

indrakhīla ឥន្ទខិល

jaṃdāv ជំទាវ

kaev preah phloeung កែវព្រះភ្លើង
kamhaeng កំហែង
kamrateṅ añ កម្រតេងអញ
kansaeng yantra កន្សែងយ័ន្ត
kap yuon កាប់យួន
kasang កសាង
katha គាថា
kathen កឋិន
kattik កត្តិក
kdei ក្ដី
khet ខេត្ត
khmer daom ខ្មែរដើម
khmoc ខ្មោច
khum ឃុំ
khyal ខ្យល់
kmeng vat ក្មេងវត្ត
kñuṃ ខ្ញុំ
kñuṃ vihāra ខ្ញុំវិហារ
kñuṃ vraḥ ខ្ញុំព្រះ
koḥ kaev tvīp laṅkā
កោះកែវត្វីបលង្កា
komnan khet កំណាន់ខេត្ត
kpoñ ក្បោញ
kram ក្រម
krang ក្រង
kse ក្សែ
kse katha ក្សែគាថា
ktom ក្ដោម
kuruṅ bnaṃ កុរុងភ្នំ

leah bang លះបង់
lekhādihikār-kun លេខាធិការគណ
lkhon khol ល្ខោនខោល
loak cah លោកចាស់
loak dhutang លោកធុតង្គ
loak song លោកសង្ឃ
loeng neak tā ឡើងអ្នកតា
lpaeng ល្បែង
luat daik លត់ដែក
lup bombat លុបបំបាត់

meakh មាឃ
meba មេបា
mekhyal មេខ្យល់
mekun មេគណ
men មេន
mevat មេវត្ត
moha មហា
mohanikay tmae មហានិកាយថ្មី
mongol tepeachar មង្គលទេពាចារ្យ
mratāñ-varman ម្រតាញវរ្ម័ន
mrenh kongveal ម្រេញកង្វាល
mul មូល

neak cheh doeng អ្នកចេះដឹង
neak mean bon អ្នកមានបុណ្យ
neak mūla kammaṭṭhāna អ្នកមូលកម្មដ្ឋាន
neak mulethan អ្នកមូលដ្ឋាន
neak saccam អ្នកសច្ចំ
neak sel អ្នកសិល
neak tā អ្នកតា
nimitta និមិត្ត
nirpean និព្វាន

oknya ឧកញ៉ា

pak spaek បកស្បែក
pandit បណ្ឌិត
paṅsukūl បង្សុកូល
pchum ben ភ្ជុំបិណ្ឌ
phalkun ផល្គុណ
phleng khmaer ភ្លេងខ្មែរ
phleng siem ភ្លេងសៀម
phluv chveng ផ្លូវឆ្វេង
phluv knong ផ្លូវក្នុង
phluv krau ផ្លូវក្រៅ

phluv sdam ផ្លូវស្ដាំ
phnom ភ្នំ
phnong ភ្នង
phtach pouch ផ្ដាច់ពូជ
pisakh ពិសាខ
poñ ពោញ
prathean ប្រធាន
pravatt'rup ប្រវត្តិរូប
pre rup ប្រែរូប
preah dīnāṃṅ ព្រះទីន័ង
preah go ព្រះគោ
preah kaev ព្រះកែវ
preah khan ព្រះខាន
preah lompeng chey ព្រះលំពែងជ័យ
Preah Nang Cam ព្រះនាងចម
Preah Nang Cek ព្រះនាងចេក
preah phang ព្រះផង់
preah sakya moni chedi
ព្រះសក្យមុនីចេតិយ
preah sasana ព្រះសាសនា
preah song snaha cheat ព្រះសង្ឃស្នហាជាតិ
preah vihear ព្រះវិហារ
prei ព្រៃ
pu caḥ añ បុចះអញ
puos muoy saṃkāṃṅ taṃrī
បួសមួយសំកាំងដំរី
puos nag បួសនាគ
puos phloeung បួសភ្លើង

raang prasut រអាងប្រសូត
reacheakhanac រាជាគណះ
rioeng lpaeng រឿងល្បែង
rup រូប
rup arak រូបអារក្ខ

sala សាលា
samdech សម្ដេច
samdech euv សម្ដេចឪ
samdech preah upayuvareach
សម្ដេចព្រះឧបយុវរាជ
samdech song santipeap
សម្ដេចសង្ឃសន្តិភាព
samne សម្មៃ
samrap សំរាប់
samuh-kun សមូហគណ
sanghareach សង្ឃរាជ
sangkum niyum preah puthasasana
សង្គមនិយមព្រះពុទ្ធសាសនា
saray andaet សារាយអន្ដែត
sasana barang សាសនាបារាំង
sasana jiet សាសនាជាតិ
sasana pritikriya សាសនាប្រតិកិរិយា
sa-uy ស្អុយ
sdach kanlong ស្ដេចគំលង់
sdach phloeung ស្ដេចភ្លើង
sdach toeuk ស្ដេចទឹក
sdach trañ ស្ដេចត្រាញ
sdap-kaset ស្ដាប់កាសែត
sgih ស្គឹះ
sloek ស្លឹក
sloek sema ស្លឹកសីមា
smut ស្មុត
sneh ស្នេហ៍
sompeah សំពះ
spaek thom ស្បែកធំ
srah ស្រះ
srap ស្រាពណ៍
srei ស្រែ
sroc toeuk ស្រោចទឹក
srok ស្រុក
sutr rah សូត្ររាស

tāṃṅ tu តាំងតុ
thmar ថ្ម
Thommakay ធម្មកាយ
Thommayut ធម្មយុត្តិ
thor cah ធម៌ចាស់
thor thmei ឃម៌ថ្មី
tnot ត្នោត
tung braling ទង់ព្រលឹង
tung kraham padevat
ទង់ក្រហមបដិវត្តន៍
tuong kaev ដួងកែវ
tuong kaev kamnot ដួងកែវកំណើត

unnalom ឧណ្ណាលោម

vassa វស្សា
vethamon វេទមន្ត
vinaythor-kun វិន័យធរគុណ
viney វិនយ
vissakh boca វិសាខបូជា

vraḥ kamratāṅ añ ព្រះកម្រតេងអញ

yaks យក្ស
yiey chi យាយជី
yogāvacara យោគាវចរ
yomareach យមរាជ

Bibliography

Ablin, David A., and Marlow Hood, eds. 1987. *The Cambodian Agony*. Armonk, NY: M. E. Sharpe.

Alkire, William H. 1972. "Concepts of Order in Southeast Asia and Micronesia." *Comparative Studies in Society and History* 14(4): 484–493.

Allman, T. D. 1982. "Cambodia: Nightmare Journey to a Doubtful Dawn." *Asia* (April): 1–12.

Anderson, Benedict. 1990. *Language and Power: Exploring Political Cultures in Indonesia*. Ithaca, NY: Cornell University Press. Quoted in Evans 1998, 188.

Ang Chouléan. 1980. "Le philtre *sneh:* De la femme humaine a la femme surnaturelle." *Seksa Khmer* 1–2:155–202.

———. 1986. *Les êtres surnaturels dans la religion populaire khmère*. Paris: CEDORECK.

———. 1987–1990. "Le sacré au féminin." *Seksa Khmer* 1013:3–30.

———. 1988. "The Place of Animism within Popular Buddhism in Cambodia: The Example of the Monastery." *Asian Folklore Studies* 47(1): 35–41.

———. 1992. "La triade de l'ensorcellement: Contribution à l'étude de la sorcellerie au Cambodge." *Kambodschanische Kultur* 4:37–49.

———. 1993. "Recherches récentes sur le culte des megaliths et des grottes au Cambodge." *Journal Asiatique* 281(1–2): 185–210.

———. 1997. "Les manuscrits Khmers: Survol thématique." *Kambodschanische Kultur* 5:53–62.

Ang Chouléan and Tan Yinh Phong. 1992. "Le monastère Khemararam: Espace identitaire de la communauté khmère." In *Habitations et habit d'Asie du sud-est continentale: Pratiques et représentations de l'espace,* ed. J. Matras-Guin and C. Taillard, 285–302. Paris: L'Harmattan.

Apter, David E. 1963. "Political Religion in the New Nations." In *Old Societies and New States,* ed. Clifford Geertz, 57–104. Glencoe, IL: Free Press.

Armstrong, John P. 1964. *Sihanouk Speaks: Cambodia's Chief of State Explains His Controversial Policies*. New York: Walker.

Aymonier, Étienne. 1883. "Notes sur les croyances superstitieuses des Cambodgiens." *Excursions et Reconnaissances* 16:133–220.

———. 1891. "Les Tchames et leurs religions." *Revue de l'Histoire des Religions* 24:187–243, 261–315.

———. 1900–1904. *Le Cambodge.* 4 vols. Paris: Ernest Leroux.

Ayres, David M. 2000. *Anatomy of a Crisis: Education, Development, and the State in Cambodia, 1953–1998.* Honolulu: University of Hawai'i Press.

Baccot, Juliette [Françoise Corrèze]. 1968. "On G'nur et Cay à O Russey: Syncrétisme religieux dans un village Cham du Cambodge." Mimeographed MS.

Bagchi, P. C. 1929. "On Some Tāntrik Texts Studied in Ancient Cambodia." *Indian Historical Quarterly* 5:754–769.

———. 1930. "On Some Tāntrik Texts Studied in Ancient Cambodia II." *Indian Historical Quarterly* 6:97–107.

Bareau, André. 1969. "Quelques ermitages et centres de méditation bouddhiques au Cambodge." *BEFEO* 56:11–28.

Barrault, Capitaine. 1927. "Les cambodgiens de cochinchine." *Extrême-Asie,* n.s., 14:67–74, 135–146.

Bauer, Christian. 1989. "Mon Honorifics." In *Linguistics and Worldview: Papers in Honor of Professor Kenneth L. Pike,* ed. Potchanat Samermit and David Thomas. Bangkok: Thammasat University.

Becchetti, Catherine. 1994. "Une ancienne tradition de manuscripts au Cambodge." In Bizot 1994b, 47–62.

Bechert, Heinz. 1998. "Remarks on Buddhist Sanskrit Literature in Sri Lanka from the Ninth Century until the End of the Dambadeniya Period." In *Sūryacandrāya: Essays in Honour of Akira Yuyama on the Occasion of His Sixty-fifth Birthday,* ed. Paul Harrison and Gregory Schopen, 1–8. Swisttal-Odendorf: Indica et Tibetica Verlag.

Becker, Elizabeth. 1979. "Communists Focus on Old Temple: Letter from Angkor Wat." *Guardian,* January 4, 6.

———. 1986. *When the War Was Over: The Voices of Cambodia's Revolution and Its People.* New York: Simon and Schuster.

Bektimirova, Nadezhda. 2002. "The Religious Situation in Cambodia in the 1990s." *Religion, State, and Society* 30(1): 63–72.

Benda, Harry J. 1962. "The Structure of Southeast Asian History: Some Preliminary Observations." *Journal of Southeast Asian History* 3:106–139.

Bernardini, P. 1974. "Le Caodaisme au Cambodge." PhD thesis, Université de Paris VII.

de Bernon, Olivier. 1992. "Le retour de l'École au Cambodge: L'implantation du FEMC." *BEFEO* 79(1): 243–246.

———. 1994. "Le Buddh Daṃnāy: Note sur un texte apocalyptique khmer." *BEFEO* 81:83–100.

———. 1997. "À propos du retour des bakous dans le palais royal de Phnom Penh." In *Renouveaux religieux en Asie,* ed. Catherine Clémentin-Ojha, Études Thématiques 6, 33–58. Paris: EFEO.

———. 1998a. “L’état des bibliothèques dans les monastères du Cambodge.” In Sorn Samnang 1998, 2:872–882.

———. 1998b. “La prédiction du Buddha.” *Aséanie* 1:43–66.

———. 1998c. *Yantra et Mantra*. Phnom Penh: Centre Culturel Français.

———. 1999. “Les inscriptions de la statue équestre du roi Norodom 1er.” *Seksa Khmer*, n.s., 1:96–97.

———. 2000. “Le rituel de la ‘grande probation annuelle’ *(mahāparivāsakamma)* des religieux du Cambodge.” *BEFEO* 87(2): 473–510.

Bertrand, Didier. 1998. “Le role social et thérapeutique des mediums cambodgiens.” In Sorn Samnang 1998, 2:1114–1130.

Bezançon, Pascale. 1992. “La rénovation des écoles de pagode au Cambodge.” *Cahiers de l’Asie du Sud-Est* 31:7–30.

———. 1998. “L’impact de la colonization française sur l’emérgence d’un système éducatif moderne au Cambodge (1863–1945).” In Sorn Samnang 1998, 2:895–910.

Bhattacharya, Kamaleswar. 1955a. “The Pāñcarātra Sect in Ancient Cambodia.” *Journal of the Greater India Society* 14:111–116.

———. 1955b. “Some Aspects of Temple Administration in the Ancient Khmer Kingdom.” *Calcutta Review* 134(2): 193–199.

———. 1961. *Les religions brahmaniques dans l’ancien Cambodge d’après l’épigraphie et l’iconographie*. Paris: EFEO.

———. 1971. “Note sur le Vedanta dans l’inscription de Prè Rup (Cambodge).” *Journal Asiatique* 259:99–101.

Bhi Dhian Lay. 1970. *Kamrang Sujivadharm* (Garland of good manners). Phnom Penh. Quoted in Marston 1997, 90.

Bilodeau, Charles. 1955. “Compulsory Education in Cambodia.” In *Compulsory Education in Cambodia, Laos, and Viet-Nam*, ed. Charles Bilodeau, Somlith Pathammavong, and Lê Quang Hông, 11–67. Paris: UNESCO.

Bizot, François. 1976. *Le figuier à cinq branches: Recherche sur le bouddhisme khmer*. Paris: EFEO.

———. 1980. “La grotte de la naissance.” *BEFEO* 67:221–273. (Recherches sur le bouddhisme khmer 2.)

———. 1981a. *Le don de soi-même*. Recherches sur le bouddhisme khmer 3. Paris: EFEO.

———. 1981b. “Notes sur les *yantra* bouddhiques d’Indochine.” In *Tantric and Taoist Studies in Honour of R. A. Stein*, ed. Michel Strickmann, *Mélanges chinois et bouddhiques* 20, 155–191. Brussels: Institut Belge des Hautes Études Chinoises.

———. 1983. “The Reamker.” In Iyengar 1983, 263–275.

———. 1988a. “Les origins du Theravada de la peninsule.” In *Premier Symposium Franco-Thaï: La Thaïlande dès débuts de son histoire jusqu’au XVe siècle*, 45–57. Bangkok: Silpakorn University.

———. 1988b. *Les traditions de la pabbajjā en Asie du Sud-Est*. Recherches sur le bouddhisme khmer 4. Göttingen: Vandenhoeck and Ruprecht.

———. 1989. *Rāmaker ou l’amour symbolique de Rām et Setā*. Recherches sur le bouddhisme khmer 5. Paris: EFEO.

———. 1992. *Le Chemin de Laṅkā.* Paris, Chiang Mai, and Phnom Penh: EFEO.

———. 1993. *Le bouddhisme des Thaïs: Brève histoire de ses mouvements et de ses idées des origins à nos jours.* Bangkok: Éditions des Cahiers de France.

———. 1994a. "La consecration des statues et la culte des morts." In Bizot 1994b, 101–139.

———, ed. 1994b. *Recherches nouvelles sur le Cambodge.* Paris: EFEO.

———. 2000. *Le portail.* Paris: Table Ronde.

Bizot, François, and Oskar von Hinüber. 1994. *La guirlande de joyaux.* Paris, Chiang Mai, Phnom Penh, and Vientiane: EFEO.

Bizot, François, and François Lagirarde. 1996. *La pureté par les mots.* Paris and Chiang Mai: EFEO.

Blackburn, Anne M. 1999. "Looking for the *Vinaya:* Monastic Discipline in the Practical Canons of the Theravāda." *Journal of the International Association of Buddhist Studies* 22(2): 281–309.

Boeles, J. J. 1966. "Two Yoginīs of Hevajra from Thailand." In *Essays Offered to G. H. Luce by His Colleagues and Friends in Honour of His Seventy-fifth Birthday,* vol. 2, ed. Ba Shin, J. Boisselier, and A. B. Griswold, 14–29. Ascona, Switzerland: Artibus Asiae.

———. 1968. "The Buddhist Tutelary Couple Harītī and Pāñcika Protectors of Children, from a Relief at the Khmer Sanctuary in Pimai." *JSS* 56(2): 187–205.

———. 1969. "A Rāmāyaṇa Relief from the Khmer Sanctuary at Pimai in North-East Thailand." *JSS* 57(1): 163–169.

Boisselier, Jean. 1952–1954. "Beṅ Mālā et la chronologie des monuments du style d'Angkor Vat." *BEFEO* 46(1): 187–226.

———. 1955. *La statuaire khmère et son évolution.* 2 vols. Saigon: EFEO.

———. 1963. *La statuaire du Champa.* Paris: EFEO.

———. 1965. "Précisions sur quelques images khmères d'Avalokiteśvara: Les bas-reliefs de Bantay Chmar." *Arts Asiatiques* 11–12:73–83.

———. 1966. *Le Cambodge.* Vol. 1, *Asie du Sud-Est—sous la direction de G. Cœdès.* Paris: A. and J. Picard.

———. 1967. "Le Buddha de Tuol-Ta-Hoy." *Annales de l'Université Royale des Beaux Arts* (Phnom Penh): 121–137.

———. 1968. "Notes sur l'art du bronze dans l'ancien Cambodge." *Artibus Asiae* 29:275–334.

———. 1970. "Pouvoir royal et symbolisme architectural Neak Pean et son importance pour la royauté Angkorienne." *Arts Asiatiques* 31:91–102.

———. 1991. "Un Buddha de bois préangkorien et ses affinités indonésiennes." *BEFEO* 78:169–178.

Bond, George D. 1996. "A. T. Ariyaratne and the Sarvodaya Shramadana Movement in Sri Lanka." In *Engaged Buddhism: Buddhist Liberation Movements in Asia,* ed. Christopher S. Queen and Sallie B. King, 121–146. Albany: State University of New York Press.

Bonnefoy, Y. 1991. *Mythologies: A Restructured Translation of* Dictionnaire des mythologies et des religions des societés traditionnelles et du monde antique *Prepared un-*

der the Direction of Wendy Doniger. Trans. Gerald Honigsblum et al. 2 vols. Chicago: University of Chicago Press.

Bou Norin, trans. 1957. *Celebration of the 2,500th Anniversary of the Buddha's Parinirvana.* Phnom Penh: Padumavati Rājavārama Pagoda.

Boulbet, J., and B. Dagens. 1973. "Les sites archéologiques de la région du Bhnaṃ Gūlen (Phnom Kulen)." *Arts Asiatiques* 27 (special issue).

Boulbet, Jean. 1970. "Kbal Spean: The Stream of a Thousand Lingas." *Nokor Khmer* (January–March): 2–17.

Boyle, Kevin, and Juliet Sheen, eds. 1997. *Freedom of Religion and Belief: A World Report.* London and New York: Routledge.

Briggs, Lawrence Palmer. 1951. "The Syncretism of Religions in Southeast Asia, Especially the Khmer Empire." *Journal of the American Oriental Society* 71:230–249.

Brocheux, Pierre. 1972. "Vietnamiens et minorités en Cochinchine pendant la période coloniale." *Modern Asian Studies* 6(4): 443–457.

———. 1995. *The Mekong Delta: Ecology, Economy, and Revolution, 1860–1960.* Madison: Center for Southeast Asian Studies, University of Wisconsin—Madison.

Broman, Barry M. 1998. "The Royal Palace of Cambodia." *Arts of Asia* 28:52–60.

Brown, R. L., and N. Eilenburg, eds. 1997. *Living Life according to the Dhamma: Papers in Honour of Professor Jean Boisselier on His Eightieth Birthday.* Bangkok: Silpakorn University.

Bruguier, Bruno. 1998a. "The Cave Temples of Kampot: A Comparative Study." In Klokke and de Bruijn 1998, 193–200.

———. 1998b. "Les vestiges archéologiques du Phnom Trotung." In Sorn Samnang 1998, vol. 1, 475–485.

Brunet, Jacques. 1967. "Le plain-chant bouddhique au Cambodge." *Annales de l'Université Royale des Beaux Arts* (Phnom Penh): 201–206.

Buch, W. J. M. 1937. "La Compagnie des Indes Neerlandaises et l'Indochine." *BEFEO* 37(1): 121–237.

Buddhism and the Development of Khmer Society: Proceedings of the First National Seminar on Buddhism and the Development of Khmer Society, Held in Phnom Penh, 21–23 November 1994. 1996. Anlongvil and Phnom Penh: Buddhism for Development in cooperation with the Ministry of Cults and Religious Affairs.

Bunchan Mul. 1971. *Kuk Niyobay* (Political prison). Phnom Penh.

———. 1982. "The Umbrella War of 1942." In Kiernan and Boua 1982, 114–127.

Bunnag, Teg. 1977. *The Provincial Administration of Siam (1892–1915).* Kuala Lumpur: Oxford University Press.

Cabaton, Antoine. 1906. "Notes sur l'Islam dans l'Indo-chine française." *Revue du Monde Musulman* 5:27–47.

———. 1907. "Les Chams Musulmans de l'Indo-chine Française." *Revue du Monde Musulman* 6:129–180.

———. 1910. "Chams." In *Encyclopedia of Religion and Ethics,* ed. J. Hastings, vol. 3, 340–350.

———. 1971. "Indochina (Islam in)." In *The Encyclopaedia of Islam,* ed. B. Lewis, V. L. Ménage, Ch. Pellat, and J. Schache, new ed., vol. 3, 1208–1212. Leiden: Brill.

Caldwell, Malcolm, and Lek Tan. 1973. *Cambodia in the Southeast Asian War.* New York and London: Monthly Review Press.

Carbonnel, J.-P. 1973. "Le stupa Cambodgien actuel." *Arts Asiatiques* 26:225–242.

Carney, Timothy Michael. 1977. *Communist Party Power in Kampuchea (Cambodia): Documents and Discussion.* Data Paper no. 106. Ithaca, NY: Southeast Asia Program, Cornell University.

Chandler, David P. 1972. "Cambodia's Relations with Siam in the Early Bangkok Period: The Politics of a Tributary State." *JSS* 60(1): 153–169.

———. 1973. "Cambodia before the French: Politics in a Tributary Kingdom, 1794–1848." PhD thesis, University of Michigan, Ann Arbor.

———. 1974. "Royally Sponsored Human Sacrifices in Nineteenth Century Cambodia: The Cult of *nak tā* Me Sa (Mahisāsuramardinī) at Ba Phnom." *JSS* 62(2): 207–222.

———. 1975a. "An Anti-Vietnamese Rebellion in Early Nineteenth Century Cambodia: Pre-colonial Imperialism and a Pre-nationalist Response." *JSEAS* 6(1): 16–24.

———. 1975b. "The Duties of the Corps of Royal Scribes: An Undated Khmer Manuscript from the Colonial Era." *JSS* 63(2): 343–348.

———. 1976a. "Folk Memories of the Decline of Angkor in Nineteenth-Century Cambodia: The Legend of the Leper King." *JSS* 67(1): 54–62.

———. 1976b. "Maps for the Ancestors: Sacralized Topography and Echoes of Angkor in Two Cambodian Texts." *JSS* 64(2): 170–187.

———. 1979. "Cambodian Palace Chronicles *(Rajabangsavatar),* 1927–1949: Kingship and Historiography at the End of the Colonial Era." In *Perceptions of the Past in Southeast Asia,* ed. Anthony Reid and David Marr, 207–217. Kuala Lumpur: Heinemann Educational.

———. 1982a. "The Assassination of Resident Bardez (1925): A Premonition of Revolt in Colonial Cambodia." *JSS* 70(1–2): 35–49.

———. 1982b. "Songs at the Edge of the Forest: Perceptions of Order in Three Cambodian Texts." In *Moral Order and the Question of Change: Essays on Southeast Asian Thought,* ed. David K. Wyatt and Alexander Woodside, Monograph Series no. 24, 53–77. New Haven, CT: Yale University Southeast Asia Series.

———. 1983. "Going through the Motions: Ritual Aspects of the Reign of King Duang of Cambodia (1848–1860)." In *Centers, Symbols, and Hierarchies: Essays on Classical States of Southeast Asia,* ed. Lorraine Gesick, Monograph Series no. 26, 106–124. New Haven, CT: Yale University Southeast Asia Series.

———. 1984. "Normative Poems (Chbap) and Pre-colonial Cambodian Society." *JSEAS* 15(2): 271–279.

———. 1985. "Cambodia in 1984: Historical Patterns Re-asserted?" *Southeast Asian Affairs:* 177–186.

———. 1986. "The Kingdom of Kampuchea, March–October 1945." *JSEAS* 17(1): 80–93.

———. 1990. "Aspects of Cambodian Politics—October 1989." In *Vietnam's Withdrawal from Cambodia: Regional Issues and Realignments*, ed. Gary Klintworth, Canberra Papers on Strategy and Defence no. 64, 55–65. Canberra: Australian National University.

———. 1991. *The Tragedy of Cambodian History: Politics, War, and Revolution since 1945*. New Haven, CT, and London: Yale University Press.

———. 1996. *A History of Cambodia*. 2nd ed., updated. Boulder, CO: Westview.

———. 1999. *Brother Number One: A Political Biography of Pol Pot*. Rev. ed. Boulder, CO: Westview.

———. 2000. *Voices from S-21: Terror and History in Pol Pot's Secret Prison*. Chiang Mai: Silkworm Books.

Chandler, David P., Ben Kiernan, and Chantou Boua, eds. 1988. *Pol Pot Plans the Future: Confidential Leadership Documents from Democratic Kampuchea, 1976–1977*. New Haven, CT: Yale University Southeast Asia Series.

Chantou Boua. 1991. "Genocide of a Religious Group: Pol Pot and Cambodia's Buddhist Monks." In *State-Organized Terror: The Case of Violent Internal Repression*, ed. Bushnell, P. Timothy, Vladimir Shlapentokh, Christopher K. Vanderpool, and Jeyaratnam Sundram, 227–240. Boulder, CO: Westview.

Chau Seng. 1962. *L'organisation bouddhique au Cambodge*. Culture et Civilisation Khmères 4. Phnom Penh: Université Bouddhique de Preah Sihanouk Raj.

———. 1970. "Éducation et développement au Cambodge." PhD diss., Sorbonne, Paris.

Chean Rithy Men. 2002. "The Changing Religious Beliefs and Ritual Practices among Cambodians in Diaspora." *Journal of Refugee Studies* 15(2): 222–233.

Chigas, George. 2000a. "A Draft Translation of the Story of *Tum Teav*, by Preah Botumthera Som." 2 vols. Master's thesis, Cornell University, Ithaca, NY.

———. 2000b. "The Emergence of Twentieth Century Cambodian Literary Institutions: The Case of *Kambujasuriya*." In Smyth 2000, 135–146.

Chirapat Prapandvidya. 1990. "The Sab Bāk Inscription: Evidence of an Early Vajrayana Buddhist Presence in Thailand." *JSS* 78(2): 10–14.

Choan and Sarin. 1970. "Le vénérable chef de la pagode de Tep Pranam." *BEFEO* 57:127–154.

Christian, Pierre. 1952a. "Son Ngoc Thanh." *Indochine Sud-Est Asiatique* (October): 48–49.

———. 1952b. "Le Viet Minh au Cambodge." *Indochine Sud-Est Asiatique* (February–March): 73–77.

Chum Ngoeun. 1996. *Guide to Wat Preah Keo Morokat (The Temple of the Emerald Buddha)*. Phnom Penh: Royal Palace.

Chuon Nath. 1918. *Samaṇa Vinaya*. Phnom Penh: Albert Portail.

———. 1938. *Vacanānukram Khmaer* (Khmer dictionary). Phnom Penh: Buddhist Institute.

Chuon Nath Jotañāno, Samdech Preah Mahāsumedhādhipatī. 1976. "The Governing of the Buddhist Order in Cambodia." *Visakha Puja* 2519 (May 13): 40–47.

Clayton, Thomas. 1995. "Restriction or Resistance? French Colonial Educational Development in Cambodia." *Education Policy Analysis Archives* 3(19) (December 1). http://epaa.asu.edu/epaa/v3n19.html.

Cœdès, G. 1908. "Les inscriptions de Bàt Čuṃ (Cambodge)." *Journal Asiatique* 12:213–254.

———. 1911. "La légende de la Nāgī. *BEFEO* 11(3–4): 391–393.

———. 1913a. "La fondation de Phnom-Penh au XVe siècle d'après la chronique cambodgienne." *BEFEO* 13(6): 6–11.

———. 1913b. "Note sur l'iconographie de Beṅ Mālā." *BEFEO* 13(1): 23–26.

———. 1915. "Notes sur les ouvrages pālis composés en pays thaï." *BEFEO* 15(3): 39–46.

———. 1918. "Essai de classification des documents historiques Cambodgiens conservé à la Bibliothèque de l'École française d'Extrême-Orient." *BEFEO* 18(9): 15–28.

———. 1931. "Deux inscriptions sanskrites du Fou-Nan." *BEFEO* 31(1–2): 1–12.

———. 1936. "La plus ancienne inscription en Pāli du Cambodge." *BEFEO* 36(1): 14–21.

———. 1938. "Review of *Vacanānukrama khmer* (Dictionnaire cambodgien, Tome I. K-M. 9,641 articles, Première Édition. Phnom Penh, Editions de la Bibliothèque Royale du Cambodge, 1938)." *BEFEO* 38(2): 314–321.

———. 1952. "Un *yantra* récemment découvert à Angkor." *Journal Asiatique* 240(4): 465–477.

———. 1964. "Some Problems in the Ancient History of the Hinduized States of South East Asia." *Journal of Southeast Asian History* 5:1–14.

———. 1966. *Inscriptions du Cambodge.* Vol. 8. Paris: EFEO.

———. 1968a. *The Indianized States of Southeast Asia.* Trans. Sue Brown Cowing. Honolulu: University of Hawai'i Press.

———. 1968b. "Une vie indochinoise du Bouddha: La Pathamasambodhi." In *Mélanges d'Indianisme à la mémoire de Louis Renou,* 217–227. Paris: E. de Boccard.

Collard, P. 1925. *Cambodge et Cambodgiens.* Paris: Société d'Éditions Géographiques, Maritimes, et Coloniales.

Collins, Steven. 1998. *Nirvana and Other Buddhist Felicities: Utopias of the Pali Imaginaire.* Cambridge: Cambridge University Press.

Collins, William. 1998a. "Grassroots Civil Society in Cambodia." Unpublished report. Phnom Penh: Center for Advanced Study.

———. 1998b. "Variation in Khmer Islam." In Sorn Samnang 1998, 2:1096–1113.

Commission des Mœurs et Coutumes du Cambodge. n.d. *Cérémonies des douze mois.* Phnom Penh.

Communist Party of Kampuchea Central Committee. 1976. "Sharpen the Consciousness of the Proletarian Class to Be as Keen and Strong as Possible." *Revolutionary Flags (Dung Pativatt)* (special issue, September–October): 33–97; trans. Kem Sos and Timothy Carney in Karl Jackson 1989, 269–291.

———. 1978. "Pay Attention to Pushing the Work of Building Party and People's Cooperative Strength to Be Even Stronger." *Revolutionary Flags (Dung Pativatt)* 3 (March): 37–53; trans. Kem Sos and Timothy Carney in Karl Jackson 1989, 293–298.

Condominas, Georges. 1975. "*Phībān* Cults in Rural Laos." In *Change and Persistence in Thai Society: Essays in Honor of Lauriston Sharp*, ed. G. William Skinner and A. Thomas Kirsch, 252–273. Ithaca, NY, and London: Cornell University Press.

de Coral-Rémusat, G. 1951. *L'Art khmer: Les grandes étapes de son évolution*. Paris: Vanoest.

Corfield, Justin. 1991. *A History of the Cambodian Non-Communist Resistance 1975–1983*. Working Paper 72. Clayton, Victoria, Australia: Centre for Southeast Asian Studies, Monash University.

———. 1994. *Khmers Stand Up! A History of the Cambodian Government 1970–1975*. Clayton, Victoria, Australia: Centre for Southeast Asian Studies, Monash University.

Coulet, Georges. 1928. "Bonzes, pagodes, et sociétés secrètes en Cochinchine." *Extrême-Asie* 25 (June): 7–13.

Cousins, L. S. 1997. "Aspects of Esoteric Southern Buddhism." In *Indian Insights: Buddhism, Brahmanism, and Bhakti*, ed. Peter Connolly and Sue Hamilton, 185–207. London: Luzac Oriental.

Crosby, Kate. 2000. "Tantric Theravāda: A Bibliographical Essay on the Writings of François Bizot and Others on the Yogāvacara Tradition." *Contemporary Buddhism* 1(2): 141–198.

Dagens, Bruno. 1988. "Autour de l'iconographie de Phimai." In *Premier Symposium Franco-Thaï: La Thaïlande dès débuts de son histoire jusqu'au XVe siècle*, 17–32. Bangkok: Silpakorn University.

Dalet, R. 1936. "Essai sur les pagodes cambodgiennes et leurs annexes." *La Géographie* 7 (February): 135–153; (March): 212–223; (April): 222–247.

Dalet, Robert. 1934. "Le Phnom-Santuk." *Extrême-Asie* 88 (July): 789–799.

Danois, Jacques. 1980. "La force du pardon." *Sudestasie* 7:72–75.

Delvert, Jean. 1956. "L'oeuvre française d'enseignement au Cambodge." *France-Asie* 13(1): 25–27, 309–320.

Descours-Gatin, Chantal. 1992. *Quand l'opium finançait la colonisation en Indochine: L'élaboration de la régie generale de l'opium (1860 à 1914)*. Paris: L'Harmattan.

DeVoss, David. 1980. "Buddhism under the Red Flag." *Time*, November 17, 62–63.

Dhaninivat Kromamun Bidyalabh Bridhyakorn, H. H. Prince. 1963. *The Royal Palaces*. Bangkok: Fine Arts Department.

Dinh Van Lien and Thach Loi. 1990. "Outline of the Khmers in the Mekong Delta." *Vietnamese Studies* 27(3): 7–30.

Dolias, Jacques. 1990. "Visvakarman: Un exemple d'adaptation des mythes indiens en pays khmer." *Cahiers de l'Asie du Sud-Est* 28:109–146.

Dossier Kampuchea. 1978. Hanoi: Le Courrier de Vietnam.

Dowling, Nancy. 1999. "A New Date for the Phnom Da Images and Its Implications for Early Cambodia." *Asian Perspectives* 38(1): 51–61.

Dumarçay, Jacques. 1991. *The Palaces of South-east Asia: Architecture and Customs*. Trans. and ed. Michael Smithies. Singapore: Oxford University Press.

Dumoulin, Heinrich, and John C. Maraldo, eds. 1976. *Buddhism in the Modern World*. New York: Collier Books.

Dupaigne, Bernard, and Khing Hoc Dy. 1981. "Les plus anciennes peintures datées du Cambodge: Quatorze episodes du Vessantara Jâtaka." *Arts Asiatiques* 36:26–36.

Dupont, Pierre. 1935. "Art de Dvāravatī et art khmèr: Les buddhas debout de l'époque du Bàyon." *Revue des Arts Asiatiques* 9(2): 63–75.

———. 1955. *La statuaire préangkorienne.* Artibus Asiae Supplementum 15. Ascona, Switzerland: Artibus Asiae.

———. 1959. *Archéologie mône de Dvāravatī.* Paris: EFEO.

Durand, R. P. 1903. "Les Chams Bani." *BEFEO* 3(1): 54–62.

Duroiselle, Charles. 1921–1922. "Wathundaye, the Earth-Goddess of Burma." *Annual Report, Archaeological Survey of India:* 144–146.

Ebihara, May. 1966. "Interrelations between Buddhism and Social Systems in Cambodian Peasant Culture." In *Anthropological Studies in Theravada Buddhism,* ed. Manning Nash, Cultural Report Series no. 13, 175–196. New Haven, CT: Yale University Southeast Asia Series.

———. 1968. "Svay: A Khmer Village in Cambodia." PhD diss., Columbia University, New York.

———. 1974. "Khmer Village Women in Cambodia: A Happy Balance." In *Many Sisters: Women in Cross-Cultural Perspective,* ed. Carolyn J. Matthiason, 305–347. New York: Free Press.

———. 1984. "Societal Organisation in Sixteenth and Seventeenth Century Cambodia." *JSEAS* 15(2): 280–295.

———. 1990. "Return to a Khmer Village." *Cultural Survival Quarterly* 14(3): 67–70.

———. 1993. "'Beyond Suffering': The Recent History of a Cambodian Village." In *The Challenge of Reform in Indochina,* ed. Börje Ljunggren, 149–166. Cambridge, MA: Harvard Institute for International Development.

———. 2002. "Memories of the Pol Pot Era in a Cambodian Village." In *Cambodia Emerges from the Past: Eight Essays,* ed. Judy Ledgerwood, 91–108. De Kalb: Center for Southeast Asian Studies, Northern Illinois University.

Ebihara, May, Judy Ledgerwood, and Carol Mortland, eds. 1994. *Cambodian Culture since 1975: Homeland and Exile.* Ithaca, NY: Cornell University Press.

Edwards, Penny. 1996. "Imaging the Other in Cambodian Nationalist Discourse before and during the UNTAC Period." In *Propaganda, Politics, and Violence in Cambodia: Democratic Transition under United Nations Peace-Keeping,* ed. Steven Heder and Judy Ledgerwood, 50–72. Armonk, NY: M. E. Sharpe.

———. 1999. "Cambodge: The Cultivation of a Nation, 1860–1945." PhD thesis, Monash University, Clayton, Victoria, Australia.

Eisenbruch, Maurice. 1992. "The Ritual Space of Patients and Traditional Healers in Cambodia." *BEFEO* 79(2): 283–316.

"Élection du chef religieux des musulmans du Cambodge." *Études Cambodgiennes* 4 (October–December): 13.

Ellul, Jean. 1980. "Le mythe de Ganeśa: Le Ganeśa cambodgien, un mythe d'origine de la magie." *Seksa Khmer* 1–2:69–153.

Engelbert, Thomas, and Christopher E. Goscha. 1995. *Falling Out of Touch: A Study on*

Vietnamese Communist Policy towards an Emerging Cambodian Communist Movement, 1930–1975. Monash Papers on Southeast Asia no. 35. Clayton, Victoria, Australia: Monash Asia Institute.

Etcheson, Craig. 1984. *The Rise and Demise of Democratic Kampuchea*. Boulder, CO: Westview; New York: Pinter.

Étudiants de la Faculté Royale d'Archéologie de Phnom Penh. 1969. "Le monastère bouddhique de Tep Pranam à Oudong." *BEFEO* 56:29–56.

Evans, Grant. 1990. *Lao Peasants under Socialism*. New Haven, CT, and London: Yale University Press.

———. 1993. "Buddhism and Economic Action in Socialist Laos." In *Socialism: Ideals, Ideologies, and Local Practice*, ed. C. M. Hann, 132–147. ASA Monographs no. 31. London and New York: Routledge.

———. 1998. *The Politics of Ritual and Remembrance: Laos since 1975*. Honolulu: University of Hawai'i Press.

Fabrice, René. 1932. "Une grande fête religieuse à Angkor." *Extrême-Asie* 63 (April): 503–508.

Fergusson, Lee C., and Gildas Le Masson. 1997. "A Culture under Siege: Post-colonial Higher Education and Teacher Education in Cambodia from 1953 to 1979." *History of Education* 26(1): 91–112.

de la Ferrière, Jacques. 1952. "Où est la grande paix du Bouddha?" *Indochine Sud-Est Asiatique* (December): 35–41.

Fillieux, Claude. 1962. *Merveilleux Cambodge*. Paris: Société Continentale d'Éditions Modernes Illustrées.

Filliozat, Jacqueline. 2000. "Pour mémoire d'un patrimonie sacré: Les manuscripts pāli du Cambodge à l'École française d'Extrême-Orient." *BEFEO* 87(2): 445–471.

Filliozat, Jean. 1954. "Le symbolisme du monument du Phnom Bakheng." *BEFEO* 44(2): 527–554.

———. 1969. "Emigration of Indian Buddhists to Indo-China c. AD 1200." In *Studies in Asian History*, ed. K. S. Lal, 45–48. London: Indian Council for Cultural Relations/ Asia Publishing House.

———. 1972. "Introduction." In *Textes sanskrits et Tamouls de Thaïlande*, ed. Neelakanta Sarma, vii–xi. Pondicherry, India: Institut Français d'Indologie.

———. 1981. "Sur le çivaïsme et le bouddhisme du Cambodge: À propos de deux livres récents." *BEFEO* 70:59–99.

———. 1983. "The Rāmāyaṇa in South-east Asian Sanskrit Epigraphy and Iconography." In Iyengar 1983, 192–205.

Finot, Louis. 1917. "Recherches sur la littérature laotienne." *BEFEO* 17(5): 1–218.

———. 1927. "Mahā Vimaladhamma." *BEFEO* 27:523.

———. 1929. *Le Bouddhisme, son origine, son evolution*. Trans. into Khmer by Choum Mau. Phnom Penh.

Flaugergues, E. 1914a. "La crémation du chef suprême des bonzes." *Revue Indochinoise*, n.s., 21:481–490.

———. 1914b. "La fête de Hèkathoen à la pagode Vat Lanka." *Revue Indochinoise*, n.s., 21:315–318.

———. 1914c. "La mort du chef suprême des bonzes." *Revue Indochinoise* 21:175–182.

Forest, Alain. 1980. *Le Cambodge et la colonisation Française: Histoire d'une colonisation sans heurts (1897–1920)*. Paris: L'Harmattan.

———. 1982. "Notes sur la royaute dechirée: À propos de quelques ouvrages recents sur le Cambodge." *ASEMI* 13(1–4): 59–80.

———. 1992. *Le culte des génies protecteurs au Cambodge: Analyse et traduction d'un corpus de textes sur les neak ta*. Paris: L'Harmattan.

Fouser, Beth. 1996. *The Lord of the Golden Tower: King Prasat Thong and the Building of Wat Chaiwatthanaram*. Bangkok: White Lotus.

Freeman, Michael. 1997. *Phimai*. Bangkok: River Books.

Frieson, Kate. 1990. "The Pol Pot Legacy in Village Life." *Cultural Survival Quarterly* 14(3): 71–73.

Frings, K. Viviane. 1994a. *Allied and Equal: The Kampuchean People's Revolutionary Party's Historiography and Its Relations with Vietnam (1979–1991)*. Working Paper no. 90. Clayton, Victoria, Australia: Centre for Southeast Asian Studies, Monash University.

———. 1994b. "The Cambodian People's Party and Sihanouk." *Journal of Contemporary Asia* 25(3): 356–365.

———. 1997. "Rewriting Cambodian History to 'Adapt' It to a New Political Context: The Kampuchean People's Revolutionary Party's Historiography (1979–1991)." *Modern Asian Studies* 31(4): 807–846.

Gaillard, Maurice. 1994. *Democratie Cambodgienne: La Constitution du 24 septembre 1993*. Paris: L'Harmattan.

Gaudes, Rüdiger. 1993. "Kauṇḍinya, Preah Thong, and the 'Nāgī Somā': Some Aspects of a Cambodian Legend." *Asian Folklore Studies* 52:333–358.

Girard-Geslan, Maud, Marijke J. Klokke, Albert Le Bonheur, Donald M. Sleadner, Valérie Zaleski, and Thierry Zéphir. 1997. *Art of Southeast Asia*. New York: Harry N. Abrams.

Girling, J. L. S. 1971. *Cambodia and the Sihanouk Myths*. Occasional Paper no. 7. Singapore: Institute of Southeast Asian Studies.

Giteau, Madeleine. 1966. "Les peintures du monastère de Kompong Tralach." *Études Cambodgiennes* 5 (January–March): 34–38.

———. 1967. "Note sur les frontons du sanctuaire central du Vatt Nagar." *Arts Asiatiques* 16:125–137.

———. 1969a. "À propos d'un episode du Rāmakertī représenté à Vatt Pūbī (Siem Reap)." *Arts Asiatiques* 19:107–121.

———. 1969b. *Le bornage rituel des temples bouddhiques au Cambodge*. Paris: EFEO.

———. 1971a. "Un court traité d'architecture cambodgienne moderne." *Arts Asiatiques* 24:103–139.

———. 1971b. "Note sur quelques pieces en bronze récemment découvertes a Vatt Deb Pranamy d'Oudong (Utun)." *Arts Asiatiques* 24:149–157.

———. 1975. *Iconographie du Cambodge post-Angkorien.* Paris: EFEO.

———. 1995. "Note sur Kumbhakarṇa dans l'iconographie khmère." *Arts Asiatiques* 50:69–75.

———. 1997. "Les represéntations du *Rāmakerti* dans les reliefs modelés de la région de Battambang (Cambodge)." In Brown and Eilenburg 1997, 229–243.

Glaize, Maurice. 1940. "Le gopura de Prah Palilai." *BEFEO* 40:363–370.

The Glass Palace Chronicle of the Kings of Burma. 1960. Trans. Pe Maung Tin and G. H. Luce. Rangoon: Burma Research Society.

Goloubew, Victor. 1925. "Mélanges sur le Cambodge ancien II. Une idole khmère de Lokeçvara au Musée de Colombo." *BEFEO* 24(3–4): 510–512.

———. 1927. "Le Cheval Balāha." *BEFEO* 27:223–237.

———. 1936. "Sylvain Lévi et l'Indochine." *BEFEO* 35(2): 551–574.

Gosling, Betty. 1991. *Sukhothai: Its History, Culture, and Art.* Singapore: Oxford University Press.

Gouvernement-Général de l'Indochine, Direction des Affaires Politiques et de La Sûreté Générale. 1933. *Contribution à l'histoire des mouvements politiques de l'Indochine Française.* Vol. 7, *Le Caodaisme.* Hanoi.

Groslier, Bernard-Philippe. 1958. *Angkor et le Cambodge au XVIe siècle d'après les sources portugaises et espagnoles.* Paris: Presses Universitaires de France.

———. 1962. *Indochina: Art in the Melting Pot of Races.* London: Methuen.

———. 1974. "Agriculture et religion dans l'empire angkorien." *Études Rurales* 53–56:95–117.

———. 1985–1986a. "For a Geographic History of Cambodia." *Seksa Khmer* 8–9:31–76.

———. 1985–1986b. "L'image d'Angkor dans la conscience khmère." *Seksa Khmer* 8–9:5–30.

Groslier, Georges. 1921. *Recherches sur les cambodgiens d'aprés les textes et les monuments depuis les premiers siècles de notre ère.* Paris: Augustin Challamel.

Guennou, J. 1967. "Cambodia." In *New Catholic Encyclopedia,* vol. 2, 1097–1098. New York: McGraw-Hill.

Guthrie-Highbee, Elizabeth. 1992. "Khmer Buddhism in New Zealand." Master's thesis, University of Otago, Dunedin, New Zealand.

Gyallay-Pap, Peter. 1989. "Reclaiming a Shattered Past: Education for the Displaced Khmer in Thailand." *Journal of Refugee Studies* 2(2): 257–275.

———. 1996. "Buddhism as a Factor of Culture and Development in Cambodia." *Cambodia Report* (special issue on Buddhism in Cambodia) 2(2): 8–13.

Gyallay-Pap, Peter, and Ruth Bottomley, eds. 1998. *Toward an Environmental Ethic in Southeast Asia.* Phnom Penh: Buddhist Institute.

Gyallay-Pap, Peter, and Michel Tranet. 1990. "Notes on the Rebirth of Khmer Buddhism." In *Radical Conservatism: Buddhism in the Contemporary World—Articles in Honour of Bhikkhu Buddhadasa's Eighty-fourth Birthday Anniversary,* 360–369. Bangkok: Thai Inter-Religious Commission for Development/INEB.

Hansen, Anne, R. 1988. "Crossing the River: The Secularization of the Khmer Religious Worldview." Master of divinity thesis, Harvard Divinity School, Cambridge, MA.

———. 1999. "Ways of the World: Moral Discernment and Narrative Ethics in a Cambodian Buddhist Text." PhD thesis, Harvard University, Cambridge, MA.

Harris, Ian. 1999a. "Buddhism *in Extremis:* The Case of Cambodia." In Harris 1999c, 54–78.

———. 1999b. "Buddhism and Politics in Asia: The Textual and Historical Roots." In Harris 1999c, 1–25.

———. 1999c. *Buddhism and Politics in Twentieth-Century Asia.* London and New York: Pinter.

———. 2000a. "Buddhism and Ecology." In *Contemporary Buddhist Ethics,* ed. Damien Keown, 113–135. Richmond, UK: Curzon.

———. 2000b. "Magician as Environmentalist: Fertility Elements in South and Southeast Asian Buddhism." *Eastern Buddhist* (Kyoto) 32(2): 128–156.

Hawixbrock, Christine. 1998. "Jayavarman VII ou le renouveau d'Angkor, entre tradition et modernité." *BEFEO* 85:63–85.

Hean Sokhom. 1996. "Notes on the Revival of Monk Education." *Cambodia Report* (special issue on Buddhism in Cambodia) 2(2): 14–16.

Heder, Stephen. 1979a. "The Kampuchean-Vietnamese Conflict." *Southeast Asian Affairs* 6:157–186.

———. 1979b. "Kampuchea's Armed Struggle: The Origins of an Independent Revolution." *Bulletin of Concerned Asian Scholars* 11(1): 2–24.

———. 1980. *Kampuchean Occupation and Resistance.* Bangkok: Institute of Asian Studies, Chulalongkorn University.

———. 1991. *Reflections on Cambodian Political History: Backgrounder to Recent Developments.* Working Paper no. 239. Canberra: Strategic and Defence Studies Centre, Australian National University.

———. 1995. "Cambodia's Democratic Transition to Neoauthoritarianism." *Current History* 94(596): 425–429.

———. 1997. "Racism, Marxism, Labelling, and Genocide in Ben Kiernan's *The Pol Pot Regime.*" *South East Asia Research* 5(2): 101–153.

Hickey, Gerald Cannon. 1982a. *Free in the Forest: Ethnohistory of the Vietnamese Central Highlands, 1954–1976.* New Haven, CT, and London: Yale University Press.

———. 1982b. *Sons of the Mountain: Ethnohistory of the Vietnamese Central Highlands to 1954.* New Haven, CT, and London: Yale University Press.

Hinton, Alexander Laban. 1997. "Cambodia's Shadow: An Examination of the Cultural Origins of Genocide." PhD thesis, Emory University, Atlanta.

———. 1998. "Why Did You Kill? The Cambodian Genocide and the Dark Side of Face and Honor." *Journal of Asian Studies* 57(1): 93–122.

———. 2002. "Purity and Contamination in the Cambodian Genocide." In *Cambodia Emerges from the Past: Eight Essays,* ed. Judy Ledgerwood, 60–90. De Kalb: Center for Southeast Asian Studies, Northern Illinois University.

von Hinüber, Oskar. 1996. *A Handbook of Pāli Literature.* Berlin and New York: de Gruyter.

Hok Sovann 1983. *Taṃnoḥsrāy Buddhasāsanā* (Buddhist solution). Montreal: Vat Kanata.

Holt, Clifford. 1991. *Buddha in the Crown: Avalokiteśvara in the Buddhist Tradition of Sri Lanka*. New York: Oxford University Press.

Houtman, Gustaaf. 1999. *Mental Culture in Burmese Crisis Politics: Aung San Suu Kyi and the National League for Democracy*. Tokyo: Institute for the Study of Languages and Cultures of Asia and Africa.

Htin Aung, Maung. 1962. *Folk Elements in Burmese Buddhism*. London: Oxford University Press.

Huber, Edouard. 1905. "Le jardinier régicide qui devint roi." *BEFEO* 5(1–2): 176–184.

Hughes, Caroline. 2000. "Cambodian Mystics and Militants: Contending Approaches to Democratic Reform." Paper presented at the Association for Asian Studies Annual Meeting, San Diego, March 11.

Huot Tath. 1929. "Tourné d'inspection dans les pagodes cambodgiennes de Sud-oeust de la Cochinchine." *Kambuja Surya* (Cambodian sun) 2:39–62.

———. 1951. *Sīmāvinicchayasaṅkhepa* (Summary of opinions on the *sīmā*). Phnom Penh: Palais Royal.

———. 1962. *L'Enseignement du bouddhisme des origines à nos jours*. Culture et civilisations khmères no. 1. Phnom Penh: Université Bouddhique de Preah Sihanouk Raj.

———. 1966. *Sattaparitta—Dvadasaparitta*. Phnom Penh: Institut Bouddhique.

———. 1970. *Kalyānamitt roboh kñom* (My intimate friend). Phnom Penh: Institut Bouddhique.

Huxley, Andrew. 1991. "Sanction in the Theravada Buddhist Kingdoms of S. E. Asia." *Receuils de la société Jean Bodin* 58:335–370.

Huxley, Tim. 1987. "Cambodia in 1986: The PRK's Eighth Year." *Southeast Asian Affairs* 14:161–173.

I Tsing: A Record of the Buddhist Religion as Practiced in the Indian and the Malay Archipelago (AD 671–695). 1896/1982. Trans. J. Takakusu. Repr. New Delhi: Munshiram Manoharlal.

Ilangasinha, H. B. M. 1998. "Some Aspects of Relations between Sri Lanka and Cambodia." In Sorn Samnang 1998, 1:186–198.

Ith Sarin. 1973. *Sranach Pralung Khmer* (Regrets for the Khmer soul). Phnom Penh.

Iv Tuot, Ven. 1930. "Historique de la pagode de Povéal (Battambang)" [in Khmer]. *Kambuja Surya* (Cambodian sun) 3(9): 99–100.

———. 1931. *Historique de la pagode de Povéal, Khum de Wat Sangker (Battambang)* [in Khmer]. Phnom Penh.

Iyengar, K. R. Srinivasa, ed. 1983. *Asian Variations in Ramayana*. Delhi: Sahitya Akademi.

Jackson, Karl D., ed. 1989. *Cambodia, 1975–1978: Rendezvous with Death*. Princeton, NJ: Princeton University Press.

Jackson, Peter A. 1989. *Buddhism, Legitimation, and Conflict: The Political Functions of Urban Thai Buddhism*. Singapore: Institute of Southeast Asian Studies.

———. 1991. "Thai-Buddhist Identity: Debates on the *Traiphum Phra Ruang*." In Reynolds 1991, 191–232.

Jacob, Judith M. 1979. "Pre-Angkor Cambodian: Evidence from the Inscriptions in Khmer concerning the Common People and Their Environment." In R. Smith and Watson 1979, 406–426.

———. 1982. "The Short Stories of Cambodian Popular Tradition." In *The Short Story in South East Asia: Aspects of a Genre*, ed. J. H. C. S. Davidson and H. Cordell, 37–61. London: School of Oriental and African Studies.

———. 1986a. "The Deliberate Use of Foreign Vocabulary by the Khmer: Changing Fashions, Methods, and Sources." In *Context, Meaning, and Power in Southeast Asia*, ed. Mark Hobart and Robert H. Taylor, 115–129. Ithaca, NY: Cornell University Studies on Southeast Asia.

———, trans. (with the assistance of Kuoch Haksrea). 1986b. *Reamker (Rāmakerti): The Cambodian Version of the Rāmāyaṇa*. Oriental Translation Fund, n.s., vol. 45. London: Royal Asiatic Society.

———. 1993a. "The Ecology of Angkor: Evidence from the Khmer Inscriptions." In Smyth 1993, 280–298.

———. 1993b. "Pre-Angkor Cambodia: Evidence from the Inscriptions in Khmer concerning the Common People and Their Environment." In Smyth 1993, 299–318.

Jacq-Hergoualc'h. 1982. *Le roman source d'inspiration de la peinture khmère à la fin du XIXe et au début du XXe siècle: L'histoire de Preah Chinavong et son illustration dans la (sala) de Vat Kieng Svay Krau*. 2 vols. Paris: EFEO.

———. 1988. "La peinture khmère." *Dossiers Histoire et Archéologie* 125 (March): 54–57.

Jacques, Claude. 1970. "The Inscriptions of Cambodia." *Nokor Khmer* (January–March): 18–25.

———. 1975. "À propos de l'esclavage dans l'ancien Cambodge." In *Le XXIXe Congrès international des orientalistes, Paris, juillet 1973*, 71–76. Paris: L'Asiathèque.

———. 1979. "'Funan,' 'Zhenla': The Reality Concealed by These Chinese Views of Indochina." In R. Smith and Watson 1979, 371–379.

———. 1982. "Nouvelles orientations pour l'étude de l'histoire du pays khmer." *ASEMI* 13(1–4): 39–58.

———. 1985. "The Kamrateṅ Jagat in Ancient Cambodia." In *Indus Valley to Mekong: Explorations in Epigraphy*, ed. Noboru Karashima, 269–286. Madras: New Era.

———. 1990. *Angkor*. Paris: Bordas.

———. 1999. "Les inscriptions du Phnom Kbal Span (K 1011, 1012, 1015, et 1016)—Études d'épigraphie cambodgienne—XI." *BEFEO* 86:357–374.

Jaini, Padmanabh S. 1965. "*Mahādibbamanta*: A *Paritta* Manuscript from Cambodia." *BSOAS* 25:61–80.

———. 1986. *Lokaneyyappakaraṇam*. London: Pali Text Society.

Jeldres, Julio A., and Somkid Chaijitvanit. 1999. *The Royal Palace of Phnom Penh and Cambodian Royal Life*. Bangkok: Post Books.

Jennar, Raoul M. 1995a. *The Cambodian Constitutions (1953–1993)*. Bangkok: White Lotus.

———. 1995b. *Les clés du Cambodge*. Paris: Maisonneuve et Larose.

Kalab, Milada. 1968. "Study of a Cambodian Village." *Geographical Journal* 134:521–537.

———. 1976. "Monastic Education, Social Mobility, and Village Structure in Cambodia." In *Changing Identities in Modern Southeast Asia*, ed. David J. Banks, 155–169. The Hague: Mouton.

———. 1990. "Buddhism and Emotional Support for Elderly People." *Journal of Cross-Cultural Gerontology* 5:7–19.

———. 1994. "Cambodian Buddhist Monasteries in Paris: Continuing Tradition and Changing Patterns." In Ebihara et al. 1994, 57–71.

Keiko Miura. 2000. "Social Anthropological Research on 'The People of Angkor Living with a World Heritage Site.'" *Siksācakr* 2 (October): 15–19.

Keng Vannsak. 1966. *Principes de Crèation des Mots Nouveaux.* Phnom Penh: Faculté des Lettres et des Sciences Humaines.

Keo-Han. 1951. "Les Étrangers dans le Cambodge." Document no. 89004, May 10, Commission des Moeurs et Coutumes. Phnom Penh: Institut Bouddhique. Quoted in Hickey 1982b, 140n35.

Kern, H. 1906. "Sur l'invocation d'une inscription bouddhique de Battambang." *Muséon*, n.s., 7:46–66.

Keston College staff members. 1988. "Religion in Kampuchea." *Religion in Communist Lands* 16:169–170.

———. 1989. "Buddhism Becomes the Cambodian State Religion." *Religion in Communist Lands* 17:337–339.

Keyes, Charles F. 1991a. "The Case of the Purloined Lintel: The Politics of a Khmer Shrine as a Thai National Treasure." In Reynolds 1991, 261–292.

———. 1991b. "The Proposed World of the School: Thai Villagers' Entry into a Bureaucratic State System." In *Reshaping Local Worlds: Formal Education and Cultural Change in Rural Southeast Asia*, ed. C. F. Keyes, Monograph no. 36, 89–130. New Haven, CT: Yale Southeast Asian Studies.

———. 1994a. "Buddhism and Revolution in Cambodia." *Cultural Survival Quarterly* 14(3): 60–63.

———. 1994b. "Communist Revolution and the Buddhist Past in Cambodia." In *Asian Visions of Authority: Religion and the Modern States of East and Southeast Asia*, ed. Charles F. Keyes, Laurel Kendall, and Helen Hardacre, 43–73. Honolulu: University of Hawai'i Press.

Khieu Chum. 1971. *Buddhasasana prajadhipateyy sadharanarath* (Buddhism, democracy, republic). Phnom Penh: Punloeu Cheat.

———. 1972. *Prajadhipateyy cas dum* (Ancient democracy). Phnom Penh: Punloeu Cheat.

Khim Tit. 1969. *Qu'est-ce que le bouddhisme?* Phnom Penh: Institut Bouddhique.

Khin Sok. 1982. "Essai d'interpretation de formules magiques des cambodgiens." *ASEMI* 13(1–4): 111–119.

———. 1988. *Chroniques royales du Cambodge de Bañā Yāt à la prise de Laṅvaek (de 1417 à 1595)*. Paris: EFEO.

Khing Hoc Dy. 1976. "L'oeuvre littéraire de Nan, auteur cambodgien de la fin du XVIIIe et du début du XIXe siècle." *ASEMI* 7:91–99.

———. 1977. "Quelques traits bouddhiques dans *Bhogakulakumar*, roman cambodgien en vers du début du XIXe siècle." *Cahiers de l'Asie du Sud-Est* 1:59–77.

———. 1981. "Santhor Mok: poète et chroniqueur du XXe siècle." *Seksa Khmer* 3–4:137–160.

———. 1985. "Oknha Sutan Preichea In (1859–1924)." In *Hommes et Destins*, vol. 6, *Asie*, 194. Paris: Académie des Sciences d'Outre-Mer.

———. 1990. *Contribution à l'histoire de la littérature khmère.* 2 vols. Paris: L'Harmattan.

———. 1994. "Khmer Literature since 1975." In Ebihara et al. 1994, 27–38.

Khmer Buddhist Society in Cambodia. n.d. "Project Rights: Training Curriculum of Human Rights and Buddhism for Buddhist Monks and Civil Servants." Phnom Penh.

Khun Ken. 1994. *De la dictature des Khmers Rouges à l'occupation vietnamienne, Cambodge 1975–1979*. Paris: L'Harmattan.

Khy Phanra. 1975. "Les Origines du Caodaisme au Cambodge (1926–1940)." *Mondes Asiatiques* 3:315–348.

———. 1977. "L'immigration vietnamienne au Cambodge à l'époque du protectorat français (1863–1940)." *Cahiers de l'Asie du Sud-Est* 2:45–58.

Kiernan, Ben. 1975. *The Samlaut Rebellion and Its Aftermath, 1967–70: The Origins of Cambodia's Liberation Movement.* Clayton, Victoria, Australia: Centre for Southeast Asian Studies, Monash University.

———. 1976. "Social Cohesion in Revolutionary Cambodia." *Australian Outlook* 30(3): 371–386.

———. 1980. "New Light on the Origins of the Vietnam-Kampuchea Conflict." *Bulletin of Concerned Asian Scholars* 12(4): 61–65.

———. 1981. "Origins of Khmer Communism." *Southeast Asian Affairs* 8:161–180.

———. 1982. "Kampuchea 1971–81: National Rehabilitation in the Eye of an International Storm." *Southeast Asian Affairs* 9:167–195.

———. 1985. *How Pol Pot Came to Power: A History of Communism in Kampuchea, 1930–1975*. London: Verso.

———. 1988. "Orphans of Genocide: The Cham Muslims of Kampuchea under Pol Pot." *Bulletin of Concerned Asian Scholars* 20(4): 2–33.

———. 1989. "The American Bombardment of Kampuchea, 1969–1973." *Vietnam Generation* 1:4–41.

———. 1990. "The Genocide in Cambodia, 1975–79." *Bulletin of Concerned Asian Scholars* 22(2): 35–40.

———. 1996. *The Pol Pot Regime: Race, Power, and Genocide in Cambodia under the Khmer Rouge, 1975–79*. New Haven, CT, and London: Yale University Press.

Kiernan, Ben, and Chantou Boua, eds. 1982. *Peasants and Politics in Kampuchea, 1942–1981*. London: Zed Books.

Klokke, Marijke J., and Thomas de Bruijn, eds. 1998. *Southeast Asian Archaeology 1996.* Hull, UK: Centre for South East Asian Studies, University of Hull.

Kong, Samphear. 1972. *Brah Palat Ghosanag Haem Ciav Virapuras Jati* (Preah Balat Khosaneak Hem Chiev: The national hero). Phnom Penh.

Kozlov, M. G., L. A. Sedov, and V. A. Churin. 1968. "Tipy ranneklassovykh gosudarstv viugovostochnoi azii" (Types of early class states in Southeast Asia). In *Problemy istorii dokapitalisticheskikh obshchestv* (Problems in the history of precapitalist societies), ed. L. V. Danilova, 516–545. Moscow: Nauka.

Kulke, Hermann. 1978. *The Devaraja Cult.* Data Paper no. 108. Ithaca, NY: Southeast Asia Program, Cornell University.

———. 1993. "The Devarāja Cult: Legitimation and Apotheosis of the Ruler in the Kingdom of Angkor." In *Kings and Cults: State Formation and Legitimation in India and Southeast Asia,* ed. Hermann Kulke, 327–381. New Delhi: Manohar.

Kulke, Hermann, and Dietmar Rothermund. 1990. *A History of India.* London: Routledge.

Kuoch Kileng. 1971. *Gamnit Nayopāy* (Political ideas). Phnom Penh.

Lafont, P.-B. 1982. "Buddhism in Contemporary Laos." In *Contemporary Laos: Studies in the Politics and Society of the Lao People's Democratic Republic,* ed. M. Stuart-Fox, 148–162. St. Lucia: University of Queensland Press.

Lamant, P.-L. 1986. "Le Cambodge et la décolonisation de l'Indochine: Les caractères particuliers du nationalisme khmer de 1936 à 1945." In *Les chemins de la décolonisation de l'empire colonial français,* ed. Colloque organisé par l'Institut d'Histoire du Temps Présent, 189–199. Paris: CNRS.

———. 1987. "Les partis politiques et les mouvements de résistance khmers vus par les services de renseignement français (1945–1952)." *Guerres Mondiales* 148:79–96.

Lamb, Alistair. 1968. *Asian Frontiers: Studies in a Continuing Problem.* London: Pall Mall Press.

de la Vallée Poussin, L. 1937. "Musīla et Nārada: Le Chemin du Nirvāṇa." *Mélanges Chinois et Bouddhiques* 5:189–222.

"Le Bouddhisme Khmer." 1969. *Études Cambodgiennes* 17 (January–March 1969): 15–22.

Leach, Edmund. 1959. "Hydraulic Society in Ceylon." *Past and Present* 15:2–26.

Leang Hap An. 1965. *Anak nibandh khmaer braḥ aṅg ḍuoṅ, jivapravatti sna ṭai* (The Khmer author Preah Ang Duong: His biography and works). Phnom Penh.

———. 1966. *Braḥ rājasambhār kavīrāj satavat(s) dī 17* (Braḥ Rājasambhār, poet-king of the seventeenth century). Phnom Penh.

———. 1970a. *Biographie de Samdech Preach Sanghareach Chuon-Nath, supérieur de l'ordre Mahanikaya.* Série de Culture et Civilisation Khmères, vol. 7. Phnom Penh: Institut Bouddhique.

———. 1970b. *Quppattihetu nai brahtraipitaka prae* (The happenings of the translated Tripitaka). Phnom Penh: Rasmei Kampuchea.

Leclère, Adhémard. 1890. *Recherches sur la législation Cambodgienne (droit privé).* Paris: Augustin Challamel.

———. 1894a. *Recherches sur le droit public des Cambodgiens.* Paris: Augustin Challamel.

———. 1894b. *Recherches sur la legislation criminelle et la procédure des Cambodgiens.* Paris: Augustin Challamel.

———. 1898. *Les codes Cambodgiens.* 2 vols. Paris: E. Leroux.

———. 1899. *Le buddhisme au Cambodge.* Paris: E. Leroux.

———. 1903. "'Sur une charte de fondation d'un monastère bouddhique où il est question du roi du feu et du roi de l'eau." *L'Académie des Inscriptions et Belles Lettres: Comptes Rendus* (July–August): 369–378.

———. 1904. "Légende Djarai sur l'origine du sabre sacré par le Roi du Feu." *Revue Indochinoise* 6:366–369.

———. 1906. *La crémation et les rites funéraires au Cambodge.* Hanoi: F. H. Schneider.

———. 1914. *Histoire du Cambodge.* Paris: Paul Geuthner.

Ledgerwood, Judy, ed. 2002. *Cambodia Emerges from the Past: Eight Essays.* De Kalb: Southeast Asia Publications, Center for Southeast Asian Studies, Northern Illinois University.

Lee, Oey Hong. 1976. *Power Struggle in South-east Asia.* Bibliotheca Asiatica 13. Zug, Switzerland: Inter Documentation Co.

Lehmann, F. K. 1981. "On the Vocabulary Semantics of 'Field' in Theravada Buddhist Society." In *Essays on Burma,* ed. John P. Ferguson, Contributions to Asian Studies vol. 16, 101–111. Leiden: E. J. Brill.

Lerner, Martin, and Steven Kossak. 1991. *The Lotus Transcendent: Indian and Southeast Asian Art from the Samuel Eilenberg Collection.* New York: Metropolitan Museum of Art.

Lewitz, Saveros. 1966–1967. "La toponymie khmère." *BEFEO* 53(2): 375–451.

———. 1970. "Inscriptions modernes d'Angkor 2 et 3." *BEFEO* 57:99–126.

———. 1971. "Inscriptions modernes d'Angkor 4, 5, 6, et 7." *BEFEO* 58:105–123.

———. 1972a. "Inscriptions modernes d'Angkor 1, 8, et 9." *BEFEO* 59:101–121.

———. 1972b. "Inscriptions modernes d'Angkor 10, 11, 12, 13, 14, 15, 16a, 16b, et 16c." *BEFEO* 59:221–249.

———. 1973a. "Inscriptions modernes d'Angkor 17–25." *BEFEO* 60:163–203.

———. 1973b. "Inscriptions modernes d'Angkor 26–33." *BEFEO* 60:205–242.

———. 1974. "Inscriptions modernes d'Angkor 35, 36, 37, et 39." *BEFEO* 61:301–337.

———. 1975. "Inscriptions modernes d'Angkor 34 et 38." *BEFEO* 62:283–353.

Lingat, Robert. 1933. "History of Wat Pavaniveca." *JSS* 26(1): 73–102.

———. 1934. "Le culte du Bouddha d'émeraude." *JSS* 27(1): 9–38.

———. 1949. "L'influence juridique de l'Inde au Champa et au Cambodge." *Journal Asiatique* 237:273–290.

———. 1958. "La double crise de l'église bouddhique au Siam (1767–1851)." *Cahiers d'Histoire Mondiale* 4:402–410.

Locard, Henri. 1996. *Le "Petit Livre Rouge" de Pol Pot ou les paroles de l'Angkar.* Paris: L'Harmattan.

———. 1998. "Les chants révolutionnaires khmers rouges et la tradition musicale cambodgienne." In Sorn Samnang 1998, 1:308–336.

———. 2002. "A Brief Overview of the History of Commune Elections: From 'Mission Civilisatrice' to 'Mission Démocratisatrice.'" *PPP* 11(3) (February): 22.

Lon Nol. 1970. *Chambang Sasana* (The religious war). N.p.

———. 1974. *Le néo-khmerisme.* Phnom Penh. Quoted in Martin 1994, 130.

Longhurst, A. H. 1930. *Pallava Architecture, Part 3.* Memoirs of the Archaeological Survey of India no. 40. Calcutta: Government of India.

Löschmann, Heike. 1989. "Die Rolle des Buddhismus in der gesellschaftlichen Entwicklung der Volksrepublik Kampuchea nach der Befreiung vom Pol-Pot-Regime 1979 bis Mitte der achtziger Jahre." PhD thesis, Humboldt-Universität zu Berlin.

———. 1991. "Buddhismus und gesellschaftliche Entwicklung in Kambodscha seit der Niederschlagung des Pol-Pot-Regimes im Jahre 1979." *Asien* 41:13–27.

———. 1997. "Re-establishing the Buddhist Institute." *Kambodschanische Kultur* 5:98–102. Orig. pub. in *Cambodia Report* (special issue: *Buddhism in Cambodia*) 2(2) (March–April 1996): 17–19.

Luciolli, Esmeralda. 1988. *Le mur de bambou: Le Cambodge après Pol Pot.* Paris: Médecins sans Frontières.

Lunet de Lajonquière, Étienne E. 1902–1911. *Inventaire descriptif des monuments du Cambodge.* 3 vols. Paris: EFEO.

Ly Vou Ong. 1967. "Les manuscripts sur feuilles de latanier." *Annales de l'Université Royale des Beaux Arts* (Phnom Penh): 97–107.

Mabbett, I. W. 1977. "*Varṇas* in Angkor and the Indian Caste System." *Journal of Asian Studies* 36(3): 429–442.

———. 1978. "Kingship in Angkor." *JSS* 66(2): 1–58.

———. 1986. "Buddhism in Champa." In *Southeast Asia in the Ninth to Fourteenth Centuries,* ed. David G. Marr and A. C. Milner, 289–313. Singapore: Institute of Southeast Asian Studies; Canberra: Australian National University.

———. 1997. "The 'Indianization' of Mainland Southeast Asia: A Reappraisal." In Brown and Eilenburg 1997, 342–355.

MacDonald, A. 1970. "Le Dhanyakaṭaka de Mans-Luns Guru." *BEFEO* 57:169–213.

Magness, T. n.d. *The Life and Teaching of the Ven. Chao Khun Mongol-Thepmuni.* Bangkok: Groarke and Co.

Mahaghosananda. 1992. *Step by Step: Meditations on Wisdom and Compassion.* Ed. Jane Sharada Mahoney and Philip Edmonds. Berkeley, CA: Parallax Press.

Majumdar, Ramesh Chandra. 1944. *Kambuja-Deça or an Ancient Hindu Colony in Cambodia.* Philadelphia: Institute for the Study of Human Issues.

———. 1953. *Inscriptions of Kambuja.* Calcutta: Asiatic Society.

Mak Phœun. 1980. "L'Introduction de la Chronique Royale du Cambodge du lettré Nong." *BEFEO* 67:135–145.

———. 1981. *Chroniques royales du Cambodge (de 1594 à 1677).* Paris: EFEO.

———. 1984. *Chroniques royales du Cambodge: Des origines légendaires jusqu'à Paramarāja 1er.* Paris: EFEO.

———. 1989. "La frontière entre le Cambodge et le Viêtnam du XVIIe siècle à l'instauration du protectorat français presentée à travers les chroniques royales khmères." In *Les frontières du Vietnam: Histoire des frontières de la péninsule indochinoise,* ed. P. B. Lafont, 136–155. Paris: L'Harmattan.

———. 1990. "La communauté Malaise musulmane au Cambodge (de la fin du XVIe siècle jusqu'au roi musulman Râmâdhipatî Ier." In *Le monde indochinois et la péninsule malaise,* 47–68. Kuala Lumpur: Ambassade de la France en Malasie.

———. 1995. *Histoire du Cambodge de la fin du XVIe siècle au début du XVIIIe.* Paris: EFEO.

Mak Phœun and Po Dharma. 1984. "La première intervention militaire Vietnamienne au Cambodge (1658–1659)." *BEFEO* 73:285–318.

Malalasekera, G. P. 1974. *Dictionary of Pāli Proper Names.* 2 vols. London: Pali Text Society.

Malleret, Louis. 1941. "Traditions légendaires des Cambodgiens de Cochinchine relevant d'une interprétation ethno-sociologique." *Institut Indochinois pour l'Étude de l'Homme: Bulletin et Travaux* 4:169–180.

———. 1942. "À la recherche de Prei Nokor: Note sur l'emplacement présumé de l'ancien Saigon khmèr." *BSEI* 17(2): 19–33.

———. 1946–1947. "La minorité cambodgienne de Cochinchine." *BSEI* 16:19–34.

Mallmann, M. Th. 1948. *Introduction à l'étude d'Avalokiteśvara.* Annales du Musée Guimet, vol. 57. Paris.

Manguin, Pierre-Yves. 1985. "L'introduction de l'Islam au Champa" [in English]. Trans. Robert Nicholl. *Journal of the Malaya Branch of the Royal Asiatic Society* 58(1): 1–28. Orig. pub. in *BEFEO* 66 (1979): 255–287.

Manipoud, Louis. 1935. *La rénovation des écoles de pagodes au Cambodge.* Phnom Penh: Albert Portail.

Mar Bo. 1969. *Kaṃṇoet prāsād aṅgar.* Phnom Penh: Librairie Phnom-Penh.

Marchal, H. 1918. "Terraces bouddhiques et monuments secondaires d'Angkor Thom." *BEFEO* 18(8): 1–40.

———. 1950. "Jeux, divertissements, et chants populaires au Cambodge." *Indochine Sud-Est Asiatique* (August): 20–27.

———. 1951. "Bonzes, Pagodes, et Fêtes en Pays Khmer." *Indochine Sud-Est Asiatique* (May): 45–46.

———. 1954. "Note sur la forme du *stūpa* au Cambodge." *BEFEO* 44(2): 581–590.

Marquis, Edouard. 1932. "Oudong la victorieuse." *Extrême-Asie* 63 (April): 475–481.

Marston, John. 1994. "Metaphors of the Khmer Rouge." In Ebihara et al. 1994, 105–118.

———. 1997. "Cambodia 1991–94: Hierarchy, Neutrality, and Etiquettes of Discourse." PhD thesis, University of Washington, Seattle.

———. 2000. "Reconstructing 'Ancient' Cambodian Buddhism." Paper presented at the Seventeenth Center for South East Asia Studies (CSEAS) Conference, University of California, Berkeley, February 12–13 (Religion, Civil Society, and NGOs in Southeast Asia).

Martel, Gabrielle. 1975. *Lovea, village des environs d'Angkor: Aspects demographiques, économiques, et sociologiques du monde rural cambodgien dans la province de Siem-Reap.* Paris: EFEO.

Martellaro, J. A., and K. Choroenthaitawee. 1987. "Buddhism and Capitalism in Thailand." *Asian Profile* 15(2): 143–155.

Martin, Marie Alexandrine. 1994. *Cambodia: A Shattered Society*. Berkeley and Los Angeles: University of California Press.

———. 1997. "L'implantation du Bouddhisme dans le Massif des Cardamones (Cambodge)." In Brown and Eilenburg 1997, 357–376.

Martini, François. 1950. "En marge du Rāmāyaṇa Cambodgien." *Journal Asiatique* 238:81–90.

———. 1952. "Note sur l'empreinte du bouddhisme dans la version Cambodgienne du Rāmāyaṇa." *Journal Asiatique* 240:67–69.

———. 1955a. "Le bonze cambodgien." *France-Asie* 12:409–415.

———. 1955b. "Organisation de clergé bouddhique au Cambodge." *France-Asie* 12:416–424.

Mazlish, Bruce. 1976. *The Revolutionary Ascetic: Evolution of a Political Type*. New York: Basic Books.

Meas-Yang, Bhikkhu. 1978. *Le Bouddhisme au Cambodge*. Études Orientales no. 6. Brussels: Thanh-Long.

Mehta, Harish C., and Julie B. Mehta. 1999. *Hun Sen: Strongman of Cambodia*. Singapore: Graham Brash.

Meillon, Gustave. 1984. "Le Caodaïsme: A. Annonce et naissance du Caodaïsme." *Cahiers de l'Asie du Sud-Est* 15–16:161–201.

Mettanando Bhikkhu. 1999. "Meditation and Healing in the Theravada Buddhist Order of Thailand and Laos." PhD thesis, University of Hamburg.

Meyer, Charles. 1965. "Les mystérieuses relations entre les rois du Cambodge et le 'Potâo' des Jarai." *Études Cambodgiennes* 4:14–26.

———. 1969. "Note sur l'introduction du bouddhisme au Cambodge." *Études Cambodgiennes* 7 (January–March): 26–30.

———. 1971. *Derrière le sourire khmer*. Paris: Plon.

Miche, Jean Claude. 1852. "Notice of the Religion of the Cambojans Extracted from a Manuscript of Monsigneur Miché, Bishop of Dansara, by the Bishop of Isauropolis." *Journal of the Indian Archipelago and Eastern Asia* 6:605–617.

Migot, O. 1947. "Le Bouddhisme en Indochine." *BSEI* 22:23–29.

Migozzi, J. 1973. *Cambodge: Faits et problèmes de population*. Paris: Éditions du CNRS.

Miller, John Francis, Jr. 1975. "Diglossia: A Centrifugal Force in Socio-Cultural Relationships—The Case of the Khmer Minority in South Vietnam." PhD thesis, Southern Illinois University, Carbondale.

Ministre de l'Information. 1962. *Aperçus religieux: Le bouddhisme au Cambodge*. Phnom Penh.

Monié, Paul. 1965. "Notes relatives à la crémation d'un personnage religieux au Cambodge." *Arts Asiatiques* 11–12:139–155.

Monographie de la circonscription résidentielle de Kompong-Cham. 1907. Saigon: F. H. Schneider.

Morris, Stephen J. 1999. *Why Vietnam Invaded Cambodia: Political Culture and the Causes of War*. Stanford, CA: Stanford University Press.

Moser-Puangsuwan, Yeshua. n.d. *One Million Kilometres for Peace: Five Years of Walking for Peace and Reconciliation in Cambodia—An Analysis of the Dhammayietra Movement*. Bangkok: Nonviolence International Southeast Asia.

Moura, J. 1883–1889. *Le Royaume du Cambodge*. 2 vols. Paris: Ernest Leroux.

Mourer, Roland. 1977. "Laang Spean and the Prehistory of Cambodia." *Modern Quaternary Research in Southeast Asia* 3:29–56.

Moussay, G. 1971. "Coup d'oeil sur les Cam d'aujourd'hui." *BSEI* 46(3): 361–370.

Mus, Paul. 1935. *Barabuḍur: Esquisse d'une histoire du Bouddhisme fondée sur la critique archéologique des textes*. Hanoi: Imprimerie d'Extrême-Orient.

———. 1937. "Angkor in the Time of Jayavarman VII." *Indian Art and Letters* 11(2): 65–75.

———. 1961. "Le sourire d'Angkor: Art, foi, et politique bouddhiques sous Jayavarman VII." *Artibus Asiae* 24:363–381.

———. 1975. "Cultes Indiens et indigènes au Champa" [in English]. Trans. Ian Mabbett. In *India Seen from the East: Indian and Indigenous Cults in Champa*, ed. I. W. Mabbett and D. P. Chandler, Monash Papers on Southeast Asia no. 3. Clayton, Victoria, Australia: Monash University, Centre of Southeast Asian Studies. Orig. pub. in *BEFEO* 33 (1933): 367–410.

Nafilyan, Jacquelin, and Guy Nafilyan. 1997. *Peintures murales des monastères bouddhiques au Cambodge*. Paris: Maisonneuve et Larose/UNESCO.

Nandana Chutiwongs. 1984. "The Iconography of Avalokitesvara in Mainland South East Asia." PhD thesis, Rijksuniversiteit te Leiden.

Népote, Jacques. 1974. "Education et développement dans le Cambodge moderne." *Mondes en Développement* 28:767–792.

———. 1980. "Pour une approche socio-historique du monachisme Théravada." *Péninsule* 1:94–135.

Népote, Jacques, and Michel Tranet. 1983. "Deux sources statistiques relatives à la monachisme Theravāda au Cambodge à la fin du XIXè siècle." *Seksa Khmer* 6:39–73.

Ner, Marcel. 1941. "Les Musulmans de l'Indochine française." *BEFEO* 16(2): 151–201.

Nhok Them. 1943. *Kulap pailin* (The rose of Pailin). Phnom Penh.

de Nike, Howard J., John Quigley, and Kenneth J. Robinson, eds. 2000. *Genocide in Cambodia: Documents from the Trial of Pol Pot and Ieng Sary*. Philadelphia: University of Pennsylvania Press.

No Na Paknam. 1981. *The Buddhist Boundary Markers of Thailand*. Bangkok: Muang Boran.

Norodom Sihanouk. 1962. "Inaugural Address: Sixth Conference of the World Fellowship of Buddhists (Phnom Penh, November 14–22, 1961)." *France-Asie* 171:25–28.

———. 1964. *Les paroles* (July–September). Phnom Penh: Ministère de l'Information.

———. 1965. "Our Buddhist Socialism." *Kambuja* 8 (November 15): 13–20.

———. 1970. "Message spécial du Prince Sihanouk aux moines bouddhistes khmers." *La Documentation Française* 50 (December 11): 16–18.

———. 1980. *War and Hope: The Case for Cambodia*. Trans. Mary Feeney. London: Sidgwick and Jackson.

———. 1981. *Souvenirs doux et amers*. Paris: Hachette.

Notton, Camille. 1933. *The Chronicle of the Emerald Buddha*. Bangkok: Bangkok Times.

Nouth Oun. 1953. "Arrivé d'une Relique du Bouddha à Phnom Penh." *France-Asie* 90 (November): 1025–1028.

Nuon Chea. 2001. "Statement of the Communist Party of Kampuchea (CPK) to the Communist Workers' Party of Denmark, July 1978." Trans. Peter Bischoff; ed., abr., and annotated by Laura Summer. *Searching for the Truth* 17 (May). Phnom Penh: Documentation Center of Cambodia. English text at http://www.bigpond.com.kh/users/dccam.genocide/posting/Nuon_Chea's_Statement.htm.

Osborne, Milton. 1973. "King-making in Cambodia: From Sisowath to Sihanouk." *JSEAS* 4(2): 169–185.

———. 1978. "Peasant Politics in Cambodia: The 1916 Affair." *Modern Asian Studies* 12(2): 217–243.

———. 1979. *Before Kampuchea: Preludes to Tragedy*. London: Allen and Unwin.

———. 1994. *Sihanouk, Prince of Light, Prince of Darkness*. St. Leonards, New South Wales: Allen and Unwin.

———. 1997. *The French Presence in Cochinchina and Cambodia*. Bangkok: White Lotus.

Osborne, Milton, and David K. Wyatt. 1968. "The Abridged Cambodian Chronicle: A Thai Version of Cambodian History." *France-Asie* 193:189–203.

Osipov, Yuriy M. 2000. "Buddhist Hagiography in Forming the Canon in the Classical Literatures of Indochina." In Smyth 2000, 1–7.

Osman, Yse. 2002. *Oukoubah*. Monograph no. 2. Phnom Penh: Documentation Center for Cambodia.

Oum Sou and Chuon Nath. 1969. *Gihipatipatti*. Phnom Penh: Institut Bouddhique.

Pachow, W. 1958. "The Voyage of Buddhist Missions to South-east Asia and the Far East." *Journal of the Greater India Society* 17(1–2): 1–22.

Panditha, Vincent. 1973. "Buddhism during the Polonnaruva Period." In *The Polonnaruva Period*, 3rd ed., ed. S. D. Saparamadu, 127–145. Dehiwala, Sri Lanka: Tisara Prakasakayo.

Paul, Diane Y. 1984. *Philosophy of Mind in Sixth-Century China: Paramārtha's "Evolution of Consciousness."* Stanford, CA: Stanford University Press.

Pavie, Auguste. 1901. *Mission Pavie Indo-Chine, 1879–1895. Geographie et voyages.* Vol. 1, *Exposé des travaux de la mission.* Paris: Leroux.

Peang-Meth, Abdulgaffar. 1991. "Understanding the Khmer: Social-Cultural Observations." *Asian Survey* 31(5): 442–455.

Pelliot, Paul. 1903. "Le fou-nan." *BEFEO* 3(2): 248–303.

———. 1951. *Mémoires et coutumes du Cambodge de Tchéou Ta-Kuan*. Paris: Adrien Maisonneuve.

Péri, N. 1923. "Essay sur les relations du Japon et de l'Indochine aux XVIe et XVIIe siècles." *BEFEO* 23(1): 1–136.

Pfanner, D. E., and J. Ingersoll. 1961–1962. "Theravada Buddhism and Village Economic Behaviour: A Burmese and Thai Comparison." *Journal of Asian Studies* 21:341–361.

Piat, Martine. 1975. "Contemporary Cambodian Literature." *JSS* 63(2): 251–259.

Pichard, Pierre. 1976. *Pimay: Étude architecturale du temple.* Paris: EFEO.

Picq, Laurence. 1989. *Beyond the Horizon: Five Years with the Khmer Rouge (Au-delà du ciel: cinq ans chez les Khmers rouges.* Trans. Patricia Norland. New York: St. Martin's.

Pin Yathay. 1980. *L'Utopie meurtrière.* Paris: Laffont.

Po Dharma 1981. "Notes sur les Caṃ du Cambodge I." *Seksa Khmer* 3–4:161–183.

———. 1982. "Notes sur les Caṃ du Cambodge II." *Seksa Khmer* 5:103–116.

———. 1991. "Le FULRO: Moment de l'histoire ou tradition de lutte des peoples du Sud du Champa." In *Deuxième symposium franco-soviétique sur l'Asie du Sud-Est,* 270–277. Moscow.

———. 1998. "Les Cham et Malais au Cambodge: Organisation socio-religieuse." In Sorn Samnang 1998, 2:1081–1095.

Ponchaud, Francois. 1978. *Cambodia Year Zero.* London: Allen Lane.

———. 1989. "Social Change in the Vortex of Revolution." In Karl Jackson 1989, 151–177.

———. 1990. *La cathédrale de la riziere: 450 ans d'histoire de l'église au Cambodge.* Paris: Fayard.

Porée, Guy, and Éveline Maspero. 1938. *Mœurs et coutumes des Khmèrs.* Paris: Payot.

Porée-Maspero, Éveline. 1951. "La cérémonie de l'appel des espirits vitaux chez les Cambodgiens." *BEFEO* 45(1): 145–183.

———. 1954. "Notes sur les particularités du culte chez les Cambodgiens." *BEFEO* 44(2): 619–641.

———. 1961a. "Kron Pali et rites de la maison." *Anthropos* 56:883–929.

———. 1961b. "Traditions orales de Pursat et de Kampot." *Artibus Asiae* 26:394–398.

———. 1962–1969. *Étude sur les rites agraires des Cambodgiens.* 3 vols. Paris: Mouton.

———. 1975. "Rites de possession au Cambodge." *Objets et Mondes* 15(1): 39–46.

———. 1983. "Le Rāmāyaṇa dans la vie des Cambodgiens." *Seksa Khmer* 6:19–24.

Pou, Saveros. 1975. "Les traits bouddhiques du *Rāmakerti.*" *BEFEO* 62:355–368.

———. 1979. "Subhāsit and Cpāp' in Khmer Literature." In *Ludwick Sternbach Felicitation Volume, Part One,* ed. J. P. Sinha, 331–348. Lucknow, India: Akhila Bharatiya Sanskrit Parishad.

———. 1980. "Some Proper Names in the Khmer Rāmakerti." *Southeast Asian Review* 5(2): 19–29.

———. 1981. "La littérature didactique khmère: Les *Cpāp'.*" *Journal Asiatique* 269(3–4): 453–466.

———. 1983. "Ramakertian Studies." In Iyengar 1983, 252–262.

———. 1986. "Sarasvatī dans la culture khmer." *Bulletin d'Études Indiennes* 4:321–339.

———. 1987–1988. "Notes on Brahmanic Gods in Theravādin Cambodia." *Indologica Taurinensia* 114:339–351.

———. 1988. *Guirlande de Cpāp'.* 2 vols. Paris: CEDORECK.

———. 1990. "From Old Khmer Epigraphy to Popular Tradition: A Study in the Names of Cambodian Monuments." In *Southeast Asian Archaeology,* ed. Ian Glover, 7–24. Hull, UK: Centre for South East Asian Studies, University of Hull.

———. 1992. "Indigenization of Rāmāyaṇa in Cambodia." *Asian Folklore Studies* 51:89–102.

———. 1995. "Indra et Brahma au Cambodge." *Orientalia Lovaniensia Periodica* 26:141–161.

———. 1998. "Ancient Cambodia's Epigraphy: A Socio-linguistic Look." In Klokke and de Bruijn 1998, 123–134.

Pou, Saveros, and K. Haksrea. 1981. "Liste d'ouvrages de *Cpāp'*." *Journal Asiatique* 269(3–4): 467–483.

Pou, Saveros, and Philip N. Jenner. 1975. "Les *Cpāp'* ou 'Codes de conduite' Khmers: I. *Cpāp' Kerti Kāl.*" *BEFEO* 62:369–394.

———. 1976. "Les *Cpāp'* ou 'Codes de conduite' Khmers: II. *Cpāp' Prus.*" *BEFEO* 63:315–350.

———. 1977. "Les *Cpāp'* ou 'Codes de conduite' Khmers: III. *Cpāp' Kūn Cau.*" *BEFEO* 64:167–215.

———. 1978. "Les *Cpāp'* ou 'Codes de conduite' Khmers: IV. *Cpāp' Rājaneti* ou *Cpāp' Braḥ Rājasambhar.*" *BEFEO* 65:361–402.

———. 1979. "Les *Cpāp'* ou 'Codes de conduite' Khmers: V. *Cpāp' Kram.*" *BEFEO* 66:129–160.

———. 1981. "Les *Cpāp'* ou 'Codes de conduite' Khmers: VI. *Cpāp' Trīneti.*" *BEFEO* 69:135–193.

Preschez, Philippe. 1961. *Essai sur la démocratie au Cambodge.* Paris: Fondation Nationale des Sciences Politiques.

Purusakara, Upasaka. 1954. "Le peuple cambodgien est plus bouddhiste que ses bonzes." *Indochine Sud-Est Asiatique* 31:25–31.

Put Tumniay: Riap riang daoy Prom Viraa. 1970. N.p.

Put Tumniay: Taam saastraa saolah nimit. 1952. Phnom Penh: Khemarak Panaakia.

Pym, Christopher. 1959. *The Road to Angkor.* London: Robert Hale.

Quinn, Kenneth M. 1976. "Political Change in Wartime: The Khmer Krahom Revolution in Southern Cambodia, 1970–1974." *Naval War College Review* 28:3–31.

———. 1982. "The Origins and Development of Radical Cambodian Communism." PhD thesis, University of Maryland, College Park.

Reynolds, Craig James. 1973. "The Buddhist Monkhood in Nineteenth Century Thailand." PhD thesis, Cornell University, Ithaca, NY.

———. 1976. "Buddhist Cosmography in Thai History with Special Reference to Nineteenth Century Culture Change." *Journal of Asian Studies* 35(2): 203–220.

———. 1979. "Monastery Lands and Labour Endowments in Thailand: Some Effects of Social and Economic Change, 1868–1910." *Journal of the Economic and Social History of the Orient* 22(2): 190–227.

———, ed. 1991. *National Identity and Its Defenders: Thailand 1939–1989.* Monash Papers on Southeast Asia no. 25. Clayton, Victoria, Australia: Monash University.

Rhum, Michael R. 1994. *The Ancestral Lords: Gender, Descent, and Spirits in a Northern Thai Village.* Monograph Series on Southeast Asia, Special Report no. 29. De Kalb: Center for Southeast Asian Studies, Northern Illinois University.

———. 1996. "'Modernity' and 'Tradition' in 'Thailand.'" *Modern Asian Studies* 30(2): 325–355.

Richardson, D. 1874. *The Dhamathat, or, the laws of Menoo, translated from the Burmese.* Rangoon: Mission Press. Quoted in A. Huxley 1991, 344n13.

Rohanadeera, Mendis. 1988. "The Noen Sa Bua Inscription of Dong Si Maha Bo, Prachinburi." *JSS* 76:89–99.

Ros Chantrabot. 1993. *La république khmère (1970–1975).* Paris: L'Harmattan.

———. 2000. *Cambodge: La répétition de l'histoire (de 1991 aux élections de juillet 1998).* Paris: You-Feng.

Ros Nol. 1997. *La culture khmère à Kampong Thom: Moeurs et coutumes, légendes et superstitions, associations et pratiques, histoires de pagodas.* Kampong Thom: GTZ. Handwritten and mimeographed MS.

Rousseau, Armand. 1904. *Le protectorat français du Cambodge.* Dijon, France: Pillu-Rolland.

Roy, Daniel. 1970. "70 000 bonzes et la guerre civile." *La Documentation Française* 50 (November 11): 14–15.

Royaume du Cambodge. 1924. *Code pénal promulgué par ordonnance royale de Sa Majesté Sisowath, Roi du Cambodge, en date du 25 Août 1924.* Phnom Penh: Imprimerie du Protectorat.

Russier, Henri. 1913. "L'enseignement élémentaire au Cambodge." *Revue Indochinoise* 19(4): 409–420.

Saddhatissa, H. 1980. "Pali Studies in Cambodia." In *Buddhist Studies in Honour of Walpola Rahula,* ed. S. Balasooriya, A. Bareau, R. Gombrich, S. Gunasingha, U. Mallawarachchi, and E. Perry, 242–250. London: Gordon Fraser.

Saddhatissa, Hammalawa. n.d. "Pāli Literature in Cambodia." In *Pāli Literature of Southeast Asia,* ed. Hammalawa Saddhatissa, 83–104. Singapore: Singapore Buddhist Meditation Centre. Orig. pub. in *Journal of the Pali Text Society* 9 (1981).

Salter, Richard C. 2000. "Time, Authority, and Ethics in the Khmer Rouge: Elements of the Millennial Vision in Year Zero." In *Millennialism, Persecution, and Violence: Historical Cases,* ed. Catherine Wessinger, 281–298. Syracuse, NY: Syracuse University Press.

Sam Nhean. 1957. *Pravatti braḥ buddhasāsanā* (History of Buddhism in Cambodia). Phnom Penh.

Sam-Ang Sam, Panya Roongrüang, and Phong T. Nguyen. 1998. "The Khmer People." In *The Garland Encyclopedia of World Music,* vol. 4, *Southeast Asia,* ed. Terry E. Miller and Sean Williams, 151–217. New York and London: Garland.

San Sarin. 1975. "Les textes liturgiques fondamentaux du bouddhisme Cambodgien actuel." PhD thesis, École Pratique des Hautes Études, Section Sciences Religieuses, Paris.

———. 1998. "Buddhism Transformed: Religious Practices and Institutional Interplay in Cambodia." *Indian Journal of Buddhist Studies* 10:116–140.

Sarkar, Kalyan. 1955. "Mahayana Buddhism in Fu-nan." *Sino-Indian Studies* 5(1): 69–75.

Sarkisyanz, Emanuel. 1958. "Communism and Lamaist Utopianism in Central Asia." *Review of Politics* 20(4): 623–633.

Schecter, Jerrold. 1967. *The New Face of Buddha: The Fusion of Religion and Politics in Contemporary Buddhism.* London: Victor Gollancz.

Schier, Peter. 1986. "Kampuchea in 1985: Between Crocodiles and Tigers." *Southeast Asian Affairs:* 139–161.

Seidenfaden, Erik. 1951. "The Kui People of Cambodia and Siam." *JSS* 39(2): 144–180.

Sem, S. 1967. "Lokhon Khol au village Vat-Svay-Andet: Son rôle dans les rites agraires." *Annales de l'Université Royale des Beaux Arts* 1:157–187.

Shapiro-Phim, Toni. 2002. "Dance, Music, and the Nature of Terror in Democratic Kampuchea." In *Annihilating Difference: The Anthropology of Genocide,* ed. A. L. Hinton, 179–193. Berkeley and Los Angeles: University of California Press.

Silva, Roland. 1988. *Religious Architecture in Early and Medieval Sri Lanka.* Leiden: Meppel.

Sirisena, W. M. 1978. *Sri Lanka and South-East Asia: Political Religions and Cultural Relations from* AD c. 1000 to c. 1500. Leiden: E. J. Brill.

Skilling, Peter. 1992. "The Rakṣā Literature of the Śāvakayāna." *Journal of the Pali Text Society* 16:109–182.

———. 1994a. "Vimuttimagga and Abhayagiri: The Form Aggregate according to the Saṃskṛtāsaṃskṛtaviniścaya." *Journal of the Pali Text Society* 20:171–210.

———, ed. 1994b. *Mahasutras: Great Discourses of the Buddha.* 2 vols. Sacred Books of the Buddhists, vols. 44 and 46. Oxford: Pali Text Society.

———. 1997. "The Advent of Theravāda Buddhism to Mainland South-east Asia." *Journal of the International Association of Buddhist Studies* 20(1): 93–107.

———. 1999. "A Buddhist Inscription from Go Xoai, Southern Vietnam, and Notes towards a Classification of *ye dharmā* Inscriptions." In *80 pi śāstrācāry dr. praḥsert a nagara: Ruam pada khwam vijākāra dan charuk lae ekasāraporāṇa* (80 years: A collection of articles on epigraphy and ancient documents published on the occasion of the celebration of the eightieth birthday of Prof. Dr. Prasert Na Nagara), 171–185. Bangkok.

———. 2001a. "The Place of South-east Asia in Buddhist Studies." *Buddhist Studies (Bukkyô Kenkyū)* 30:19–43.

———. 2001b. "Some Literary References in the *Grande Inscription d'Angkor* (IMA38)." *Aséanie* 8:57–66.

Smith, Donald Eugene. 1965. *Religion and Politics in Burma.* Princeton, NJ: Princeton University Press.

Smith, Frank. 1989. *Interpretive Accounts of the Khmer Rouge Years: Personal Experience in Cambodian Peasant World View.* Occasional Paper no. 18. Madison: Center for Southeast Asian Studies, University of Wisconsin.

Smith, R. B. 1970a. "An Introduction to Caodaism, I. Origins and Early History." *BSOAS* 33:335–349.

———. 1970b. "An Introduction to Caodaism, II. Beliefs and Organisation." *BSOAS* 33:572–587.

Smith, R. B., and W. Watson, eds. 1979. *Early South East Asia: Essays in Archaeology,*

History, and Historical Geography. New York and Kuala Lumpur: Oxford University Press.

Smith-Hefner, Nancy J. 1999. *Khmer American: Identity and Moral Education in a Diasporic Community*. Berkeley and Los Angeles: University of California Press.

Smyth, David A., ed. 1993. *Cambodian Linguistics, Literature, and History: Collected Articles*. London: School of Oriental and African Studies.

———, ed. 2000. *The Canon in Southeast Asian Literatures: Literatures of Burma, Cambodia, Indonesia, Laos, Malaysia, the Philippines, Thailand, and Vietnam*. Richmond, UK: Curzon.

Snellgrove, David. 2000. *Asian Commitment: Travels and Studies in the Indian Subcontinent and South-east Asia*. Bangkok: Orchid Press.

Sok Sakhom and Didier Bertrand. 1998. "Étude des noms et de l'identité des borameï chez les mediums cambodgiens." In Sorn Samnang 1998, 1131–1138.

Sok Vanny. 1984. "Réflexion sur la khmèritude." *ASEMI: Cambodge II* 15(1–4): 141–144.

Solomon, Robert L. 1970. *Aspects of State, Kingship, and Succession in Southeast Asia*. Santa Monica, CA: Rand Corp.

Somboon Suksamran. 1993. "Buddhism, Political Authority, and Legitimacy in Thailand and Cambodia." In *Buddhist Trends in Southeast Asia*, ed. Trevor Ling, 101–153. Singapore: Institute of Southeast Asian Studies.

Son Soubert, et al. 1986. *Buddhism and the Future of Cambodia*. Rithisen, Thailand: Khmer Buddhist Research Center.

Sorn Samnang, ed. 1998. *Khmer Studies: Knowledge of the Past and Its Contributions to the Rehabilitation and Reconstruction of Cambodia—Proceedings of the International Conference on Khmer Studies, Phnom Penh, 26–30 August 1996*. 2 vols. Phnom Penh.

Souyris-Roland, André. 1951a. "Contribution à l'étude du culte des génies tutélaires ou 'Neak ta' chez les Cambodgiens du Sud." *BSEI* 26(2): 161–174.

———. 1951b. "Les procédés magiques d'immunisation chez les Cambodgiens." *BSEI* 26(2): 175–187.

Spiro, Melford. 1966. "Buddhism and Economic Action in Burma." *American Anthropologist* 68(5): 1163–1173.

Stanic, S. 1978. "Cambodia: A Path without a Model. Buddha Is Dead! Long Live the Revolution." Belgrade Domestic Service. *FBIS* 4, April 24.

Steinberg, David J., in collaboration with Chester A. Bain, Lloyd Burlingham, Russell G. Daft, Bernard B. Fall, Ralph Greenhouse, Lucy Kramer, and Robert S. McLellan. 1959. *Cambodia: Its People, Its Society, Its Culture*. New Haven, CT: HRAF Press.

Stott, Philip. 1992. "Angkor: Shifting the Hydraulic Paradigm." In *The Gift of Water: Water Management, Cosmology, and the State in South East Asia*, ed. Jonathan Rigg, 47–58. London: School of Oriental and African Studies.

Syed-Leo, Yasmeen. 1993. "Buddhism, Socialism, and Democracy: Democratic Kampuchea 1975–1979." Master's thesis, Université Laval, Quebec.

Taillard, Christian. 1977. "Le village Lao de la région de Vientiane: Un pouvoir local face au pouvoir étatique." *L'Homme* 17(2–3): 71–100.

Tambiah, S. J. 1992. *Buddhism Betrayed? Religion, Politics, and Violence in Sri Lanka.* Chicago: University of Chicago Press.

Tandart, S. 1910. *Dictionnaire cambodgien-français.* Hong Kong: Imprimerie MEP. Quoted in Tauch Chhuong 1994, 100.

Tannenbaum, Nicola. 1987. "Tattoos: Invulnerability and Power in Shan Cosmology." *American Ethnologist* 14(4): 693–711.

Tauch Chhuong. 1994. *Battambang during the Time of the Lord Governor.* Trans. Hin Sithan, Carol Mortland, and Judy Ledgerwood. Phnom Penh: CEDORECK.

Taylor, Charles. 1989. *Sources of the Self.* Cambridge, MA: Harvard University Press.

Témoignages: Les moines bouddhistes Khmers krom parlent. . . . 1963. *Les persécutions religieuses au sud Vietnam.* Phnom Penh.

Terwiel, B. J. 1991. "Thai Nationalism and Identity: Popular Themes of the 1930s." In Reynolds 1991, 133–154.

———. 1994. *Monks and Magic: An Analysis of Religious Ceremonies in Central Thailand.* 3rd rev. ed. Bangkok: White Lotus.

Thach Bunroeun. 1993. "Santiphum Khmer: A Buddhist Way to Peace." PhD thesis, University of Hawai'i, Honolulu.

Thach Reaksa. n.d. *Au Sud-Vietnam 2,600,000 Khmers-Krom revendiquent.* Paris.

Thayer, Nate. 1997. "Forbidden City." *Far Eastern Economic Review* (October): 22–23.

Thierry, Solange. 1959. "La personne sacrée du roi dans la littérature populaire Cambodgienne." In *The Sacral Kingship: Contributions to the Central Theme of the Seventh International Congress of the History of Religions, Rome 1955,* 219–230. Leiden: Brill.

———. 1968. "La place des textes de sagesse dans la littérature cambodgienne." *Revue de l'École Nationale des Langues Orientales* 5:163–184.

———. 1982. "*Brai* et *Himavant:* Les thèmes de la forêt dans la tradition khmère." *ASEMI* 13(1–4): 121–133.

———. 1984. *Le popil: Objet rituel Cambodgien.* Paris: CEDORECK.

Thion, Serge. 1983. "Chronology of Khmer Communism." In *Revolution and Its Aftermath in Kampuchea: Eight Essays,* ed. David P. Chandler and Ben Kiernan, 291–319. New Haven, CT: Yale University Southeast Asia Series.

———. 1987. "The Pattern of Cambodian Politics." In Ablin and Hood 1987, 149–164.

———. 1988. "Remodelling Broken Images: Manipulation of Identities towards and beyond the Nation—an Asian Perspective." In *Ethnicities and Nations: Processes of Interethnic Relations in Latin America, Southeast Asia, and the Pacific,* ed. Remo Guidieri, Francesco Pellizzi, and Stanley J. Tambiah, 229–258. Houston: Rothko Chapel.

———. 1993. *Watching Cambodia: Ten Paths to Enter the Cambodian Tangle.* Bangkok: White Lotus.

Thion, Serge, and Ben Kiernan. 1981. *Khmers rouges: Matériaux pour l'histoire du communisme au Cambodge.* Paris: J. E. Hallier–Ablin Michel.

Thompson, Ashley. 1996. *The Calling of the Souls: A Study of the Khmer Ritual Hau Braliṅ.* Working Paper no. 98. Clayton, Victoria, Australia: Monash Asia Institute.

———. 1998. "The Ancestral Cult in Transition: Reflections on Spatial Organisation in Cambodia's Early Theravāda Complex." In Klokke and de Bruijn 1998, 273–295.

———. 1999. "Mémoires du Cambodge." 2 vols. PhD thesis, Université de Paris VIII.

———. 2000. "Lost and Found: The Stupa, the Four-faced Buddha, and the Seat of Royal Power in Middle Cambodia." In *Southeast Asian Archaeology 1998,* ed. Wibke Lobo and Stephanie Reimann, 245–264. Hull, UK: Centre for South East Asian Studies, University of Hull; Berlin: Ethnologisches Museum, Staatliche Museen zu Berlin.

Thompson, Virginia, and Richard Adloff. 1955. *Minority Problems in Southeast Asia.* Stanford, CA: Stanford University Press.

Thongchai Winichakal. 1994. *Siam Mapped: A History of the Geo-Body of a Nation.* Honolulu: University of Hawai'i Press.

Tranet, Michel. 1983. "Étude sur la Sāvatār Vatt Saṃpuk." *Seksa Khmer* 6:75–107.

———. 1997. *Sambaur-Prei-Kuk: Monuments d'Içanavarman (615–628).* 2 vols. Phnom Penh.

———. 1998. "Les premières représentations de Bouddha au Cambodge ancien." In Sorn Samnang 1998, vol. 1, 427–473.

Trán-quan-Thuận. 1905. *Notice sur la pagode appelée Wott Préas Buonn Muc en Cambodgien et Chùa Phật Bôn Mặt en Annamite.* Saigon: Imprimerie Saigonnaise.

Try, Jean-Samuel S. 1991. "Le bouddhisme dans la société khmère moderne." PhD thesis, École Pratique des Hautes Études, Section Sciences Religieuses, Paris.

Tully, John. 1996. *Cambodia under the Tricolour: King Sisowath and the "Mission Civilisatrice" 1904–1927.* Monash Papers on Southeast Asia no. 37. Clayton, Victoria, Australia: Monash Asia Institute.

Van Liere, W. J. 1982. "Was Angkor a Hydraulic Society?" *Ruam Botkwam Prawatisat* 4:36–48.

Vickery, Michael. 1973. "The Khmer Inscriptions of Tenasserim: A Reinterpretation." *JSS* 61(1): 51–70.

———. 1977. "Cambodia after Angkor: The Chronicular Evidence for the Fourteenth to Sixteenth Centuries." 2 vols. PhD thesis, University of Michigan, Ann Arbor.

———. 1982. "Qui était Naṅ/Nong, savant(s) cambodgien(s) des XIIIe–XIXe siècles?" *ASEMI* 13(1–4): 81–86.

———. 1984. *Cambodia 1975–1982.* Sydney and Boston: Allen and Unwin.

———. 1986. *Kampuchea: Politics, Economics, and Society.* Marxist Regimes Series. London: Pinter; Boulder, CO: Rienner.

———. 1987. "Refugee Politics: The Khmer Camp System in Thailand." In Ablin and Hood 1987, 293–331.

———. 1988. "Letter to the Editor." *Bulletin of Concerned Asian Scholars* 20:70–73.

———. 1990. "Cultural Survival in Cambodian Language and Literature." *Cultural Survival Quarterly* 14(3): 49–52.

———. 1992. "Comments on Cham Population Figures." *Bulletin of Concerned Asian Scholars* 22(1): 31–33.

———. 1994. "The Cambodian People's Party: Where Has It Come From, Where Is It Going?" *Southeast Asian Affairs:* 102–117.

———. 1998. *Society, Economics, and Politics in Pre-Angkor Cambodia: The Seventh–Eighth Centuries.* Tokyo: Centre for East Asian Cultural Studies for UNESCO, Toyo Bunko.

"Village Cham au Cambodge, Chrui Chanva." 1951. *Indochine Sud-Est Asiatique* (special issue 21): 80–89.

Vollman, Wolfgang. 1973. "Notes sur les relations inter-ethniques au Cambodge du XIXe siècle." *ASEMI* 4:171–208.

Vorvong and Saurivong. 1971. Série de Culture et Civilisation Khmères, vol. 5. Phnom Penh: Institut Bouddhique.

Vu Can. 1982. "Buddhism and Socialism in Kampuchea." *Vietnam Courier* 18(9): 28–30.

Wales, H. G. Quaritch. 1992. *Siamese State Ceremonies.* Richmond, UK: Curzon.

Walker, Andrew. 1999. *The Legend of the Golden Boat: Regulation, Trade, and Traders in the Borderlands of Laos, Thailand, China, and Burma.* Honolulu: University of Hawai'i Press.

Weggel, Oskar. 1984. "Buddhismus und Sozialismus: Die Völker Indochinas auf der Suche nach der verlorenen Identität." *Südostasien Aktuell* 3(1): 47–65.

Wijayaratna, Mohan. 1991. *Les moniales bouddhistes: Naissance et développement du monachisme féminine.* Paris: Cerf.

Wijeyewardene, Gehan. 1991. "The Frontiers of Thailand." In Reynolds 1991, 157–190.

Willmott, W. E. 1966. "History and Sociology of the Chinese in Cambodia Prior to the French Protectorate." *Journal of Southeast Asian History* 7(1): 15–38.

———. 1970. *The Political Structure of the Chinese Community in Cambodia.* London School of Economics Monographs on Social Anthropology no. 42. London: Athlone Press.

———. 1981. "Analytical Errors of the Kampuchean Communist Party." *Pacific Affairs* 54:209–227.

Wolters, O. W. 1979. "Khmer 'Hinduism' in the Seventh Century." In R. Smith and Watson 1979, 427–442.

Woodward, Hiram W., Jr. 1980. "Some Buddha Images and the Cultural Developments of the Late Angkorian Period." *Artibus Asiae* 42:155–174.

———. 1981. "Tantric Buddhism at Angkor Thom." *Ars Orientalis* 12:57–67.

———. 1994–1995. "The Jayabuddhamahānātha Images of Cambodia." *Journal of the Walters Art Gallery* 52–53:105–111.

———. 1997. "The Emerald and Sihing Buddhas: Interpretations of Their Significance." In Brown and Eilenburg 1997, 502–513.

———. 2001. "Practice and Belief in Ancient Cambodia: Claude Jacques, *Angkor,* and the *Devarāja* Question." *JSEAS* 32(2): 249–261.

Wright, Michael. 1990. "Sacrifice and the Underworld: Death and Fertility in Siamese Myth and Ritual." *JSS* 78(1): 43–54.

Wyatt, David K. 1984. *Thailand: A Short History.* New Haven, CT, and London: Yale University Press.

Yang Baoyun. 1994. "Les sources historiques en caractères chinois: Un trésor pour les recherches sur l'histoire du Cambodge." *Péninsule* 28:45–50.

———. 1998. "Les relations historiques entre la Chine et le Cambodge ainsi que leurs caractéristiques." In Sorn Samnang 1998, 1:130–144.

Yang Sam. 1987. *Khmer Buddhism and Politics from 1954 to 1984*. Newington, CT: Khmer Studies Institute.

———. 1990. "Buddhism in Cambodia, 1795–1954." Master's thesis, Cornell University, Ithaca, NY.

———. 1998. "Battambang as a Tributary State: Religion and Society." In Sorn Samnang 1998, 1:230–256.

Yoshiaki Ishizawa. 1998. "Les relations entre le Cambodge et le Japon au XVIIe siècle." In Sorn Samnang 1998, 1:75–82.

Yu, David. 1987. "Religion and Politics in Asian Communist Nations." In *Movements and Issues in World Religions: A Sourcebook and Analysis of Developments since 1945*, ed. C. Wei-hsun Fu and G. E. Spiegler, 371–392. New York and Westport, CT: Greenwood Press.

Yukiko Yonekura. 1999. "Case Studies of Civil Associations in Cambodia: Their Advantages and Limitations in the Struggle for Democracy." Paper delivered at Cambodia: Moving Towards a Better Future Conference, Oxford, June 5, 1999.

Zago, Marcello. 1976a. "Buddhism in Contemporary Laos." In Dumoulin and Maraldo, 120–129.

———. 1976b. "Contemporary Khmer Buddhism." In Dumoulin and Maraldo, 109–119.

Zigmund-Cerbu, A. 1961. "À propos d'un vajra Khmer." *Artibus Asiae* 24(3–4): 425–431.

Index

Abhayagirivihāra, 94, 268n.65
Abhidhamma, 6, 30, 35, 83; and death rites, 99; magical significances, 59, 95, 101
achar yogi, 77, 99
achar, 77–78
Aggabodhi IV, king of Sri Lanka (c. 626–641), 62
amulets, 45, 60–61, 112, 133, 168
Anavatāpta, 20, 22
Ang Chan, king of Cambodia (1794–1835), 41, 44, 45, 47; and Khleang Moeung, 33–34, 53; legislator, 51; Buddhist patronage, 33, 40
Ang Duang, king of Cambodia (1848–1860), 44, 45, 58, 105; Buddhist and cultural activities, 46–47, 85; founds Thommayut, 106, 109, 213; relations with Islam, 47–48
Ang Eng, king of Cambodia (1779–1794), 44
Ang Jī, king of Cambodia (1673–1677), 43
Ang Mey, princess (1835–1841), 44
Ang Sūr, king of Cambodia (1659–1672), 43, 72
angkar padevat, 175, 183, 184, 187
angkarviney, 182
Angkor Borei, 1, 4, 5, 8
Angkor Wat, 42, 68, 90; Ang Chan and, 33; Buddhist appropriation, 35–36, 38; dedicated to Viṣṇu, 18, 19; and legend, 29–30; Mongkut and, 32; Sihanouk and, 153; under Khmer Rouge, 180
anti-Vietnamese massacres, 165–166. *See also* Vietnam
anukun, 123
anusamvacchara-mahāsannipāt, 123
appanages, 111–112, 122
arak, 58–59
Ârchoun, 155, 184
ascetic practices, 98–100, 182, 186
Asian Buddhists' Conference for Peace, 190–191
Aśoka: as *cakravartin*, 22, 47, 113; Edicts of, 148; in legend, 20, 29
Avalokiteśvara, 11, 20, 243n.29; iconography of, 8, 21, 22, 242n.21; inscriptions to, 10; in pantheon, 15
Ayutthaya, 31, 40, 41, 84, 131

Ba Phnom, 4, 51; sacred site, 45, 54, 62, 131; and sacrifice, 53
Bakan, 35
Bakheng, 14, 33, 244nn.44, 46
Bakong, 13, 89, 234nn.39, 41
Baksei Chamkrong temple, 15
Baksei Chamkrong, 64, 251n.44
baku, 51, 114, 255n.6
Bālaputra, 11